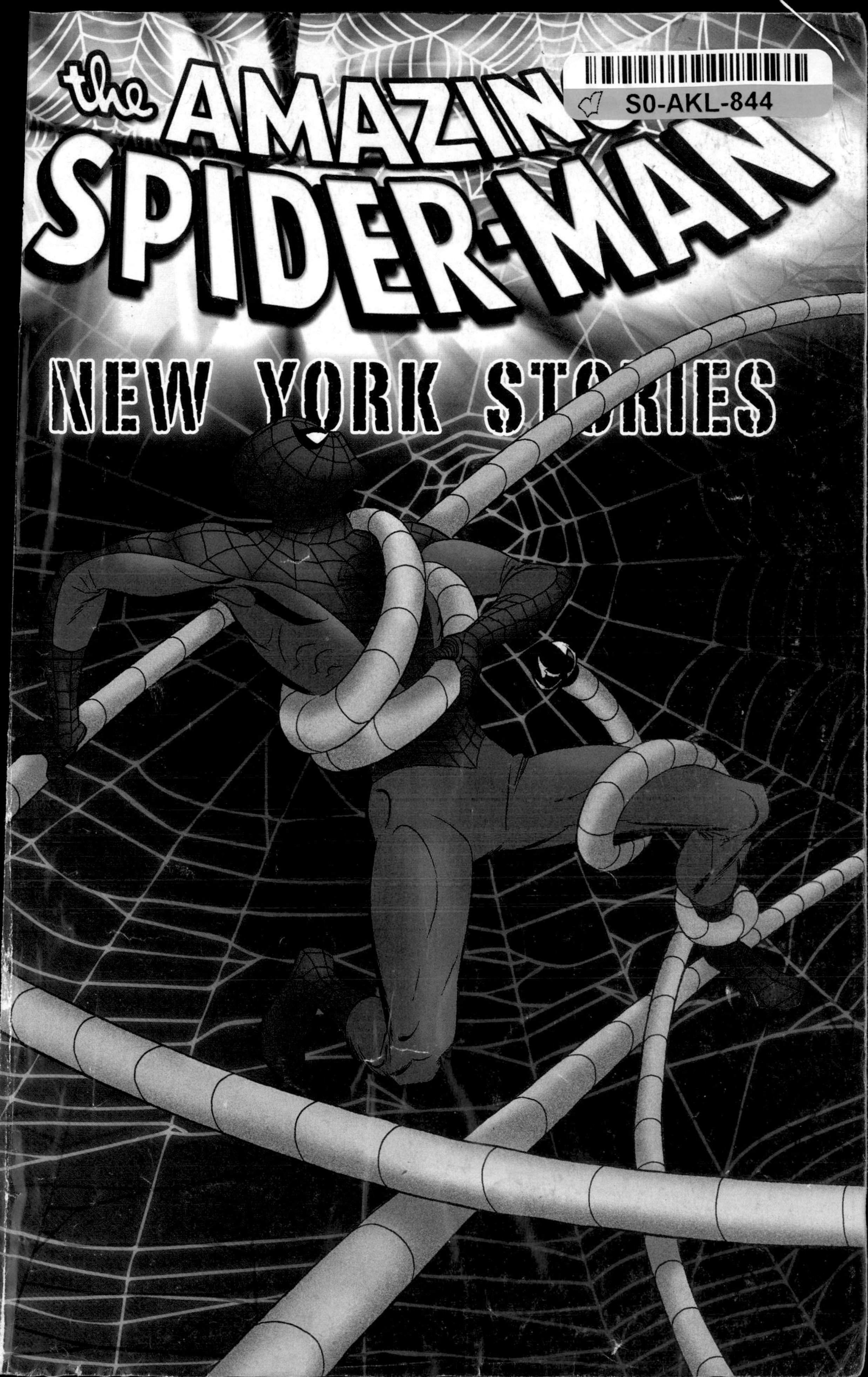
the AMAZING
SPIDER-MAN
NEW YORK STORIES

the AMAZING SPIDER-MAN

NEW YORK STORIES

"LAST STAND OF FROGMAN"
from *Web of Spider-Man #1*
Writer: **SEAN McKEEVER**
Artist: **STEPHANIE BUSCEMA**
Letterer: **JARED K. FLETCHER**

"LOVE & MARRIAGE"
from *Web of Spider-Man #3*
Writer: **J.M. DeMATTEIS**
Penciler: **VAL SEMEIKS**
Inker: **DAN GREEN**
Colorist: **ANDRES MOSSA**
Letterer: **JARED K. FLETCHER**

"WESTERN PROMISES"
from *Web of Spider-Man #4*
Writer: **FRANK TIERI**
Artist: **ERIC CANETE**
Colorist: **ANDRES MOSSA**
Letterer: **JARED K. FLETCHER**

"NOBODY"
from *Web of Spider-Man #5*
Writer: **J.M. DeMATTEIS**
Penciler: **CHAD HARDIN**
Inkers: **WAYNE FAUCHER**
with **ROB CAMPANELLA**
Colorist: **JEROMY COX**
Letterer: **DAVE SHARPE**

"FASHION SPREAD"
from *Web of Spider-Man #7*
Writer: **JOE CASEY**
Artist: **JIM MAHFOOD**
Colorist: **JUSTIN STEWART**
Letterer: **VC'S JOE CARAMAGNA**

"UN NUOVO INIZIO"
from *Web of Spider-Man #8*
Writer: **J.M. DeMATTEIS**
Penciler: **VAL SEMEIKS**
Inker: **DAN GREEN**
Colorist: **CHRIS SOTOMAYOR**
Letterer: **DAVE SHARPE**
Special Thanks to **CARLO CARLEI**

"REFLECTIONS", "NEGATIVE REINFORCEMENT", & "DOUBLE-EDGED SWORD"
from *Web of Spider-Man #9-11*
Writer: **MARC GUGGENHEIM**
Artist: **SANA TAKEDA**
Letterer: **DAVE SHARPE**

"THE SPIDER AND THE SHIELD!"
from *Amazing Spider-Man Annual #37*
Writer: **KARL KESEL**
Artist: **PAULO SIQUEIRA**
Colorist: **FABIO D'AURIA**
Letterer: **VC'S JOE CARAMAGNA**

"MAKE MINE MARVEL!"
from *Amazing Spider-Man Annual #37*
Writer: **KURT BUSIEK**
Artist: **PAT OLLIFFE**
Colorist: **STEVE BUCCELLATO**
Letterer: **COMICRAFT**
Cover Artist: **MARCOS MARTIN**

"SPIDEY SUNDAY SPECTACULAR"
from *Amazing Spider-Man #634-645*
Writer: **STAN LEE**
Artist: **MARCOS MARTIN**
Colorist: **MUNTSA VINCENTE**
Letterer: **VC'S JOE CARAMAGNA**

Editors: **THOMAS BRENNAN** & **STEPHEN WACKER**
Executive Editor: **TOM BREVOORT**

Collection Editor: **CORY LEVINE**
Editorial Assistants: **JAMES EMMETT** & **JOE HOCHSTEIN**
Assistant Editors: **MATT MASDEU, ALEX STARBUCK** & **NELSON RIBEIRO**
Editors, Special Projects: **JENNIFER GRÜNWALD** & **MARK D. BEAZLEY**
Senior Editor, Special Projects: **JEFF YOUNGQUIST**
Senior Vice President of Sales: **DAVID GABRIEL**
Collection Cover Artist: **PASQUAL FERRY**

Editor in Chief: **AXEL ALONSO**
Chief Creative Officer: **JOE QUESADA**
Publisher: **DAN BUCKLEY**
Executive Producer: **ALAN FINE**

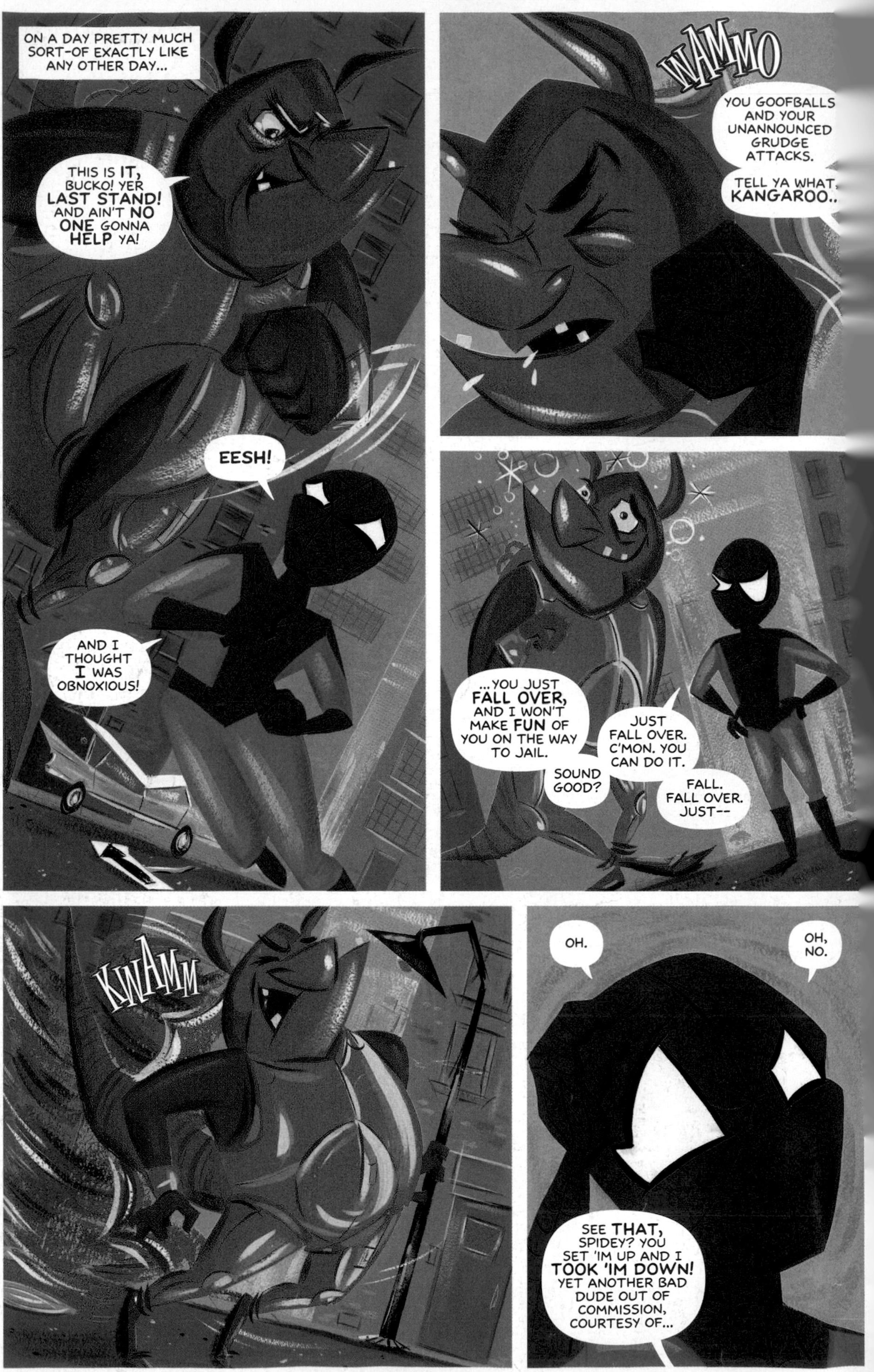
ON A DAY PRETTY MUCH SORT-OF EXACTLY LIKE ANY OTHER DAY...
THIS IS IT, BUCKO! YER LAST STAND! AND AIN'T NO ONE GONNA HELP YA!
EESH!
AND I THOUGHT I WAS OBNOXIOUS!
WAMMO
YOU GOOFBALLS AND YOUR UNANNOUNCED GRUDGE ATTACKS.
TELL YA WHAT, KANGAROO..
...YOU JUST FALL OVER, AND I WON'T MAKE FUN OF YOU ON THE WAY TO JAIL.
SOUND GOOD?
JUST FALL OVER. C'MON. YOU CAN DO IT.
FALL. FALL OVER. JUST--
KWAMM
OH.
OH, NO.
SEE THAT, SPIDEY? YOU SET 'IM UP AND I TOOK 'IM DOWN! YET ANOTHER BAD DUDE OUT OF COMMISSION, COURTESY OF...

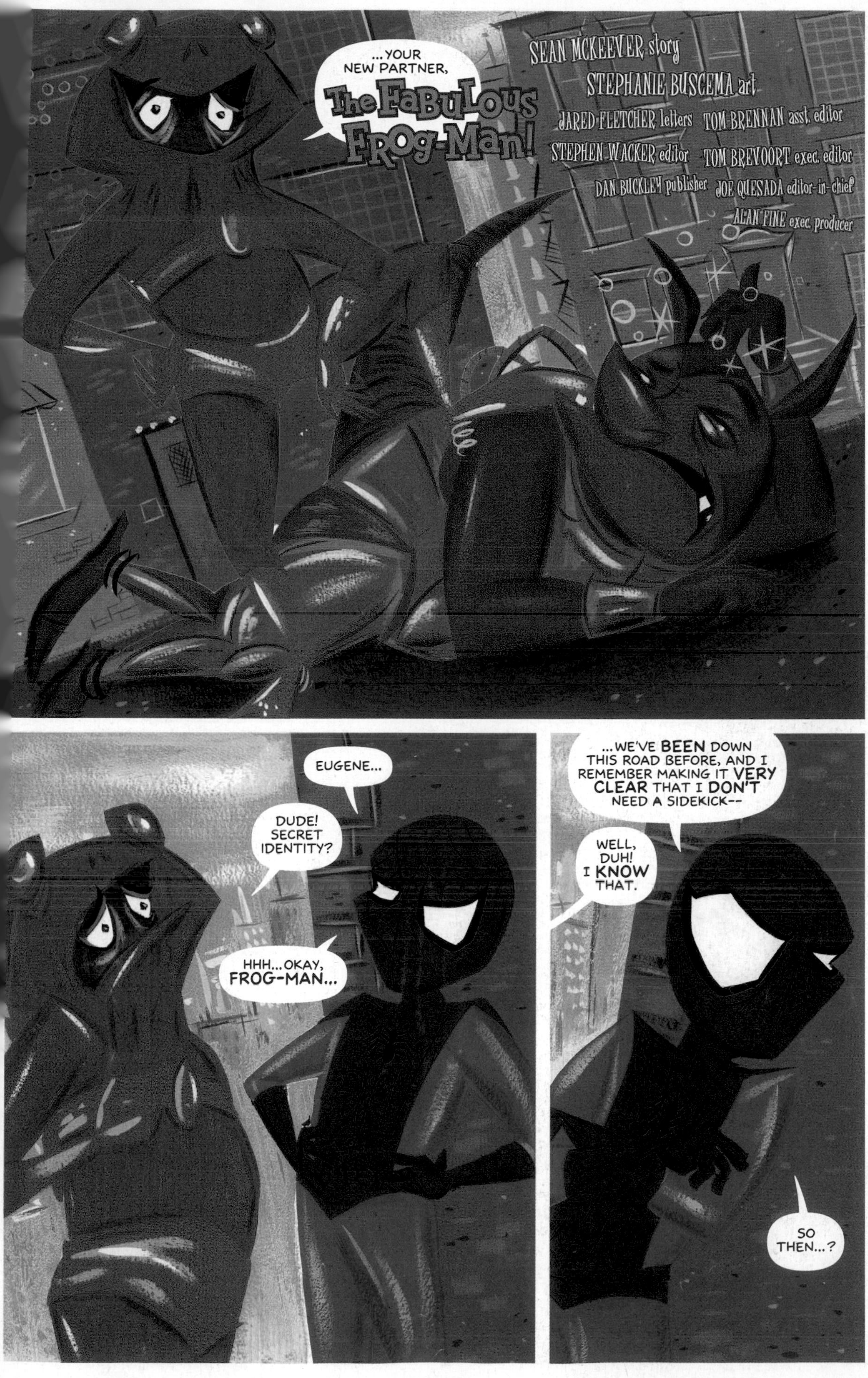
...YOUR NEW PARTNER, THE FABULOUS FROG-MAN!
SEAN MCKEEVER story
STEPHANIE BUSCEMA art
JARED FLETCHER letters TOM BRENNAN asst. editor
STEPHEN WACKER editor TOM BREVOORT exec. editor
DAN BUCKLEY publisher JOE QUESADA editor-in-chief
ALAN FINE exec. producer
EUGENE...
DUDE! SECRET IDENTITY?
HHH...OKAY, FROG-MAN...
...WE'VE BEEN DOWN THIS ROAD BEFORE, AND I REMEMBER MAKING IT VERY CLEAR THAT I DON'T NEED A SIDEKICK--
WELL, DUH! I KNOW THAT.
SO THEN...?

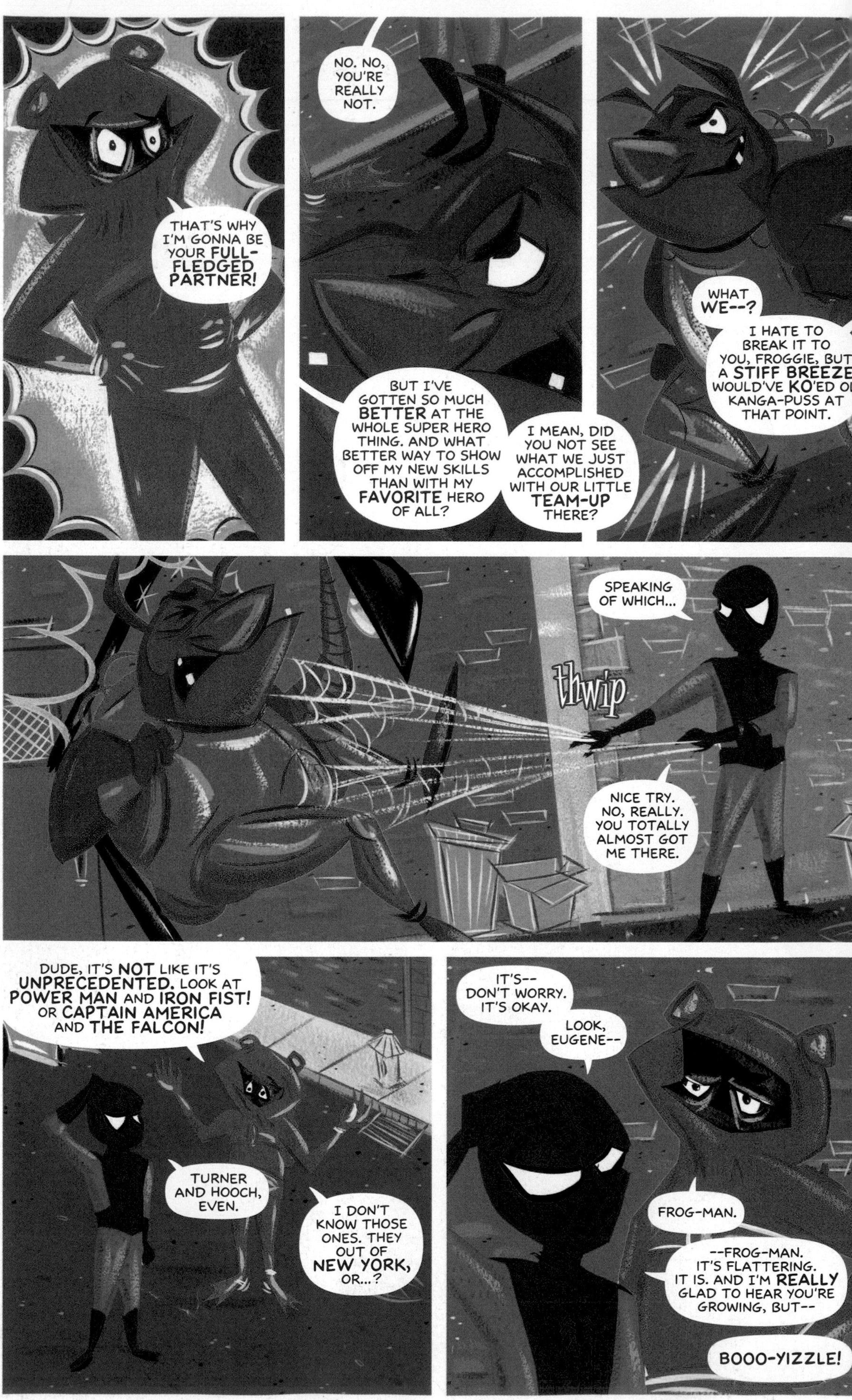
THAT'S WHY I'M GONNA BE YOUR FULL-FLEDGED PARTNER!
NO. NO, YOU'RE REALLY NOT.
BUT I'VE GOTTEN SO MUCH BETTER AT THE WHOLE SUPER HERO THING. AND WHAT BETTER WAY TO SHOW OFF MY NEW SKILLS THAN WITH MY FAVORITE HERO OF ALL?
I MEAN, DID YOU NOT SEE WHAT WE JUST ACCOMPLISHED WITH OUR LITTLE TEAM-UP THERE?
WHAT WE--?
I HATE TO BREAK IT TO YOU, FROGGIE, BUT A STIFF BREEZE WOULD'VE KO'ED OL' KANGA-PUSS AT THAT POINT.
SPEAKING OF WHICH...
thwip
NICE TRY. NO, REALLY. YOU TOTALLY ALMOST GOT ME THERE.
DUDE, IT'S NOT LIKE IT'S UNPRECEDENTED. LOOK AT POWER MAN AND IRON FIST! OR CAPTAIN AMERICA AND THE FALCON!
TURNER AND HOOCH, EVEN.
I DON'T KNOW THOSE ONES. THEY OUT OF NEW YORK, OR...?
IT'S-- DON'T WORRY. IT'S OKAY.
LOOK, EUGENE--
FROG-MAN.
--FROG-MAN. IT'S FLATTERING. IT IS. AND I'M REALLY GLAD TO HEAR YOU'RE GROWING, BUT--
BOOO-YIZZLE!

IT'S ME-- The Tenacious Tadpole!
ANYWAY, LIKE I WAS SAYING--
DAAAG!
WHAT'S WITH THE BEING A TOOL WHILE I'M INTRODUCING MYSELF TO MY IDOL?
WHAT AN EGO ON YOU! "OH, I'M SPIDER-MAN! STOP EVERYTHING FOR ME AND MY RIDICULOUS COSTUME!"
UH--
I'VE BEEN DRUGGED. OR SUCKED INTO AN ALTERNATE REALITY. SOMETHING.
HEY, DUDE, YOU CAN'T GO TALKING TO SPIDEY LIKE--
WAIT. DID YOU JUST REFER TO ME AS YOUR IDOL?
YOU GOT NO IDEA! I CELEBRATE YOUR ENTIRE CAREER!

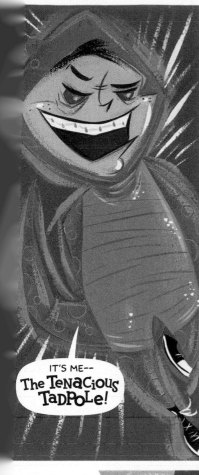

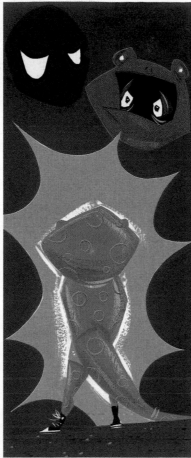

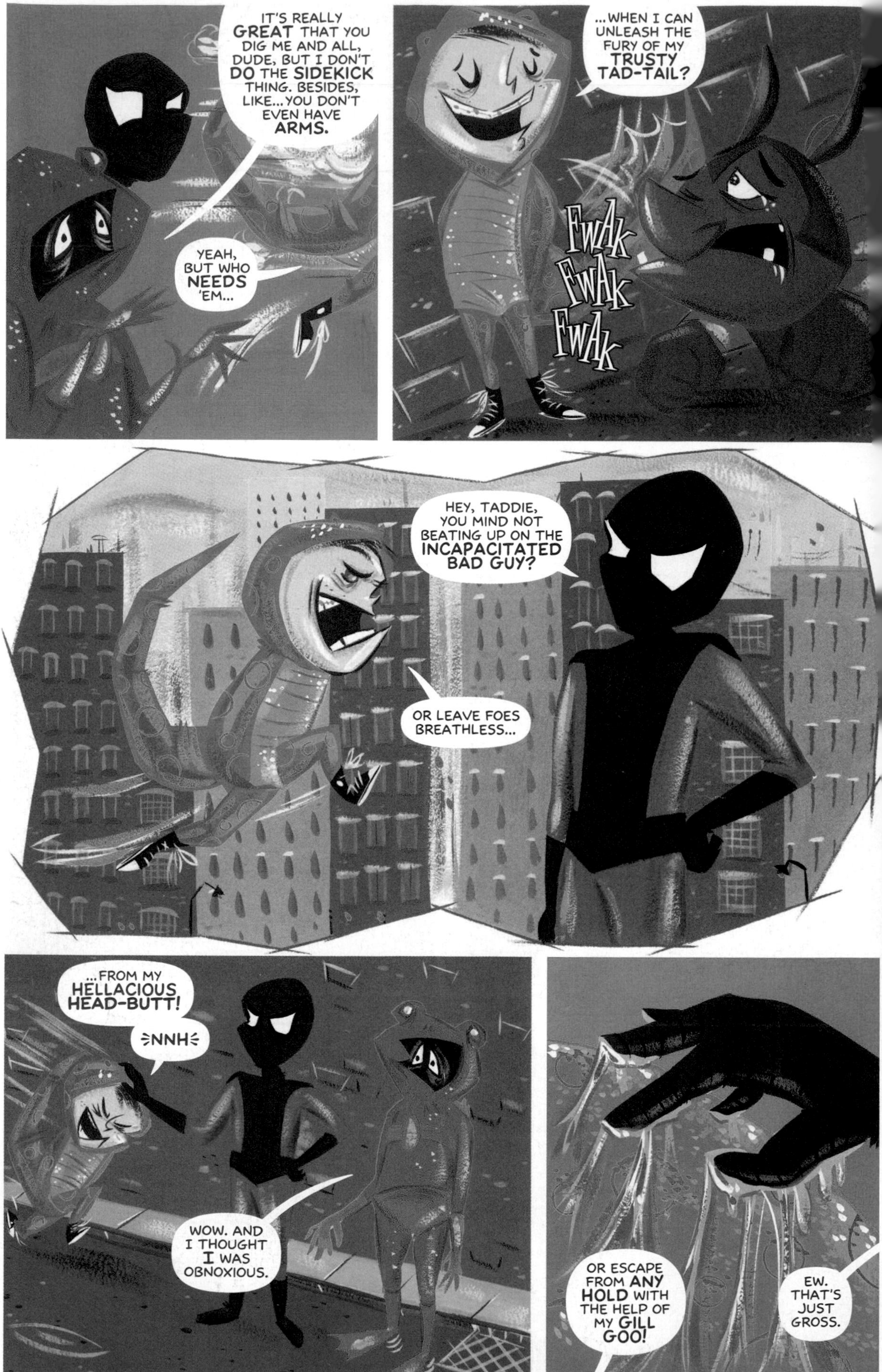
IT'S REALLY GREAT THAT YOU DIG ME AND ALL, DUDE, BUT I DON'T DO THE SIDEKICK THING. BESIDES, LIKE...YOU DON'T EVEN HAVE ARMS.
YEAH, BUT WHO NEEDS 'EM...
...WHEN I CAN UNLEASH THE FURY OF MY TRUSTY TAD-TAIL?
FWAK
FWAK
FWAK
HEY, TADDIE, YOU MIND NOT BEATING UP ON THE INCAPACITATED BAD GUY?
OR LEAVE FOES BREATHLESS...
...FROM MY HELLACIOUS HEAD-BUTT!
NNH
WOW. AND I THOUGHT I WAS OBNOXIOUS.
OR ESCAPE FROM ANY HOLD WITH THE HELP OF MY GILL GOO!
EW. THAT'S JUST GROSS.

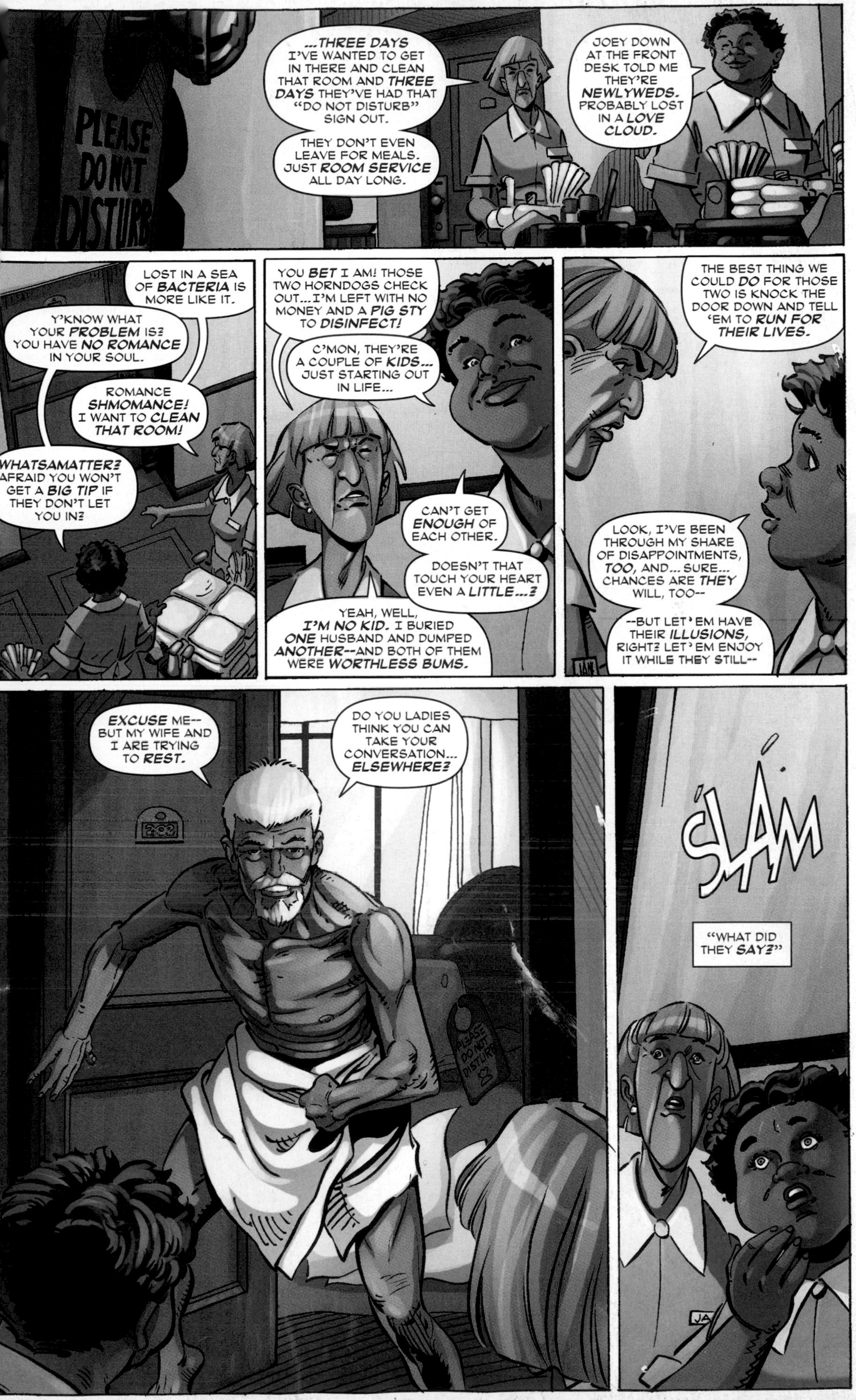
PLEASE DO NOT DISTURB
...THREE DAYS I'VE WANTED TO GET IN THERE AND CLEAN THAT ROOM AND THREE DAYS THEY'VE HAD THAT "DO NOT DISTURB" SIGN OUT.
THEY DON'T EVEN LEAVE FOR MEALS. JUST ROOM SERVICE ALL DAY LONG.
JOEY DOWN AT THE FRONT DESK TOLD ME THEY'RE NEWLYWEDS. PROBABLY LOST IN A LOVE CLOUD.
LOST IN A SEA OF BACTERIA IS MORE LIKE IT.
Y'KNOW WHAT YOUR PROBLEM IS? YOU HAVE NO ROMANCE IN YOUR SOUL.
ROMANCE SHMOMANCE! I WANT TO CLEAN THAT ROOM!
WHATSAMATTER? AFRAID YOU WON'T GET A BIG TIP IF THEY DON'T LET YOU IN?
YOU BET I AM! THOSE TWO HORNDOGS CHECK OUT...I'M LEFT WITH NO MONEY AND A PIG STY TO DISINFECT!
C'MON, THEY'RE A COUPLE OF KIDS... JUST STARTING OUT IN LIFE...
CAN'T GET ENOUGH OF EACH OTHER.
DOESN'T THAT TOUCH YOUR HEART EVEN A LITTLE...?
YEAH, WELL, I'M NO KID. I BURIED ONE HUSBAND AND DUMPED ANOTHER--AND BOTH OF THEM WERE WORTHLESS BUMS.
THE BEST THING WE COULD DO FOR THOSE TWO IS KNOCK THE DOOR DOWN AND TELL 'EM TO RUN FOR THEIR LIVES.
LOOK, I'VE BEEN THROUGH MY SHARE OF DISAPPOINTMENTS, TOO, AND... SURE... CHANCES ARE THEY WILL, TOO--
--BUT LET'EM HAVE THEIR ILLUSIONS, RIGHT? LET'EM ENJOY IT WHILE THEY STILL--
EXCUSE ME-- BUT MY WIFE AND I ARE TRYING TO REST.
DO YOU LADIES THINK YOU CAN TAKE YOUR CONVERSATION... ELSEWHERE?
SLAM
"WHAT DID THEY SAY?"

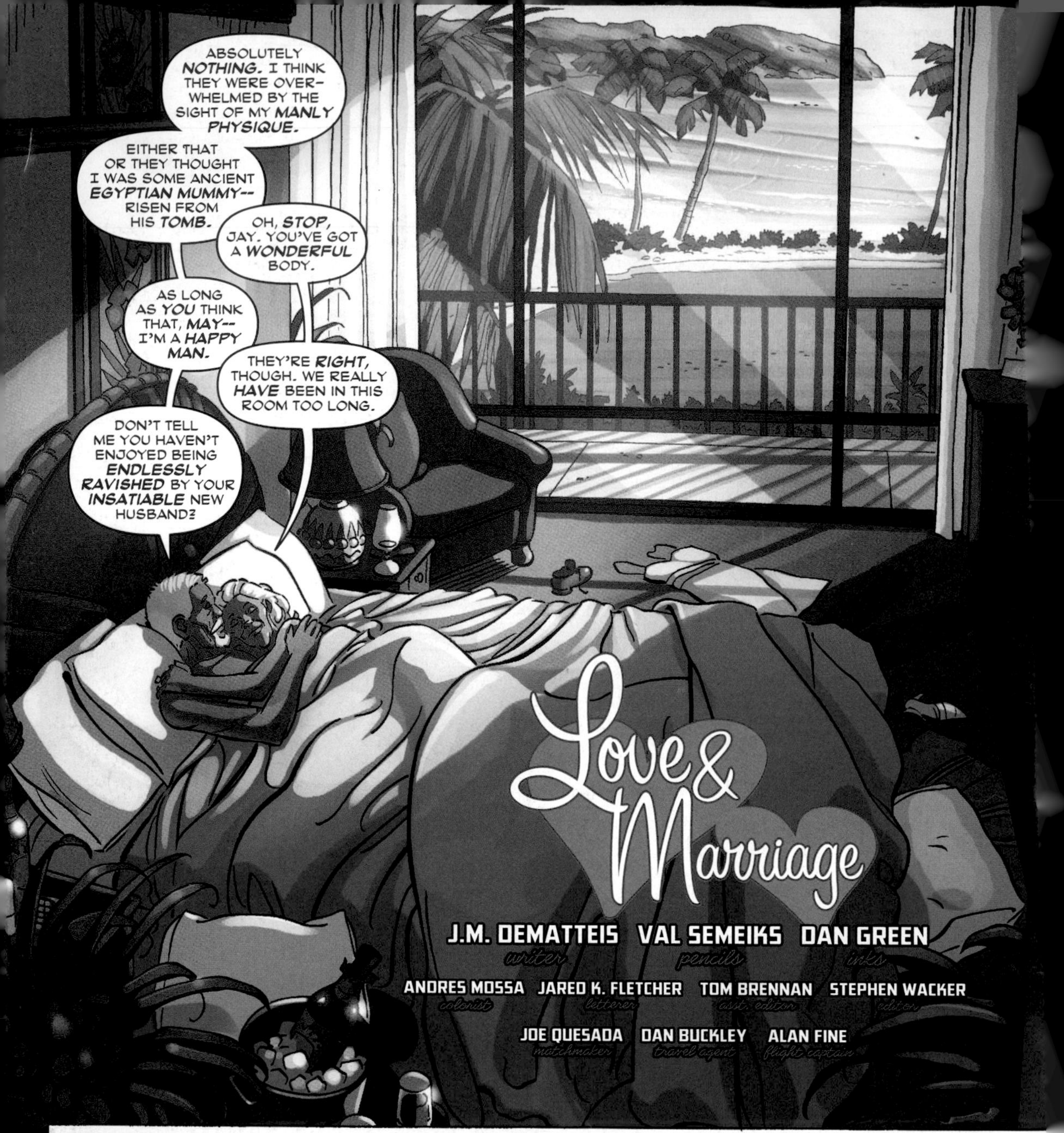
ABSOLUTELY NOTHING. I THINK THEY WERE OVER-WHELMED BY THE SIGHT OF MY MANLY PHYSIQUE.
EITHER THAT OR THEY THOUGHT I WAS SOME ANCIENT EGYPTIAN MUMMY--RISEN FROM HIS TOMB.
OH, STOP, JAY. YOU'VE GOT A WONDERFUL BODY.
AS LONG AS YOU THINK THAT, MAY--I'M A HAPPY MAN.
THEY'RE RIGHT, THOUGH. WE REALLY HAVE BEEN IN THIS ROOM TOO LONG.
DON'T TELL ME YOU HAVEN'T ENJOYED BEING ENDLESSLY RAVISHED BY YOUR INSATIABLE NEW HUSBAND?
Love & Marriage
J.M. DEMATTEIS writer
VAL SEMEIKS pencils
DAN GREEN inks
ANDRES MOSSA colorist
JARED K. FLETCHER letterer
TOM BRENNAN asst. editor
STEPHEN WACKER editor
JOE QUESADA matchmaker
DAN BUCKLEY travel agent
ALAN FINE flight captain

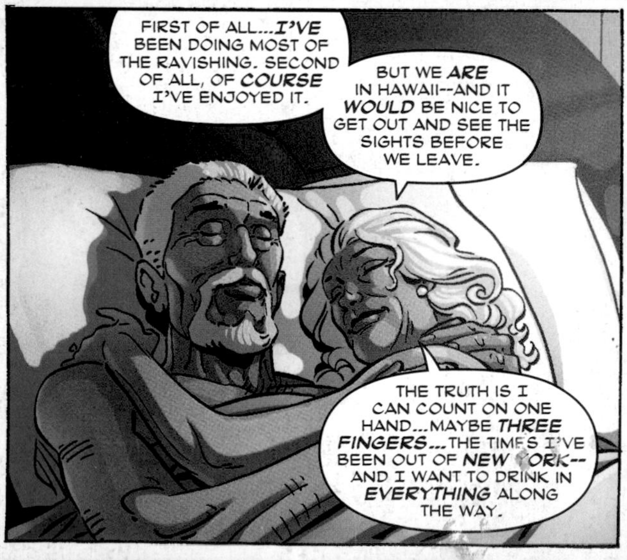
FIRST OF ALL...I'VE BEEN DOING MOST OF THE RAVISHING. SECOND OF ALL, OF COURSE I'VE ENJOYED IT.
BUT WE ARE IN HAWAII--AND IT WOULD BE NICE TO GET OUT AND SEE THE SIGHTS BEFORE WE LEAVE.
THE TRUTH IS I CAN COUNT ON ONE HAND...MAYBE THREE FINGERS...THE TIMES I'VE BEEN OUT OF NEW YORK--AND I WANT TO DRINK IN EVERYTHING ALONG THE WAY.

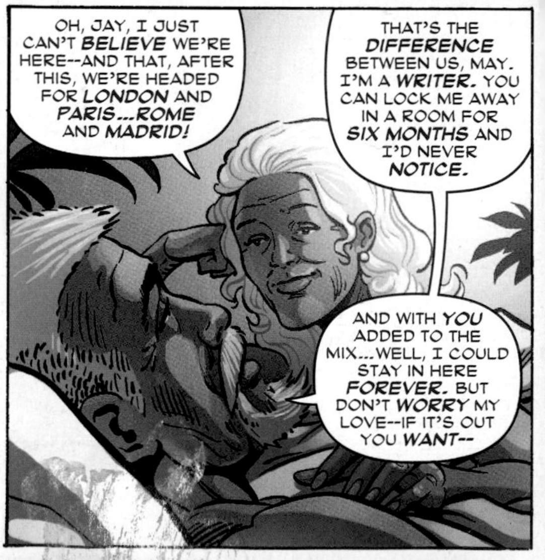
OH, JAY, I JUST CAN'T BELIEVE WE'RE HERE--AND THAT, AFTER THIS, WE'RE HEADED FOR LONDON AND PARIS...ROME AND MADRID!
THAT'S THE DIFFERENCE BETWEEN US, MAY. I'M A WRITER. YOU CAN LOCK ME AWAY IN A ROOM FOR SIX MONTHS AND I'D NEVER NOTICE.
AND WITH YOU ADDED TO THE MIX...WELL, I COULD STAY IN HERE FOREVER. BUT DON'T WORRY MY LOVE--IF IT'S OUT YOU WANT--

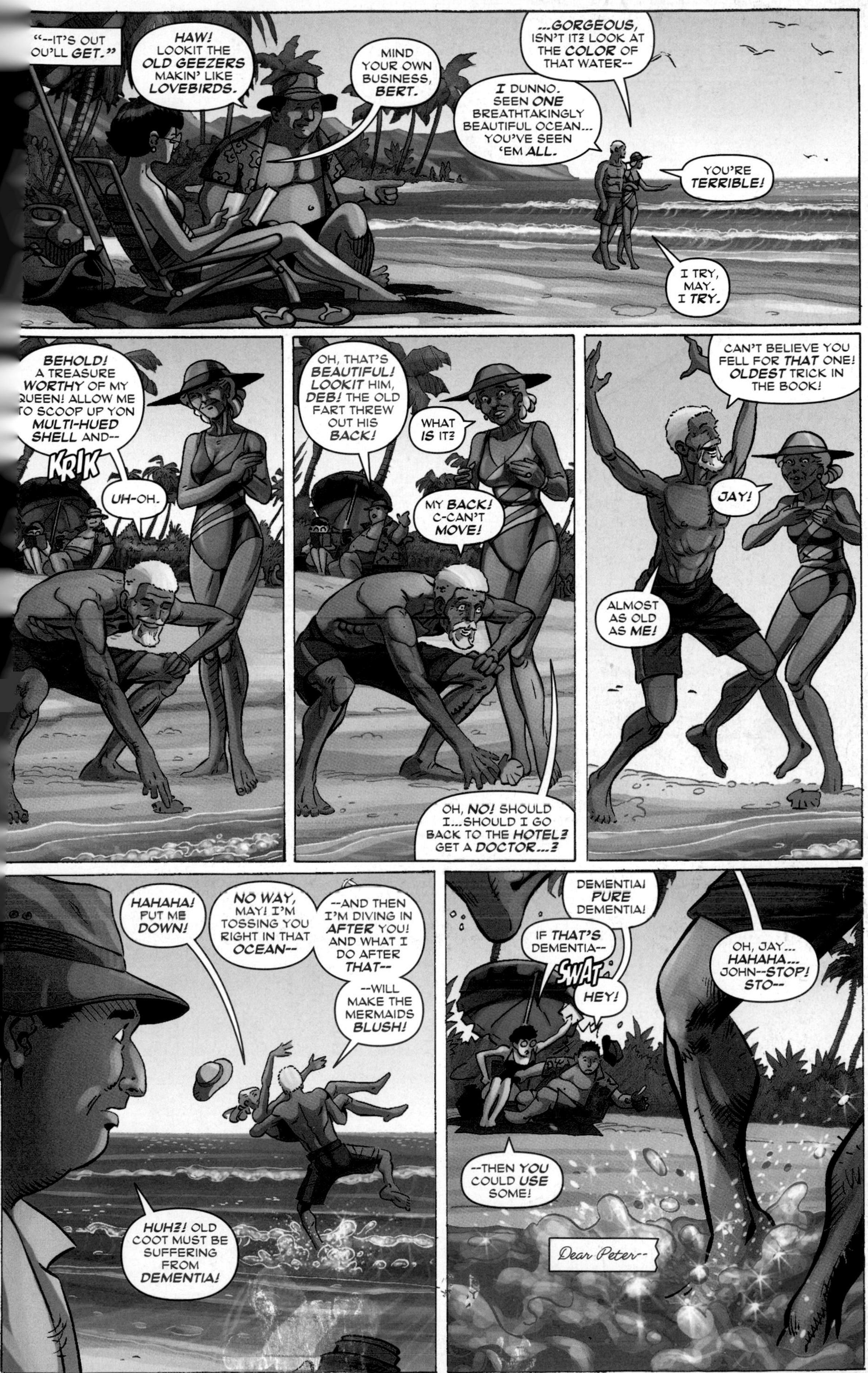
"--IT'S OUT
OU'LL GET."
HAW! LOOKIT THE OLD GEEZERS MAKIN' LIKE LOVEBIRDS.
MIND YOUR OWN BUSINESS, BERT.
...GORGEOUS, ISN'T IT? LOOK AT THE COLOR OF THAT WATER--
I DUNNO. SEEN ONE BREATHTAKINGLY BEAUTIFUL OCEAN... YOU'VE SEEN 'EM ALL.
YOU'RE TERRIBLE!
I TRY, MAY. I TRY.
BEHOLD! A TREASURE WORTHY OF MY QUEEN! ALLOW ME TO SCOOP UP YON MULTI-HUED SHELL AND--
KRIK
UH-OH.
OH, THAT'S BEAUTIFUL! LOOKIT HIM, DEB! THE OLD FART THREW OUT HIS BACK!
WHAT IS IT?
MY BACK! C-CAN'T MOVE!
OH, NO! SHOULD I...SHOULD I GO BACK TO THE HOTEL? GET A DOCTOR...?
CAN'T BELIEVE YOU FELL FOR THAT ONE! OLDEST TRICK IN THE BOOK!
JAY!
ALMOST AS OLD AS ME!
HAHAHA! PUT ME DOWN!
NO WAY, MAY! I'M TOSSING YOU RIGHT IN THAT OCEAN--
--AND THEN I'M DIVING IN AFTER YOU! AND WHAT I DO AFTER THAT--
--WILL MAKE THE MERMAIDS BLUSH!
HUH?! OLD COOT MUST BE SUFFERING FROM DEMENTIA!
DEMENTIA! PURE DEMENTIA!
IF THAT'S DEMENTIA--
SWAT
HEY!
--THEN YOU COULD USE SOME!
OH, JAY... HAHAHA... JOHN--STOP! STO--
Dear Peter--

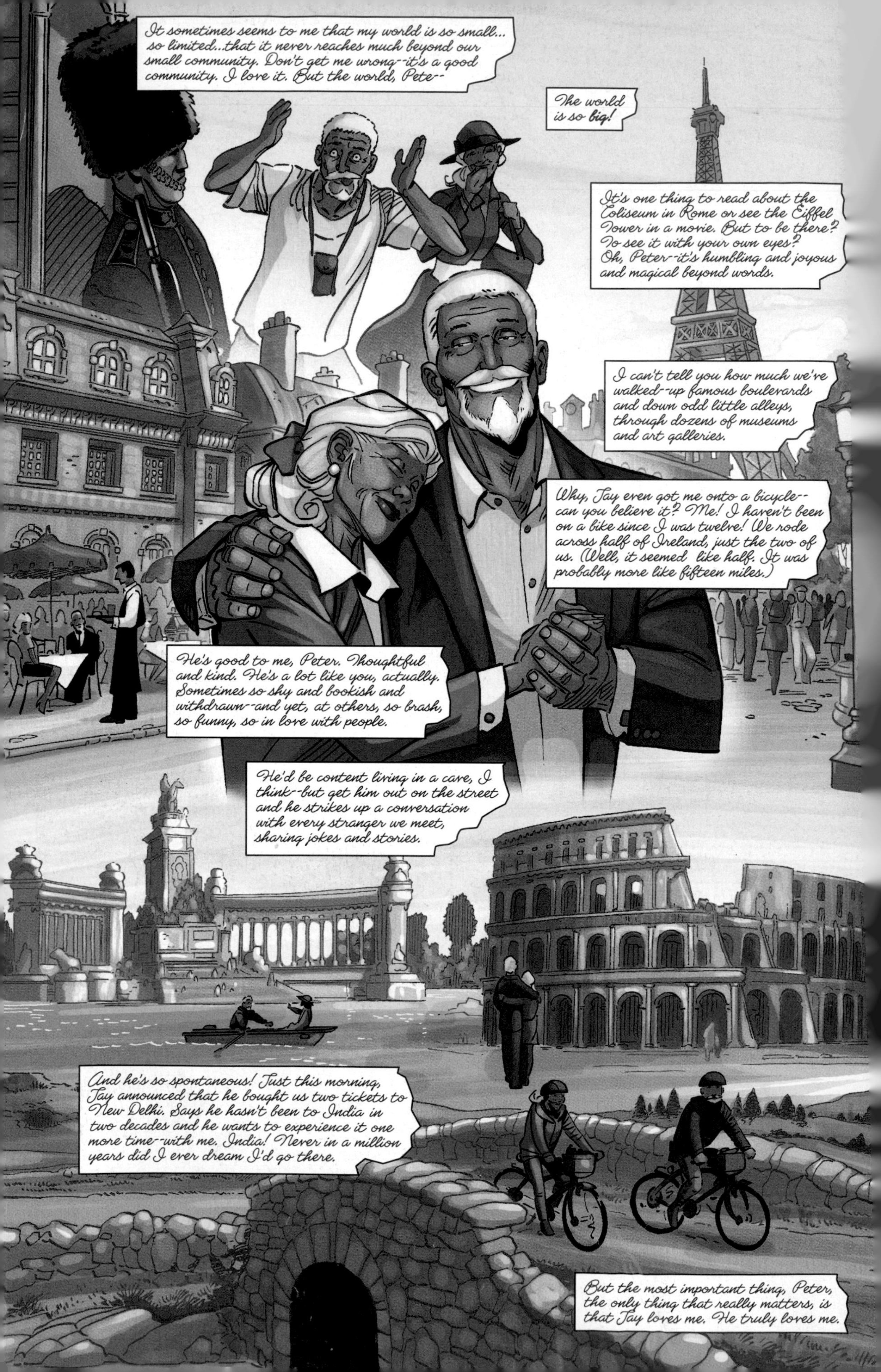
It sometimes seems to me that my world is so small... so limited...that it never reaches much beyond our small community. Don't get me wrong--it's a good community. I love it. But the world, Pete--
The world is so big!
It's one thing to read about the Coliseum in Rome or see the Eiffel Tower in a movie. But to be there? To see it with your own eyes? Oh, Peter--it's humbling and joyous and magical beyond words.
I can't tell you how much we've walked--up famous boulevards and down odd little alleys, through dozens of museums and art galleries.
Why, Jay even got me onto a bicycle--can you believe it? Me! I haven't been on a bike since I was twelve! We rode across half of Ireland, just the two of us. (Well, it seemed like half. It was probably more like fifteen miles.)
He's good to me, Peter. Thoughtful and kind. He's a lot like you, actually. Sometimes so shy and bookish and withdrawn--and yet, at others, so brash, so funny, so in love with people.
He'd be content living in a cave, I think--but get him out on the street and he strikes up a conversation with every stranger we meet, sharing jokes and stories.
And he's so spontaneous! Just this morning, Jay announced that he bought us two tickets to New Delhi. Says he hasn't been to India in two decades and he wants to experience it one more time--with me. India! Never in a million years did I ever dream I'd go there.
But the most important thing, Peter, the only thing that really matters, is that Jay loves me. He truly loves me.

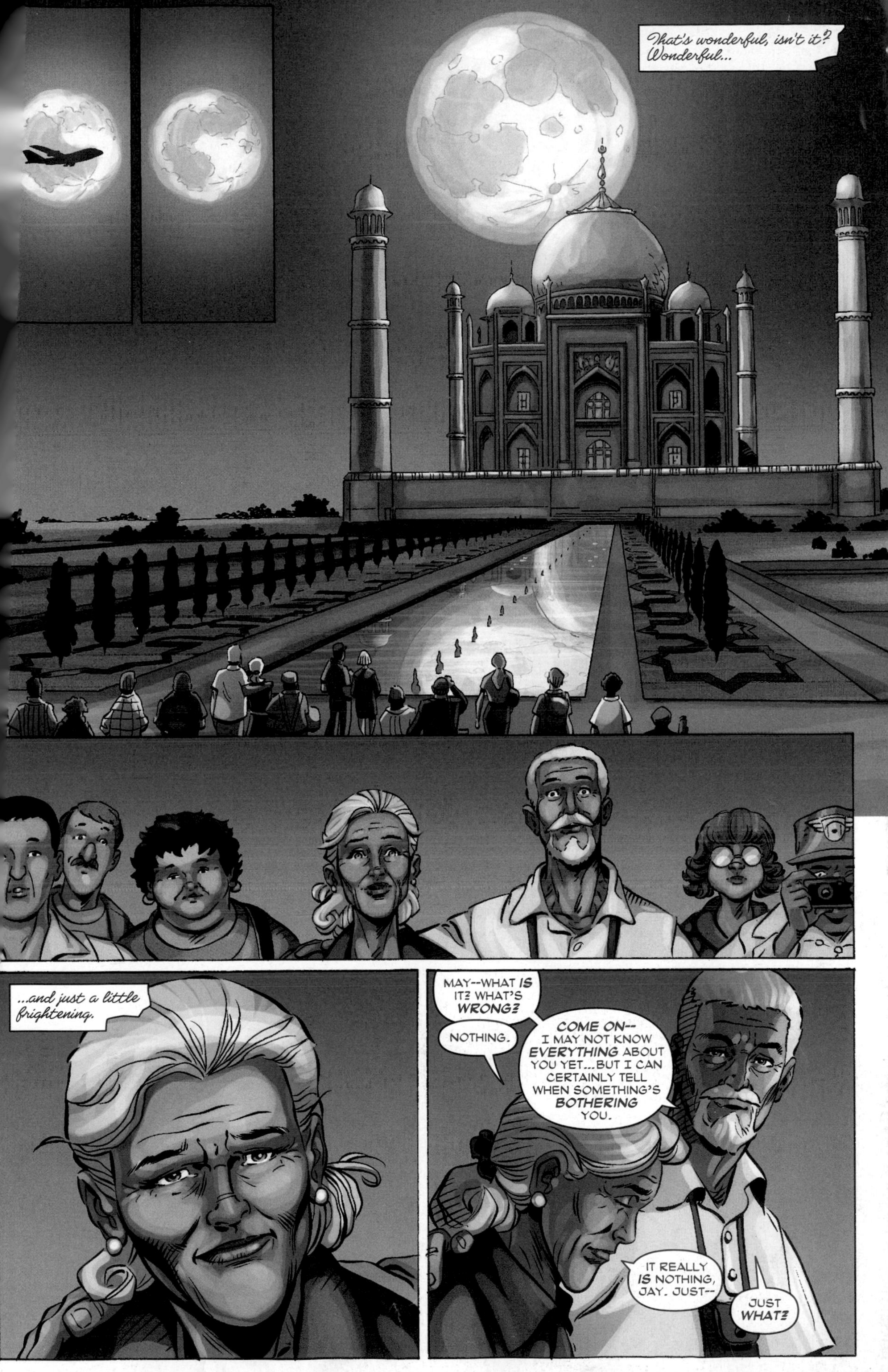
That's wonderful, isn't it? Wonderful...
...and just a little frightening.
MAY--WHAT IS IT? WHAT'S WRONG?
NOTHING.
COME ON-- I MAY NOT KNOW EVERYTHING ABOUT YOU YET...BUT I CAN CERTAINLY TELL WHEN SOMETHING'S BOTHERING YOU.
IT REALLY IS NOTHING, JAY. JUST--
JUST WHAT?

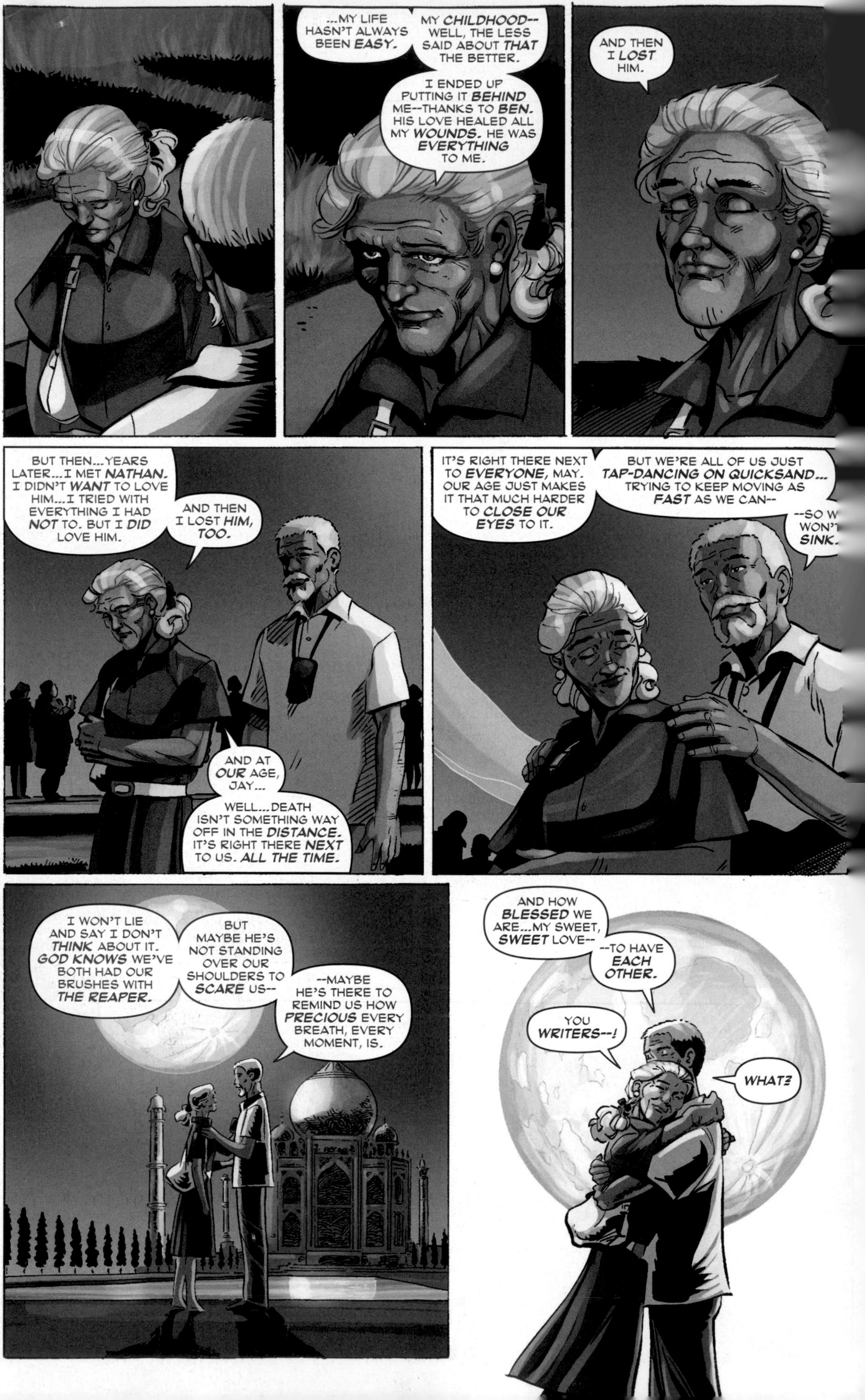
...MY LIFE HASN'T ALWAYS BEEN EASY.
MY CHILDHOOD-- WELL, THE LESS SAID ABOUT THAT THE BETTER.
I ENDED UP PUTTING IT BEHIND ME--THANKS TO BEN. HIS LOVE HEALED ALL MY WOUNDS. HE WAS EVERYTHING TO ME.
AND THEN I LOST HIM.
BUT THEN...YEARS LATER...I MET NATHAN. I DIDN'T WANT TO LOVE HIM...I TRIED WITH EVERYTHING I HAD NOT TO. BUT I DID LOVE HIM.
AND THEN I LOST HIM, TOO.
AND AT OUR AGE, JAY...
WELL...DEATH ISN'T SOMETHING WAY OFF IN THE DISTANCE. IT'S RIGHT THERE NEXT TO US. ALL THE TIME.
IT'S RIGHT THERE NEXT TO EVERYONE, MAY. OUR AGE JUST MAKES IT THAT MUCH HARDER TO CLOSE OUR EYES TO IT.
BUT WE'RE ALL OF US JUST TAP-DANCING ON QUICKSAND... TRYING TO KEEP MOVING AS FAST AS WE CAN--
I WON'T LIE AND SAY I DON'T THINK ABOUT IT. GOD KNOWS WE'VE BOTH HAD OUR BRUSHES WITH THE REAPER.
BUT MAYBE HE'S NOT STANDING OVER OUR SHOULDERS TO SCARE US--
--MAYBE HE'S THERE TO REMIND US HOW PRECIOUS EVERY BREATH, EVERY MOMENT, IS.
AND HOW BLESSED WE ARE...MY SWEET, SWEET LOVE--
--TO HAVE EACH OTHER.
YOU WRITERS--!
WHAT?

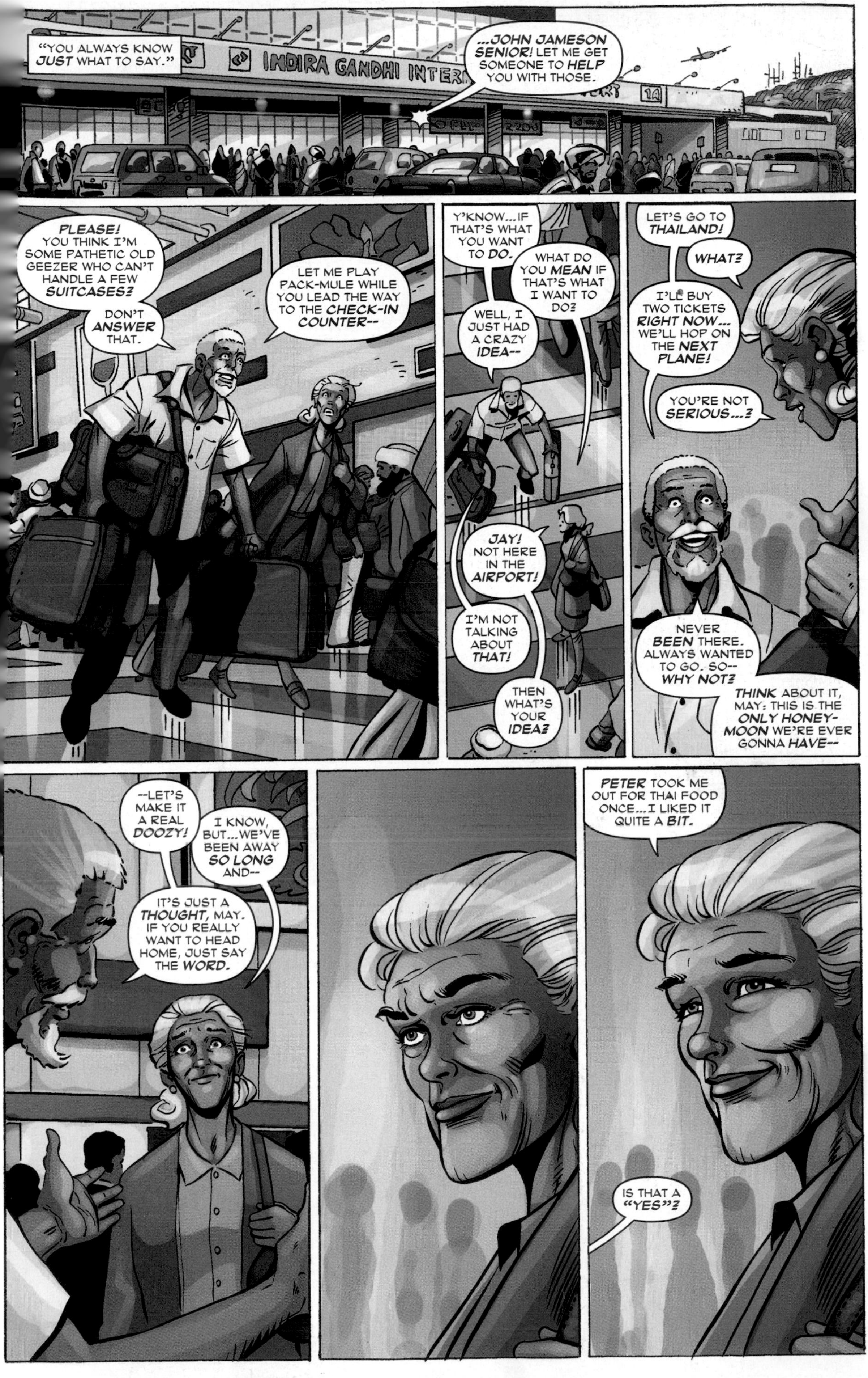
"YOU ALWAYS KNOW JUST WHAT TO SAY."
INDIRA GANDHI INTER
...JOHN JAMESON SENIOR! LET ME GET SOMEONE TO HELP YOU WITH THOSE.
PLEASE! YOU THINK I'M SOME PATHETIC OLD GEEZER WHO CAN'T HANDLE A FEW SUITCASES?
DON'T ANSWER THAT.
LET ME PLAY PACK-MULE WHILE YOU LEAD THE WAY TO THE CHECK-IN COUNTER--
Y'KNOW...IF THAT'S WHAT YOU WANT TO DO.
WHAT DO YOU MEAN IF THAT'S WHAT I WANT TO DO?
WELL, I JUST HAD A CRAZY IDEA--
JAY! NOT HERE IN THE AIRPORT!
I'M NOT TALKING ABOUT THAT!
THEN WHAT'S YOUR IDEA?
LET'S GO TO THAILAND!
WHAT?
I'LL BUY TWO TICKETS RIGHT NOW... WE'LL HOP ON THE NEXT PLANE!
YOU'RE NOT SERIOUS...?
NEVER BEEN THERE. ALWAYS WANTED TO GO. SO-- WHY NOT?
THINK ABOUT IT, MAY: THIS IS THE ONLY HONEY-MOON WE'RE EVER GONNA HAVE--
--LET'S MAKE IT A REAL DOOZY!
I KNOW, BUT...WE'VE BEEN AWAY SO LONG AND--
IT'S JUST A THOUGHT, MAY. IF YOU REALLY WANT TO HEAD HOME, JUST SAY THE WORD.
PETER TOOK ME OUT FOR THAI FOOD ONCE...I LIKED IT QUITE A BIT.
IS THAT A "YES"?

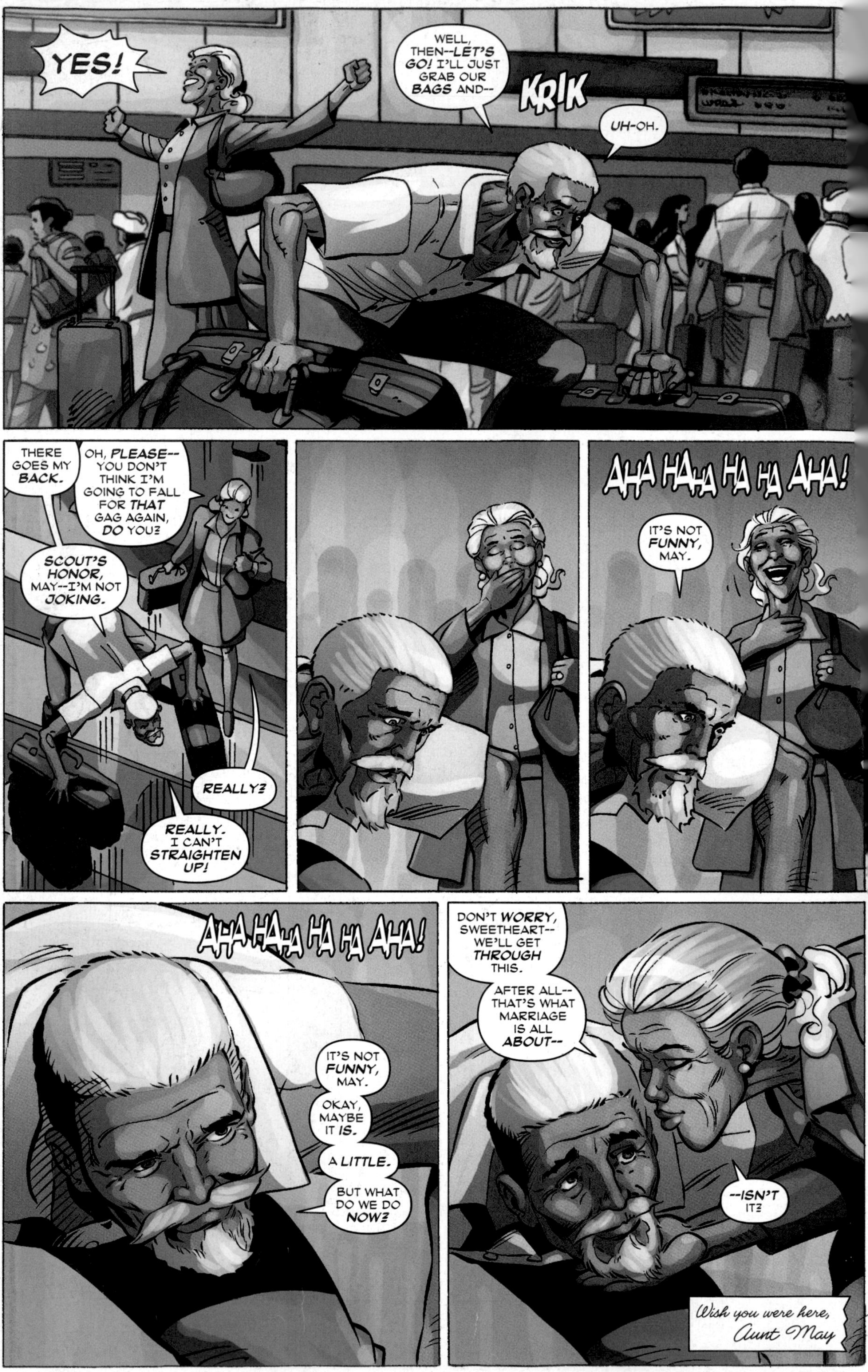
YES!
WELL, THEN--LET'S GO! I'LL JUST GRAB OUR BAGS AND--
KRIK
UH-OH.
THERE GOES MY BACK.
OH, PLEASE--YOU DON'T THINK I'M GOING TO FALL FOR THAT GAG AGAIN, DO YOU?
SCOUT'S HONOR, MAY--I'M NOT JOKING.
REALLY?
REALLY. I CAN'T STRAIGHTEN UP!
AHA HAHA HA HA AHA!
IT'S NOT FUNNY, MAY.
AHA HAHA HA HA AHA!
IT'S NOT FUNNY, MAY.
OKAY, MAYBE IT IS.
A LITTLE.
BUT WHAT DO WE DO NOW?
DON'T WORRY, SWEETHEART--WE'LL GET THROUGH THIS.
AFTER ALL--THAT'S WHAT MARRIAGE IS ALL ABOUT--
--ISN'T IT?
Wish you were here,
Aunt May

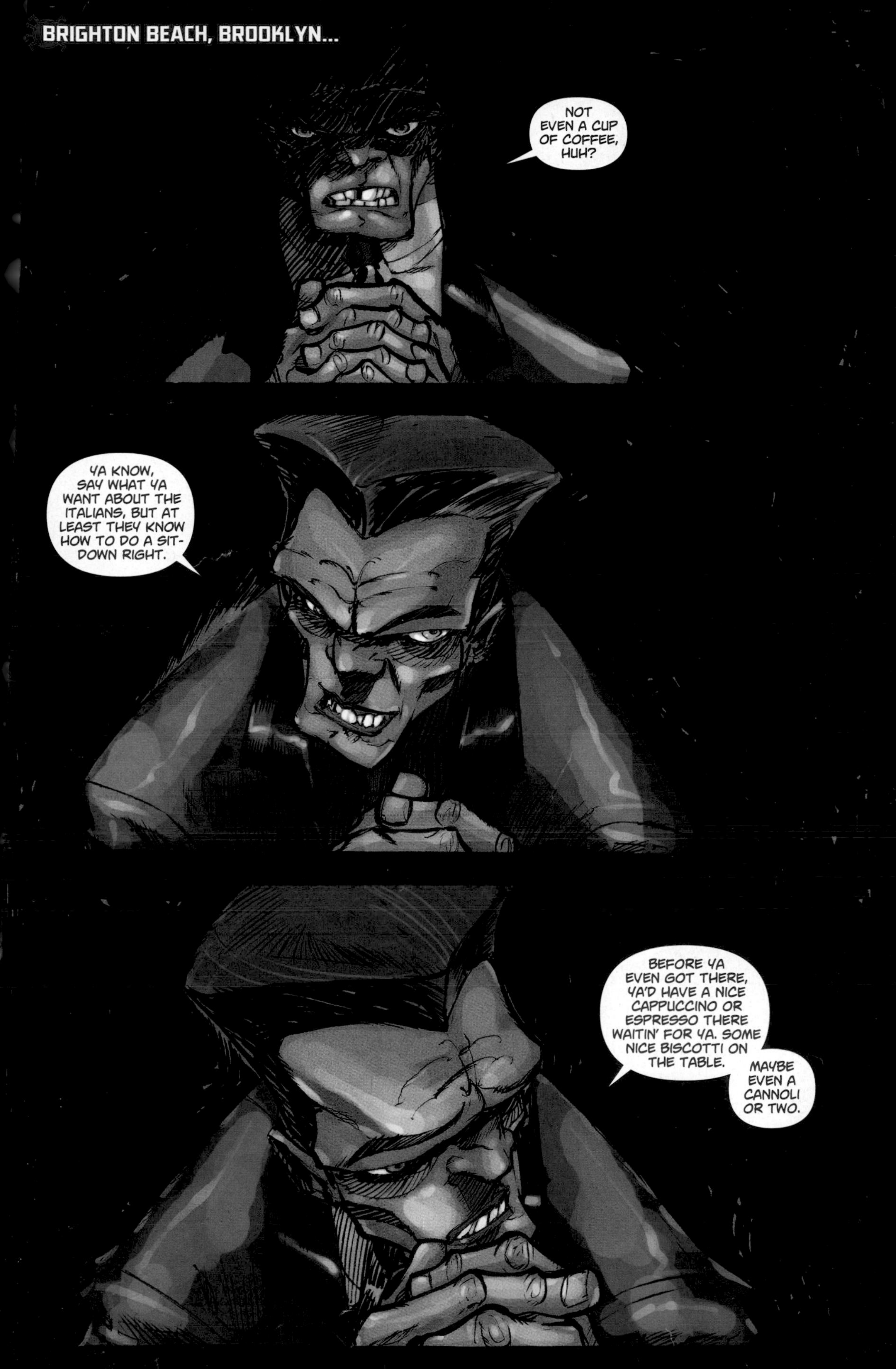
BRIGHTON BEACH, BROOKLYN...
NOT EVEN A CUP OF COFFEE, HUH?
YA KNOW, SAY WHAT YA WANT ABOUT THE ITALIANS, BUT AT LEAST THEY KNOW HOW TO DO A SIT-DOWN RIGHT.
BEFORE YA EVEN GOT THERE, YA'D HAVE A NICE CAPPUCCINO OR ESPRESSO THERE WAITIN' FOR YA. SOME NICE BISCOTTI ON THE TABLE.
MAYBE EVEN A CANNOLI OR TWO.

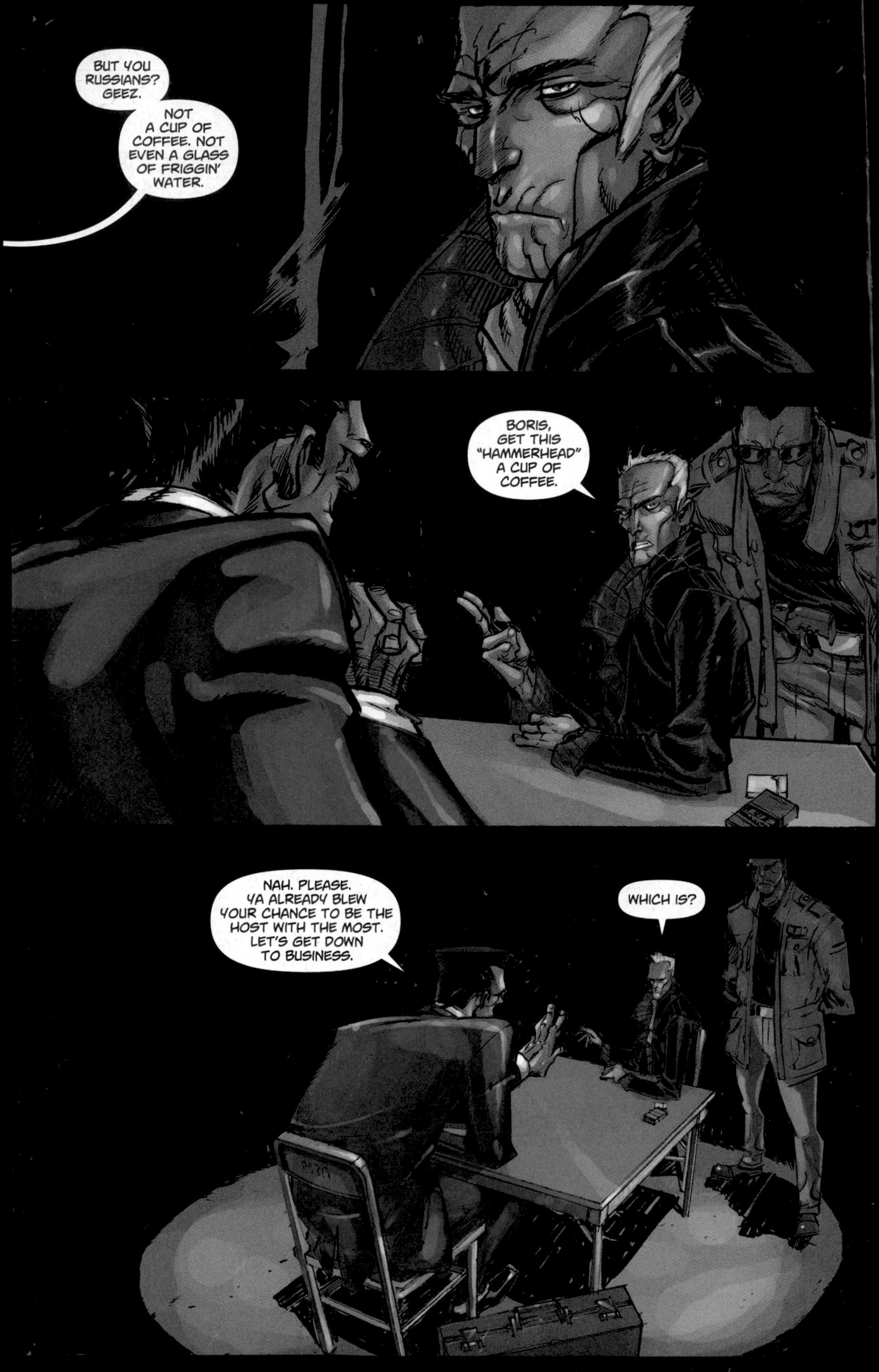
BUT YOU RUSSIANS? GEEZ.
NOT A CUP OF COFFEE. NOT EVEN A GLASS OF FRIGGIN' WATER.
BORIS, GET THIS "HAMMERHEAD" A CUP OF COFFEE.
NAH. PLEASE. YA ALREADY BLEW YOUR CHANCE TO BE THE HOST WITH THE MOST. LET'S GET DOWN TO BUSINESS.
WHICH IS?

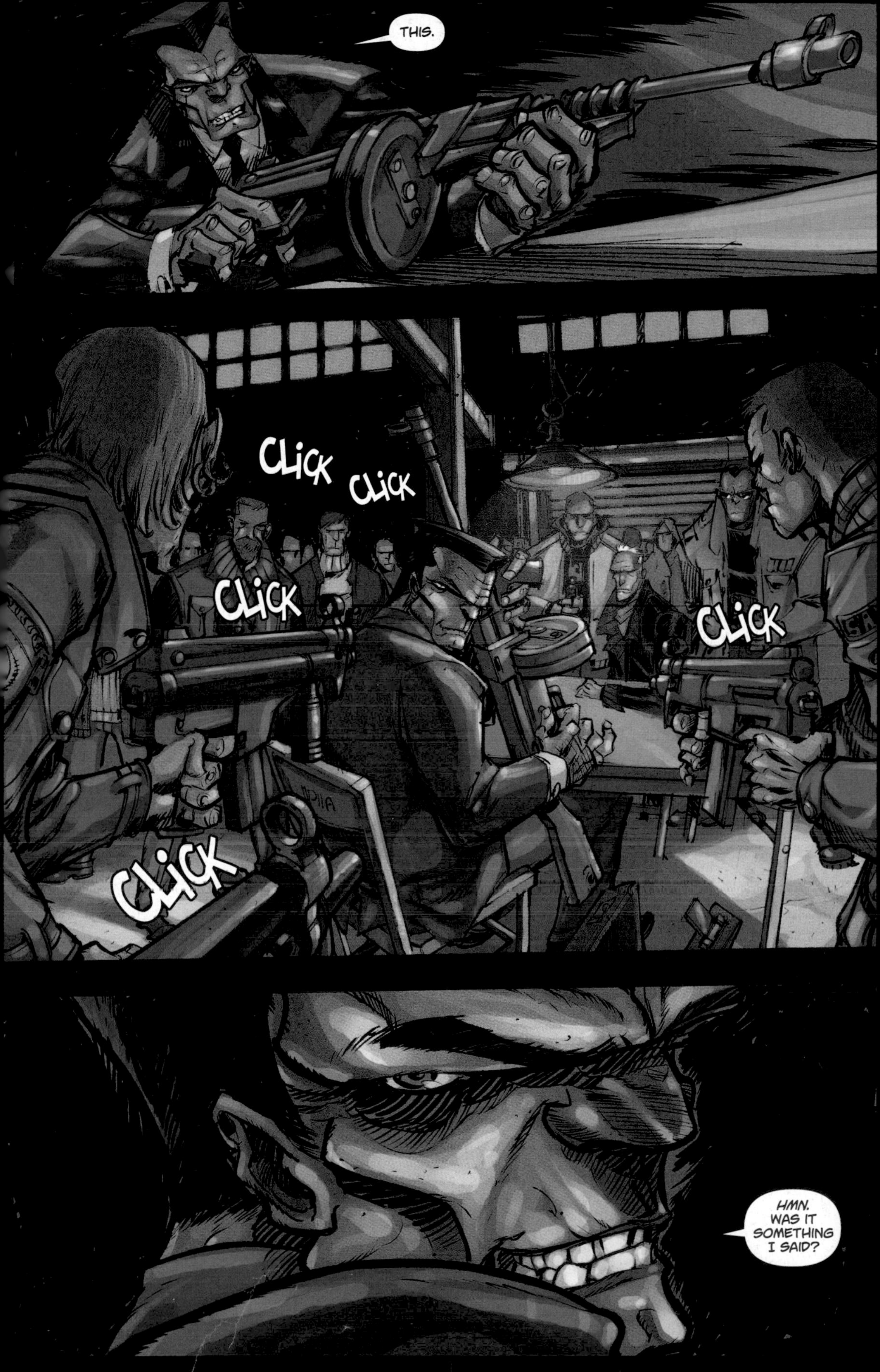
THIS.
CLICK
CLICK
CLICK
CLICK
CLICK
HMN. WAS IT SOMETHING I SAID?

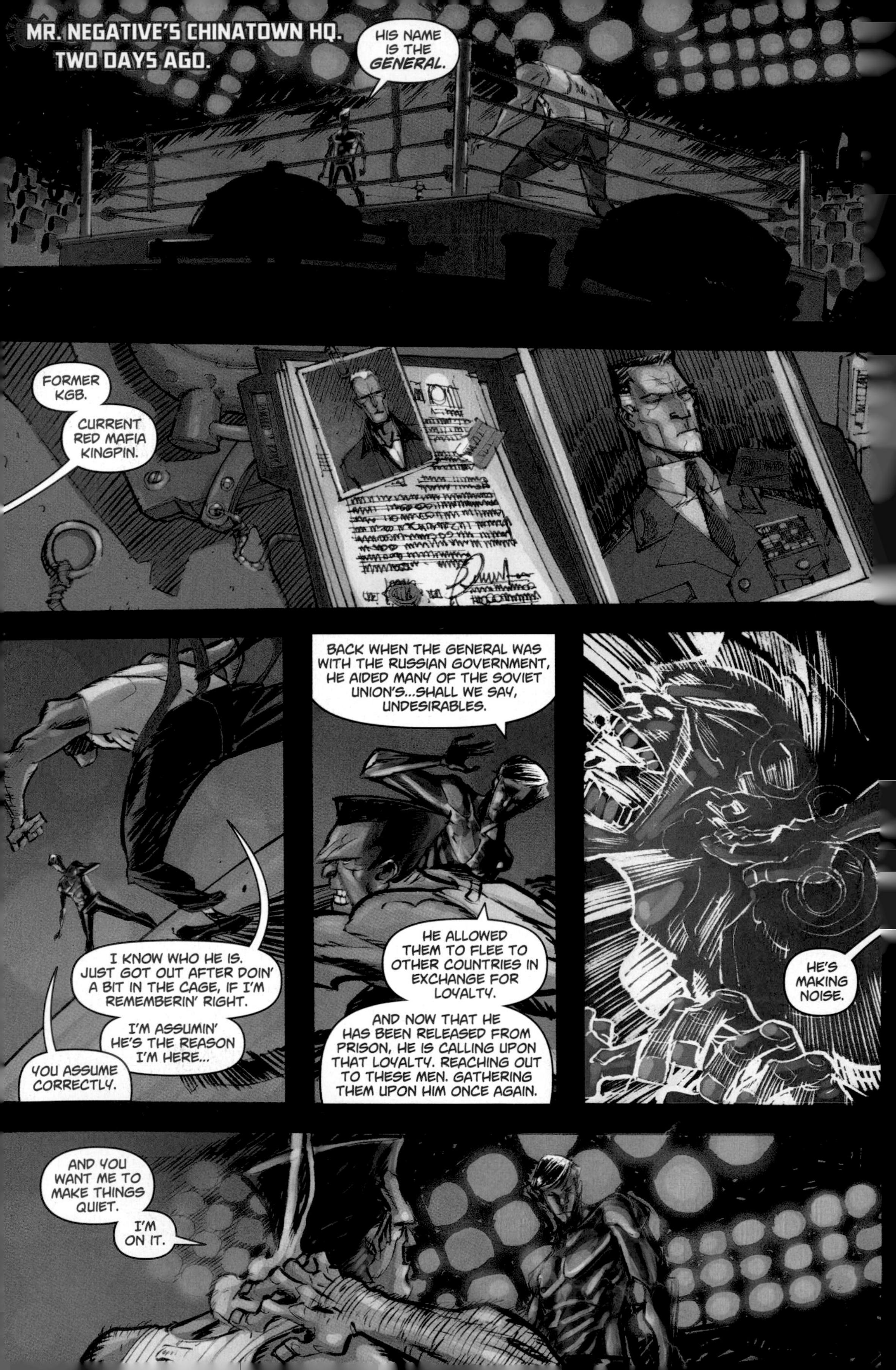
MR. NEGATIVE'S CHINATOWN HQ. TWO DAYS AGO.
HIS NAME IS THE GENERAL.
FORMER KGB.
CURRENT RED MAFIA KINGPIN.
I KNOW WHO HE IS. JUST GOT OUT AFTER DOIN' A BIT IN THE CAGE, IF I'M REMEMBERIN' RIGHT.
I'M ASSUMIN' HE'S THE REASON I'M HERE...
YOU ASSUME CORRECTLY.
BACK WHEN THE GENERAL WAS WITH THE RUSSIAN GOVERNMENT, HE AIDED MANY OF THE SOVIET UNION'S...SHALL WE SAY, UNDESIRABLES.
HE ALLOWED THEM TO FLEE TO OTHER COUNTRIES IN EXCHANGE FOR LOYALTY.
AND NOW THAT HE HAS BEEN RELEASED FROM PRISON, HE IS CALLING UPON THAT LOYALTY. REACHING OUT TO THESE MEN. GATHERING THEM UPON HIM ONCE AGAIN.
HE'S MAKING NOISE.
AND YOU WANT ME TO MAKE THINGS QUIET.
I'M ON IT.

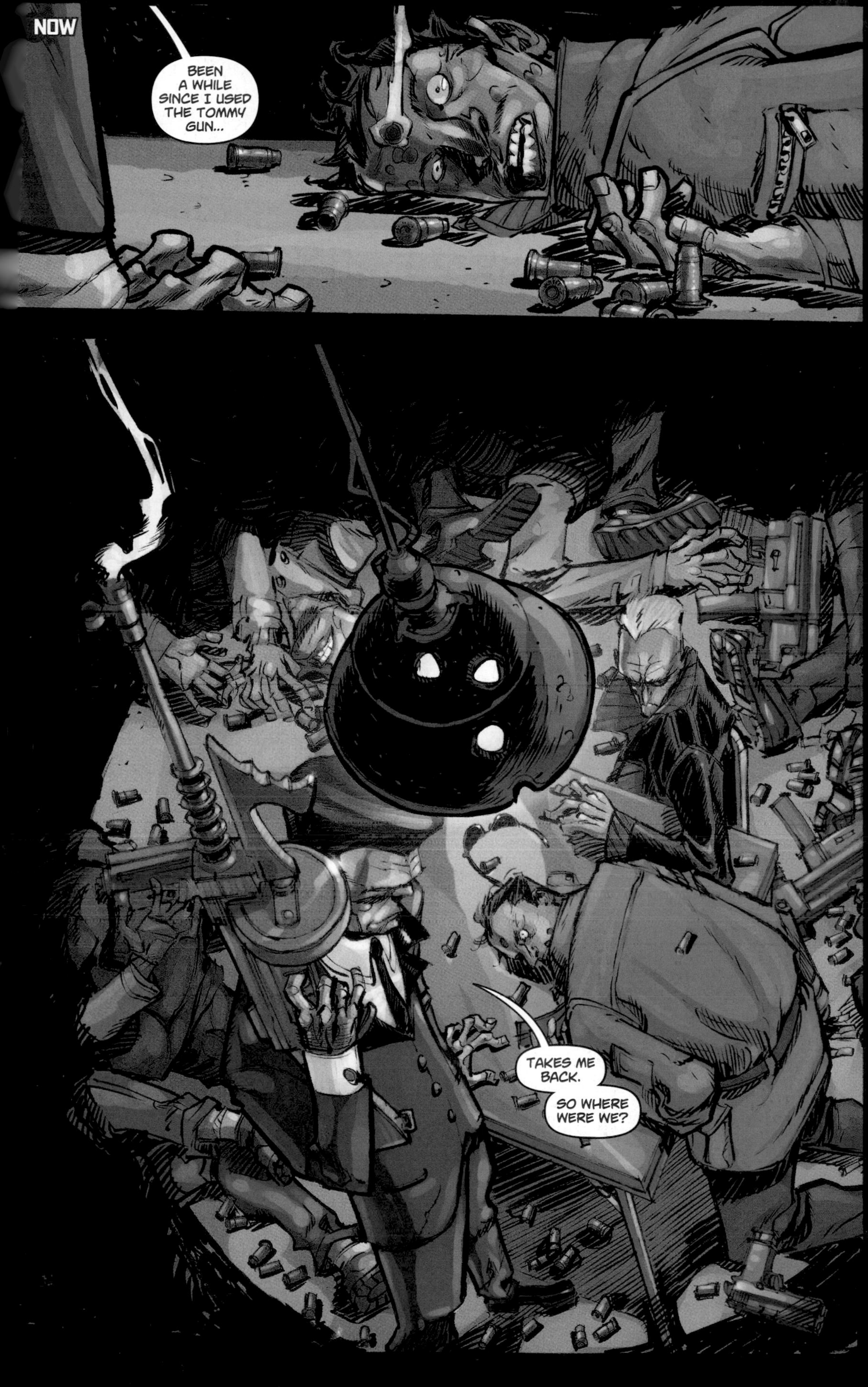
NOW
BEEN A WHILE SINCE I USED THE TOMMY GUN...
TAKES ME BACK.
SO WHERE WERE WE?

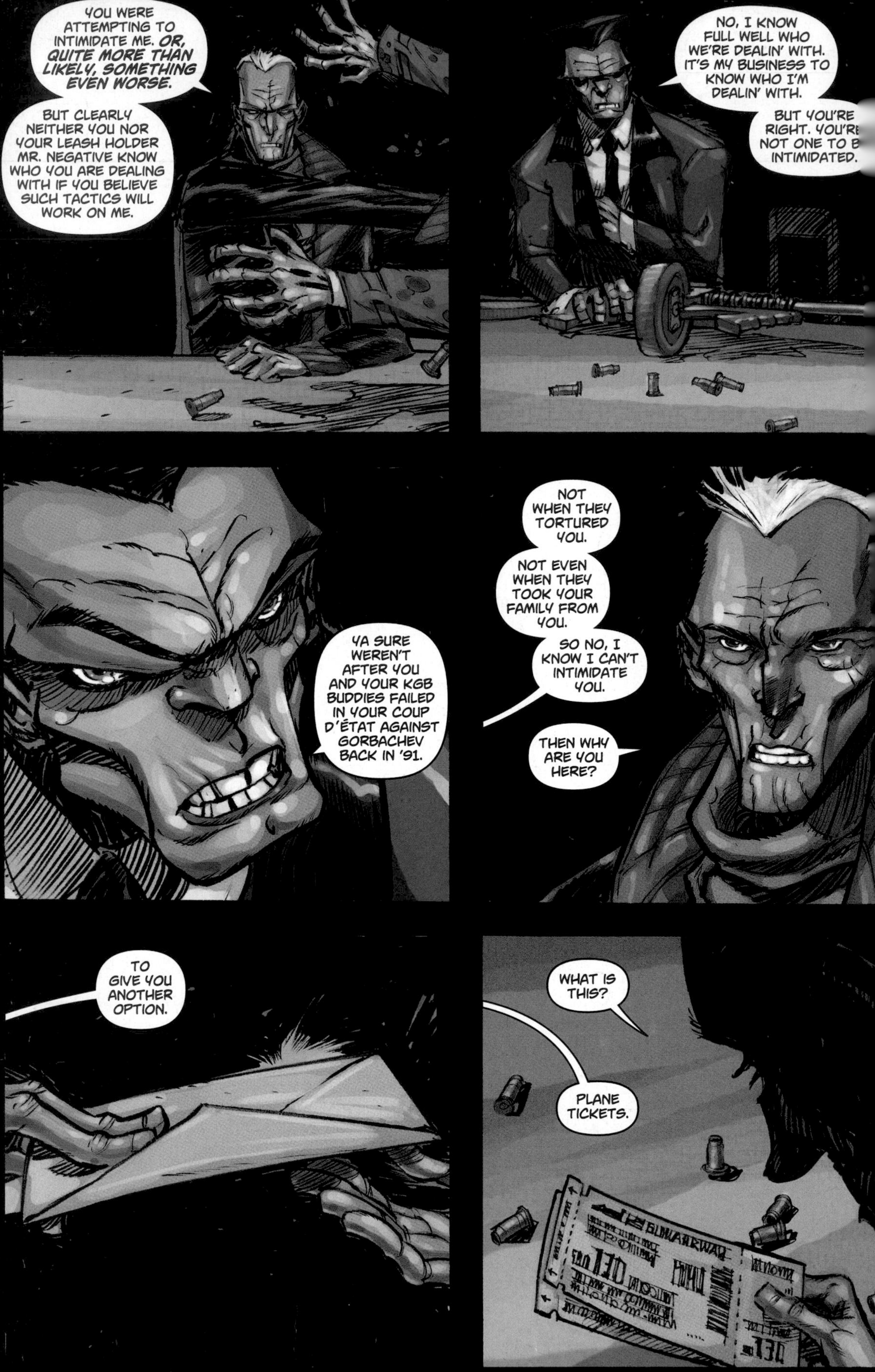
YOU WERE ATTEMPTING TO INTIMIDATE ME. *OR, QUITE MORE THAN LIKELY, SOMETHING EVEN WORSE.*
BUT CLEARLY NEITHER YOU NOR YOUR LEASH HOLDER MR. NEGATIVE KNOW WHO YOU ARE DEALING WITH IF YOU BELIEVE SUCH TACTICS WILL WORK ON ME.
NO, I KNOW FULL WELL WHO WE'RE DEALIN' WITH. IT'S MY BUSINESS TO KNOW WHO I'M DEALIN' WITH.
BUT YOU'RE RIGHT. YOU'R NOT ONE TO B INTIMIDATED.
YA SURE WEREN'T AFTER YOU AND YOUR KGB BUDDIES FAILED IN YOUR COUP D'ÉTAT AGAINST GORBACHEV BACK IN '91.
NOT WHEN THEY TORTURED YOU.
NOT EVEN WHEN THEY TOOK YOUR FAMILY FROM YOU.
SO NO, I KNOW I CAN'T INTIMIDATE YOU.
THEN WHY ARE YOU HERE?
TO GIVE YOU ANOTHER OPTION.
WHAT IS THIS?
PLANE TICKETS.

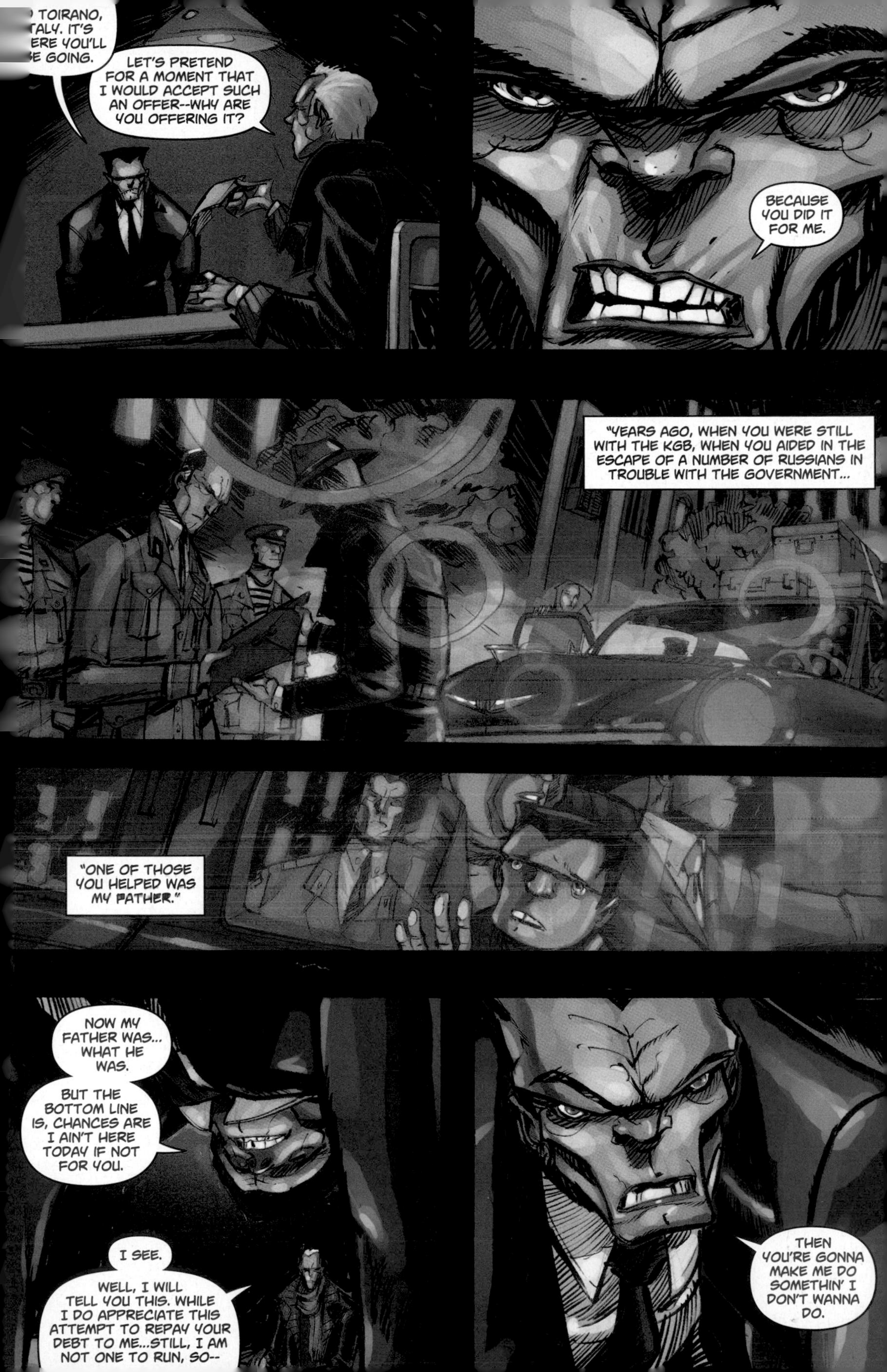

TOIRANO, ITALY. IT'S ERE YOU'LL E GOING.
LET'S PRETEND FOR A MOMENT THAT I WOULD ACCEPT SUCH AN OFFER--WHY ARE YOU OFFERING IT?
BECAUSE YOU DID IT FOR ME.
"YEARS AGO, WHEN YOU WERE STILL WITH THE KGB, WHEN YOU AIDED IN THE ESCAPE OF A NUMBER OF RUSSIANS IN TROUBLE WITH THE GOVERNMENT...
"ONE OF THOSE YOU HELPED WAS MY FATHER."
NOW MY FATHER WAS... WHAT HE WAS.
BUT THE BOTTOM LINE IS, CHANCES ARE I AIN'T HERE TODAY IF NOT FOR YOU.
I SEE.
WELL, I WILL TELL YOU THIS. WHILE I DO APPRECIATE THIS ATTEMPT TO REPAY YOUR DEBT TO ME...STILL, I AM NOT ONE TO RUN, SO--
THEN YOU'RE GONNA MAKE ME DO SOMETHIN' I DON'T WANNA DO.

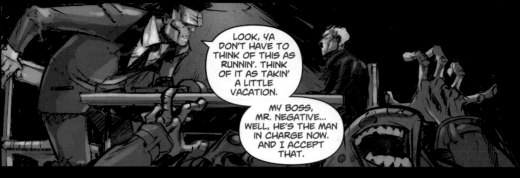

LOOK, YA DON'T HAVE TO THINK OF THIS AS RUNNIN'. THINK OF IT AS TAKIN' A LITTLE VACATION.

MY BOSS, MR. NEGATIVE... WELL, HE'S THE MAN IN CHARGE NOW. AND I ACCEPT THAT.

FOR NOW.

THERE'LL COME A DAY WHEN THAT'LL CHANGE. WHEN I WON'T BE SO ACCEPTIN' OF THAT.

WHEN I MIGHT NEED TO CALL ON AN OLD FRIEND VACATIONIN' IN TOIRANO.

SO... WHAT'S ITALY LIKE THIS TIME OF YEAR?

HMN. YA KNOW...

I THINK I'LL HAVE THAT COFFEE NOW...

Western promises

FRANK TIERI words
ERIC CANETE art

ANDRES MOSSA color
JARED K. FLETCHER letters

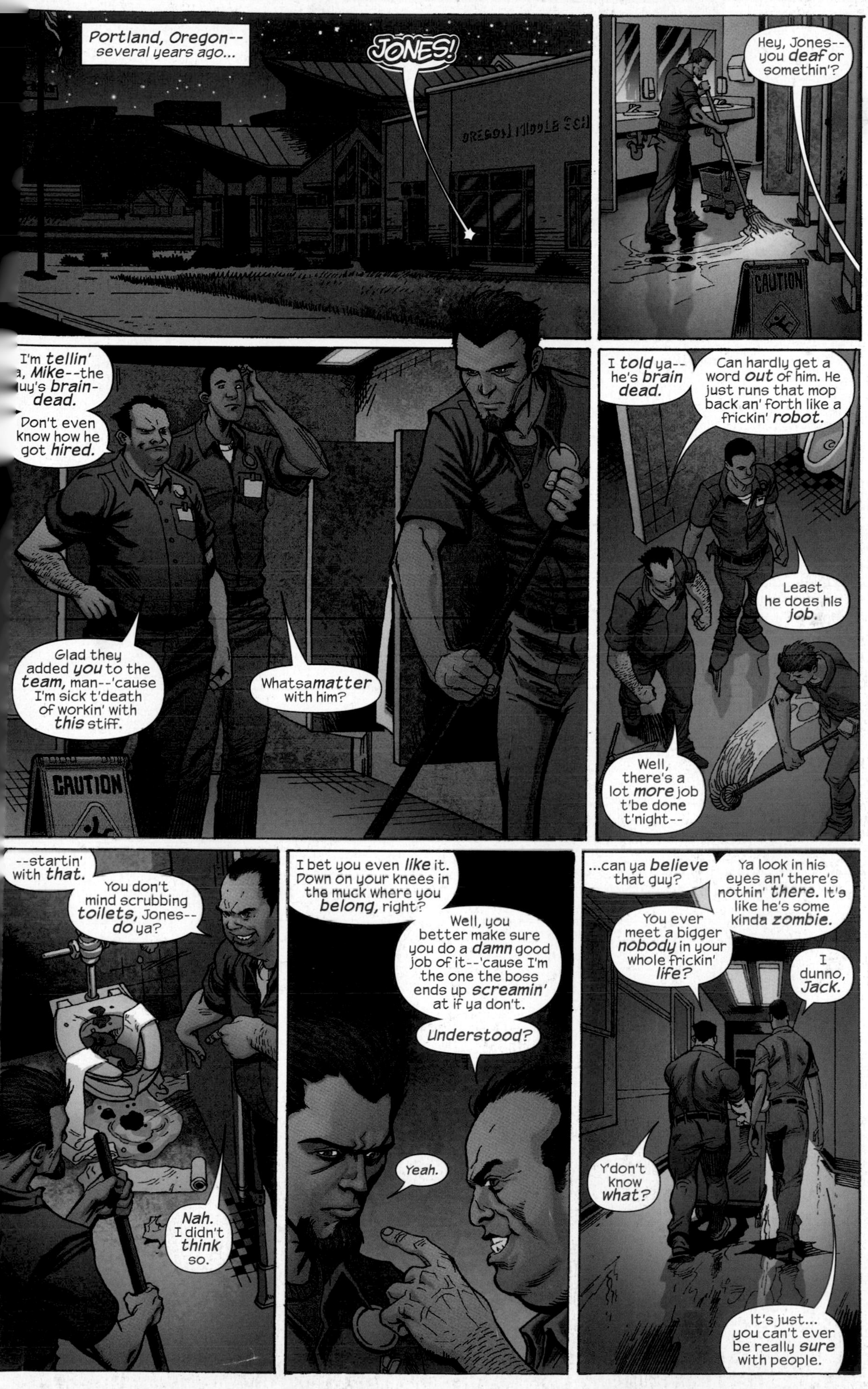
Portland, Oregon-- several years ago...
JONES!
OREGON MIDDLE SCH
Hey, Jones-- you deaf or somethin'?
CAUTION
I'm tellin' ya, Mike--the guy's brain-dead.
Don't even know how he got hired.
Glad they added you to the team, man--'cause I'm sick t'death of workin' with this stiff.
Whatsamatter with him?
CAUTION
I told ya-- he's brain dead.
Can hardly get a word out of him. He just runs that mop back an' forth like a frickin' robot.
Least he does his job.
Well, there's a lot more job t'be done t'night--
--startin' with that.
You don't mind scrubbing toilets, Jones-- do ya?
Nah. I didn't think so.
I bet you even like it. Down on your knees in the muck where you belong, right?
Well, you better make sure you do a damn good job of it--'cause I'm the one the boss ends up screamin' at if ya don't.
Understood?
Yeah.
...can ya believe that guy?
Ya look in his eyes an' there's nothin' there. It's like he's some kinda zombie.
You ever meet a bigger nobody in your whole frickin' life?
I dunno, Jack.
Y'don't know what?
It's just... you can't ever be really sure with people.

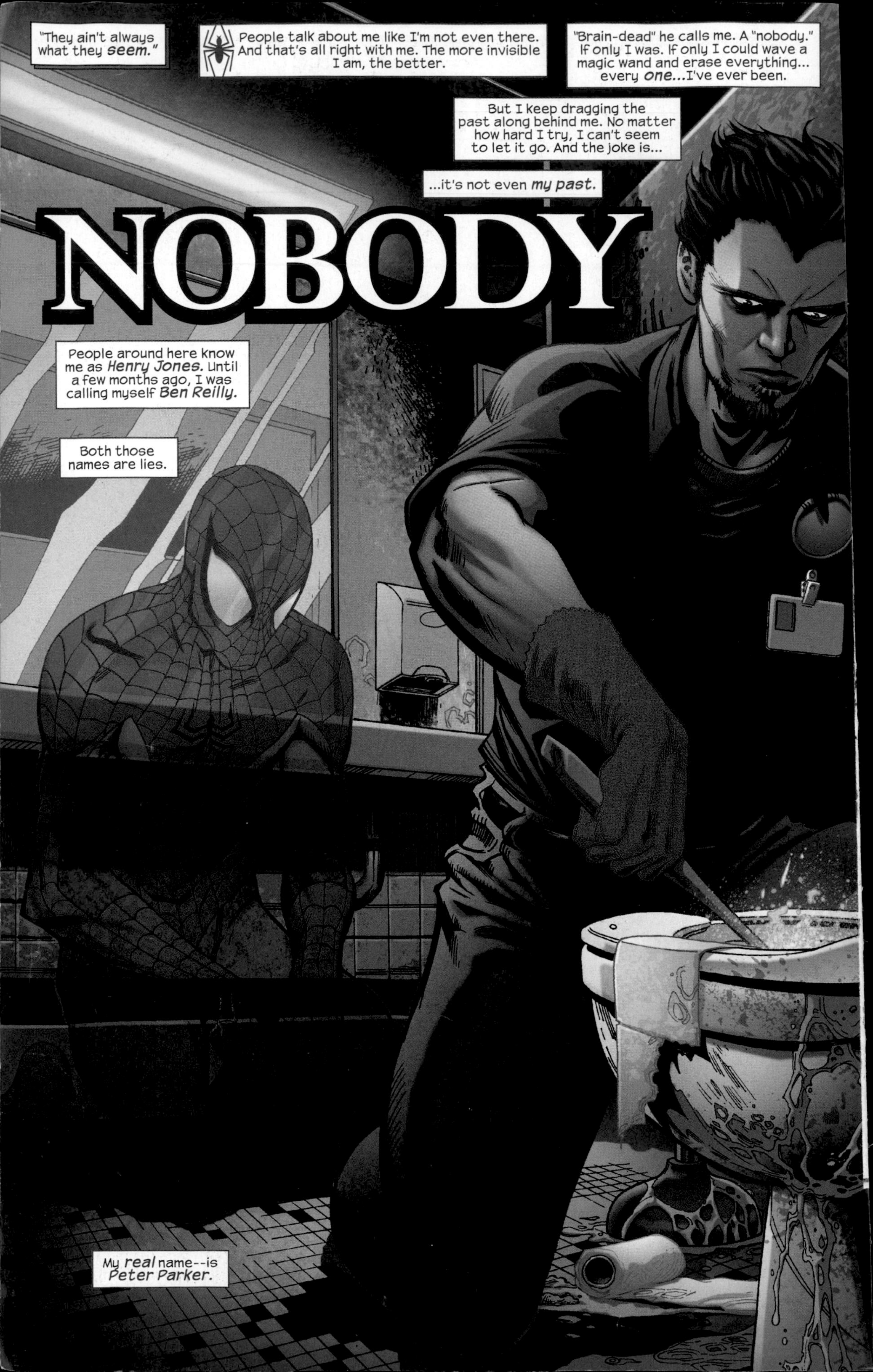
"They ain't always what they seem."
People talk about me like I'm not even there. And that's all right with me. The more invisible I am, the better.
"Brain-dead" he calls me. A "nobody." If only I was. If only I could wave a magic wand and erase everything... every one...I've ever been.
But I keep dragging the past along behind me. No matter how hard I try, I can't seem to let it go. And the joke is...
...it's not even my past.
NOBODY
People around here know me as Henry Jones. Until a few months ago, I was calling myself Ben Reilly.
Both those names are lies.
My real name--is Peter Parker.

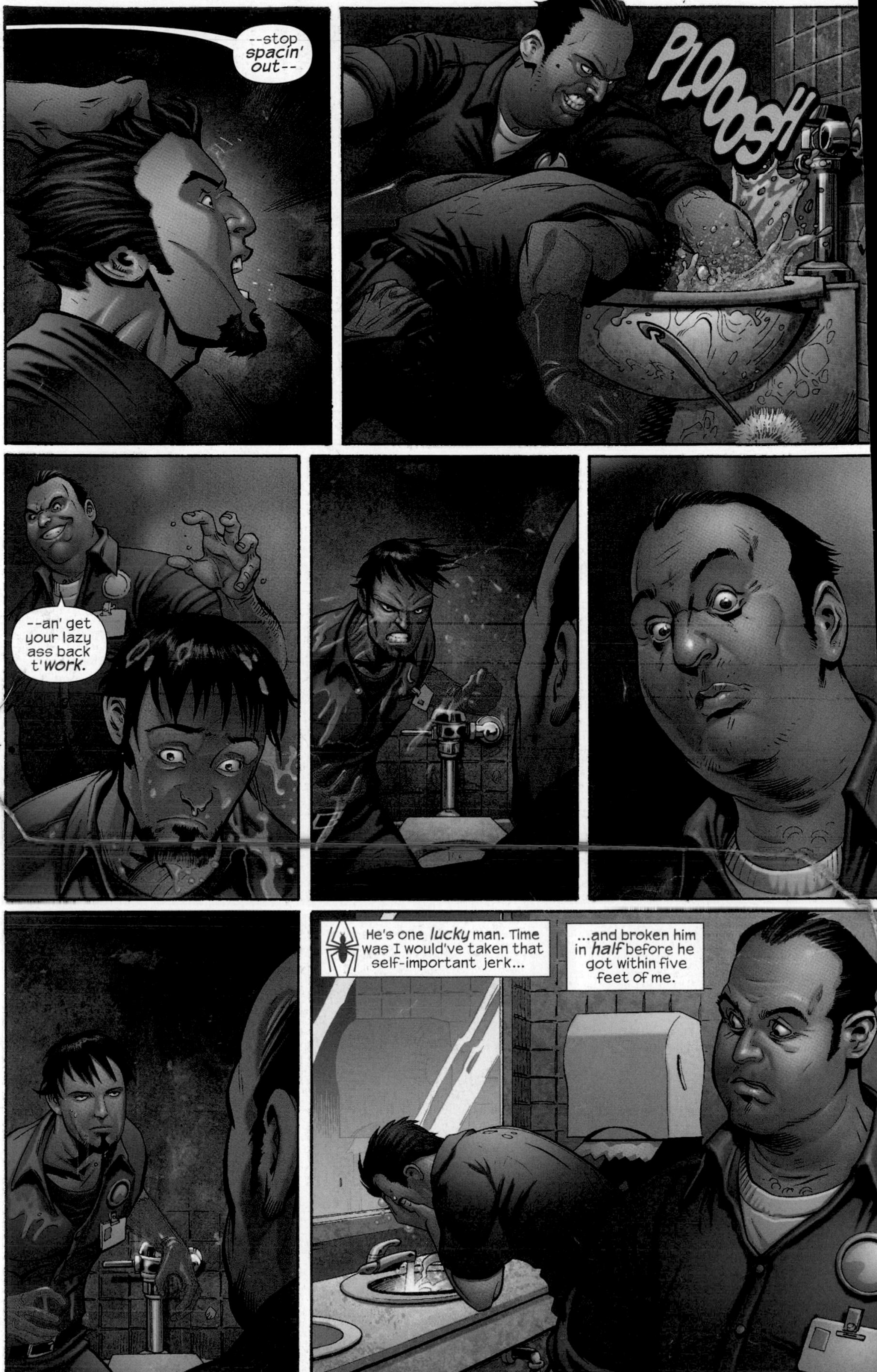
--stop spacin' out--
PLOOOSH
--an' get your lazy ass back t'work.
He's one lucky man. Time was I would've taken that self-important jerk...
...and broken him in half before he got within five feet of me.

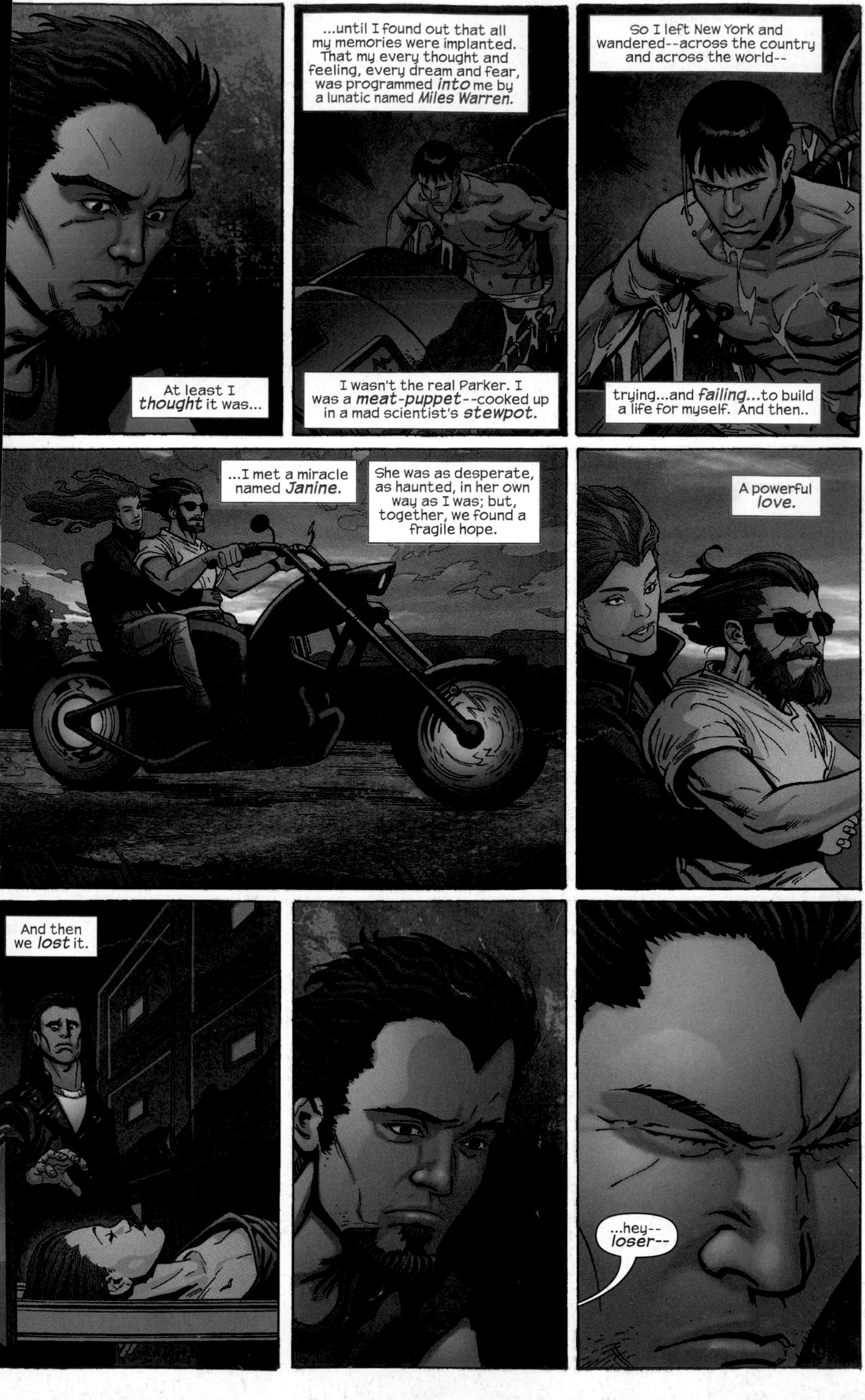
At least I thought it was...
...until I found out that all my memories were implanted. That my every thought and feeling, every dream and fear, was programmed into me by a lunatic named Miles Warren.
I wasn't the real Parker. I was a meat-puppet--cooked up in a mad scientist's stewpot.
So I left New York and wandered--across the country and across the world--
trying...and failing...to build a life for myself. And then..
...I met a miracle named Janine.
She was as desperate, as haunted, in her own way as I was; but, together, we found a fragile hope.
A powerful love.
And then we lost it.
...hey--loser--

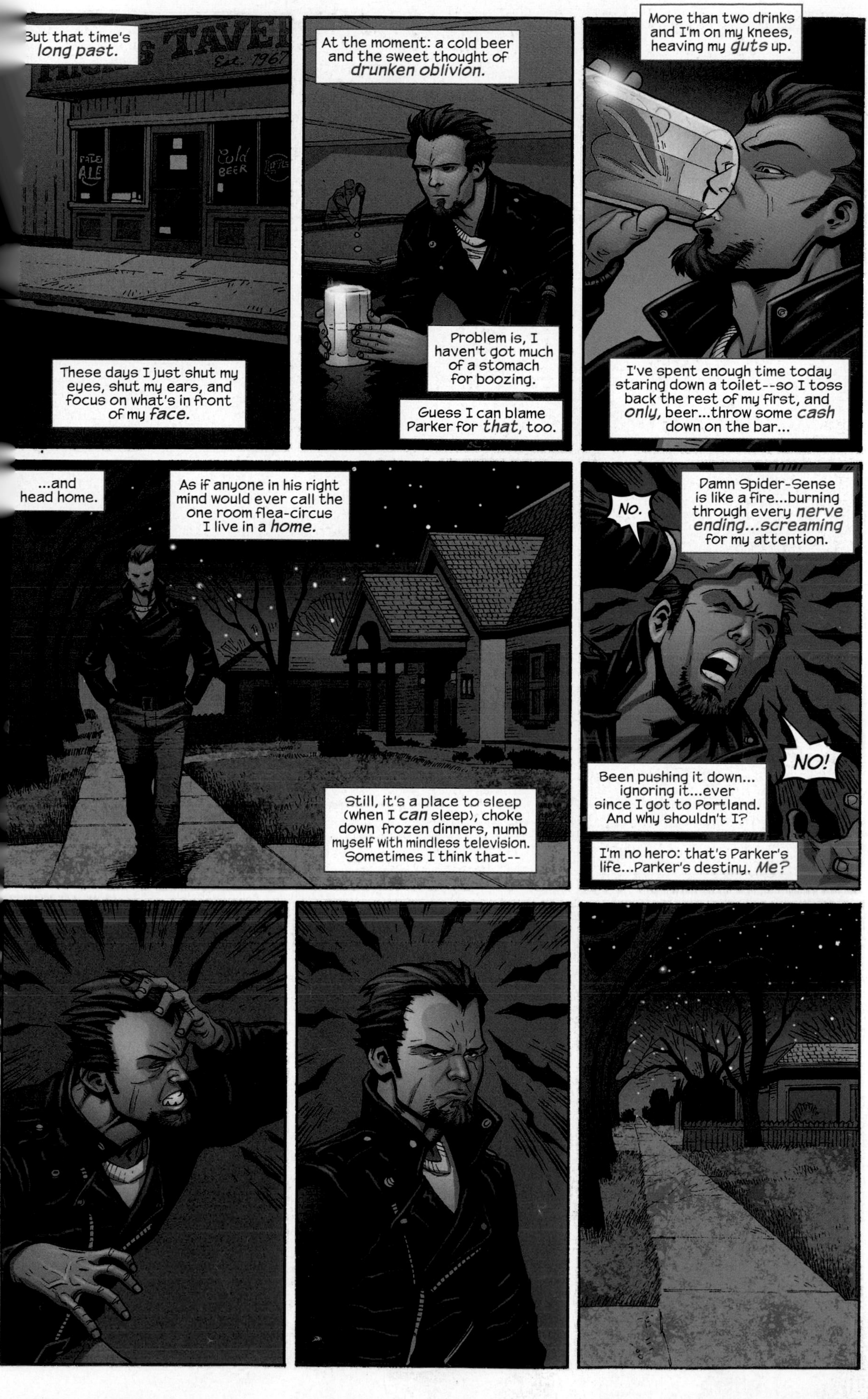
But that time's *long past.*
These days I just shut my eyes, shut my ears, and focus on what's in front of my *face.*
At the moment: a cold beer and the sweet thought of *drunken oblivion.*
Problem is, I haven't got much of a stomach for boozing.
Guess I can blame Parker for *that*, too.
More than two drinks and I'm on my knees, heaving my *guts* up.
I've spent enough time today staring down a toilet--so I toss back the rest of my first, and *only*, beer...throw some *cash* down on the bar...
...and head home.
As if anyone in his right mind would ever call the one room flea-circus I live in a *home.*
Still, it's a place to sleep (when I *can* sleep), choke down frozen dinners, numb myself with mindless television. Sometimes I think that--
No.
Damn Spider-Sense is like a fire...burning through every *nerve ending...screaming* for my attention.
NO!
Been pushing it down... ignoring it...ever since I got to Portland. And why shouldn't I?
I'm no hero: that's Parker's life...Parker's destiny. *Me?*

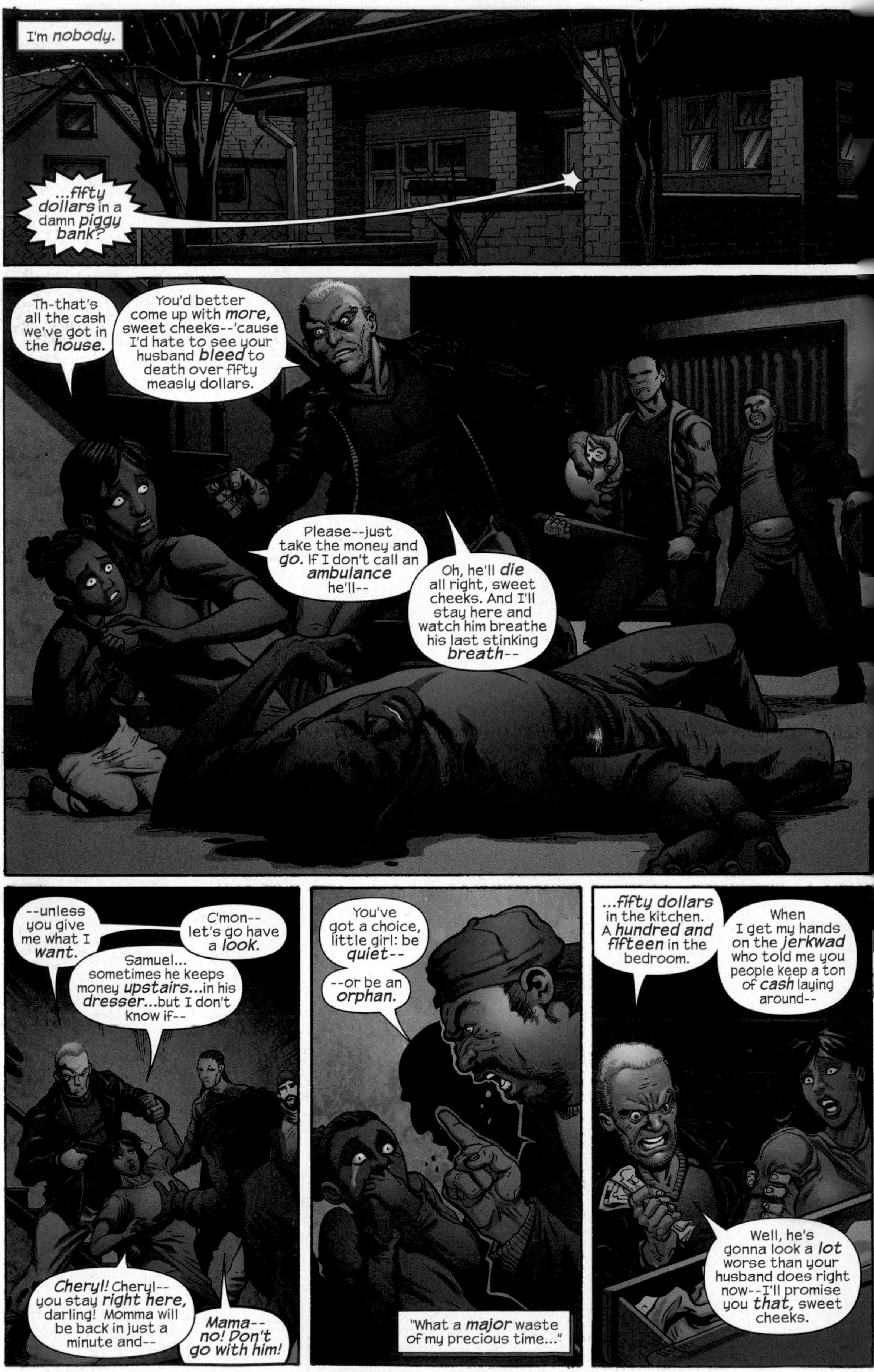
I'm nobody.
...fifty dollars in a damn piggy bank?
Th-that's all the cash we've got in the house.
You'd better come up with more, sweet cheeks--'cause I'd hate to see your husband bleed to death over fifty measly dollars.
Please--just take the money and go. If I don't call an ambulance he'll--
Oh, he'll die all right, sweet cheeks. And I'll stay here and watch him breathe his last stinking breath--
--unless you give me what I want.
C'mon-- let's go have a look.
Samuel... sometimes he keeps money upstairs...in his dresser...but I don't know if--
Cheryl! Cheryl-- you stay right here, darling! Momma will be back in just a minute and--
Mama-- no! Don't go with him!
You've got a choice, little girl: be quiet--
--or be an orphan.
"What a major waste of my precious time..."
...fifty dollars in the kitchen. A hundred and fifteen in the bedroom.
When I get my hands on the jerkwad who told me you people keep a ton of cash laying around--
Well, he's gonna look a lot worse than your husband does right now--I'll promise you that, sweet cheeks.

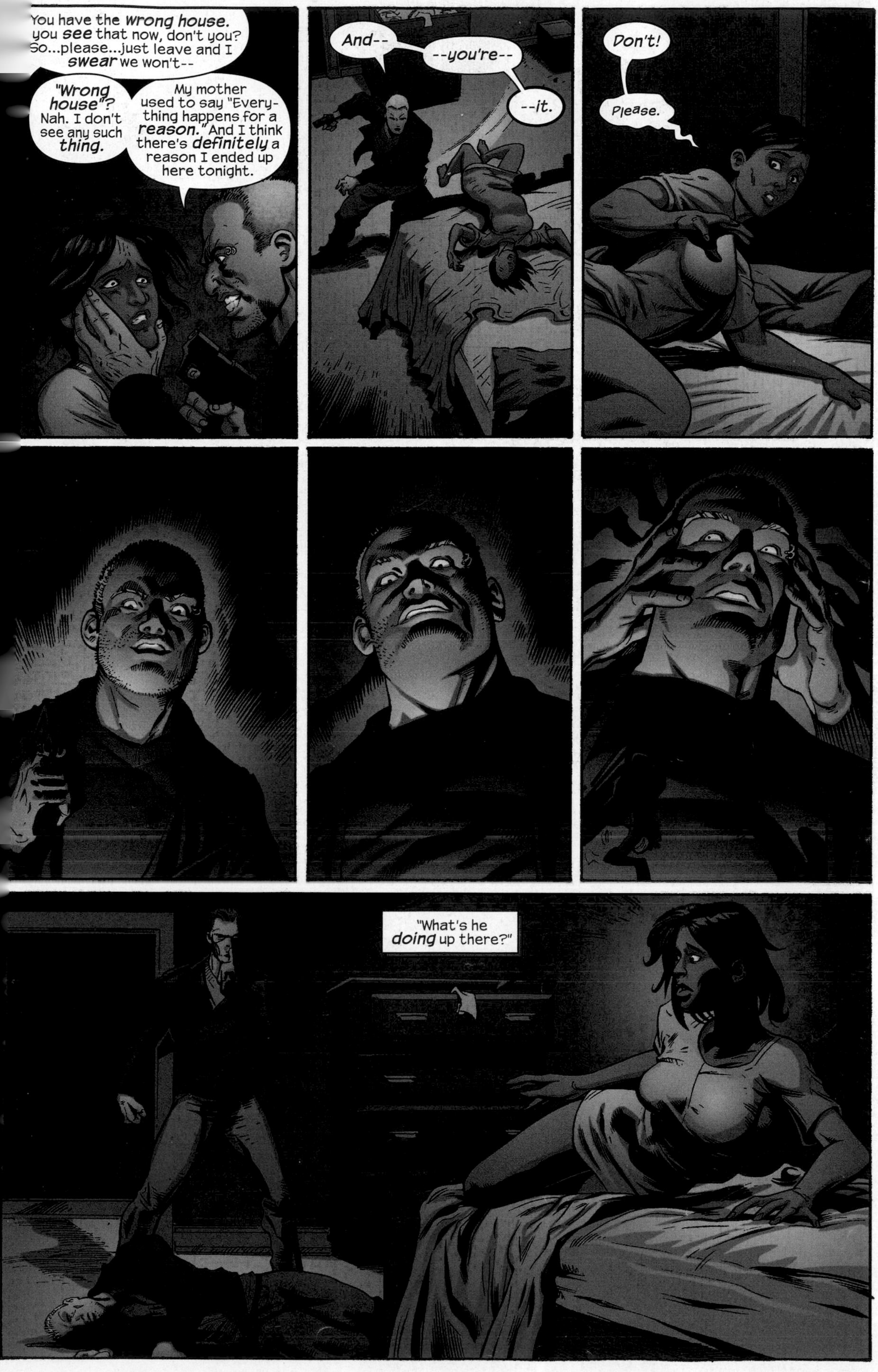

You have the wrong house. you see that now, don't you? So...please...just leave and I swear we won't--
"Wrong house"? Nah. I don't see any such thing.
My mother used to say "Everything happens for a reason." And I think there's definitely a reason I ended up here tonight.
And--
--you're--
--it.
Don't!
Please.
"What's he doing up there?"

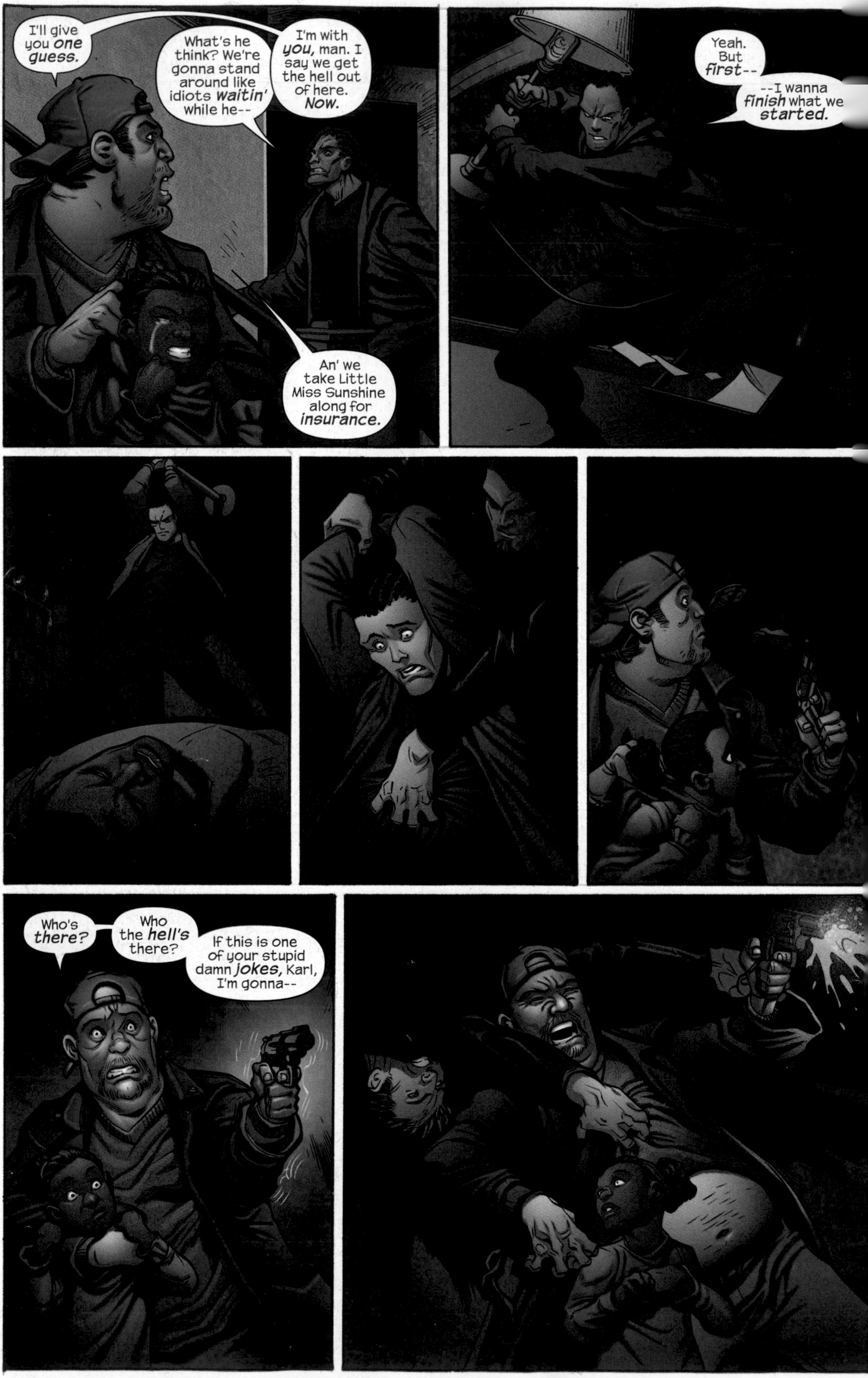

I'll give you one guess.
What's he think? We're gonna stand around like idiots waitin' while he--
I'm with you, man. I say we get the hell out of here. Now.
An' we take Little Miss Sunshine along for insurance.
Yeah. But first--
--I wanna finish what we started.
Who's there?
Who the hell's there?
If this is one of your stupid damn jokes, Karl, I'm gonna--

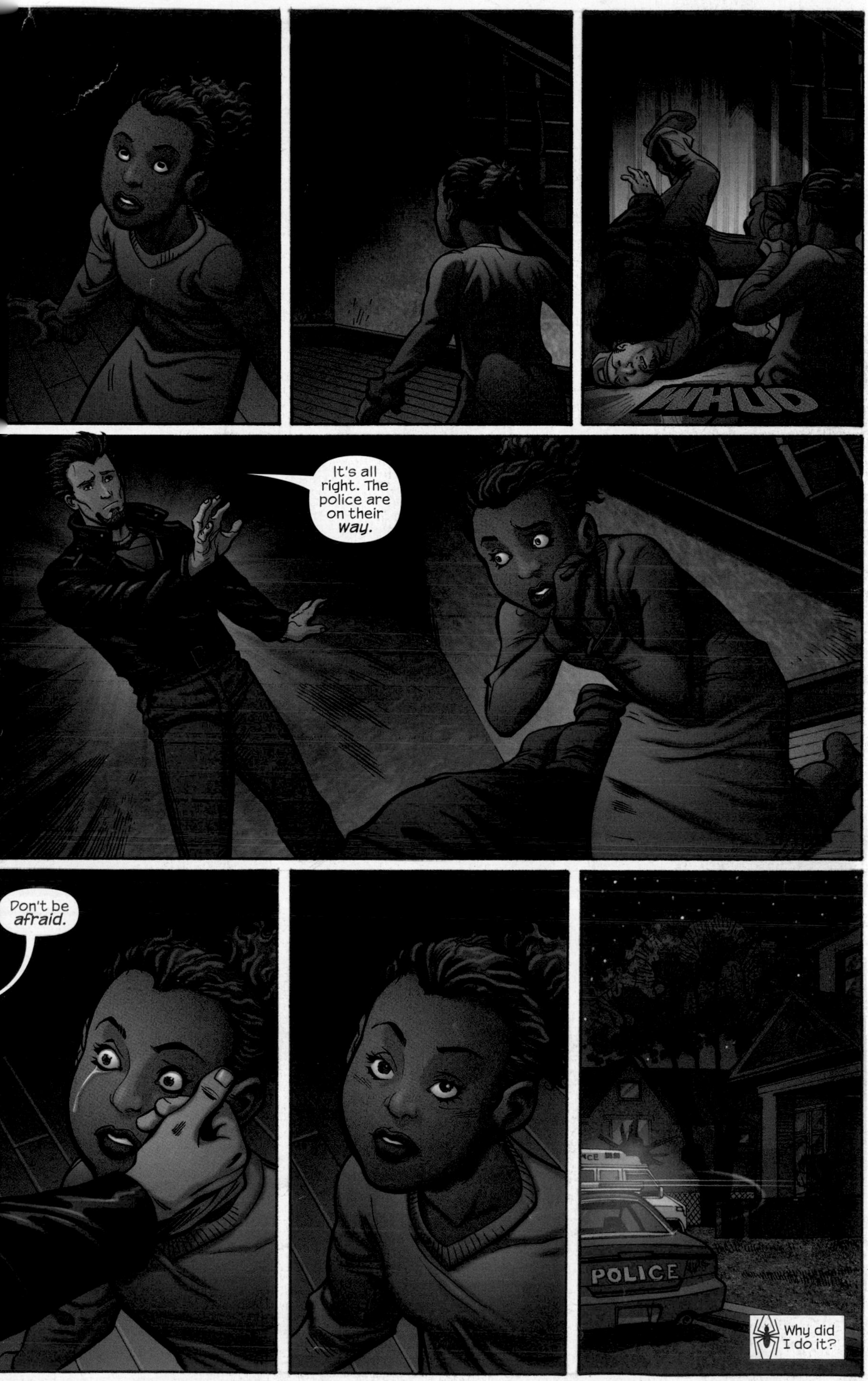
WHUD
It's all right. The police are on their *way*.
Don't be *afraid*.
POLICE
Why did I do it?

OREGON TRIBUNE

MYSTERY MAN SAVES FAMILY!

Sure I spared those people some suffering *today*; but who knows what new miseries are waiting for them...for *any* of us...*tomorrow?*

I'm not Peter Parker. I haven't deluded myself into thinking I can *change the world.* The best any of us can do is duck the bullets as long as we can...

...and try to find a little *love* along the way. But love, like everything *else* in this rotten life, *doesn't last.*

So, in the end, it's better to just keep your head down. Stay off the grid. Don't get involved. Be a *nothing.* A...

Hey... *Jones!*

OREGON MYS SAVE

EARTHQUAKE SHAKES TONGA

BSG H

You think you're gettin' paid t'stand around reading the *newspaper?*

Reading? *Haw!* You probably just lookin' at the pretty pictures! Now, *c'mon,* moron--

--get your butt t'*work* before I--

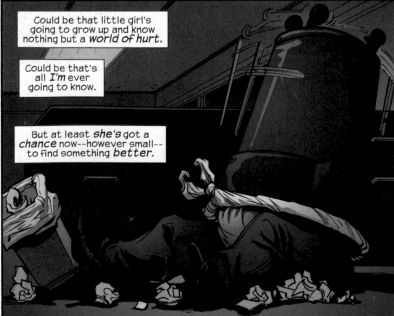

Could be that little girl's going to grow up and know nothing but a *world of hurt.*

Could be that's all *I'm* ever going to know.

But at least *she's* got a *chance* now--however small-- to find something *better.*

Guess I'm as delusional as Parker, after all. But it's a *good* delusion, I think.

And it sure as hell beats being a *nobody.*

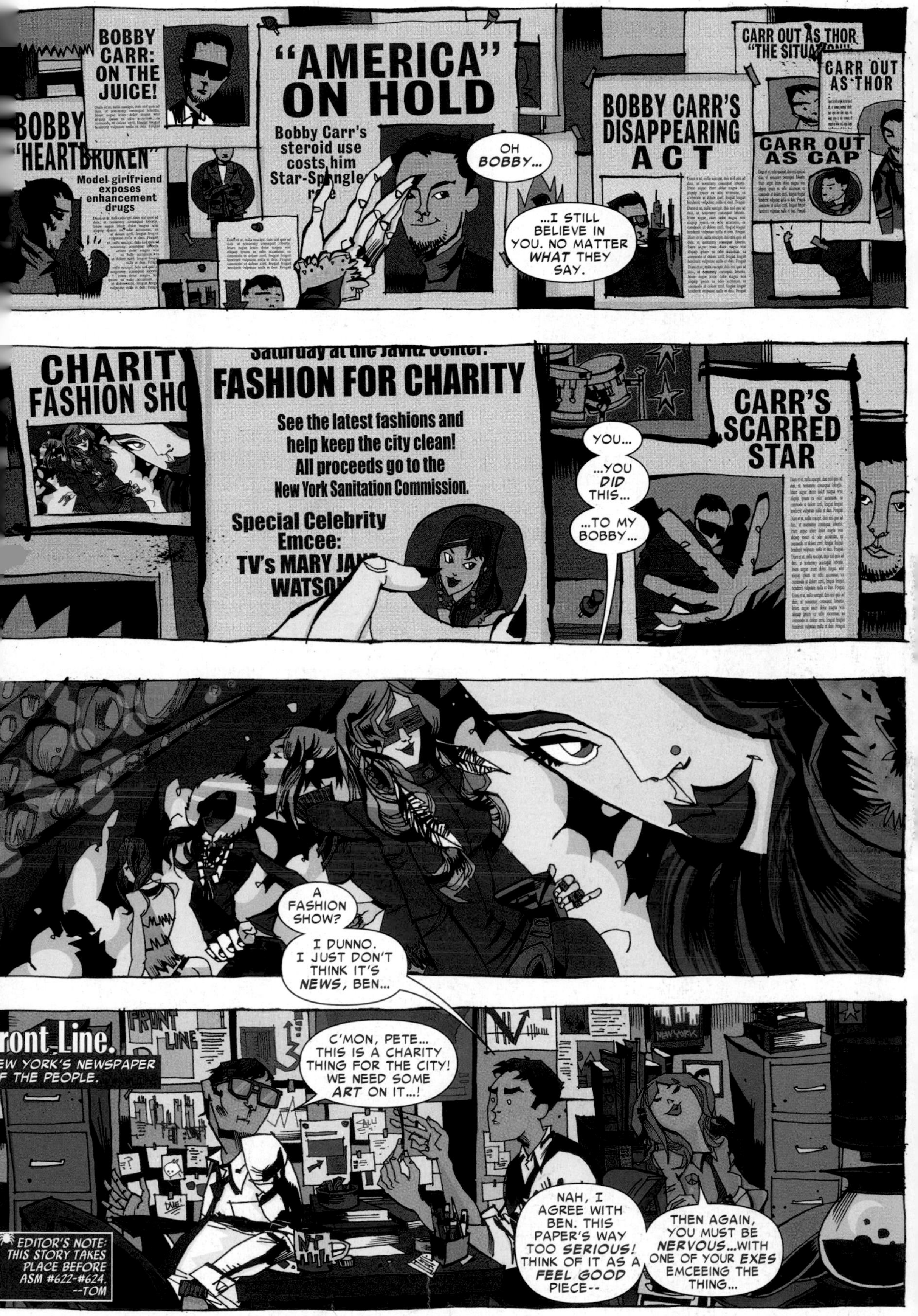
BOBBY CARR: ON THE JUICE!
"AMERICA" ON HOLD
Bobby Carr's steroid use costs him Star-Spangle role
BOBBY "HEARTBROKEN"
Model-girlfriend exposes enhancement drugs
BOBBY CARR'S DISAPPEARING ACT
CARR OUT AS THOR "THE SITUA
CARR OUT AS THOR
CARR OUT AS CAP
OH BOBBY...
...I STILL BELIEVE IN YOU. NO MATTER WHAT THEY SAY.
CHARIT FASHION SHO
Saturday at the Javitz Center:
FASHION FOR CHARITY
See the latest fashions and help keep the city clean! All proceeds go to the New York Sanitation Commission.
Special Celebrity Emcee: TV's MARY JANE WATSON
CARR'S SCARRED STAR
YOU...
...YOU DID THIS...
...TO MY BOBBY...
A FASHION SHOW?
I DUNNO. I JUST DON'T THINK IT'S NEWS, BEN...
Front Line. NEW YORK'S NEWSPAPER OF THE PEOPLE.
C'MON, PETE... THIS IS A CHARITY THING FOR THE CITY! WE NEED SOME ART ON IT...!
NAH, I AGREE WITH BEN. THIS PAPER'S WAY TOO SERIOUS! THINK OF IT AS A FEEL GOOD PIECE--
THEN AGAIN, YOU MUST BE NERVOUS...WITH ONE OF YOUR EXES EMCEEING THE THING...
EDITOR'S NOTE: THIS STORY TAKES PLACE BEFORE ASM #622-#624. --TOM

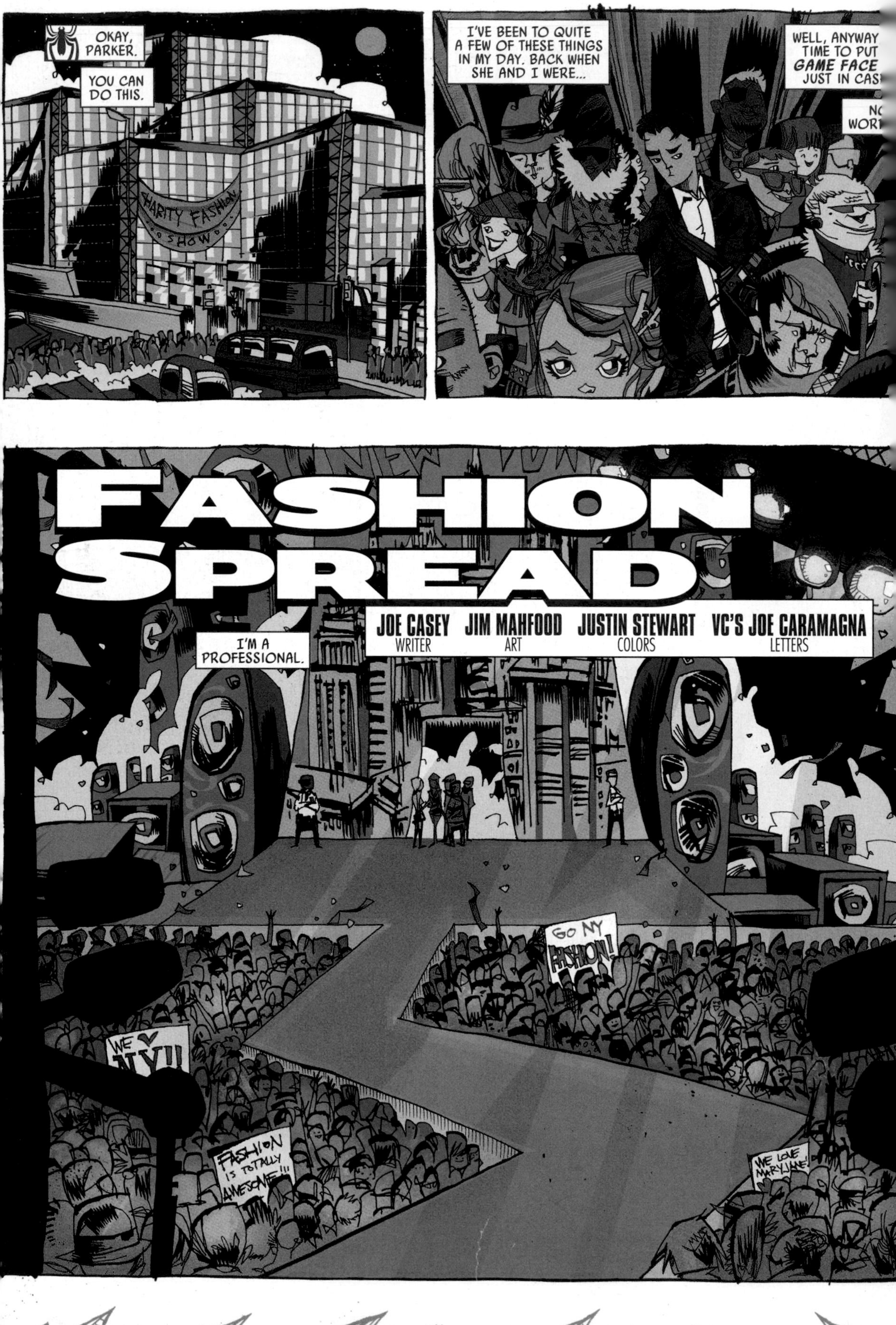
OKAY, PARKER.
YOU CAN DO THIS.
CHARITY FASHION SHOW
I'VE BEEN TO QUITE A FEW OF THESE THINGS IN MY DAY. BACK WHEN SHE AND I WERE...
WELL, ANYWAY TIME TO PUT GAME FACE JUST IN CAS
NO WOR
FASHION SPREAD
JOE CASEY WRITER
JIM MAHFOOD ART
JUSTIN STEWART COLORS
VC'S JOE CARAMAGNA LETTERS
I'M A PROFESSIONAL.
GO NY FASHION!
WE ♥ NYU
FASHION IS TOTALLY AWESOME!!!
WE LOVE MARY JANE!

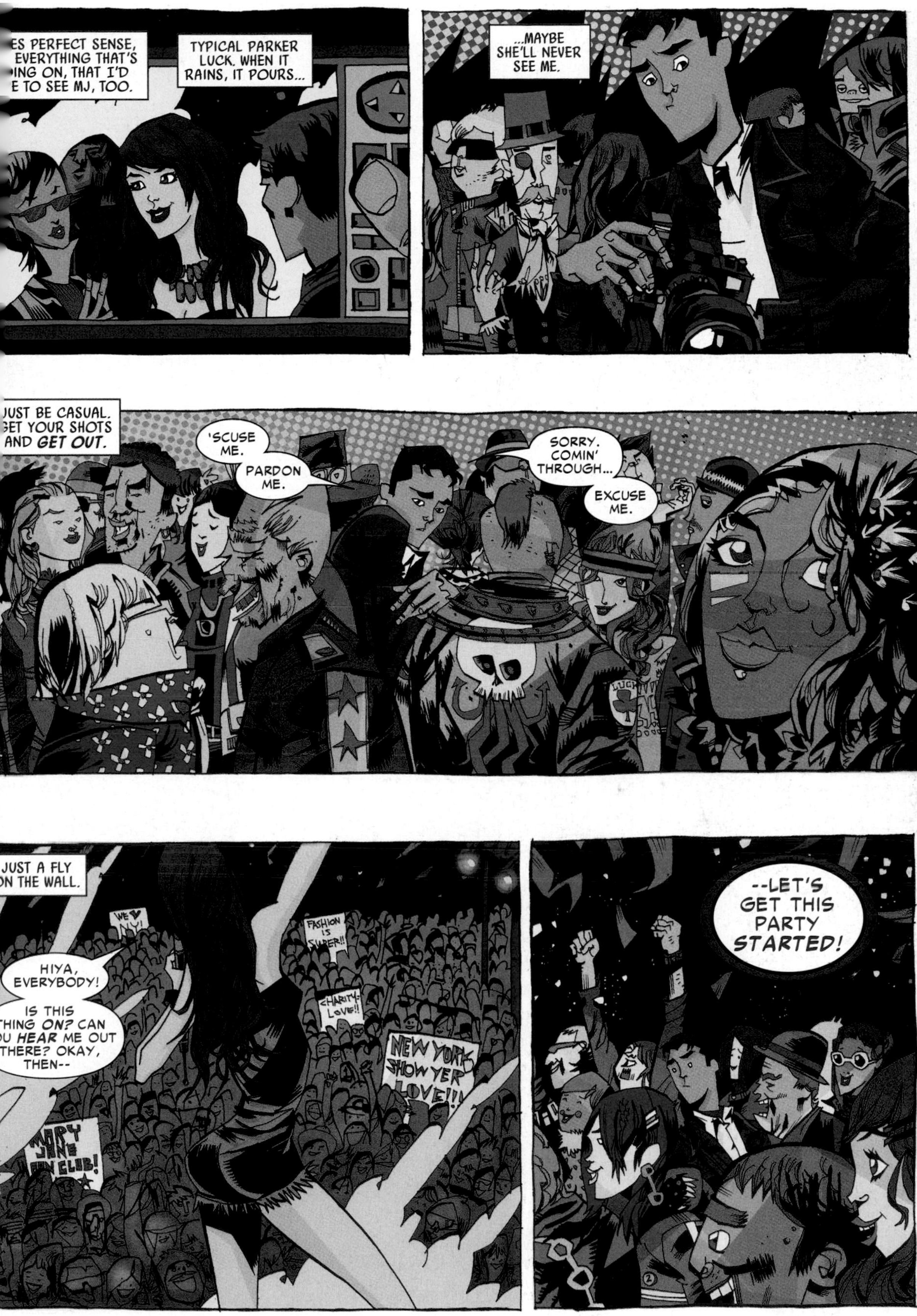
ES PERFECT SENSE, EVERYTHING THAT'S ING ON, THAT I'D E TO SEE MJ, TOO.
TYPICAL PARKER LUCK. WHEN IT RAINS, IT POURS...
...MAYBE SHE'LL NEVER SEE ME.
JUST BE CASUAL. GET YOUR SHOTS AND GET OUT.
'SCUSE ME.
PARDON ME.
SORRY. COMIN' THROUGH...
EXCUSE ME.
JUST A FLY ON THE WALL.
WE ♥ NY!
FASHION IS SUPER!!
CHARITY-LOVE!!
NEW YORK SHOW YER LOVE!!!
MARY JANE FAN CLUB!
HIYA, EVERYBODY!
IS THIS THING ON? CAN YOU HEAR ME OUT THERE? OKAY, THEN--
--LET'S GET THIS PARTY STARTED!

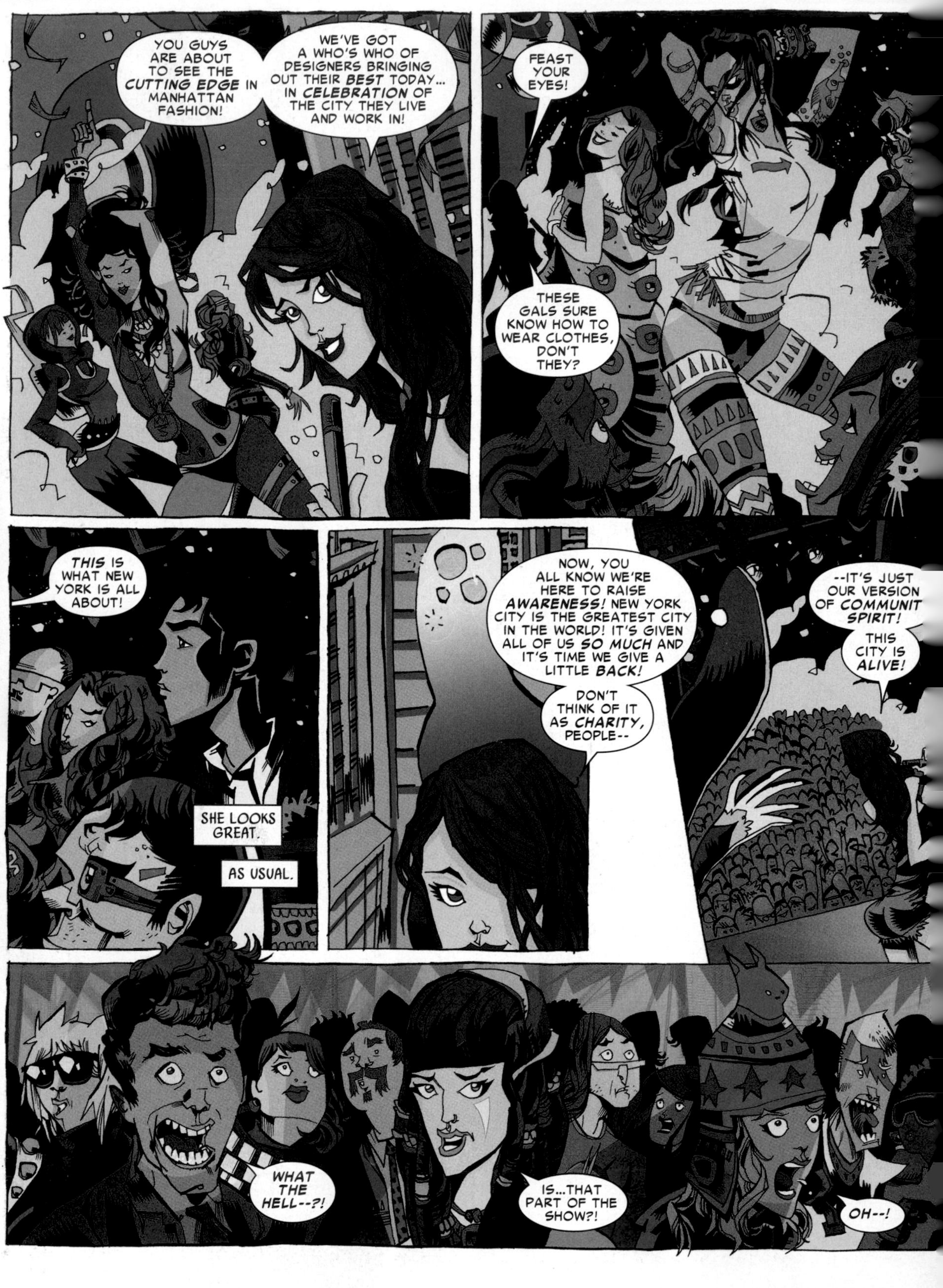
YOU GUYS ARE ABOUT TO SEE THE CUTTING EDGE IN MANHATTAN FASHION!
WE'VE GOT A WHO'S WHO OF DESIGNERS BRINGING OUT THEIR BEST TODAY... IN CELEBRATION OF THE CITY THEY LIVE AND WORK IN!
FEAST YOUR EYES!
THESE GALS SURE KNOW HOW TO WEAR CLOTHES, DON'T THEY?
THIS IS WHAT NEW YORK IS ALL ABOUT!
SHE LOOKS GREAT.
AS USUAL.
NOW, YOU ALL KNOW WE'RE HERE TO RAISE AWARENESS! NEW YORK CITY IS THE GREATEST CITY IN THE WORLD! IT'S GIVEN ALL OF US SO MUCH AND IT'S TIME WE GIVE A LITTLE BACK!
DON'T THINK OF IT AS CHARITY, PEOPLE--
--IT'S JUST OUR VERSION OF COMMUNIT SPIRIT!
THIS CITY IS ALIVE!
WHAT THE HELL--?!
IS...THAT PART OF THE SHOW?!
OH--!

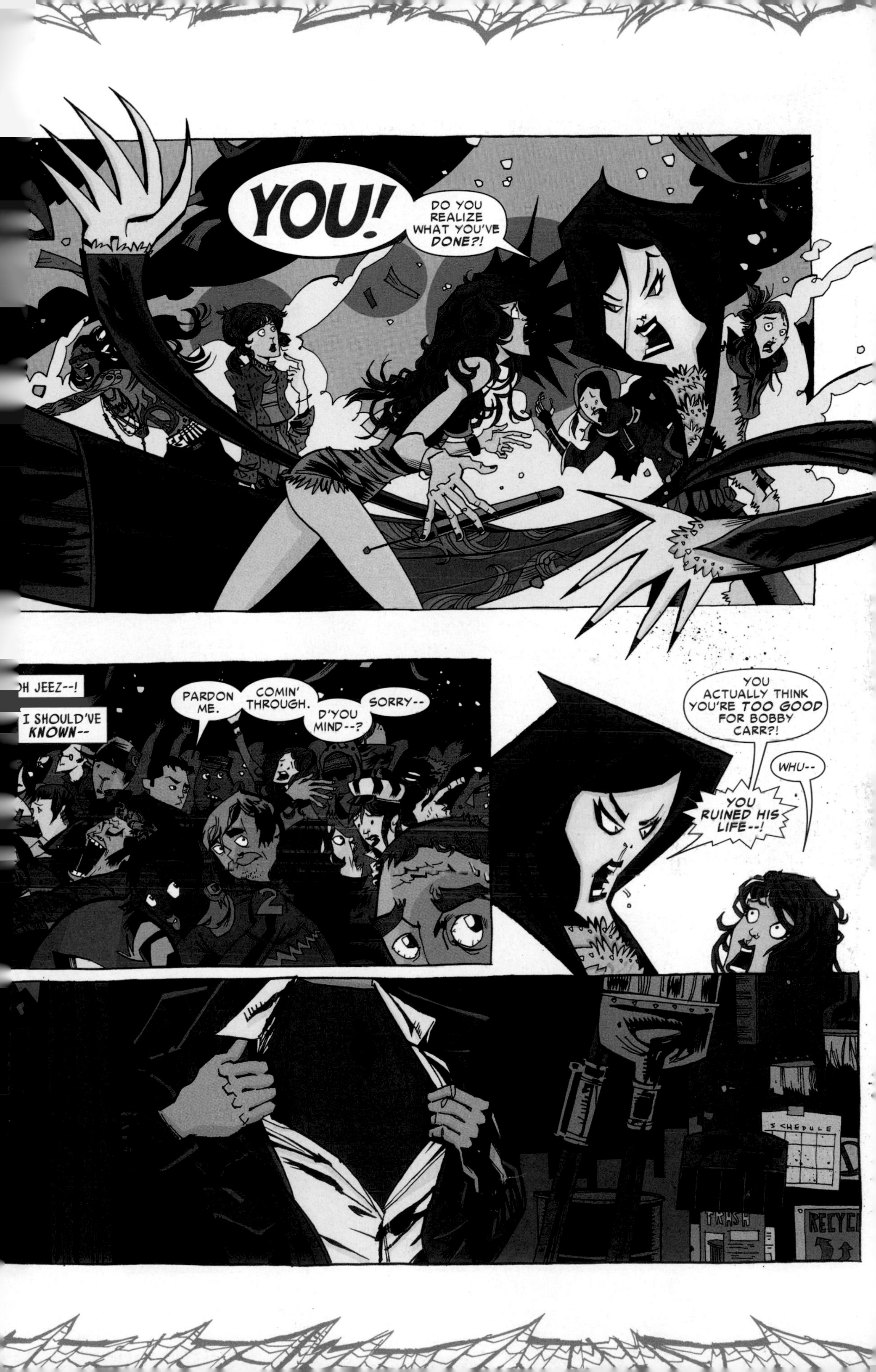

YOU!
DO YOU REALIZE WHAT YOU'VE DONE?!
OH JEEZ--!
I SHOULD'VE KNOWN--
PARDON ME.
COMIN' THROUGH.
D'YOU MIND--?
SORRY--
YOU ACTUALLY THINK YOU'RE TOO GOOD FOR BOBBY CARR?!
YOU RUINED HIS LIFE--!
WHU--
SCHEDULE
TRASH
RECYC

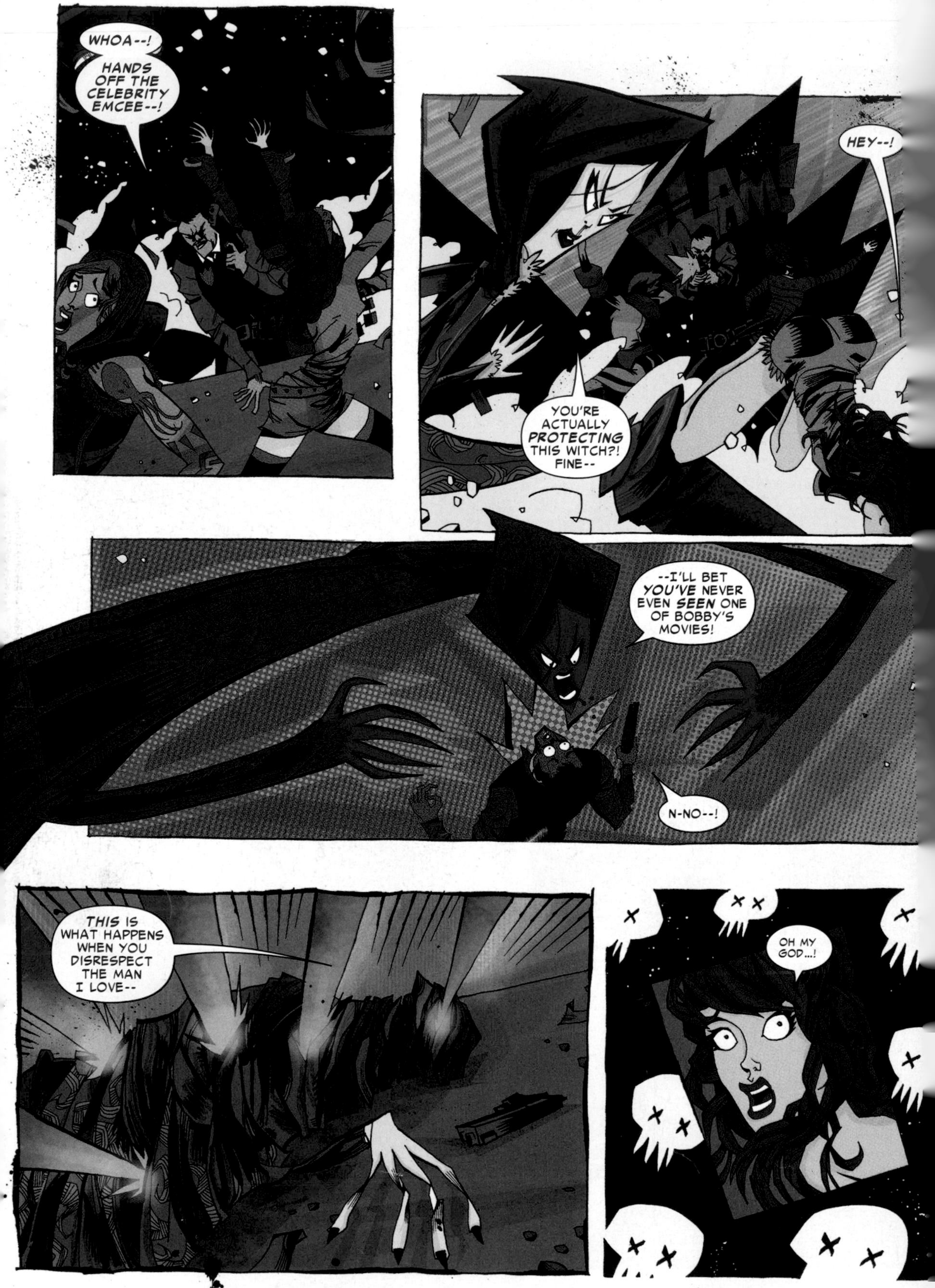
WHOA--! HANDS OFF THE CELEBRITY EMCEE--!
HEY--!
YOU'RE ACTUALLY *PROTECTING* THIS WITCH?! FINE--
--I'LL BET *YOU'VE* NEVER EVEN *SEEN* ONE OF BOBBY'S MOVIES!
N-NO--!
THIS IS WHAT HAPPENS WHEN YOU DISRESPECT THE MAN I LOVE--
OH MY GOD...!

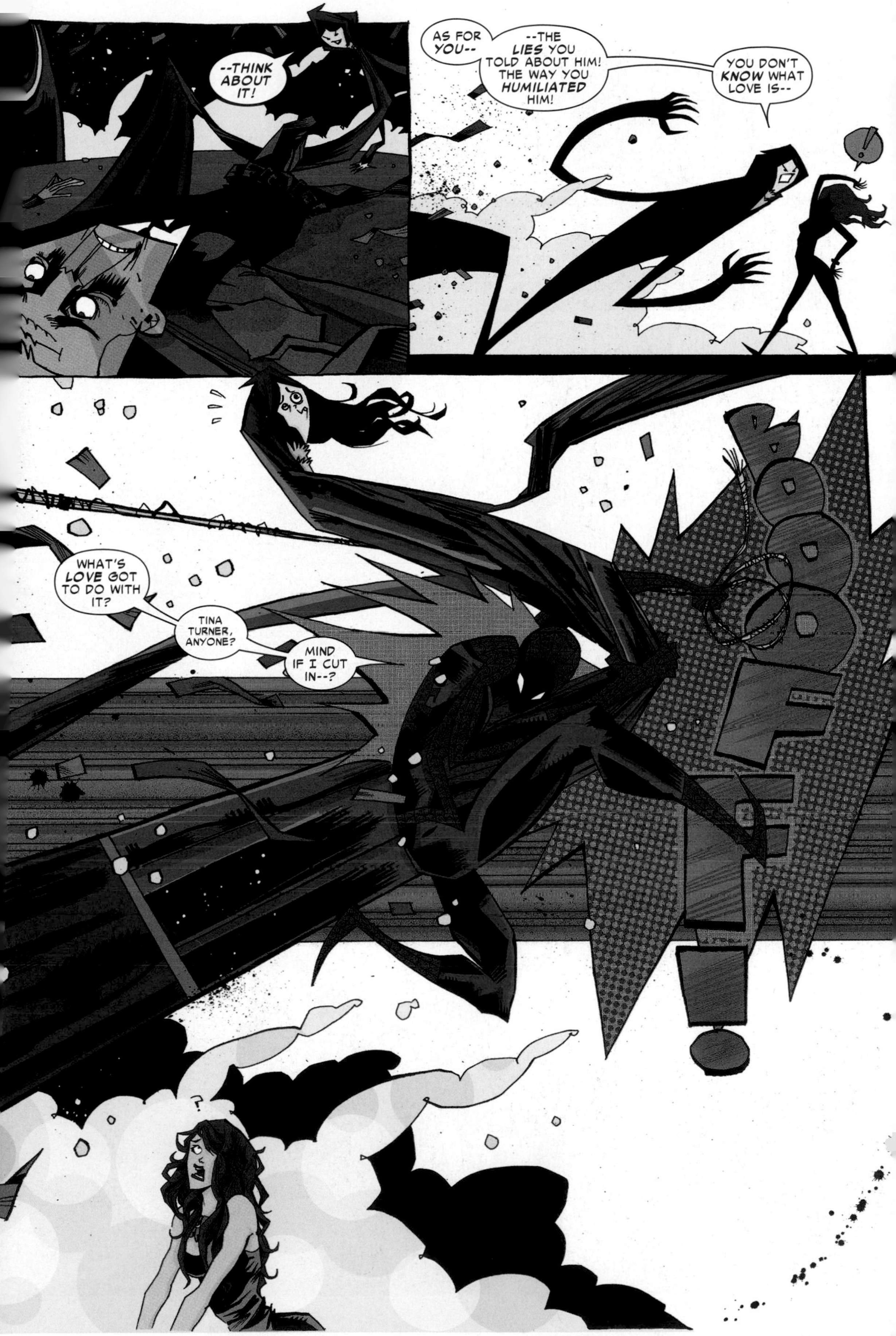
--THINK ABOUT IT!
AS FOR YOU--
--THE LIES YOU TOLD ABOUT HIM! THE WAY YOU HUMILIATED HIM!
YOU DON'T KNOW WHAT LOVE IS--
!
WHAT'S LOVE GOT TO DO WITH IT?
TINA TURNER, ANYONE?
MIND IF I CUT IN--?
BOOOOFF!
?

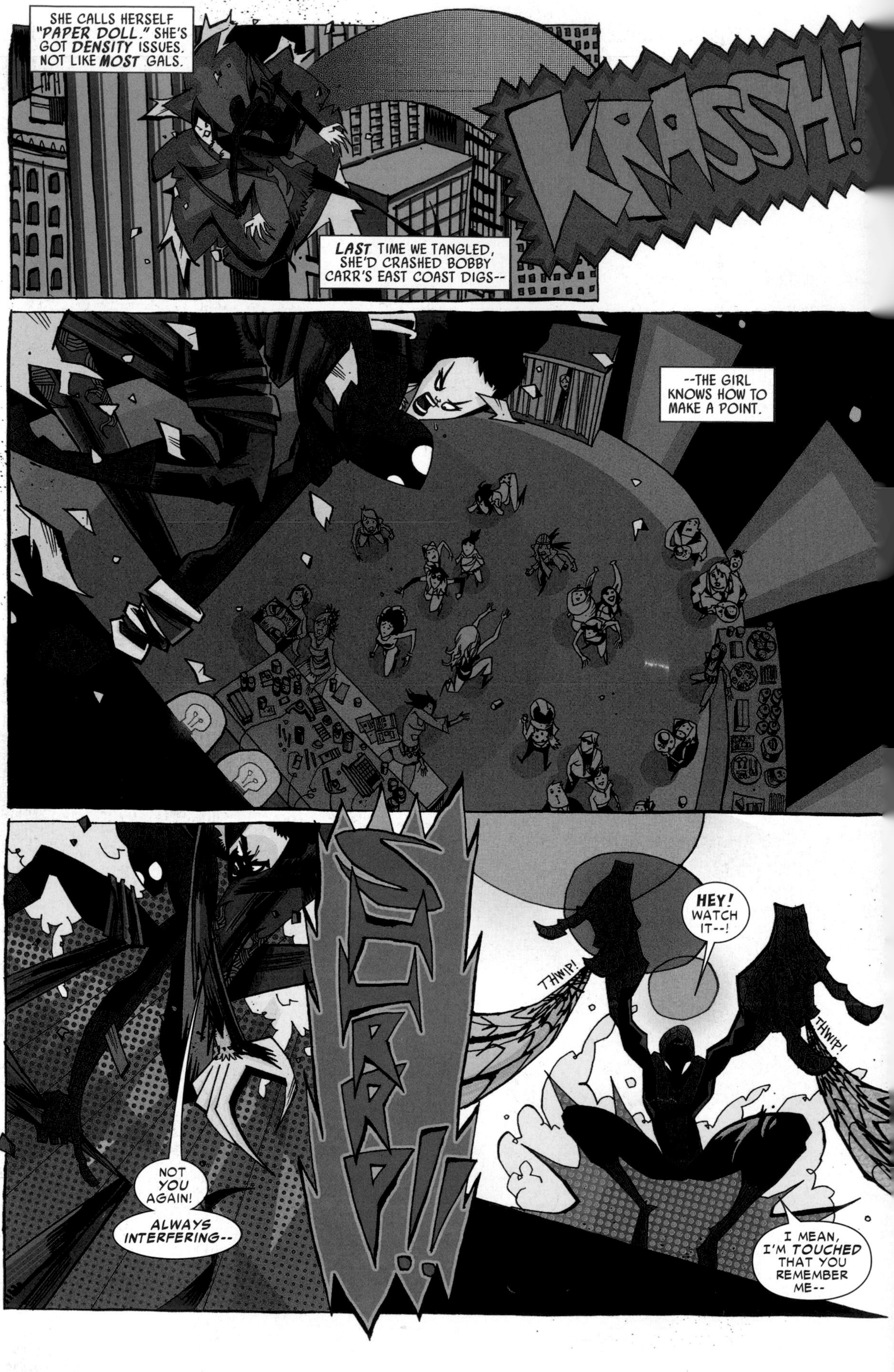

SHE CALLS HERSELF "PAPER DOLL." SHE'S GOT DENSITY ISSUES. NOT LIKE MOST GALS.
KRASSH!
LAST TIME WE TANGLED, SHE'D CRASHED BOBBY CARR'S EAST COAST DIGS--
--THE GIRL KNOWS HOW TO MAKE A POINT.
HEY! WATCH IT--!
THWIP!
THWIP!
NOT YOU AGAIN!
ALWAYS INTERFERING--
I MEAN, I'M TOUCHED THAT YOU REMEMBER ME--

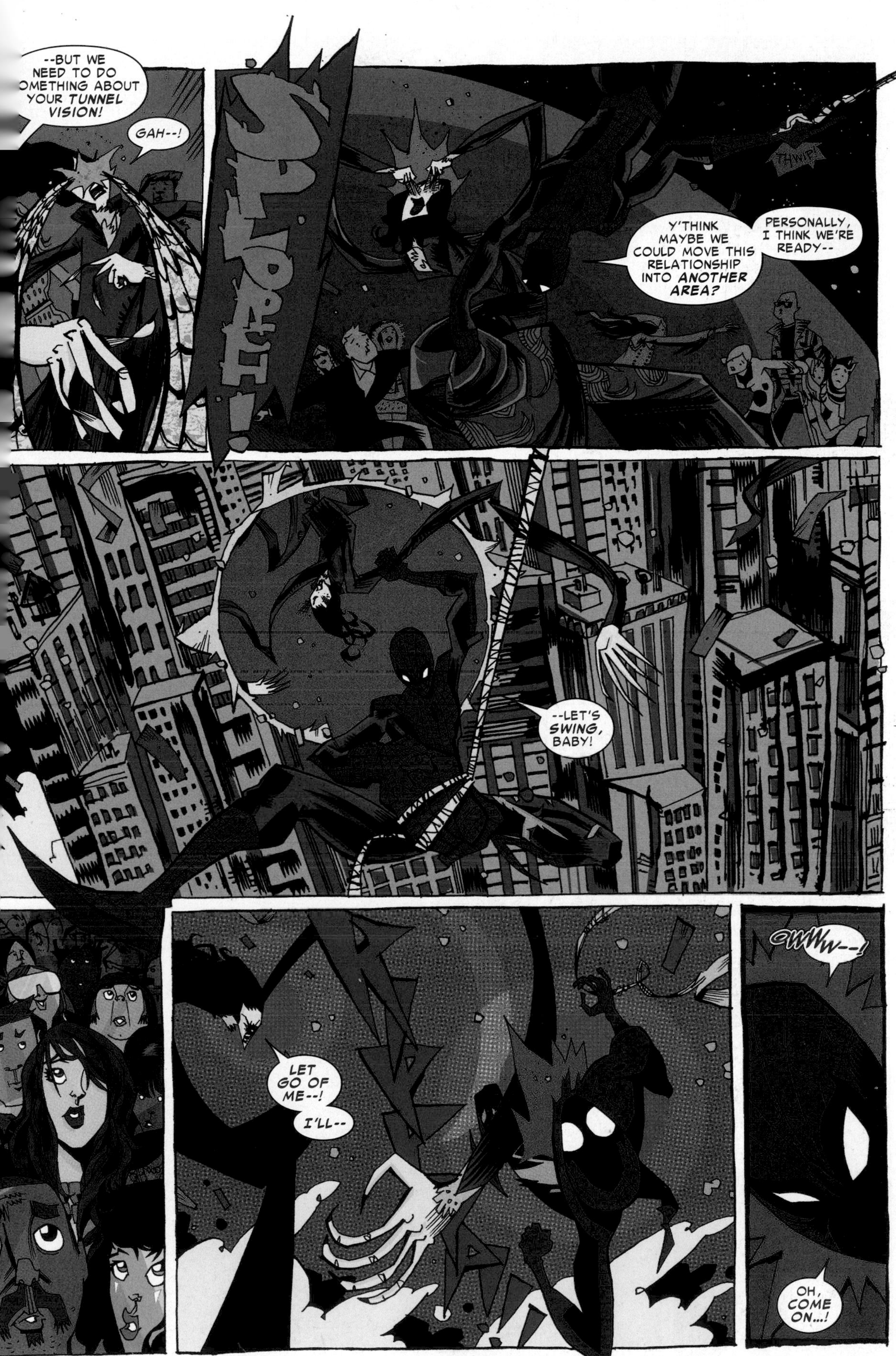
--BUT WE NEED TO DO SOMETHING ABOUT YOUR TUNNEL VISION!
GAH--!
SPLORCH!
THWIP!
Y'THINK MAYBE WE COULD MOVE THIS RELATIONSHIP INTO ANOTHER AREA?
PERSONALLY, I THINK WE'RE READY--
--LET'S SWING, BABY!
LET GO OF ME--!
I'LL--
OWWW--!
OH, COME ON...!

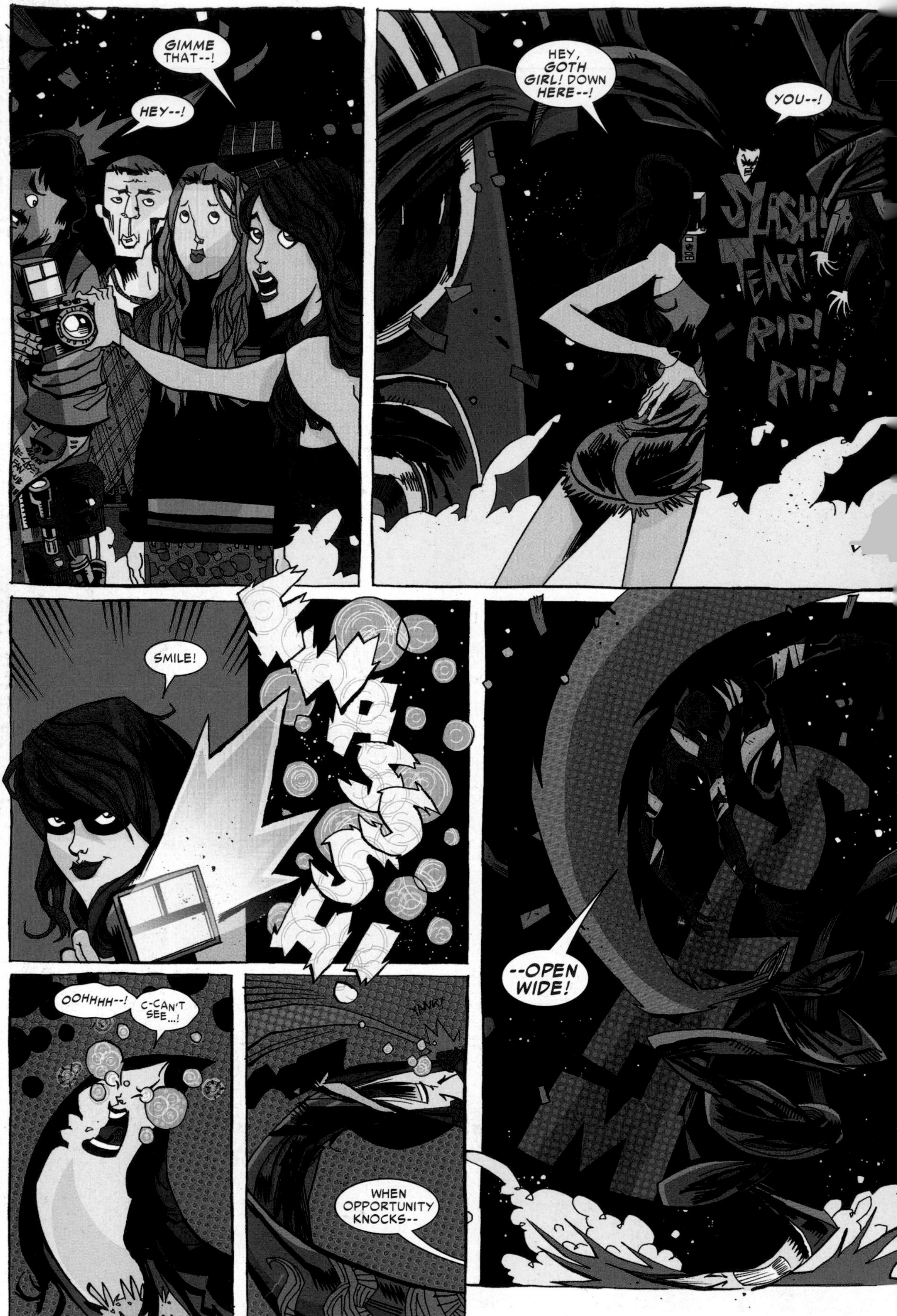

GIMME THAT--!
HEY--!
HEY, GOTH GIRL! DOWN HERE--!
YOU--!
SLASH!
TEAR!
RIP!
RIP!
SMILE!
FWASSH!
--OPEN WIDE!
OOHHHH--!
C-CAN'T SEE...!
YANK!
WHEN OPPORTUNITY KNOCKS--

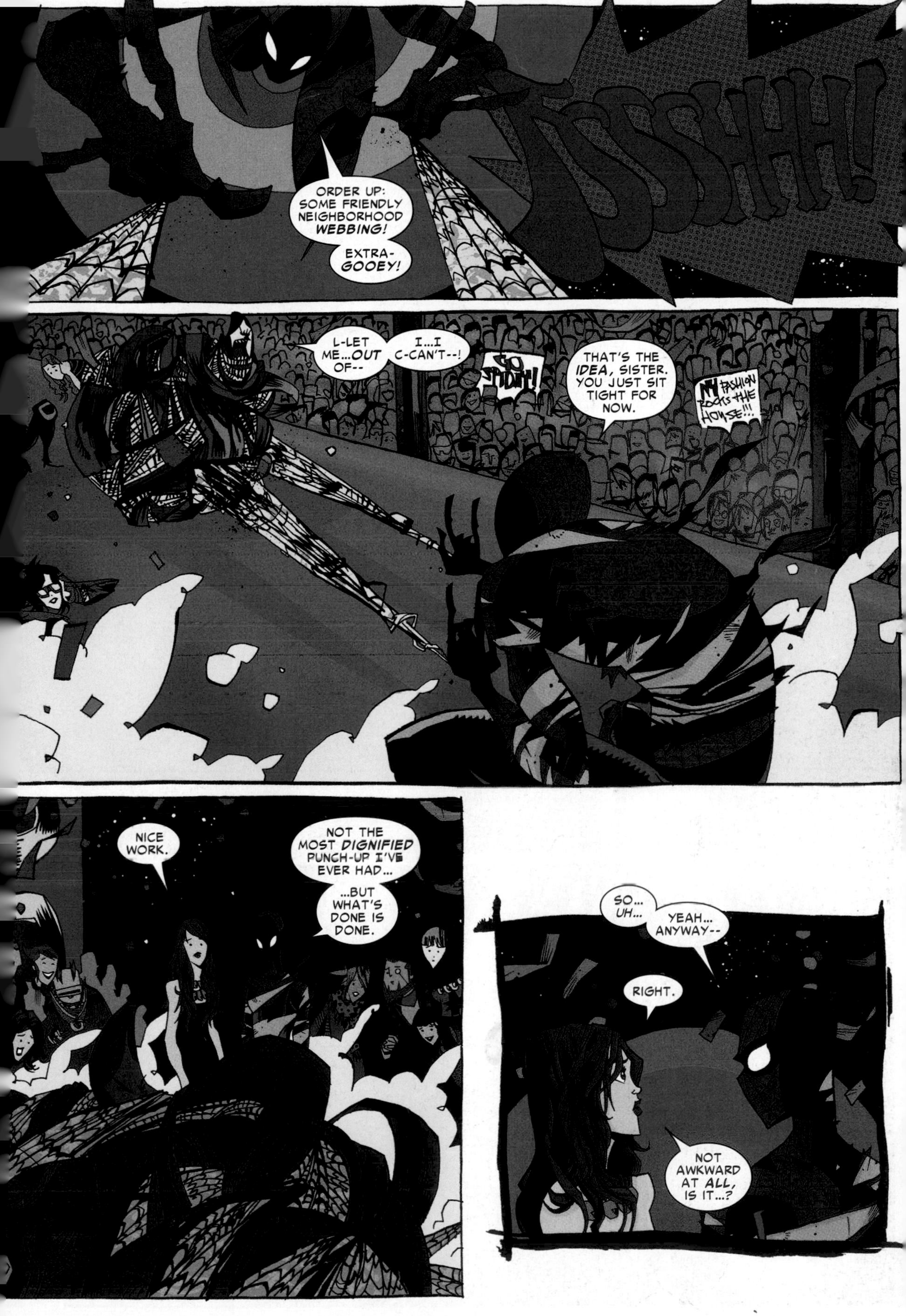
TSSSHHH!
ORDER UP: SOME FRIENDLY NEIGHBORHOOD *WEBBING!*
EXTRA-*GOOEY!*
L-LET ME...*OUT* OF--
I...I C-CAN'T--!
GO SPIDEY!
THAT'S THE *IDEA*, SISTER. YOU JUST SIT TIGHT FOR NOW.
NY FASHION ROCKS THE HOUSE!!!
NICE WORK.
NOT THE MOST *DIGNIFIED* PUNCH-UP I'VE EVER HAD...
...BUT WHAT'S DONE IS DONE.
SO... UH...
YEAH... ANYWAY--
RIGHT.
NOT AWKWARD AT *ALL*, IS IT...?

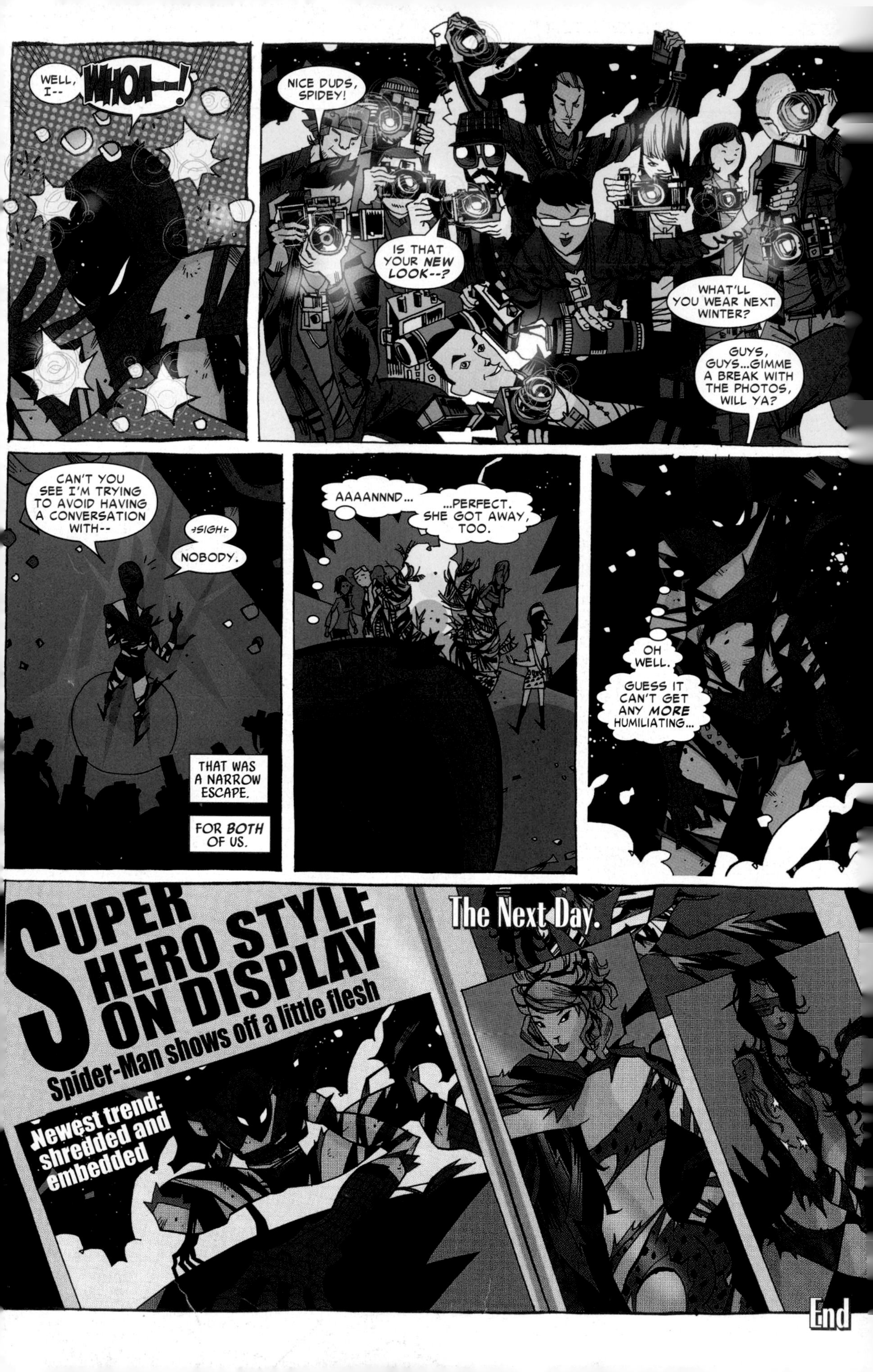

WELL, I--
WHOA--!
NICE DUDS, SPIDEY!
IS THAT YOUR NEW LOOK--?
WHAT'LL YOU WEAR NEXT WINTER?
GUYS, GUYS...GIMME A BREAK WITH THE PHOTOS, WILL YA?
CAN'T YOU SEE I'M TRYING TO AVOID HAVING A CONVERSATION WITH--
SIGH
NOBODY.
THAT WAS A NARROW ESCAPE.
FOR BOTH OF US.
AAAANNND...
...PERFECT. SHE GOT AWAY, TOO.
OH WELL.
GUESS IT CAN'T GET ANY MORE HUMILIATING...
SUPER HERO STYLE ON DISPLAY
Spider-Man shows off a little flesh
Newest trend: shredded and embedded
The Next Day.
End

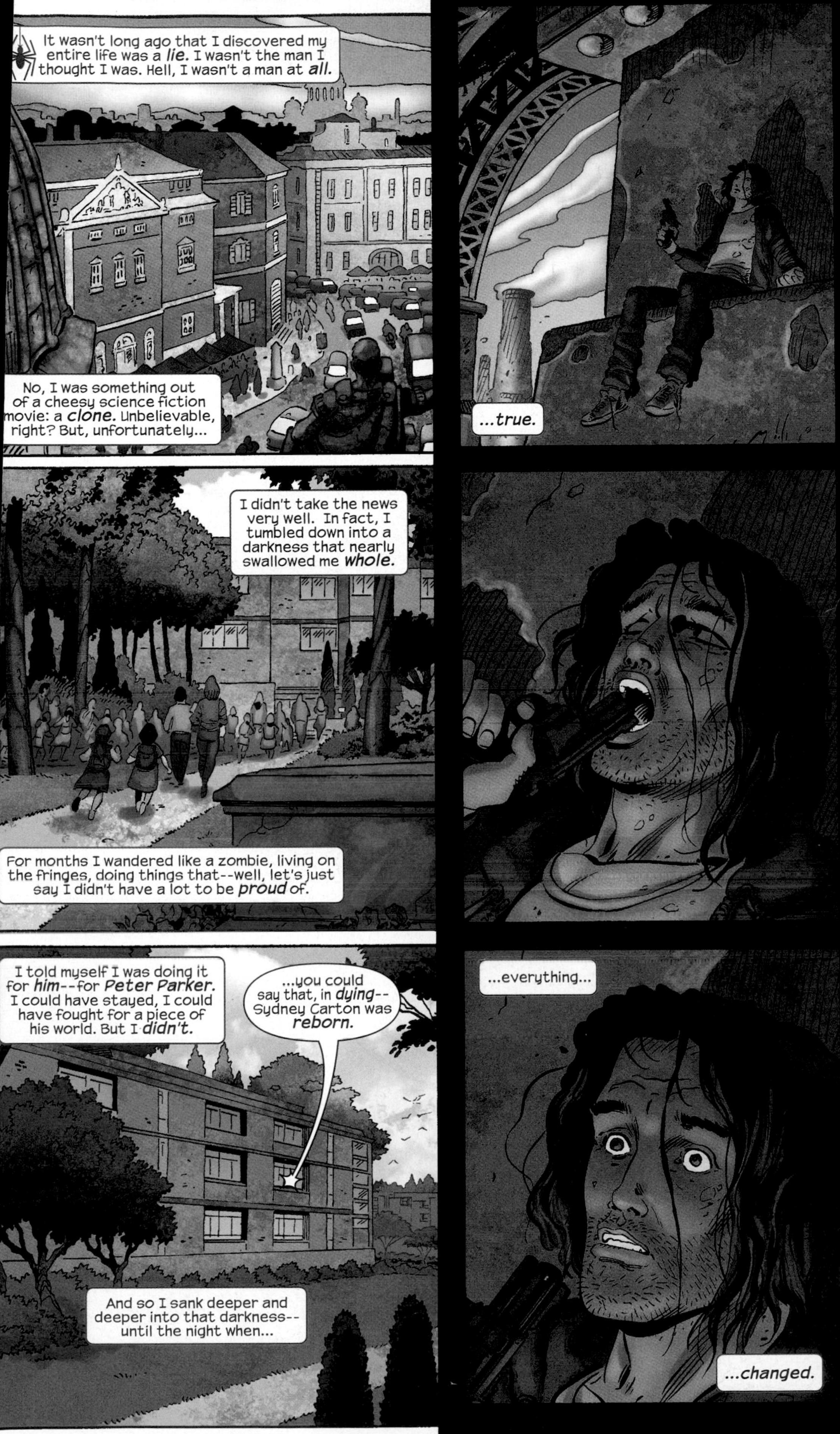
It wasn't long ago that I discovered my entire life was a lie. I wasn't the man I thought I was. Hell, I wasn't a man at all.
No, I was something out of a cheesy science fiction movie: a clone. Unbelievable, right? But, unfortunately...
...true.
I didn't take the news very well. In fact, I tumbled down into a darkness that nearly swallowed me whole.
For months I wandered like a zombie, living on the fringes, doing things that--well, let's just say I didn't have a lot to be proud of.
I told myself I was doing it for him--for Peter Parker. I could have stayed, I could have fought for a piece of his world. But I didn't.
...you could say that, in dying--Sydney Carton was reborn.
And so I sank deeper and deeper into that darkness--until the night when...
...everything...
...changed.

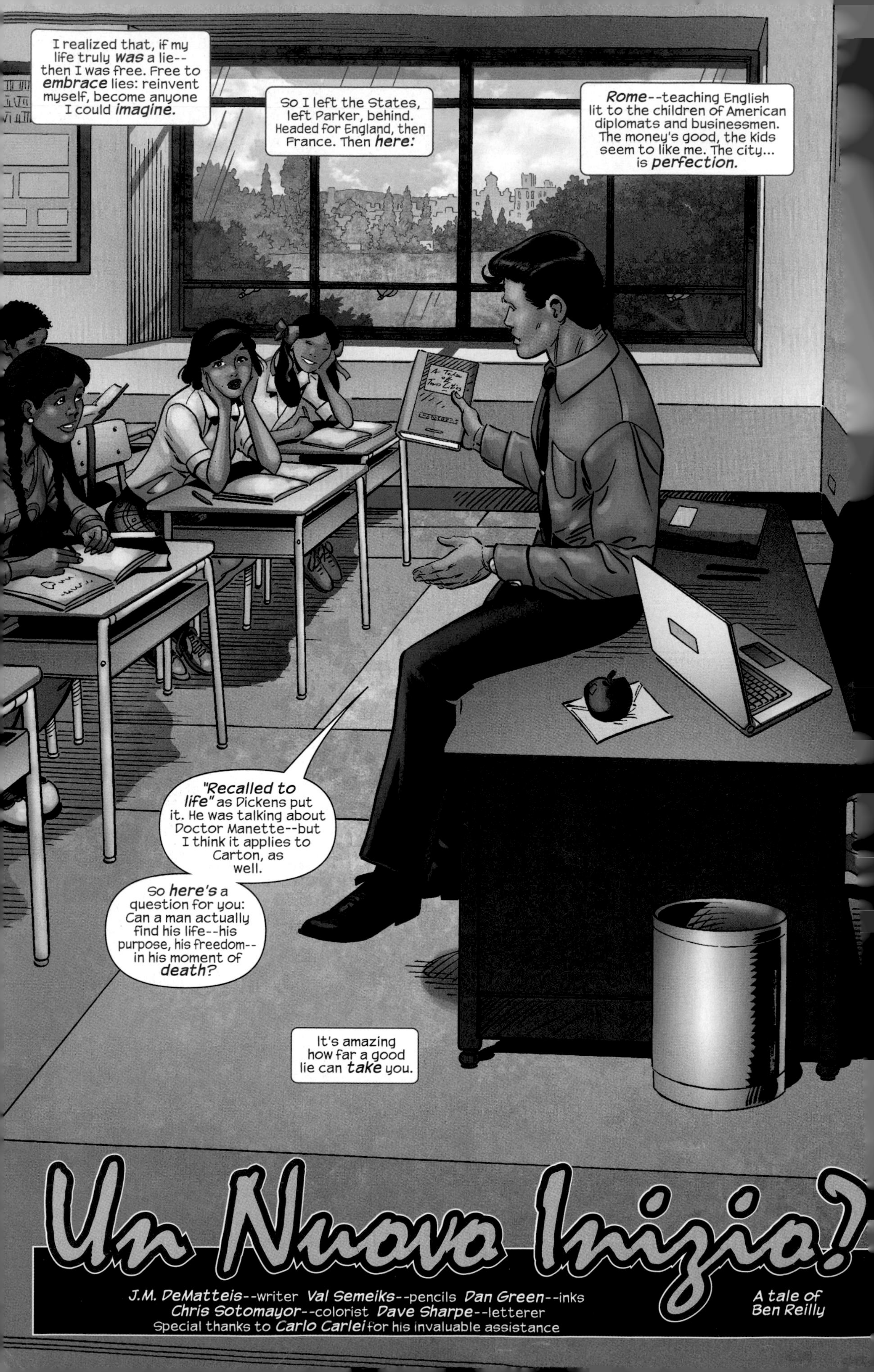
I realized that, if my life truly *was* a lie--then I was free. Free to *embrace* lies: reinvent myself, become anyone I could *imagine.*
So I left the States, left Parker, behind. Headed for England, then France. Then *here:*
Rome--teaching English lit to the children of American diplomats and businessmen. The money's good, the kids seem to like me. The city... is *perfection.*
"Recalled to life" as Dickens put it. He was talking about Doctor Manette--but I think it applies to Carton, as well.
So *here's* a question for you: Can a man actually find his life--his purpose, his freedom--in his moment of *death?*
It's amazing how far a good lie can *take* you.
Un Nuovo Inizio?
J.M. DeMatteis--writer *Val Semeiks*--pencils *Dan Green*--inks
Chris Sotomayor--colorist *Dave Sharpe*--letterer
Special thanks to *Carlo Carlei* for his invaluable assistance
A tale of Ben Reilly

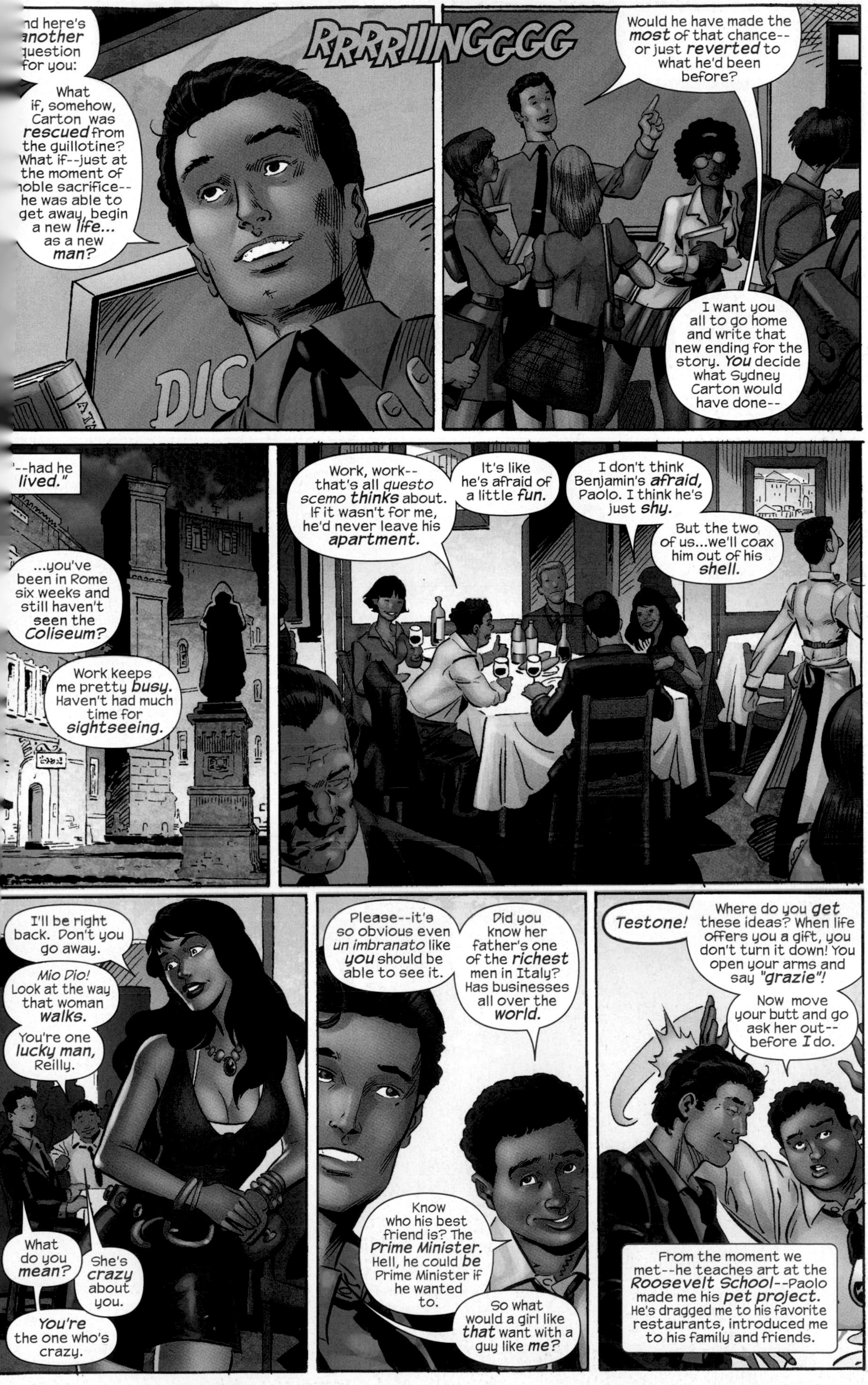
nd here's another question for you:
What if, somehow, Carton was rescued from the guillotine? What if--just at the moment of noble sacrifice--he was able to get away, begin a new life... as a new man?
RRRRIIINGGGG
Would he have made the most of that chance--or just reverted to what he'd been before?
I want you all to go home and write that new ending for the story. You decide what Sydney Carton would have done--
"--had he lived."
...you've been in Rome six weeks and still haven't seen the Coliseum?
Work keeps me pretty busy. Haven't had much time for sightseeing.
Work, work--that's all questo scemo thinks about. If it wasn't for me, he'd never leave his apartment.
It's like he's afraid of a little fun.
I don't think Benjamin's afraid, Paolo. I think he's just shy.
But the two of us...we'll coax him out of his shell.
I'll be right back. Don't you go away.
Mio Dio! Look at the way that woman walks.
You're one lucky man, Reilly.
What do you mean?
She's crazy about you.
You're the one who's crazy.
Please--it's so obvious even un imbranato like you should be able to see it.
Did you know her father's one of the richest men in Italy? Has businesses all over the world.
Know who his best friend is? The Prime Minister. Hell, he could be Prime Minister if he wanted to.
So what would a girl like that want with a guy like me?
Testone!
Where do you get these ideas? When life offers you a gift, you don't turn it down! You open your arms and say "grazie"!
Now move your butt and go ask her out--before I do.
From the moment we met--he teaches art at the Roosevelt School--Paolo made me his pet project. He's dragged me to his favorite restaurants, introduced me to his family and friends.

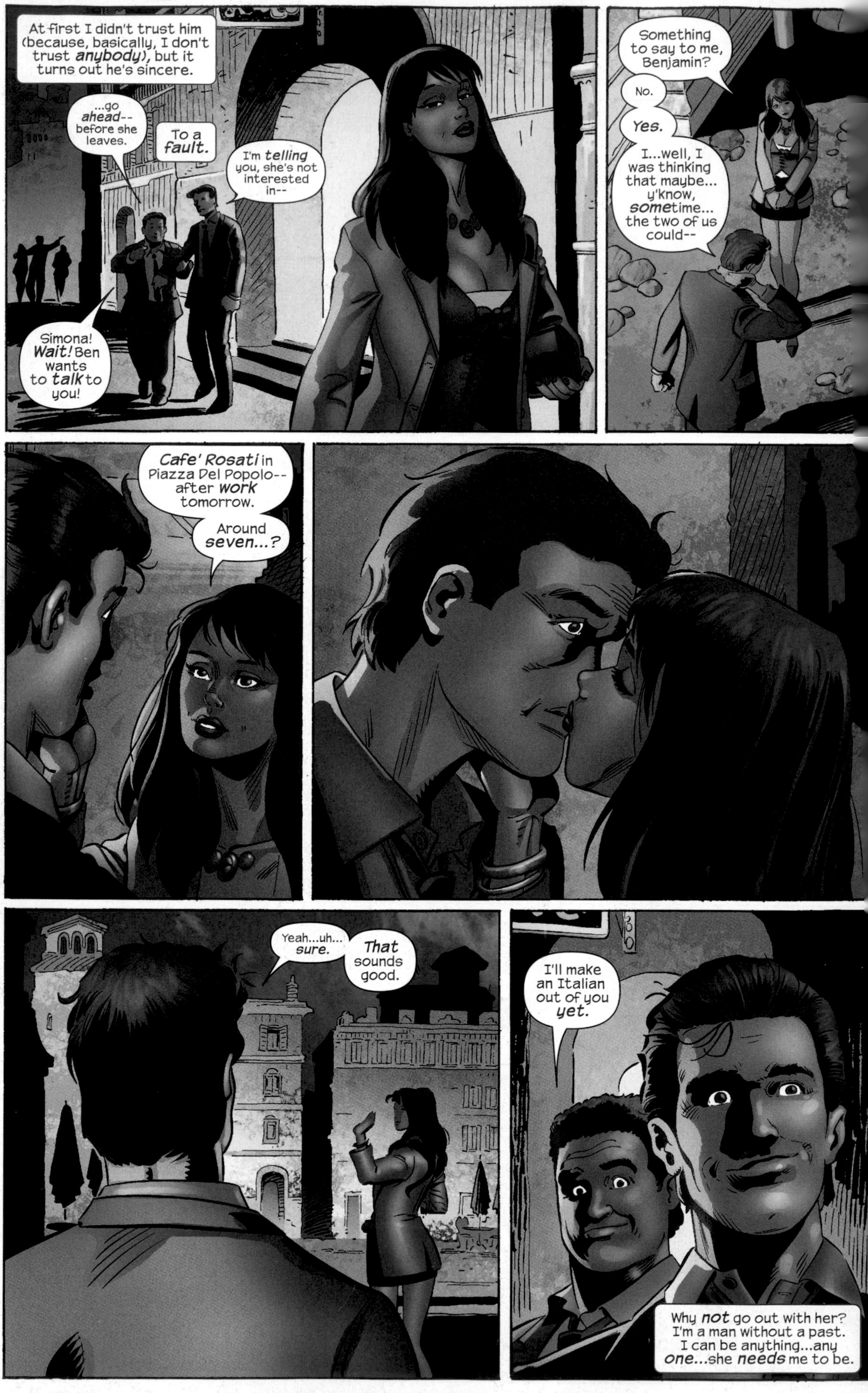
At first I didn't trust him (because, basically, I don't trust anybody), but it turns out he's sincere.
...go ahead-- before she leaves.
To a fault.
I'm telling you, she's not interested in--
Simona! Wait! Ben wants to talk to you!
Something to say to me, Benjamin?
No.
Yes.
I...well, I was thinking that maybe... y'know, sometime... the two of us could--
Cafe' Rosati in Piazza Del Popolo-- after work tomorrow.
Around seven...?
Yeah...uh... sure.
That sounds good.
I'll make an Italian out of you yet.
Why not go out with her? I'm a man without a past. I can be anything...any one...she needs me to be.

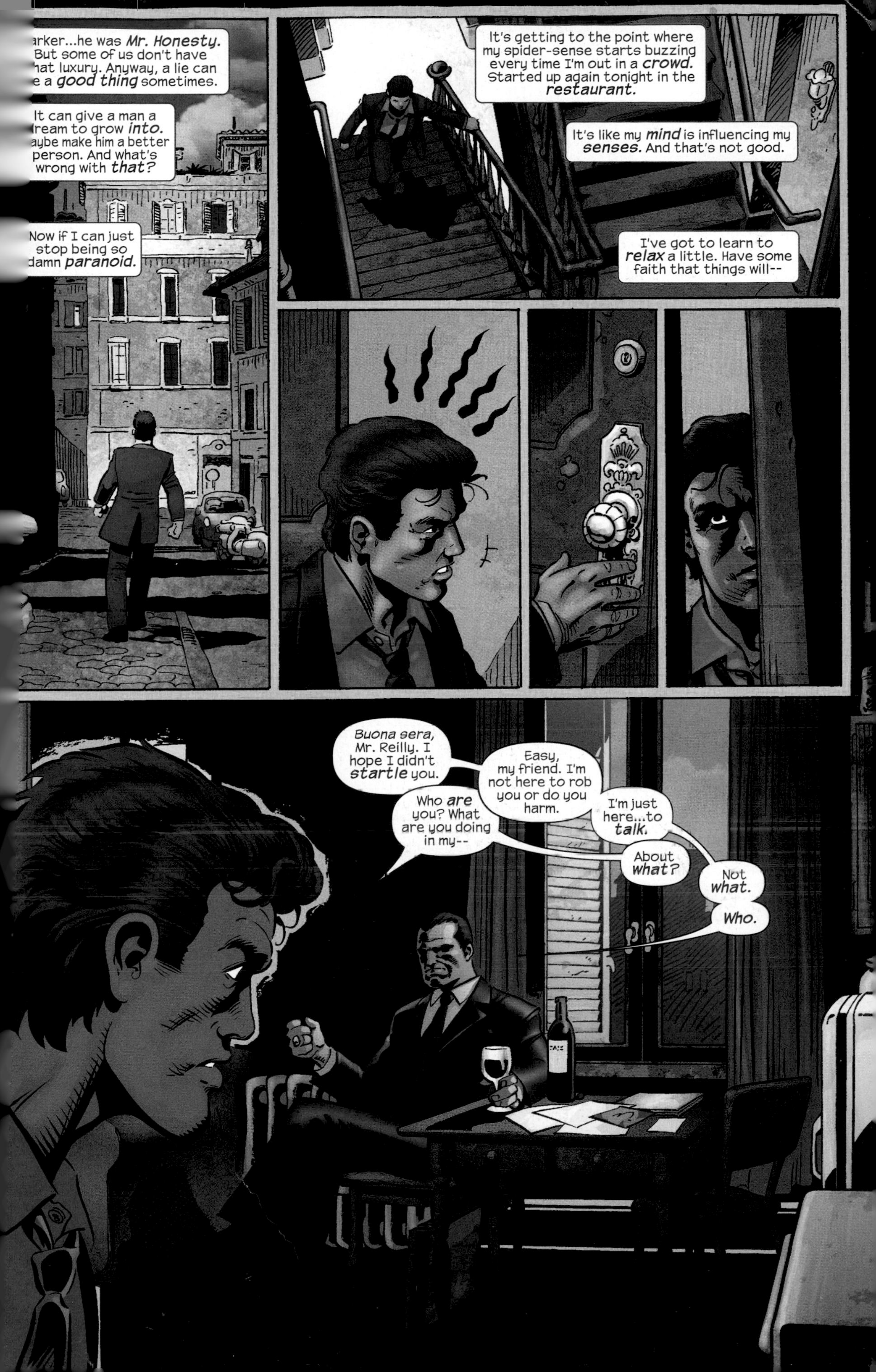
arker...he was Mr. Honesty. But some of us don't have hat luxury. Anyway, a lie can e a good thing sometimes.
It can give a man a ream to grow into. aybe make him a better person. And what's wrong with that?
Now if I can just stop being so damn paranoid.
It's getting to the point where my spider-sense starts buzzing every time I'm out in a crowd. Started up again tonight in the restaurant.
It's like my mind is influencing my senses. And that's not good.
I've got to learn to relax a little. Have some faith that things will--
Buona sera, Mr. Reilly. I hope I didn't startle you.
Who are you? What are you doing in my--
Easy, my friend. I'm not here to rob you or do you harm.
I'm just here...to talk.
About what?
Not what.
Who.

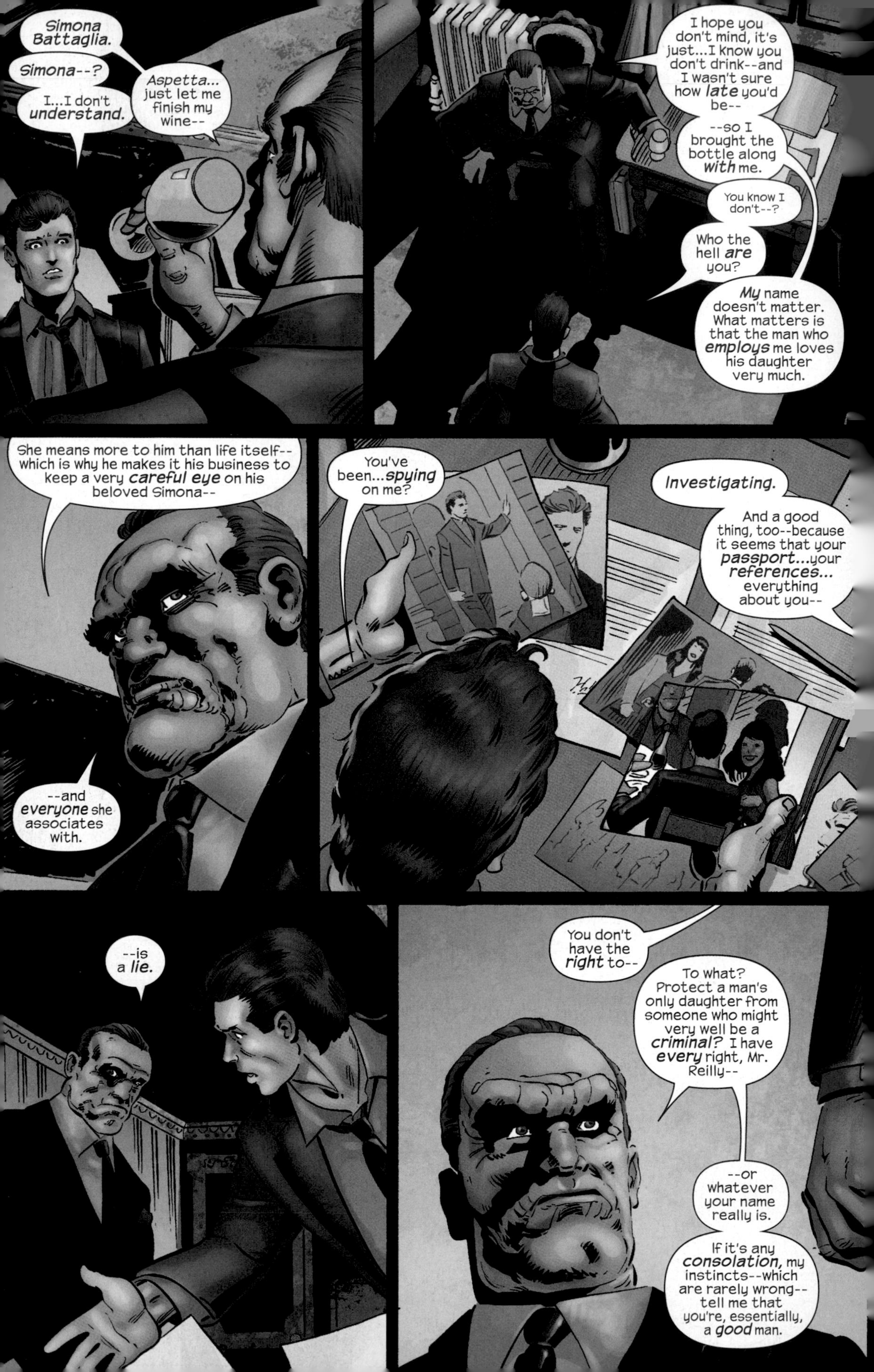
Simona Battaglia.
Simona--?
I...I don't understand.
Aspetta... just let me finish my wine--
I hope you don't mind, it's just...I know you don't drink--and I wasn't sure how late you'd be--
--so I brought the bottle along with me.
You know I don't--?
Who the hell are you?
My name doesn't matter. What matters is that the man who employs me loves his daughter very much.
She means more to him than life itself--which is why he makes it his business to keep a very careful eye on his beloved Simona--
--and everyone she associates with.
You've been...spying on me?
Investigating.
And a good thing, too--because it seems that your passport...your references... everything about you--
--is a lie.
You don't have the right to--
To what? Protect a man's only daughter from someone who might very well be a criminal? I have every right, Mr. Reilly--
--or whatever your name really is.
If it's any consolation, my instincts--which are rarely wrong--tell me that you're, essentially, a good man.

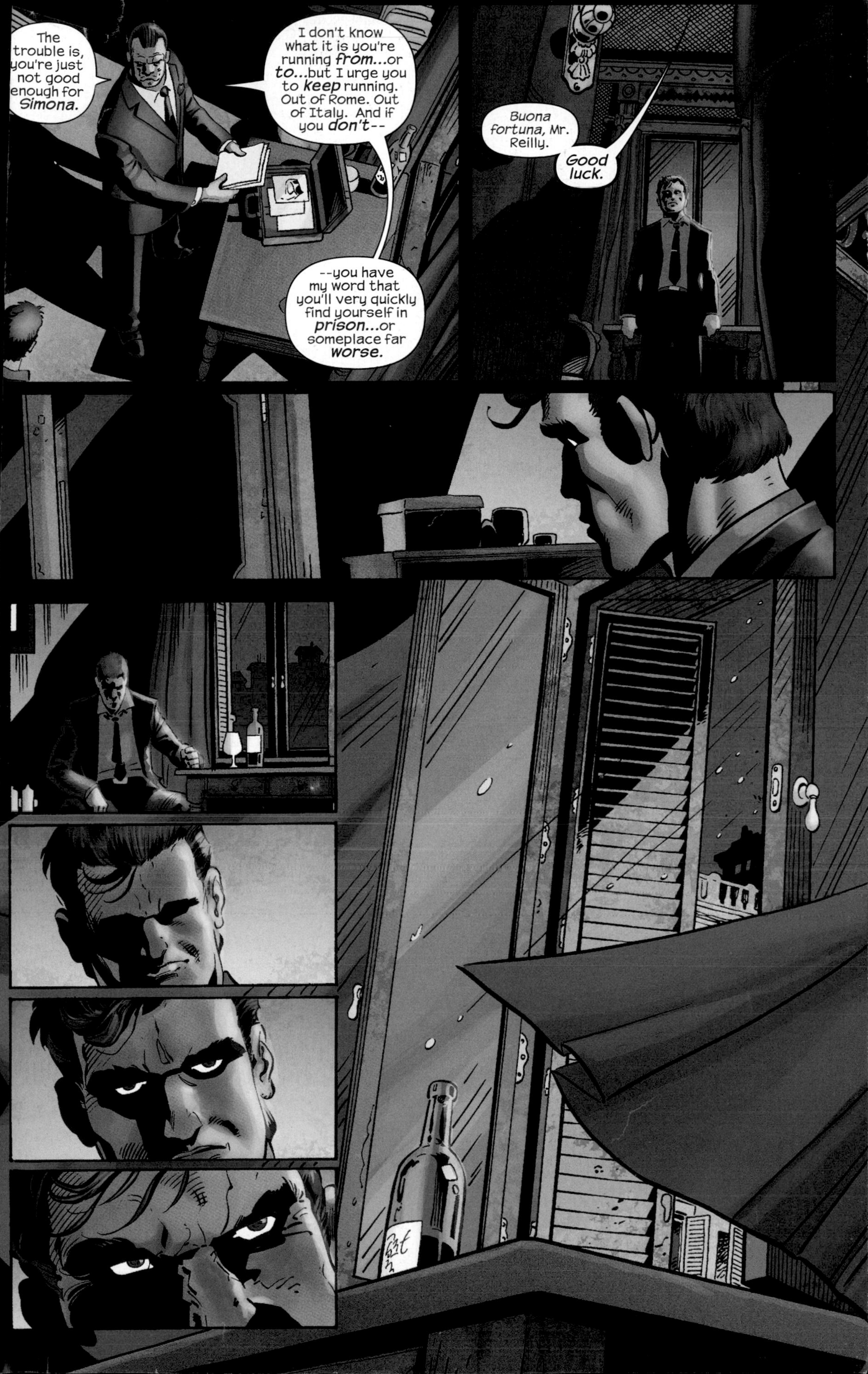
The trouble is, you're just not good enough for Simona.
I don't know what it is you're running from...or to...but I urge you to keep running. Out of Rome. Out of Italy. And if you don't--
--you have my word that you'll very quickly find yourself in prison...or someplace far worse.
Buona fortuna, Mr. Reilly.
Good luck.

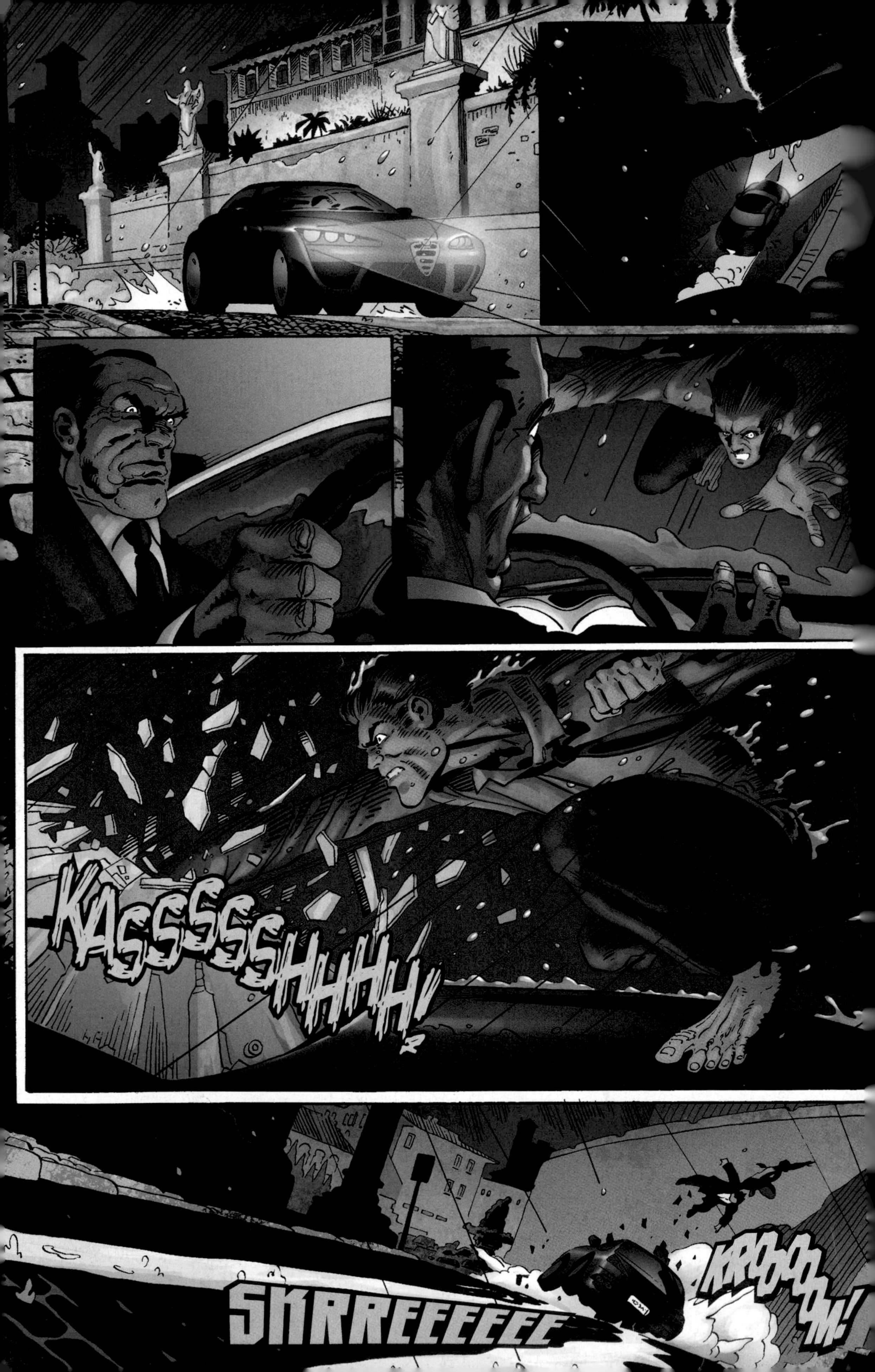
KASSSSSHHHH!
SKRREEEEEEE
KRROOOOOM!

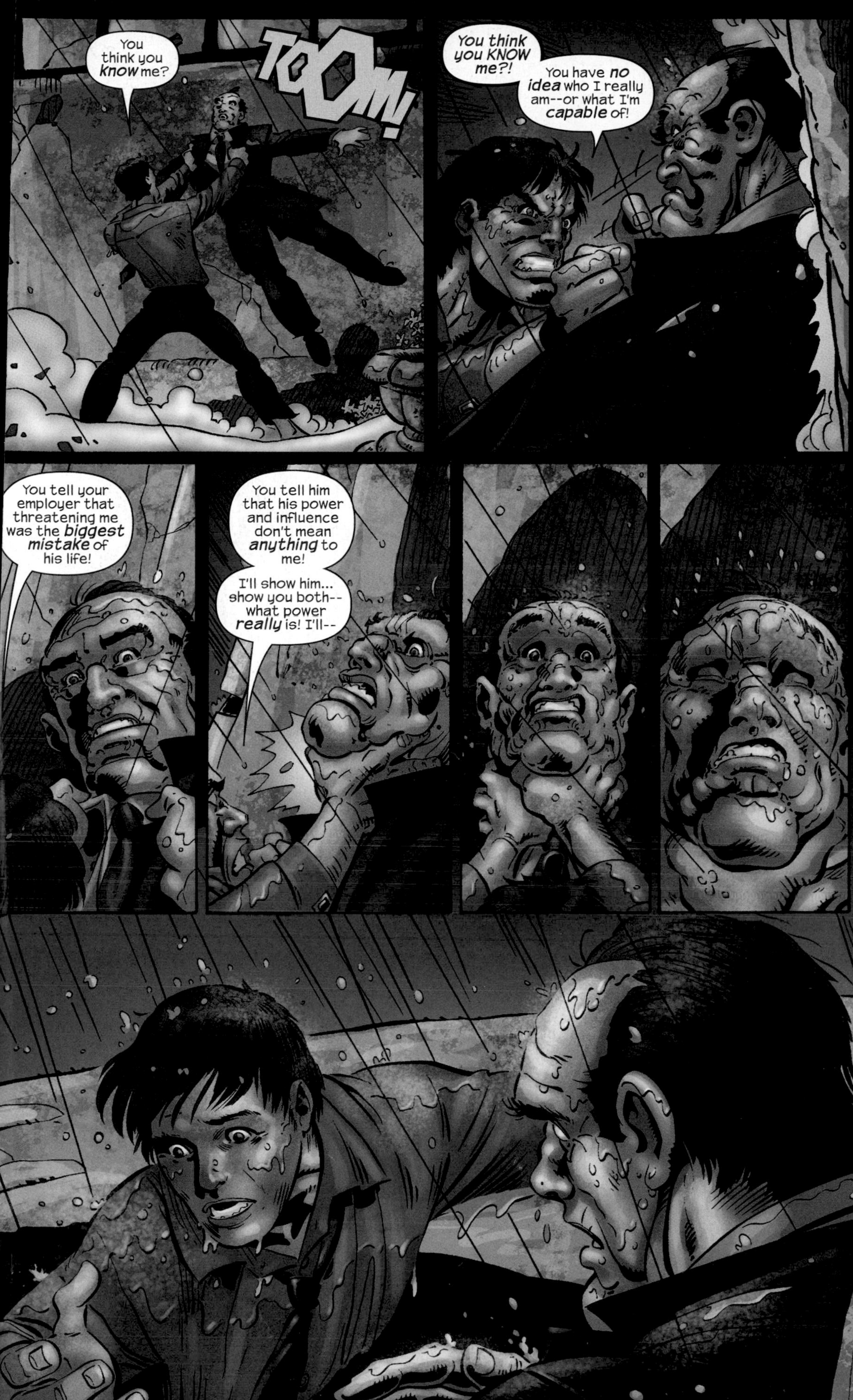
You think you know me?
TOOOM!
You think you KNOW me?!
You have no idea who I really am--or what I'm capable of!
You tell your employer that threatening me was the biggest mistake of his life!
You tell him that his power and influence don't mean anything to me!
I'll show him... show you both--what power really is! I'll--

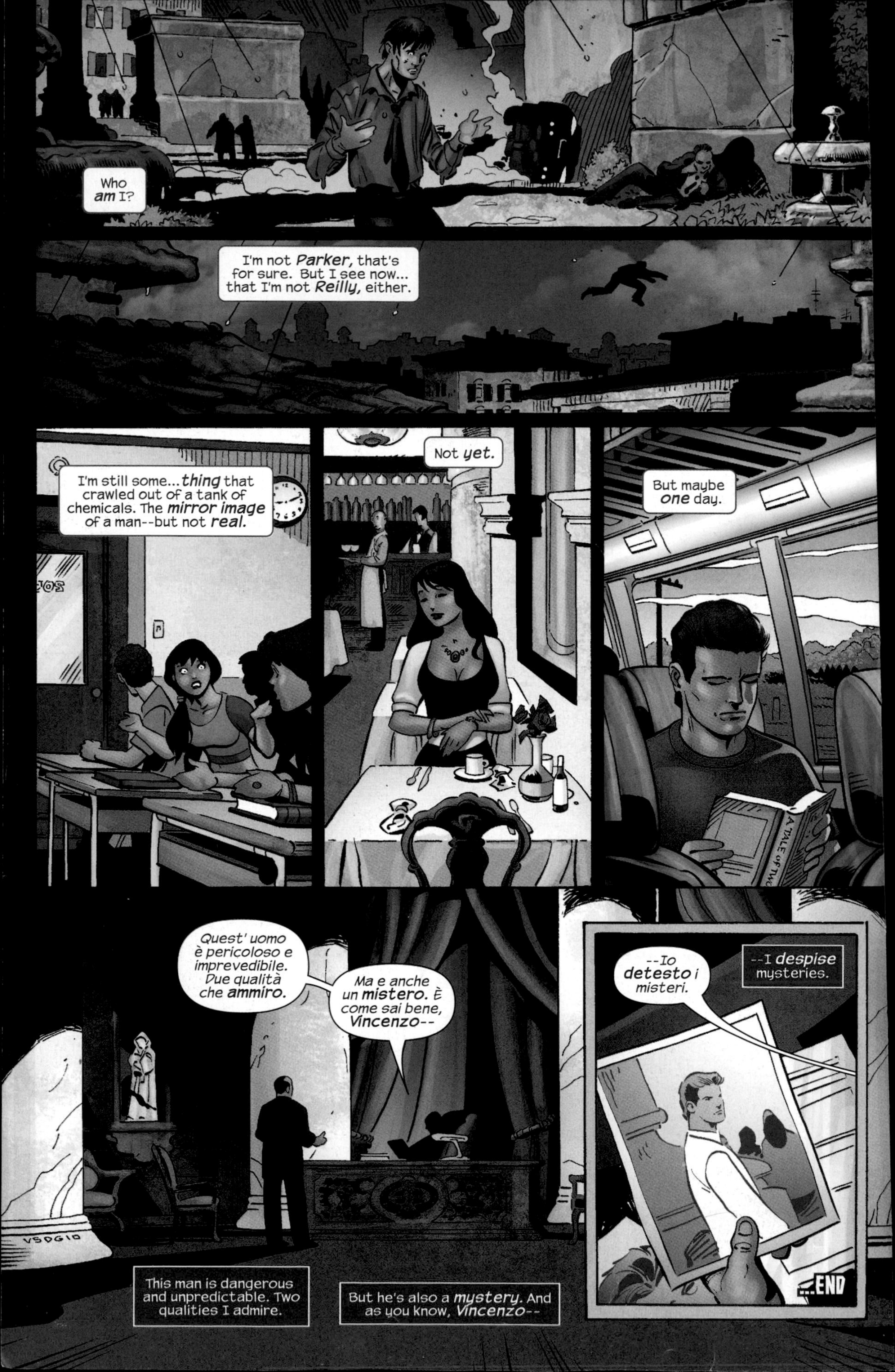
Who am I?
I'm not Parker, that's for sure. But I see now... that I'm not Reilly, either.
I'm still some...thing that crawled out of a tank of chemicals. The mirror image of a man--but not real.
Not yet.
But maybe one day.
Quest' uomo è pericoloso e imprevedibile. Due qualità che ammiro.
This man is dangerous and unpredictable. Two qualities I admire.
Ma e anche un mistero. È come sai bene, Vincenzo--
But he's also a mystery. And as you know, Vincenzo--
--Io detesto i misteri.
--I despise mysteries.
...END

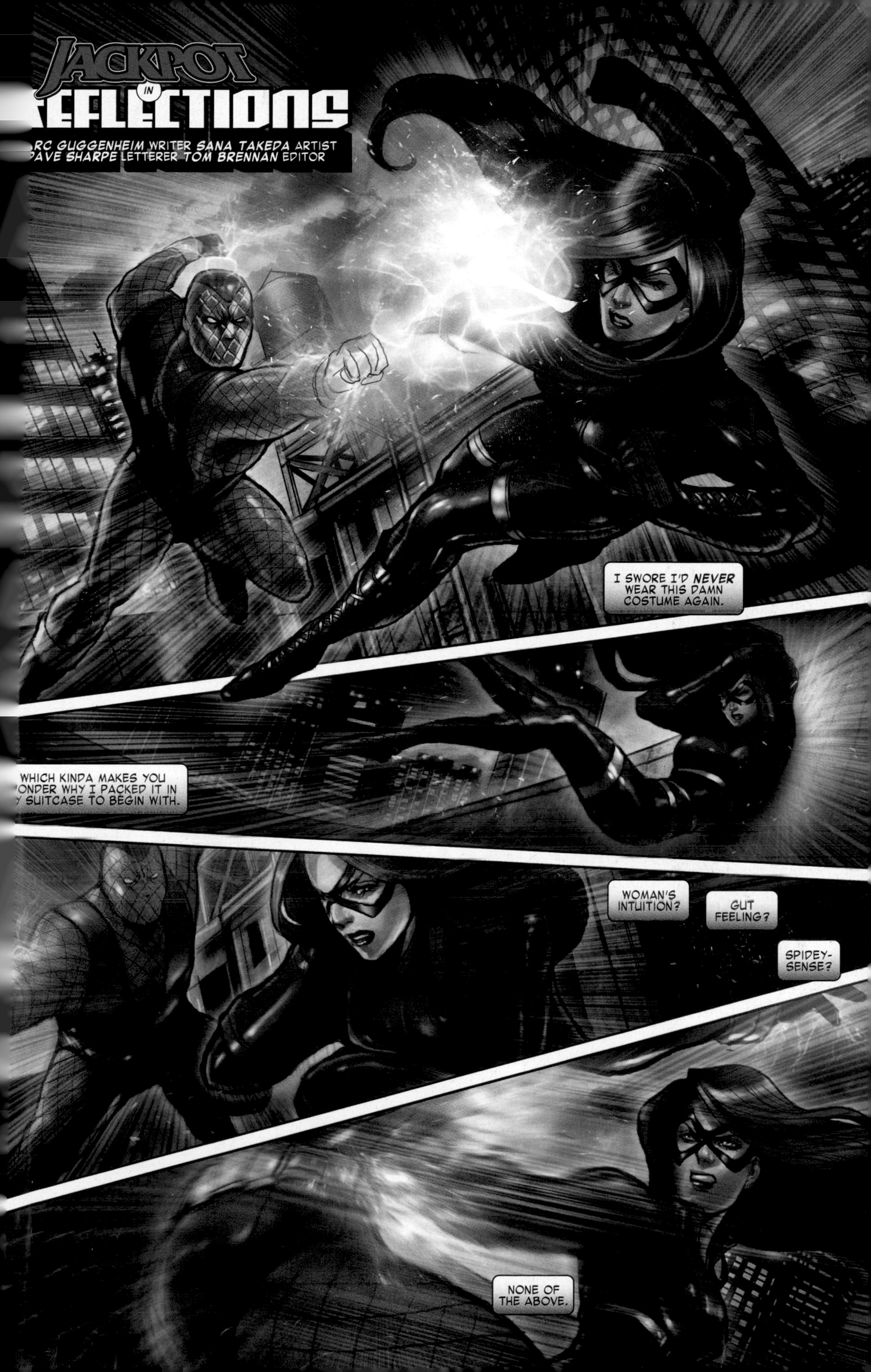
JACKPOT IN
EFLECTIONS
RC GUGGENHEIM WRITER SANA TAKEDA ARTIST
DAVE SHARPE LETTERER TOM BRENNAN EDITOR
I SWORE I'D NEVER WEAR THIS DAMN COSTUME AGAIN.
WHICH KINDA MAKES YOU ONDER WHY I PACKED IT IN SUITCASE TO BEGIN WITH.
WOMAN'S INTUITION?
GUT FEELING?
SPIDEY-SENSE?
NONE OF THE ABOVE.

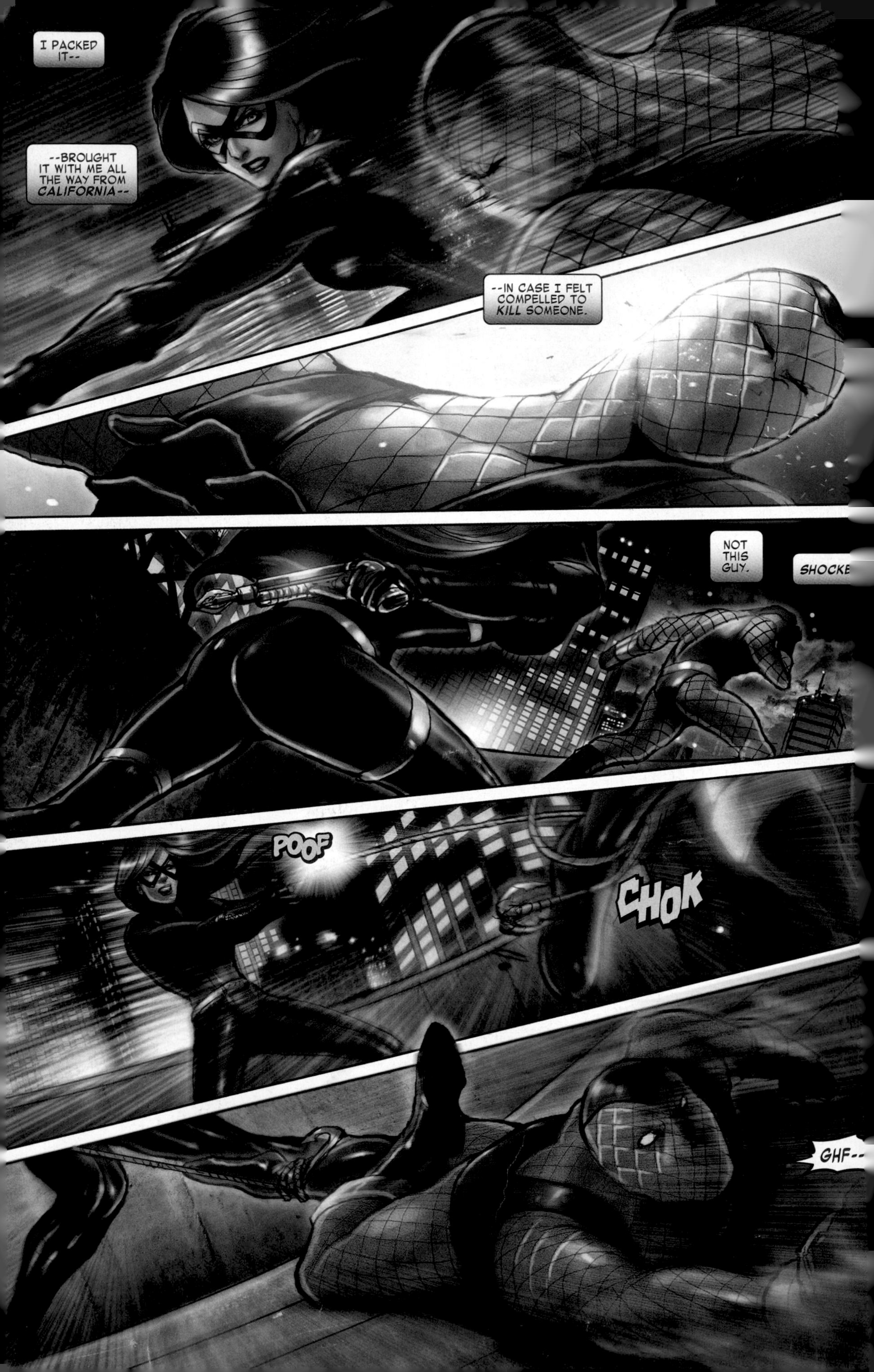
I PACKED IT--
--BROUGHT IT WITH ME ALL THE WAY FROM CALIFORNIA--
--IN CASE I FELT COMPELLED TO KILL SOMEONE.
NOT THIS GUY.
SHOCKE
POOF
CHOK
GHF--

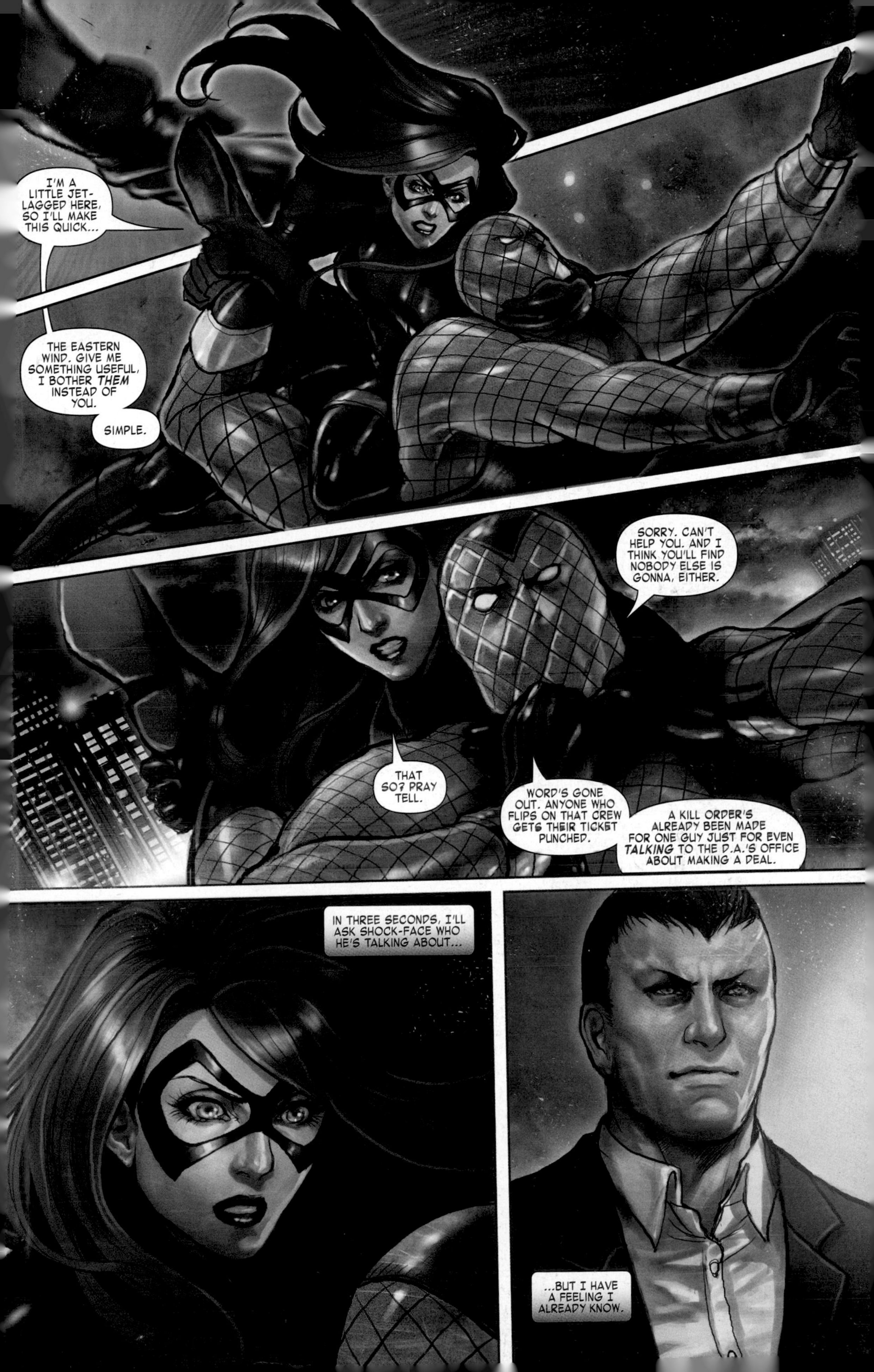
I'M A LITTLE JET-LAGGED HERE, SO I'LL MAKE THIS QUICK...
THE EASTERN WIND. GIVE ME SOMETHING USEFUL, I BOTHER *THEM* INSTEAD OF YOU.
SIMPLE.
SORRY. CAN'T HELP YOU. AND I THINK YOU'LL FIND NOBODY ELSE IS GONNA, EITHER.
THAT SO? PRAY TELL.
WORD'S GONE OUT. ANYONE WHO FLIPS ON THAT CREW GETS THEIR TICKET PUNCHED.
A KILL ORDER'S ALREADY BEEN MADE FOR ONE GUY JUST FOR EVEN *TALKING* TO THE D.A.'S OFFICE ABOUT MAKING A DEAL.
IN THREE SECONDS, I'LL ASK SHOCK-FACE WHO HE'S TALKING ABOUT...
...BUT I HAVE A FEELING I ALREADY KNOW.

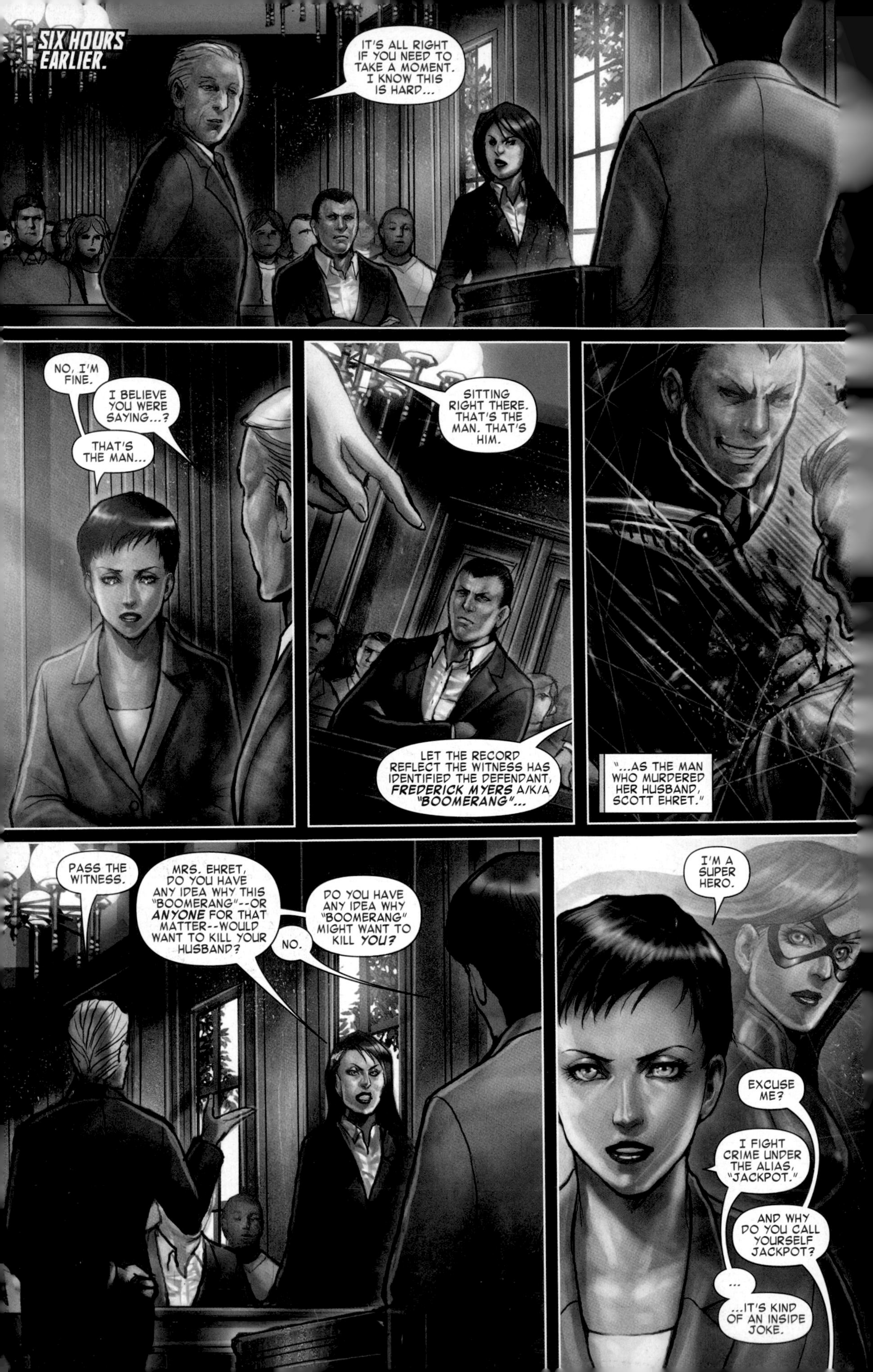
SIX HOURS EARLIER.
IT'S ALL RIGHT IF YOU NEED TO TAKE A MOMENT. I KNOW THIS IS HARD...
NO, I'M FINE.
I BELIEVE YOU WERE SAYING...?
THAT'S THE MAN...
SITTING RIGHT THERE. THAT'S THE MAN. THAT'S HIM.
LET THE RECORD REFLECT THE WITNESS HAS IDENTIFIED THE DEFENDANT, FREDERICK MYERS A/K/A "BOOMERANG"...
"...AS THE MAN WHO MURDERED HER HUSBAND, SCOTT EHRET."
PASS THE WITNESS.
MRS. EHRET, DO YOU HAVE ANY IDEA WHY THIS "BOOMERANG"--OR ANYONE FOR THAT MATTER--WOULD WANT TO KILL YOUR HUSBAND?
NO.
DO YOU HAVE ANY IDEA WHY "BOOMERANG" MIGHT WANT TO KILL YOU?
I'M A SUPER HERO.
EXCUSE ME?
I FIGHT CRIME UNDER THE ALIAS, "JACKPOT."
AND WHY DO YOU CALL YOURSELF JACKPOT?
...
...IT'S KIND OF AN INSIDE JOKE.

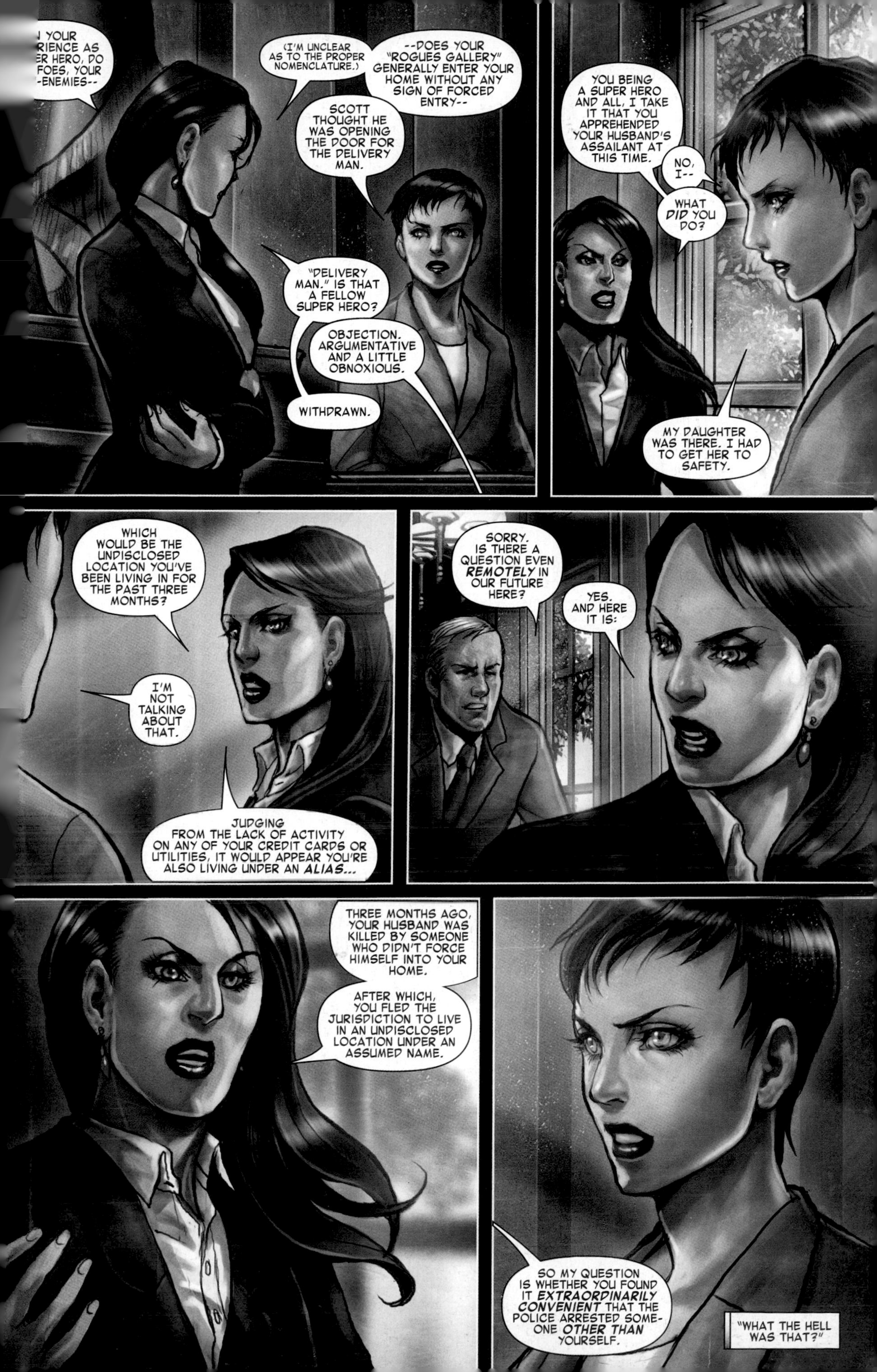
...N YOUR
...RIENCE AS
...R HERO, DO
...FOES, YOUR
...-ENEMIES--
(I'M UNCLEAR AS TO THE PROPER NOMENCLATURE.)
--DOES YOUR "ROGUES GALLERY" GENERALLY ENTER YOUR HOME WITHOUT ANY SIGN OF FORCED ENTRY--
SCOTT THOUGHT HE WAS OPENING THE DOOR FOR THE DELIVERY MAN.
"DELIVERY MAN." IS THAT A FELLOW SUPER HERO?
OBJECTION. ARGUMENTATIVE AND A LITTLE OBNOXIOUS.
WITHDRAWN.
YOU BEING A SUPER HERO AND ALL, I TAKE IT THAT YOU APPREHENDED YOUR HUSBAND'S ASSAILANT AT THIS TIME.
NO, I--
WHAT DID YOU DO?
MY DAUGHTER WAS THERE. I HAD TO GET HER TO SAFETY.
WHICH WOULD BE THE UNDISCLOSED LOCATION YOU'VE BEEN LIVING IN FOR THE PAST THREE MONTHS?
I'M NOT TALKING ABOUT THAT.
JUDGING FROM THE LACK OF ACTIVITY ON ANY OF YOUR CREDIT CARDS OR UTILITIES, IT WOULD APPEAR YOU'RE ALSO LIVING UNDER AN ALIAS...
SORRY. IS THERE A QUESTION EVEN REMOTELY IN OUR FUTURE HERE?
YES. AND HERE IT IS:
THREE MONTHS AGO, YOUR HUSBAND WAS KILLED BY SOMEONE WHO DIDN'T FORCE HIMSELF INTO YOUR HOME.
AFTER WHICH, YOU FLED THE JURISDICTION TO LIVE IN AN UNDISCLOSED LOCATION UNDER AN ASSUMED NAME.
SO MY QUESTION IS WHETHER YOU FOUND IT EXTRAORDINARILY CONVENIENT THAT THE POLICE ARRESTED SOMEONE OTHER THAN YOURSELF.
"WHAT THE HELL WAS THAT?"

IT'S CALLED CROSS-EXAMINATION.

SHE ACCUSED ME OF MURDERING MY HUSBAND!

WHEN I TOLD YOU THIS WOULD BE HARD, CONVICTING MYERS WITHOUT YOUR DAUGHTER'S CORROBORATION...

WITHOUT REVEALING THE ALIAS YOU'RE LIVING UNDER...WHEN I TOLD YOU THIS WAS A LONG SHOT...

WHAT D YOU THIN WAS TALK ABOUT

I KNOW YOU'LL HATE THIS... BUT WHAT IF MATTIE...

NO. I WASN'T WILLING TO EXPOSE MATTIE BEFORE. AND WHAT I JUST ENJOYED IN THERE DOESN'T EXACTLY CHANGE MY MIND.

THEN I THINK WE HAVE TO GO TO PLAN B.

THERE'S A PLAN B? WHY DIDN'T YOU SAY ANY-THING?

'CAUSE YOU'RE GONNA HATE IT.

I DOUBT IT.

MY BOSS...SHE'S PUTTING TOGETHER A CASE AGAINST A SUSPECTED ORGANIZED CRIME GROUP CALLED THE EASTERN WIND.

MYERS CLAIMS TO HAVE DONE SOME WORK FOR THEM.

AND HE'S WILLING TO NAME NAMES.

IN EXCHANGE FOR...

WITNESS PROTECTION.

YOU'RE RIGHT. I HATE IT.

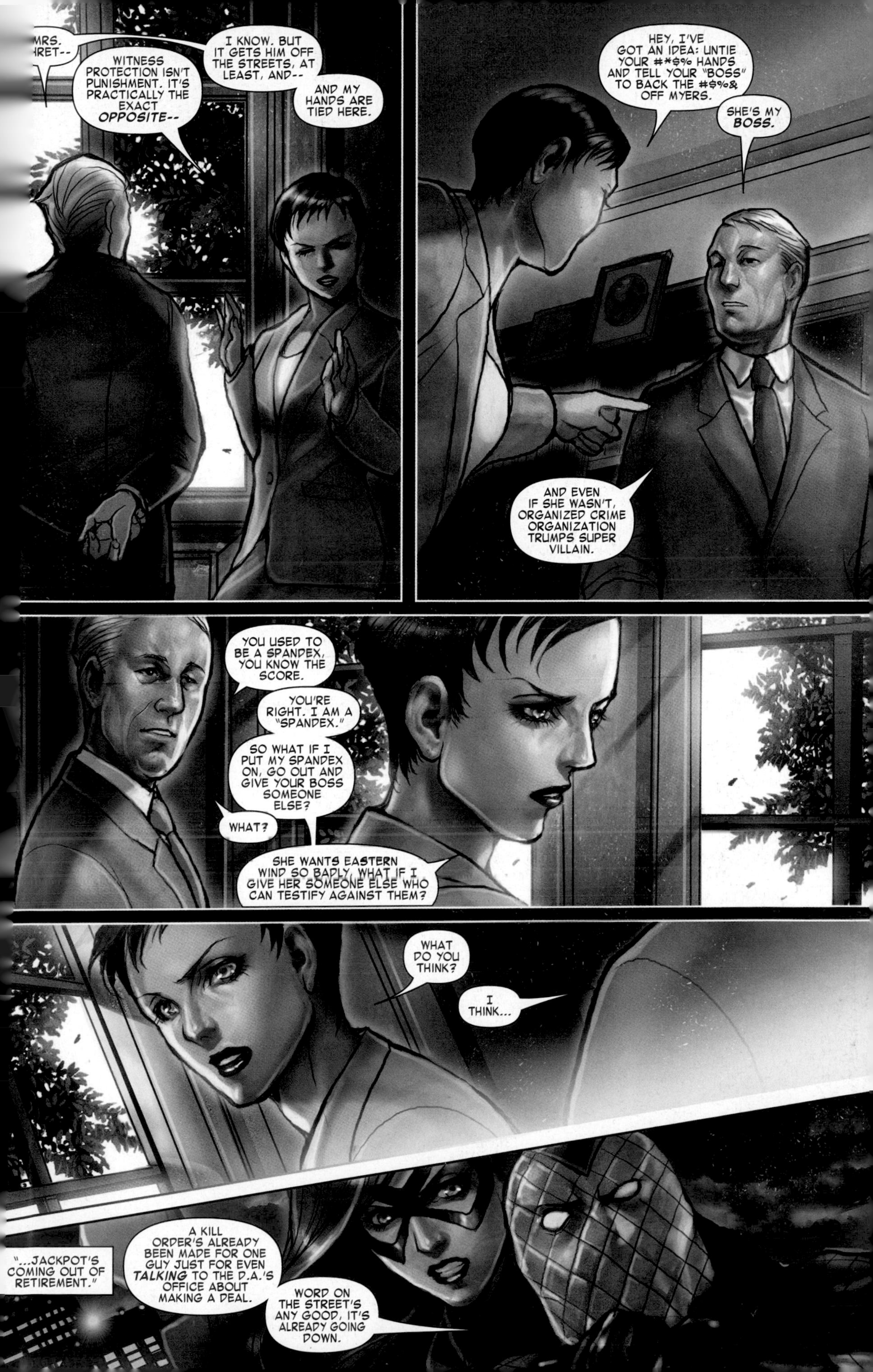
MRS. [cut off] HRET--
WITNESS PROTECTION ISN'T PUNISHMENT. IT'S PRACTICALLY THE EXACT OPPOSITE--
I KNOW. BUT IT GETS HIM OFF THE STREETS, AT LEAST, AND--
AND MY HANDS ARE TIED HERE.
HEY, I'VE GOT AN IDEA: UNTIE YOUR #*$% HANDS AND TELL YOUR "BOSS" TO BACK THE #$%& OFF MYERS.
SHE'S MY BOSS.
AND EVEN IF SHE WASN'T, ORGANIZED CRIME ORGANIZATION TRUMPS SUPER VILLAIN.
YOU USED TO BE A SPANDEX, YOU KNOW THE SCORE.
YOU'RE RIGHT. I AM A "SPANDEX."
SO WHAT IF I PUT MY SPANDEX ON, GO OUT AND GIVE YOUR BOSS SOMEONE ELSE?
WHAT?
SHE WANTS EASTERN WIND SO BADLY, WHAT IF I GIVE HER SOMEONE ELSE WHO CAN TESTIFY AGAINST THEM?
WHAT DO YOU THINK?
I THINK...
"...JACKPOT'S COMING OUT OF RETIREMENT."
A KILL ORDER'S ALREADY BEEN MADE FOR ONE GUY JUST FOR EVEN TALKING TO THE D.A.'S OFFICE ABOUT MAKING A DEAL.
WORD ON THE STREET'S ANY GOOD, IT'S ALREADY GOING DOWN.

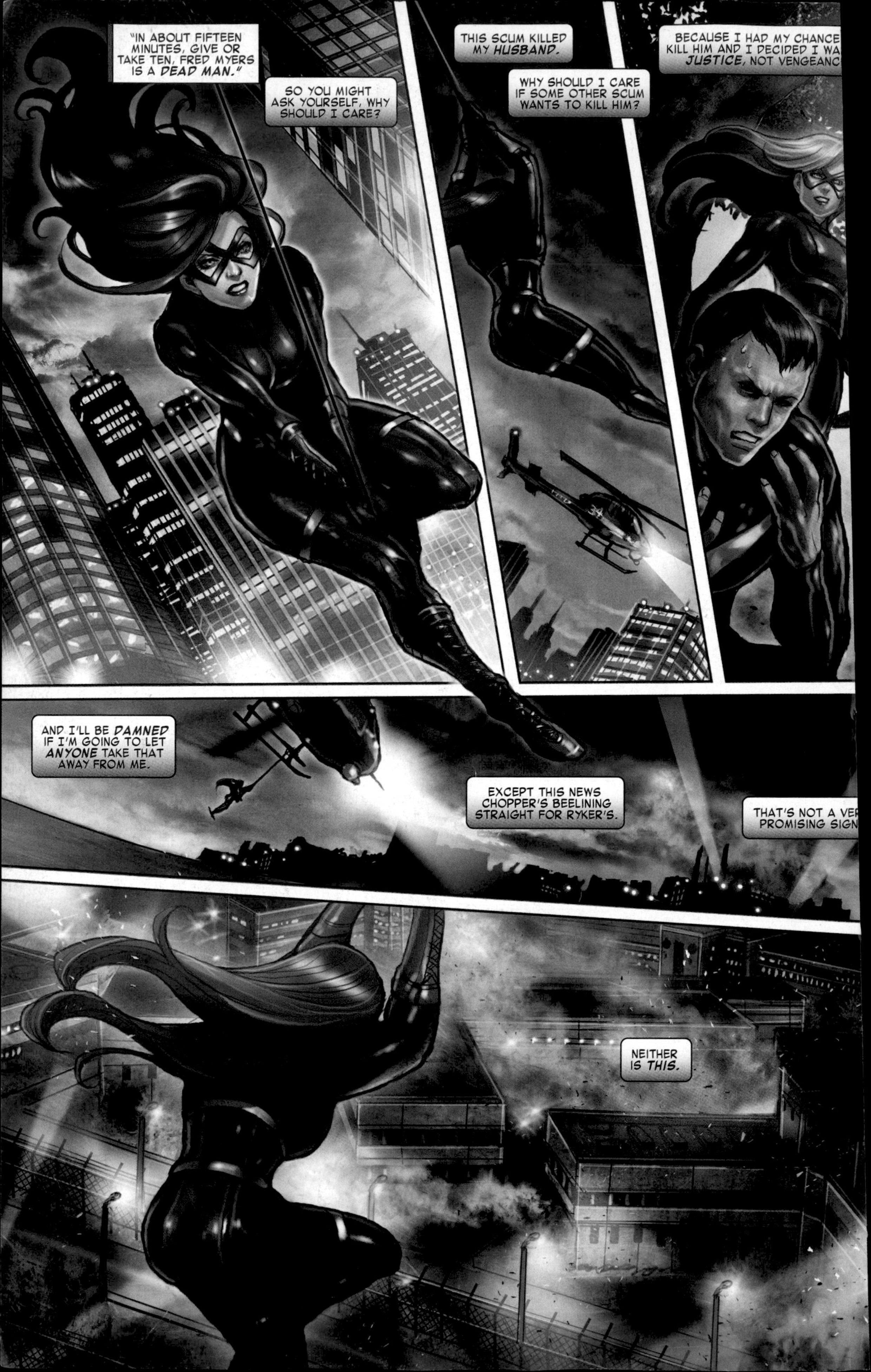
"IN ABOUT FIFTEEN MINUTES, GIVE OR TAKE TEN, FRED MYERS IS A DEAD MAN."
SO YOU MIGHT ASK YOURSELF, WHY SHOULD I CARE?
THIS SCUM KILLED MY HUSBAND.
WHY SHOULD I CARE IF SOME OTHER SCUM WANTS TO KILL HIM?
BECAUSE I HAD MY CHANCE KILL HIM AND I DECIDED I WA JUSTICE, NOT VENGEANC
AND I'LL BE DAMNED IF I'M GOING TO LET ANYONE TAKE THAT AWAY FROM ME.
EXCEPT THIS NEWS CHOPPER'S BEELINING STRAIGHT FOR RYKER'S.
THAT'S NOT A VER PROMISING SIGN
NEITHER IS THIS.

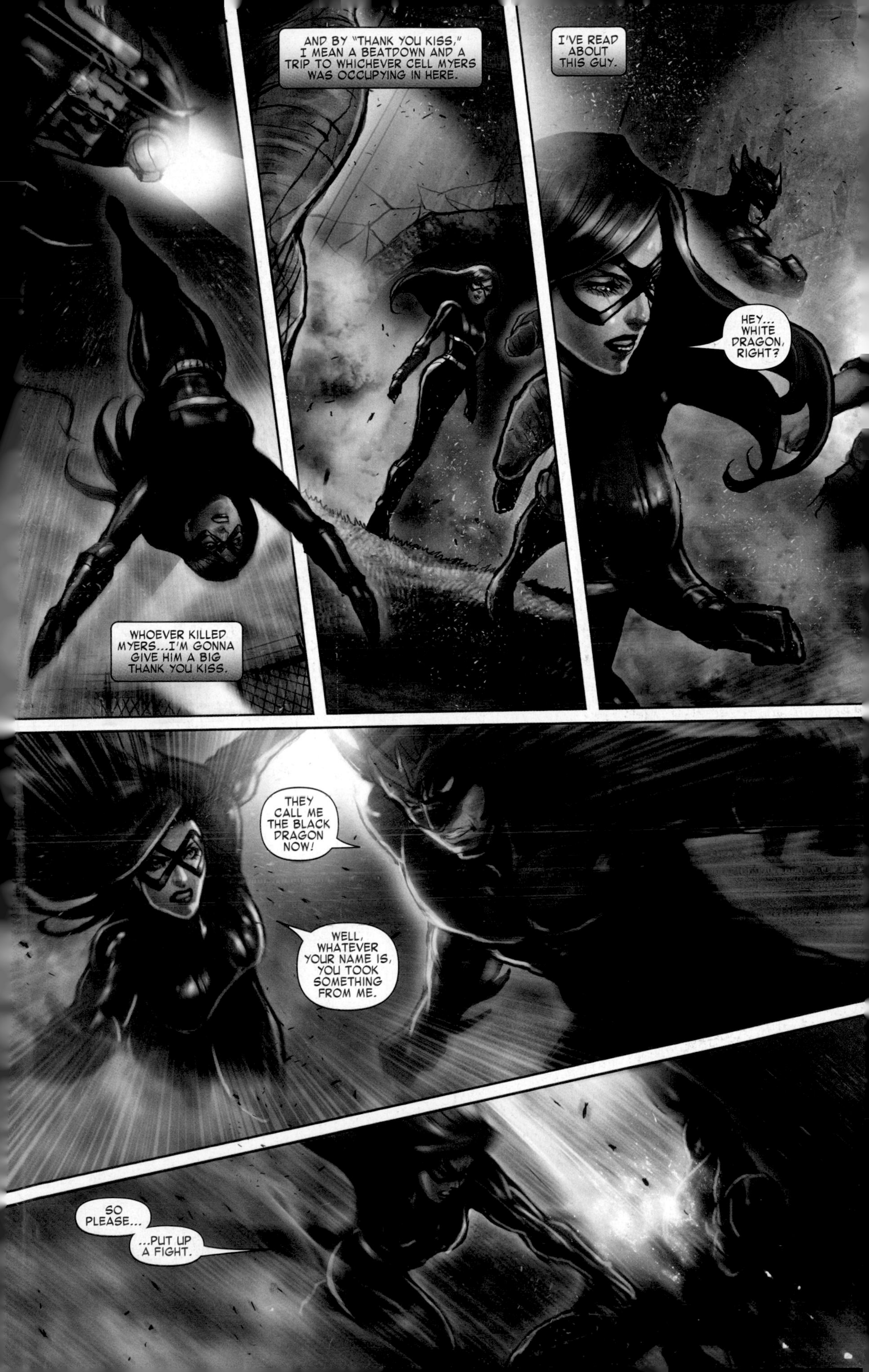
WHOEVER KILLED MYERS...I'M GONNA GIVE HIM A BIG THANK YOU KISS.
AND BY "THANK YOU KISS," I MEAN A BEATDOWN AND A TRIP TO WHICHEVER CELL MYERS WAS OCCUPYING IN HERE.
I'VE READ ABOUT THIS GUY.
HEY... WHITE DRAGON, RIGHT?
THEY CALL ME THE BLACK DRAGON NOW!
WELL, WHATEVER YOUR NAME IS, YOU TOOK SOMETHING FROM ME.
SO PLEASE...
...PUT UP A FIGHT.

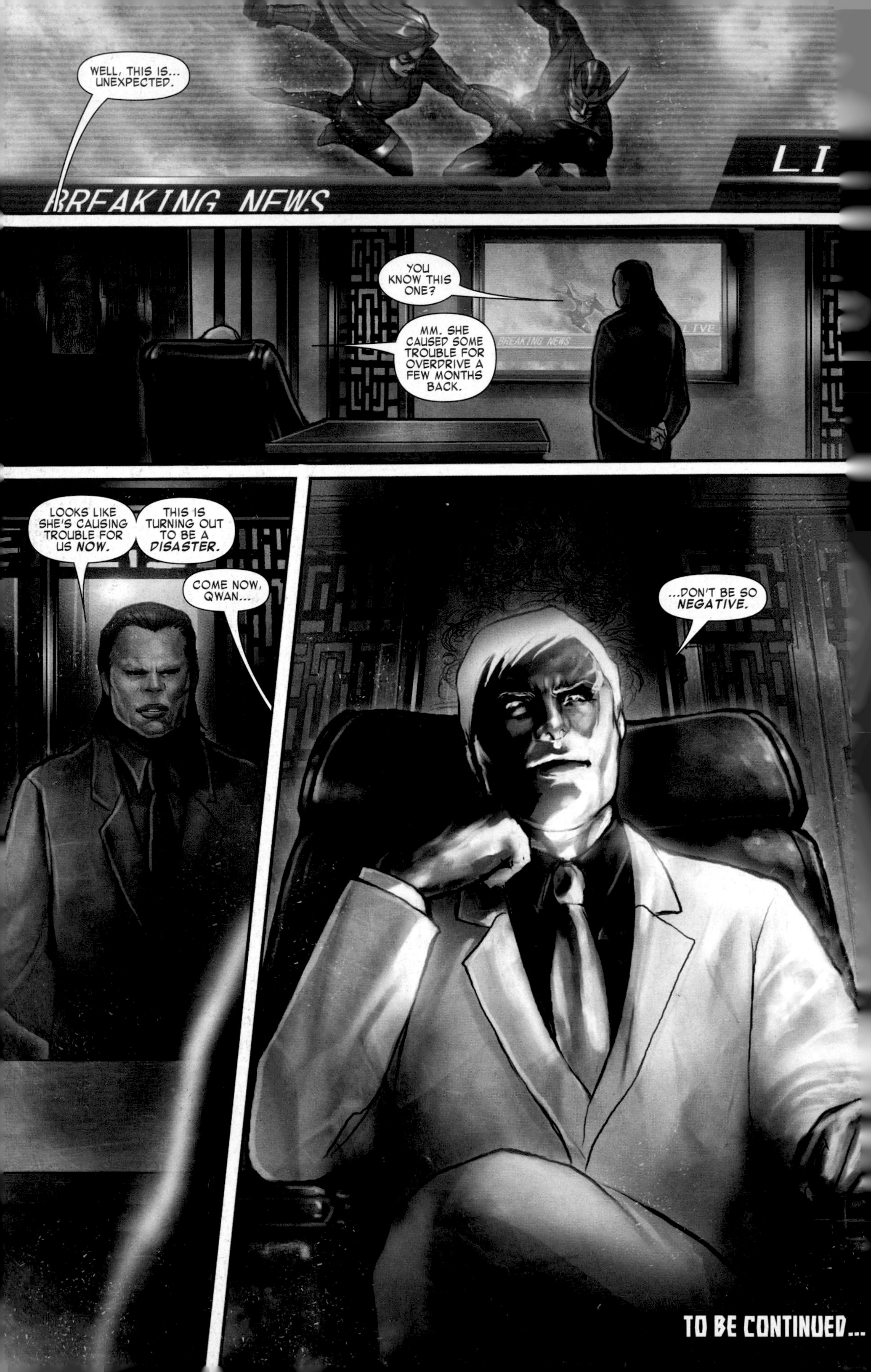
WELL, THIS IS... UNEXPECTED.
LI
BREAKING NEWS
YOU KNOW THIS ONE?
LIVE
BREAKING NEWS
MM. SHE CAUSED SOME TROUBLE FOR OVERDRIVE A FEW MONTHS BACK.
LOOKS LIKE SHE'S CAUSING TROUBLE FOR US NOW.
THIS IS TURNING OUT TO BE A DISASTER.
COME NOW, QWAN...
...DON'T BE SO NEGATIVE.
TO BE CONTINUED...

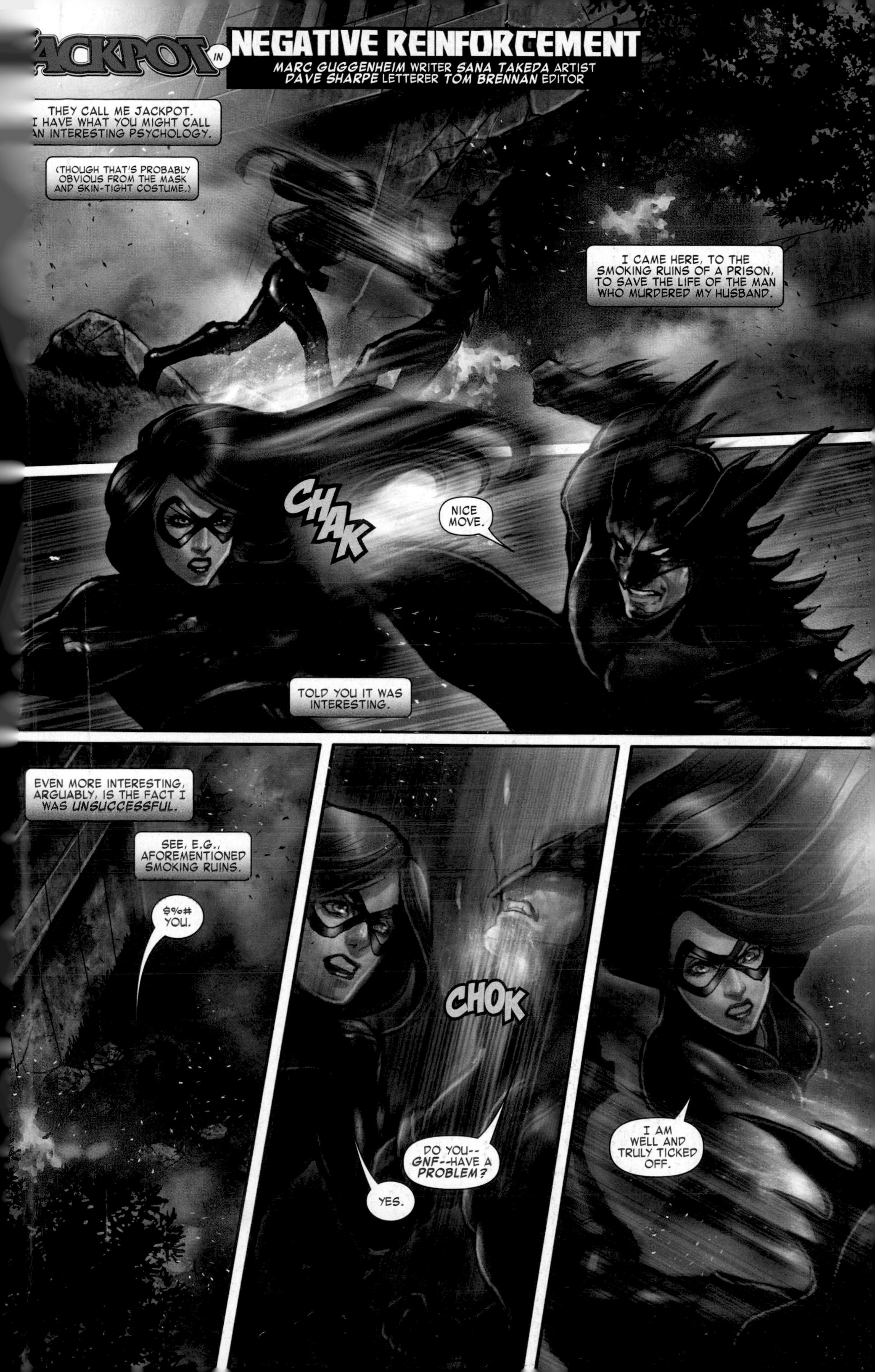
JACKPOT IN NEGATIVE REINFORCEMENT
MARC GUGGENHEIM WRITER SANA TAKEDA ARTIST
DAVE SHARPE LETTERER TOM BRENNAN EDITOR
THEY CALL ME JACKPOT. I HAVE WHAT YOU MIGHT CALL AN INTERESTING PSYCHOLOGY.
(THOUGH THAT'S PROBABLY OBVIOUS FROM THE MASK AND SKIN-TIGHT COSTUME.)
I CAME HERE, TO THE SMOKING RUINS OF A PRISON, TO SAVE THE LIFE OF THE MAN WHO MURDERED MY HUSBAND.
CHAK
NICE MOVE.
TOLD YOU IT WAS INTERESTING.
EVEN MORE INTERESTING, ARGUABLY, IS THE FACT I WAS UNSUCCESSFUL.
SEE, E.G., AFOREMENTIONED SMOKING RUINS.
$%# YOU.
CHOK
DO YOU--GNF--HAVE A PROBLEM?
YES.
I AM WELL AND TRULY TICKED OFF.

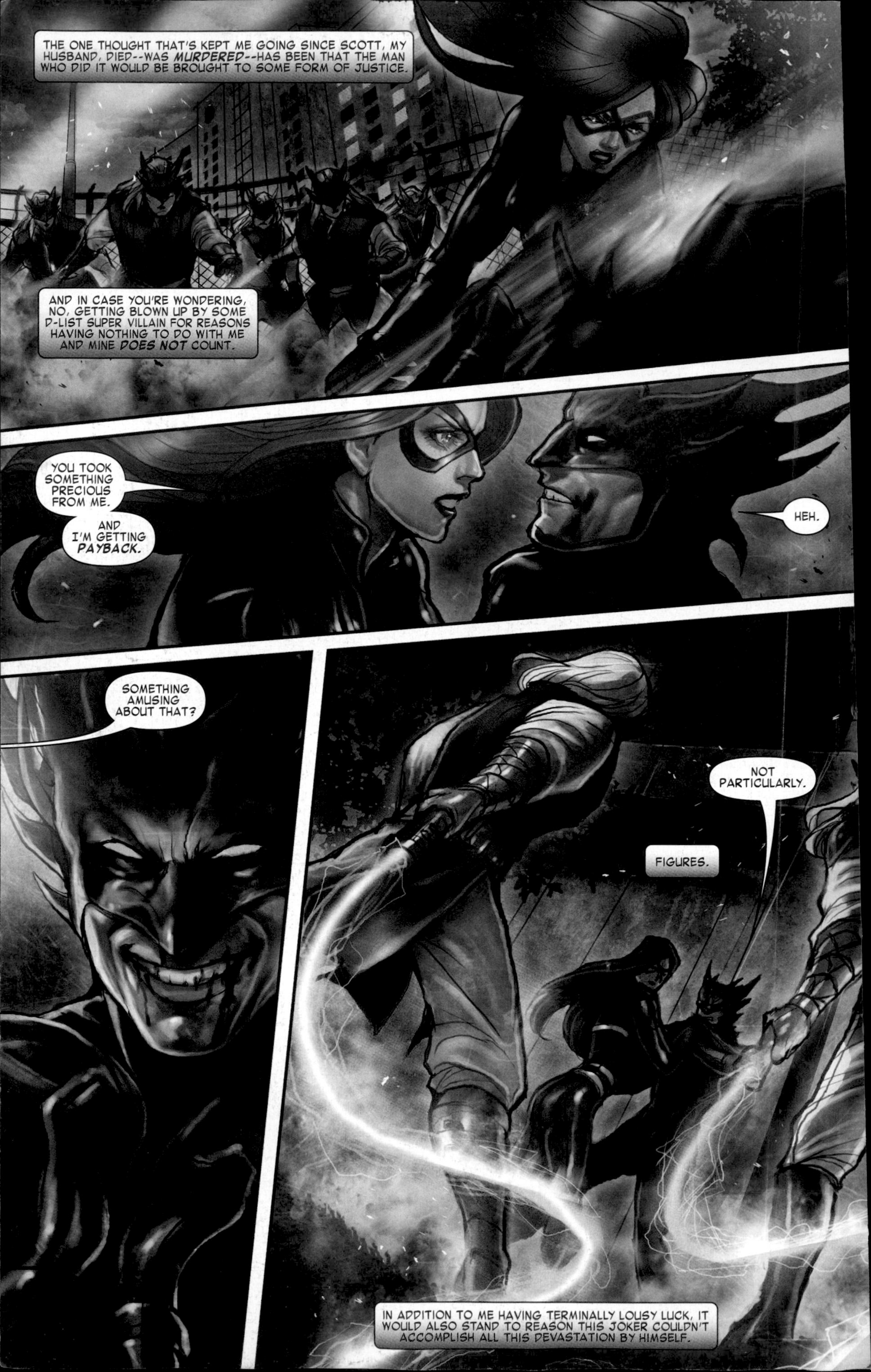
THE ONE THOUGHT THAT'S KEPT ME GOING SINCE SCOTT, MY HUSBAND, DIED--WAS MURDERED--HAS BEEN THAT THE MAN WHO DID IT WOULD BE BROUGHT TO SOME FORM OF JUSTICE.
AND IN CASE YOU'RE WONDERING, NO, GETTING BLOWN UP BY SOME D-LIST SUPER VILLAIN FOR REASONS HAVING NOTHING TO DO WITH ME AND MINE DOES NOT COUNT.
YOU TOOK SOMETHING PRECIOUS FROM ME.
AND I'M GETTING PAYBACK.
HEH.
SOMETHING AMUSING ABOUT THAT?
NOT PARTICULARLY.
FIGURES.
IN ADDITION TO ME HAVING TERMINALLY LOUSY LUCK, IT WOULD ALSO STAND TO REASON THIS JOKER COULDN'T ACCOMPLISH ALL THIS DEVASTATION BY HIMSELF.

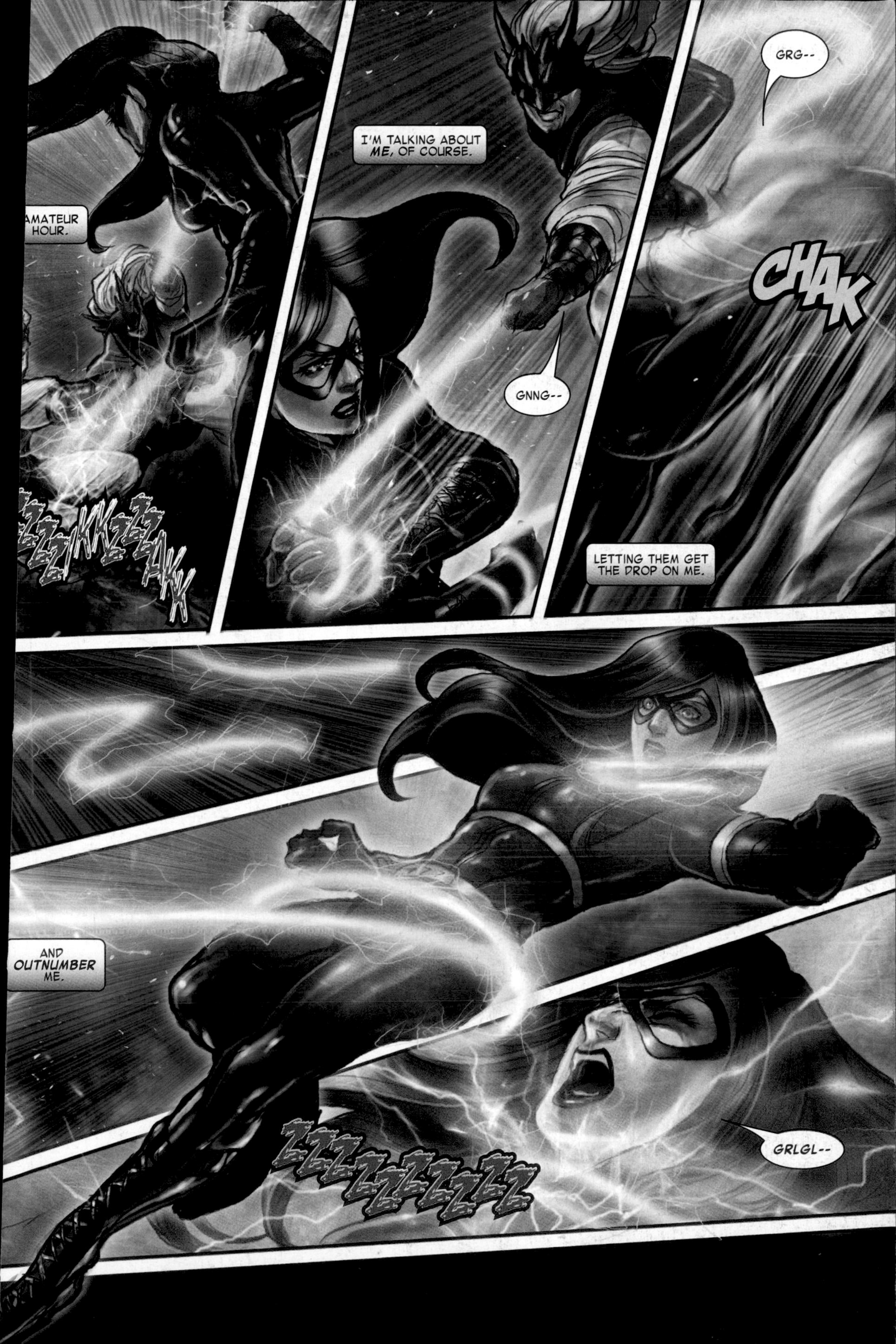

AMATEUR HOUR.
ZZZZZIKKZZZZAKK
I'M TALKING ABOUT ME, OF COURSE.
GNNG--
GRG--
CHAK
LETTING THEM GET THE DROP ON ME.
AND OUTNUMBER ME.
ZZZZZZZZZZZZ
GRLGL--

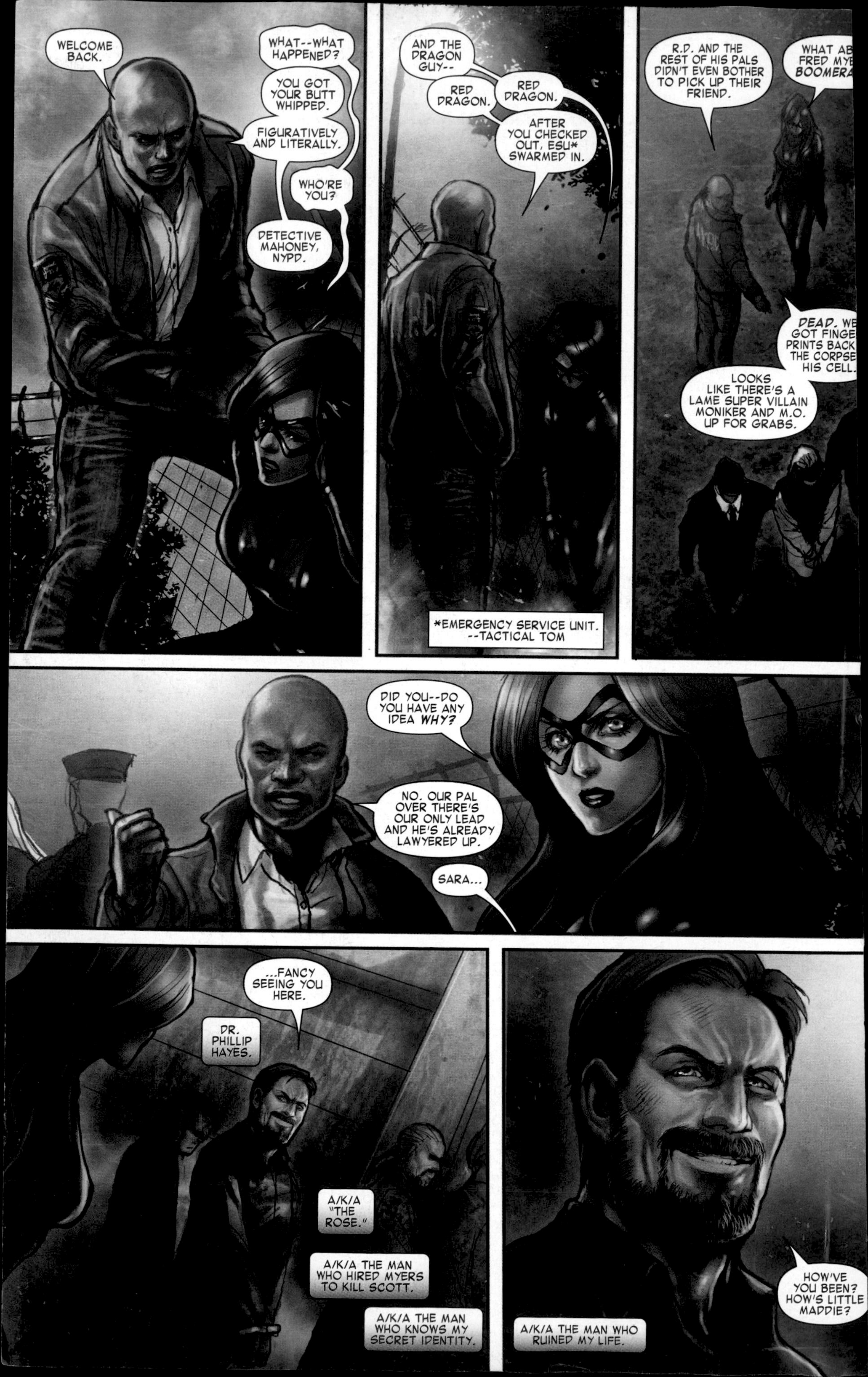
WELCOME BACK.
WHAT--WHAT HAPPENED?
YOU GOT YOUR BUTT WHIPPED.
FIGURATIVELY AND LITERALLY.
WHO'RE YOU?
DETECTIVE MAHONEY, NYPD.
AND THE DRAGON GUY--
RED DRAGON.
RED DRAGON.
AFTER YOU CHECKED OUT, ESU* SWARMED IN.
*EMERGENCY SERVICE UNIT. --TACTICAL TOM
R.D. AND THE REST OF HIS PALS DIDN'T EVEN BOTHER TO PICK UP THEIR FRIEND.
WHAT AB FRED MYE BOOMERA
DEAD. WE GOT FINGE PRINTS BACK THE CORPSE HIS CELL.
LOOKS LIKE THERE'S A LAME SUPER VILLAIN MONIKER AND M.O. UP FOR GRABS.
DID YOU--DO YOU HAVE ANY IDEA WHY?
NO. OUR PAL OVER THERE'S OUR ONLY LEAD AND HE'S ALREADY LAWYERED UP.
SARA...
...FANCY SEEING YOU HERE.
DR. PHILLIP HAYES.
A/K/A "THE ROSE."
A/K/A THE MAN WHO HIRED MYERS TO KILL SCOTT.
A/K/A THE MAN WHO KNOWS MY SECRET IDENTITY.
A/K/A THE MAN WHO RUINED MY LIFE.
HOW'VE YOU BEEN? HOW'S LITTLE MADDIE?

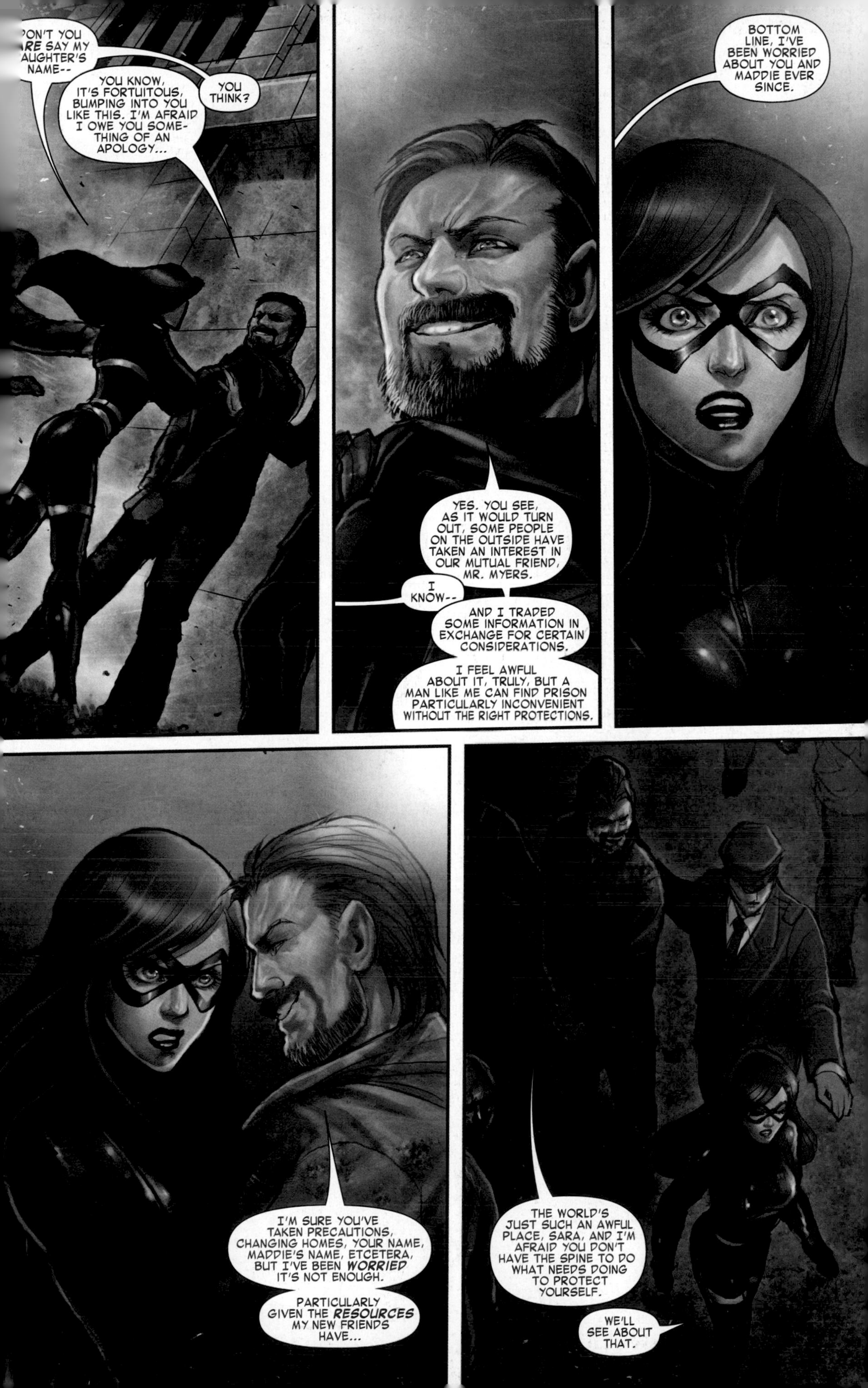
DON'T YOU DARE SAY MY DAUGHTER'S NAME--
YOU KNOW, IT'S FORTUITOUS, BUMPING INTO YOU LIKE THIS. I'M AFRAID I OWE YOU SOMETHING OF AN APOLOGY...
YOU THINK?
YES. YOU SEE, AS IT WOULD TURN OUT, SOME PEOPLE ON THE OUTSIDE HAVE TAKEN AN INTEREST IN OUR MUTUAL FRIEND, MR. MYERS.
I KNOW--
AND I TRADED SOME INFORMATION IN EXCHANGE FOR CERTAIN CONSIDERATIONS.
I FEEL AWFUL ABOUT IT, TRULY, BUT A MAN LIKE ME CAN FIND PRISON PARTICULARLY INCONVENIENT WITHOUT THE RIGHT PROTECTIONS.
BOTTOM LINE, I'VE BEEN WORRIED ABOUT YOU AND MADDIE EVER SINCE.
I'M SURE YOU'VE TAKEN PRECAUTIONS, CHANGING HOMES, YOUR NAME, MADDIE'S NAME, ETCETERA, BUT I'VE BEEN WORRIED IT'S NOT ENOUGH.
PARTICULARLY GIVEN THE RESOURCES MY NEW FRIENDS HAVE...
THE WORLD'S JUST SUCH AN AWFUL PLACE, SARA, AND I'M AFRAID YOU DON'T HAVE THE SPINE TO DO WHAT NEEDS DOING TO PROTECT YOURSELF.
WE'LL SEE ABOUT THAT.

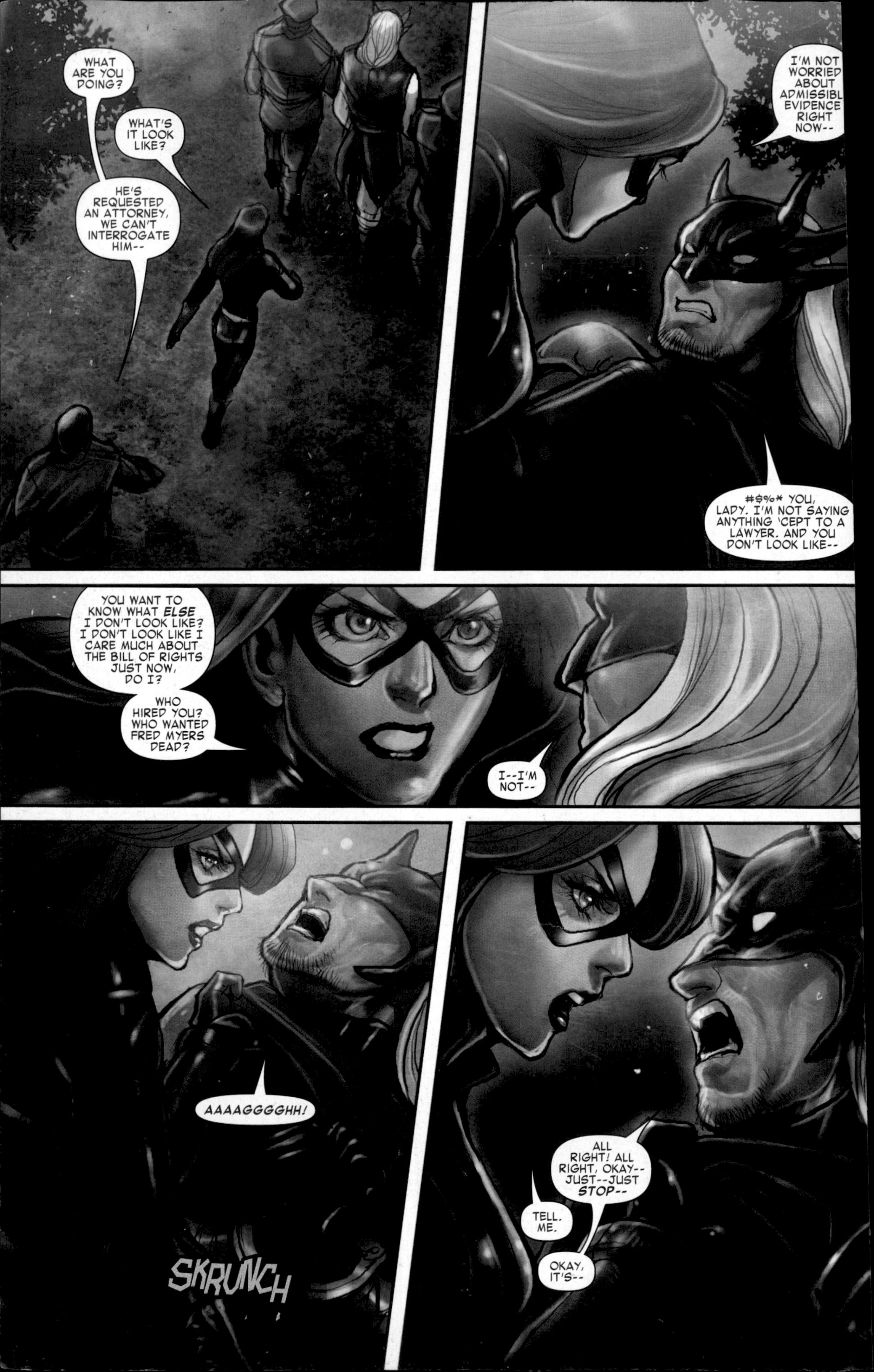
WHAT ARE YOU DOING?
WHAT'S IT LOOK LIKE?
HE'S REQUESTED AN ATTORNEY, WE CAN'T INTERROGATE HIM--
I'M NOT WORRIED ABOUT ADMISSIBL EVIDENCE RIGHT NOW--
#$%* YOU, LADY. I'M NOT SAYING ANYTHING 'CEPT TO A LAWYER. AND YOU DON'T LOOK LIKE--
YOU WANT TO KNOW WHAT *ELSE* I DON'T LOOK LIKE? I DON'T LOOK LIKE I CARE MUCH ABOUT THE BILL OF RIGHTS JUST NOW, DO I?
WHO HIRED YOU? WHO WANTED FRED MYERS DEAD?
I--I'M NOT--
AAAAGGGGHH!
SKRUNCH
ALL RIGHT! ALL RIGHT, OKAY-- JUST--JUST *STOP*--
TELL. ME.
OKAY, IT'S--

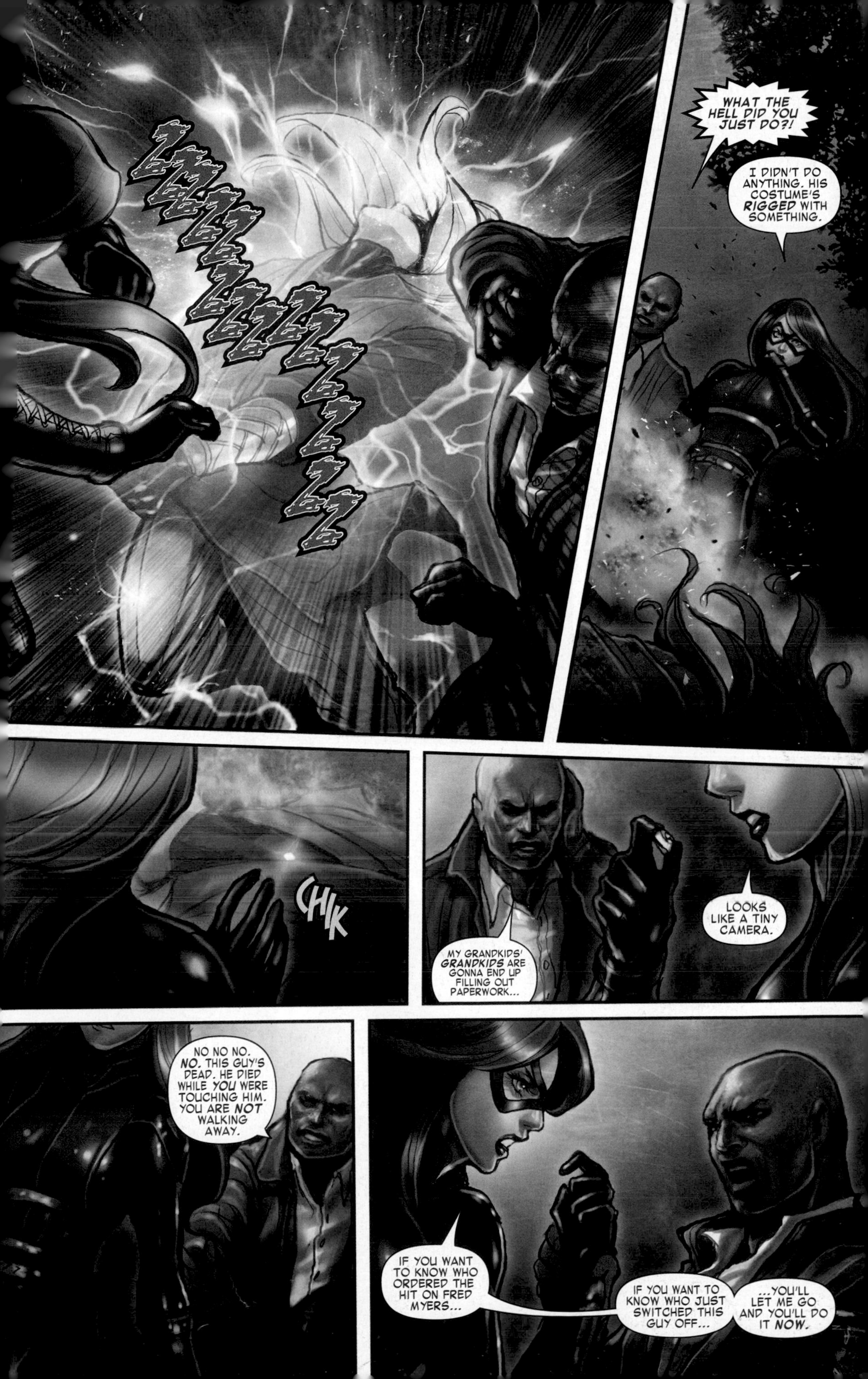
ZZZZZZZZZZZZZZZZ
WHAT THE HELL DID YOU JUST DO?!
I DIDN'T DO ANYTHING. HIS COSTUME'S RIGGED WITH SOMETHING.
CHIK
LOOKS LIKE A TINY CAMERA.
MY GRANDKIDS' GRANDKIDS ARE GONNA END UP FILLING OUT PAPERWORK...
NO NO NO. NO. THIS GUY'S DEAD. HE DIED WHILE YOU WERE TOUCHING HIM. YOU ARE NOT WALKING AWAY.
IF YOU WANT TO KNOW WHO ORDERED THE HIT ON FRED MYERS...
IF YOU WANT TO KNOW WHO JUST SWITCHED THIS GUY OFF...
...YOU'LL LET ME GO AND YOU'LL DO IT NOW.

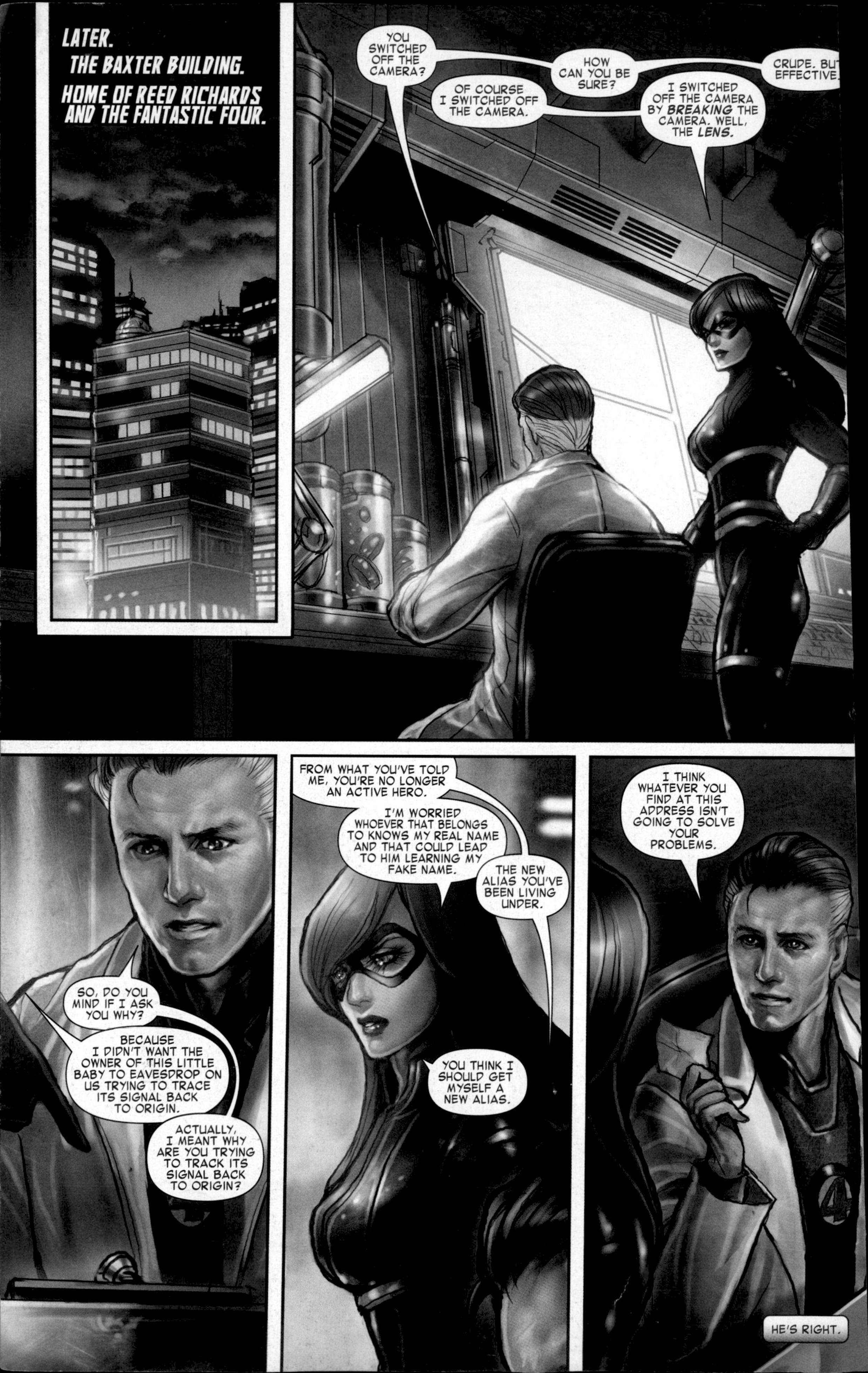
LATER.
THE BAXTER BUILDING.
HOME OF REED RICHARDS AND THE FANTASTIC FOUR.
YOU SWITCHED OFF THE CAMERA?
OF COURSE I SWITCHED OFF THE CAMERA.
HOW CAN YOU BE SURE?
I SWITCHED OFF THE CAMERA BY BREAKING THE CAMERA. WELL, THE LENS.
CRUDE. BUT EFFECTIVE.
SO, DO YOU MIND IF I ASK YOU WHY?
BECAUSE I DIDN'T WANT THE OWNER OF THIS LITTLE BABY TO EAVESDROP ON US TRYING TO TRACE ITS SIGNAL BACK TO ORIGIN.
ACTUALLY, I MEANT WHY ARE YOU TRYING TO TRACK ITS SIGNAL BACK TO ORIGIN?
FROM WHAT YOU'VE TOLD ME, YOU'RE NO LONGER AN ACTIVE HERO.
I'M WORRIED WHOEVER THAT BELONGS TO KNOWS MY REAL NAME AND THAT COULD LEAD TO HIM LEARNING MY FAKE NAME.
THE NEW ALIAS YOU'VE BEEN LIVING UNDER.
YOU THINK I SHOULD GET MYSELF A NEW ALIAS.
I THINK WHATEVER YOU FIND AT THIS ADDRESS ISN'T GOING TO SOLVE YOUR PROBLEMS.
HE'S RIGHT.

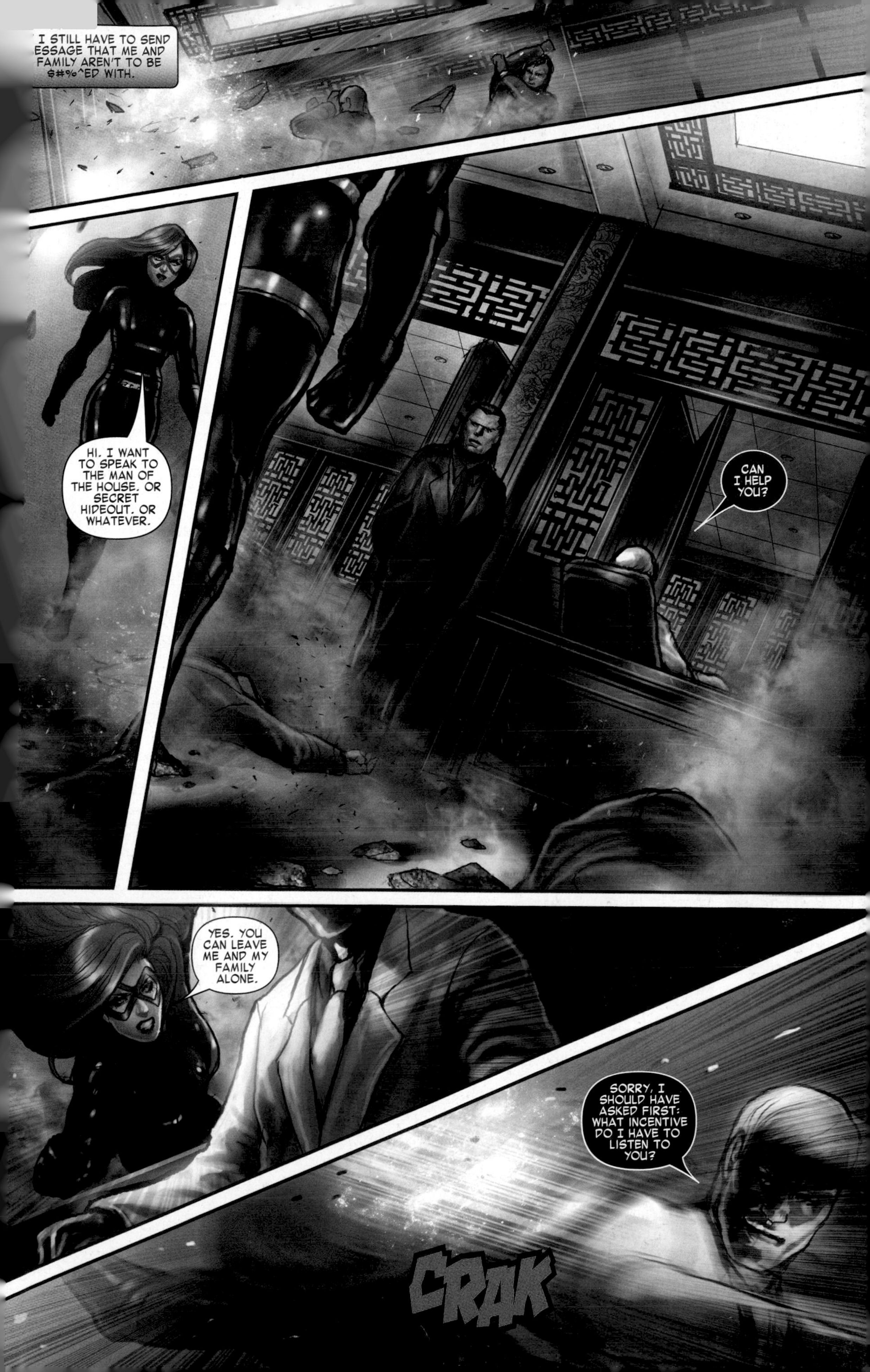
I STILL HAVE TO SEND
ESSAGE THAT ME AND
FAMILY AREN'T TO BE
$#%^ED WITH.
HI. I WANT TO SPEAK TO THE MAN OF THE HOUSE. OR SECRET HIDEOUT. OR WHATEVER.
CAN I HELP YOU?
YES. YOU CAN LEAVE ME AND MY FAMILY ALONE.
SORRY, I SHOULD HAVE ASKED FIRST: WHAT INCENTIVE DO I HAVE TO LISTEN TO YOU?
CRAK

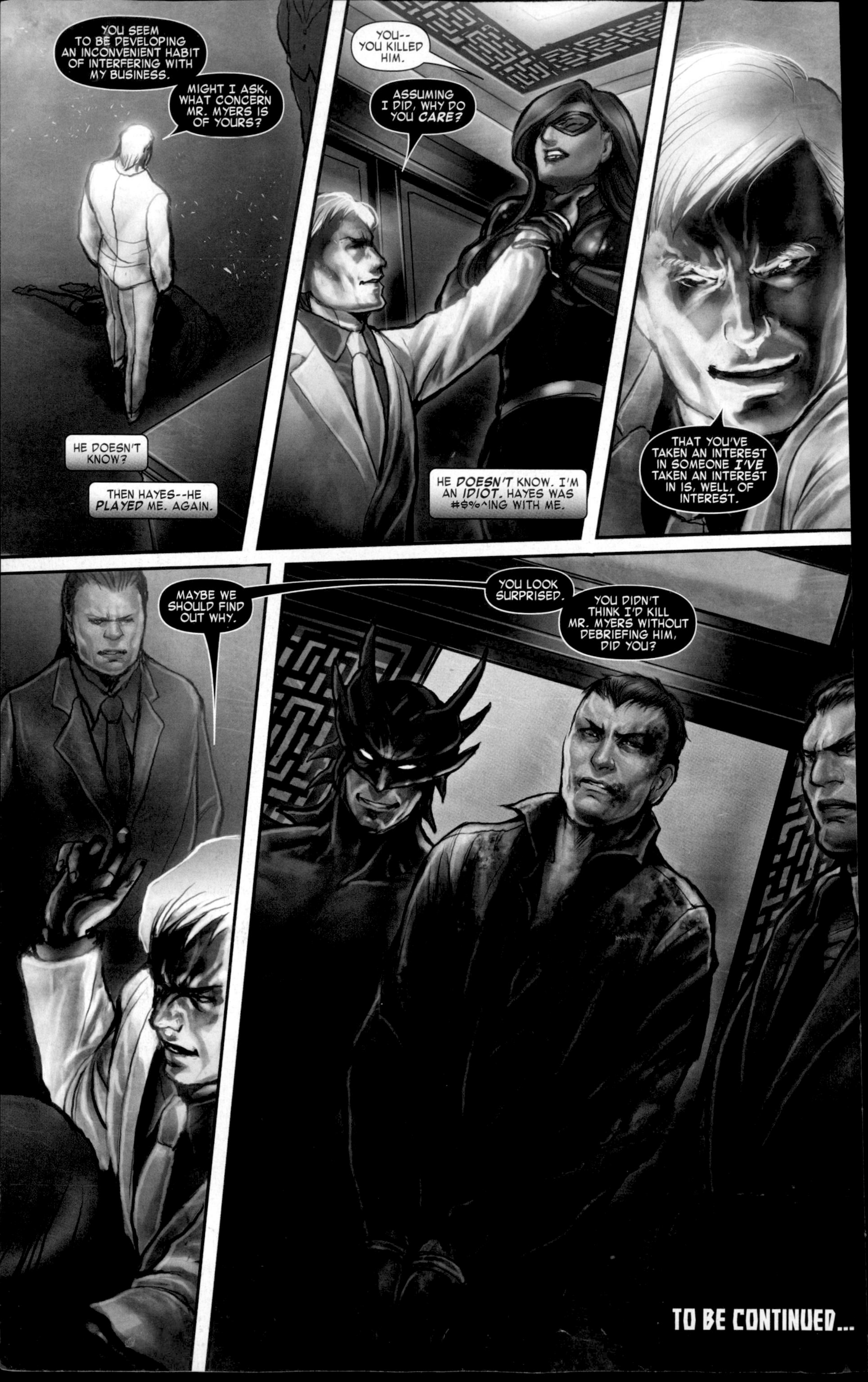
YOU SEEM TO BE DEVELOPING AN INCONVENIENT HABIT OF INTERFERING WITH MY BUSINESS.
MIGHT I ASK, WHAT CONCERN MR. MYERS IS OF YOURS?
HE DOESN'T KNOW?
THEN HAYES--HE PLAYED ME. AGAIN.
YOU-- YOU KILLED HIM.
ASSUMING I DID, WHY DO YOU CARE?
HE DOESN'T KNOW. I'M AN IDIOT. HAYES WAS #$%^ING WITH ME.
THAT YOU'VE TAKEN AN INTEREST IN SOMEONE I'VE TAKEN AN INTEREST IN IS, WELL, OF INTEREST.
MAYBE WE SHOULD FIND OUT WHY.
YOU LOOK SURPRISED.
YOU DIDN'T THINK I'D KILL MR. MYERS WITHOUT DEBRIEFING HIM, DID YOU?
TO BE CONTINUED...

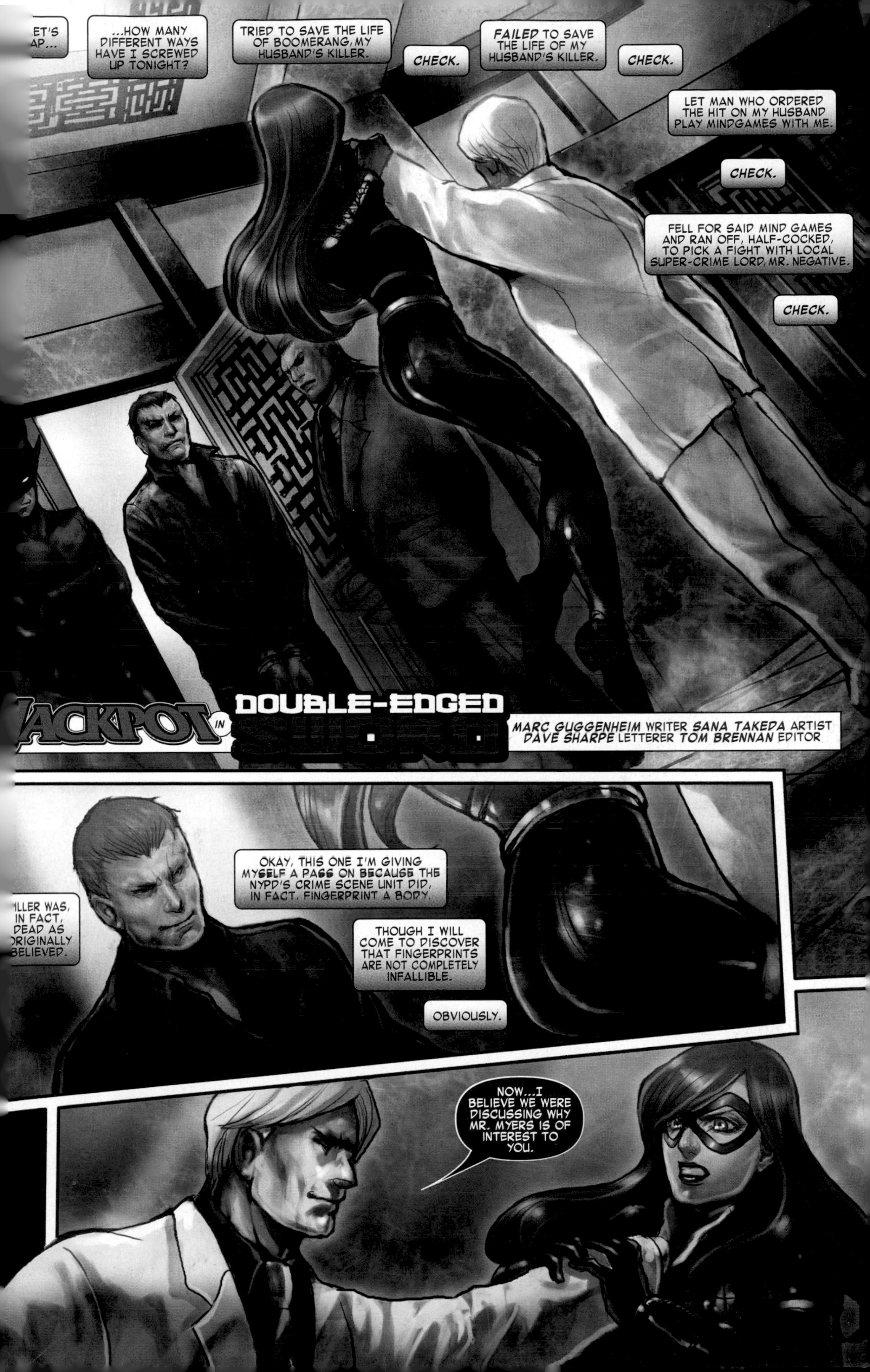

ET'S
AP...
...HOW MANY DIFFERENT WAYS HAVE I SCREWED UP TONIGHT?
TRIED TO SAVE THE LIFE OF BOOMERANG, MY HUSBAND'S KILLER.
CHECK.
FAILED TO SAVE THE LIFE OF MY HUSBAND'S KILLER.
CHECK.
LET MAN WHO ORDERED THE HIT ON MY HUSBAND PLAY MINDGAMES WITH ME.
CHECK.
FELL FOR SAID MIND GAMES AND RAN OFF, HALF-COCKED, TO PICK A FIGHT WITH LOCAL SUPER-CRIME LORD, MR. NEGATIVE.
CHECK.
ACKPOT IN DOUBLE-EDGED SWORD
MARC GUGGENHEIM WRITER SANA TAKEDA ARTIST
DAVE SHARPE LETTERER TOM BRENNAN EDITOR
ILLER WAS, IN FACT, DEAD AS ORIGINALLY BELIEVED.
OKAY, THIS ONE I'M GIVING MYSELF A PASS ON BECAUSE THE NYPD'S CRIME SCENE UNIT DID, IN FACT, FINGERPRINT A BODY.
THOUGH I WILL COME TO DISCOVER THAT FINGERPRINTS ARE NOT COMPLETELY INFALLIBLE.
OBVIOUSLY.
NOW...I BELIEVE WE WERE DISCUSSING WHY MR. MYERS IS OF INTEREST TO YOU.

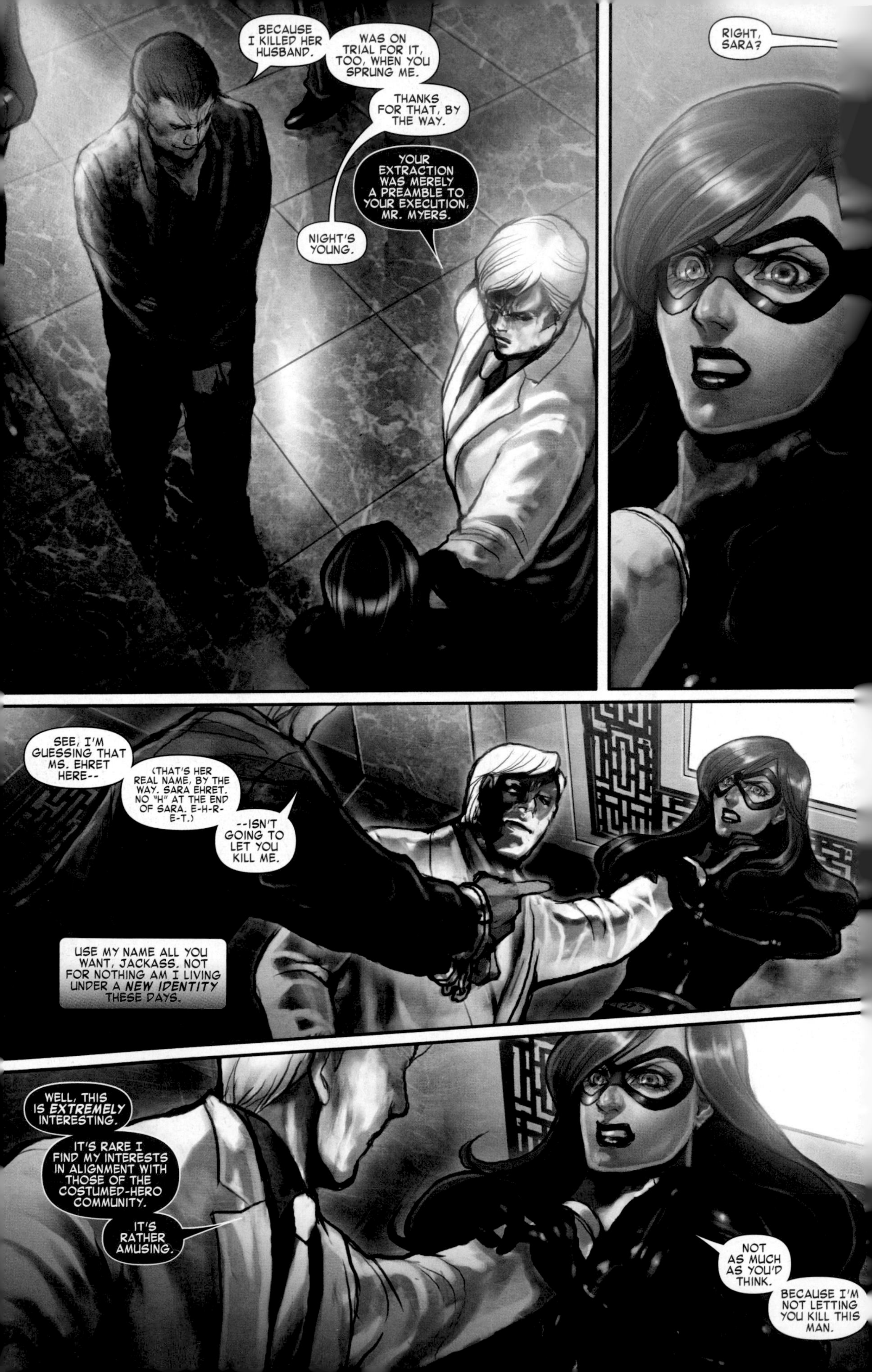

BECAUSE I KILLED HER HUSBAND.
WAS ON TRIAL FOR IT, TOO, WHEN YOU SPRUNG ME.
THANKS FOR THAT, BY THE WAY.
YOUR EXTRACTION WAS MERELY A PREAMBLE TO YOUR EXECUTION, MR. MYERS.
NIGHT'S YOUNG.
RIGHT, SARA?
SEE, I'M GUESSING THAT MS. EHRET HERE--
(THAT'S HER REAL NAME, BY THE WAY. SARA EHRET. NO "H" AT THE END OF SARA. E-H-R-E-T.)
--ISN'T GOING TO LET YOU KILL ME.
USE MY NAME ALL YOU WANT, JACKASS. NOT FOR NOTHING AM I LIVING UNDER A *NEW IDENTITY* THESE DAYS.
WELL, THIS IS *EXTREMELY* INTERESTING.
IT'S RARE I FIND MY INTERESTS IN ALIGNMENT WITH THOSE OF THE COSTUMED-HERO COMMUNITY.
IT'S RATHER AMUSING.
NOT AS MUCH AS YOU'D THINK.
BECAUSE I'M NOT LETTING YOU KILL THIS MAN.

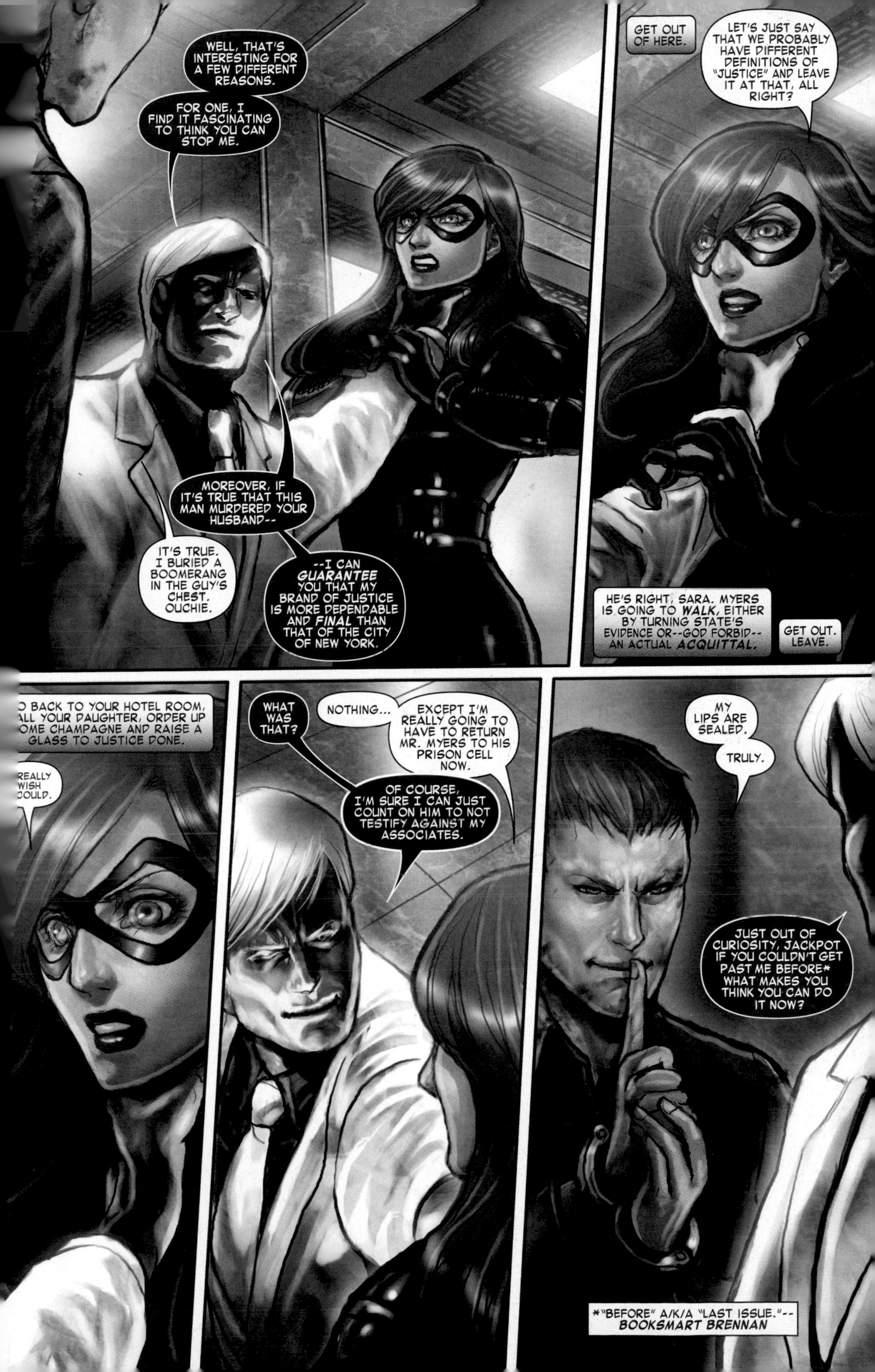
WELL, THAT'S INTERESTING FOR A FEW DIFFERENT REASONS.
FOR ONE, I FIND IT FASCINATING TO THINK YOU CAN STOP ME.
MOREOVER, IF IT'S TRUE THAT THIS MAN MURDERED YOUR HUSBAND--
IT'S TRUE. I BURIED A BOOMERANG IN THE GUY'S CHEST. OUCHIE.
--I CAN GUARANTEE YOU THAT MY BRAND OF JUSTICE IS MORE DEPENDABLE AND FINAL THAN THAT OF THE CITY OF NEW YORK.
GET OUT OF HERE.
LET'S JUST SAY THAT WE PROBABLY HAVE DIFFERENT DEFINITIONS OF "JUSTICE" AND LEAVE IT AT THAT, ALL RIGHT?
HE'S RIGHT, SARA. MYERS IS GOING TO WALK, EITHER BY TURNING STATE'S EVIDENCE OR--GOD FORBID--AN ACTUAL ACQUITTAL.
GET OUT. LEAVE.
O BACK TO YOUR HOTEL ROOM, ALL YOUR DAUGHTER, ORDER UP OME CHAMPAGNE AND RAISE A GLASS TO JUSTICE DONE.
REALLY WISH COULD.
WHAT WAS THAT?
NOTHING...
EXCEPT I'M REALLY GOING TO HAVE TO RETURN MR. MYERS TO HIS PRISON CELL NOW.
OF COURSE, I'M SURE I CAN JUST COUNT ON HIM TO NOT TESTIFY AGAINST MY ASSOCIATES.
MY LIPS ARE SEALED.
TRULY.
JUST OUT OF CURIOSITY, JACKPOT IF YOU COULDN'T GET PAST ME BEFORE* WHAT MAKES YOU THINK YOU CAN DO IT NOW?
*"BEFORE" A/K/A "LAST ISSUE."--BOOKSMART BRENNAN

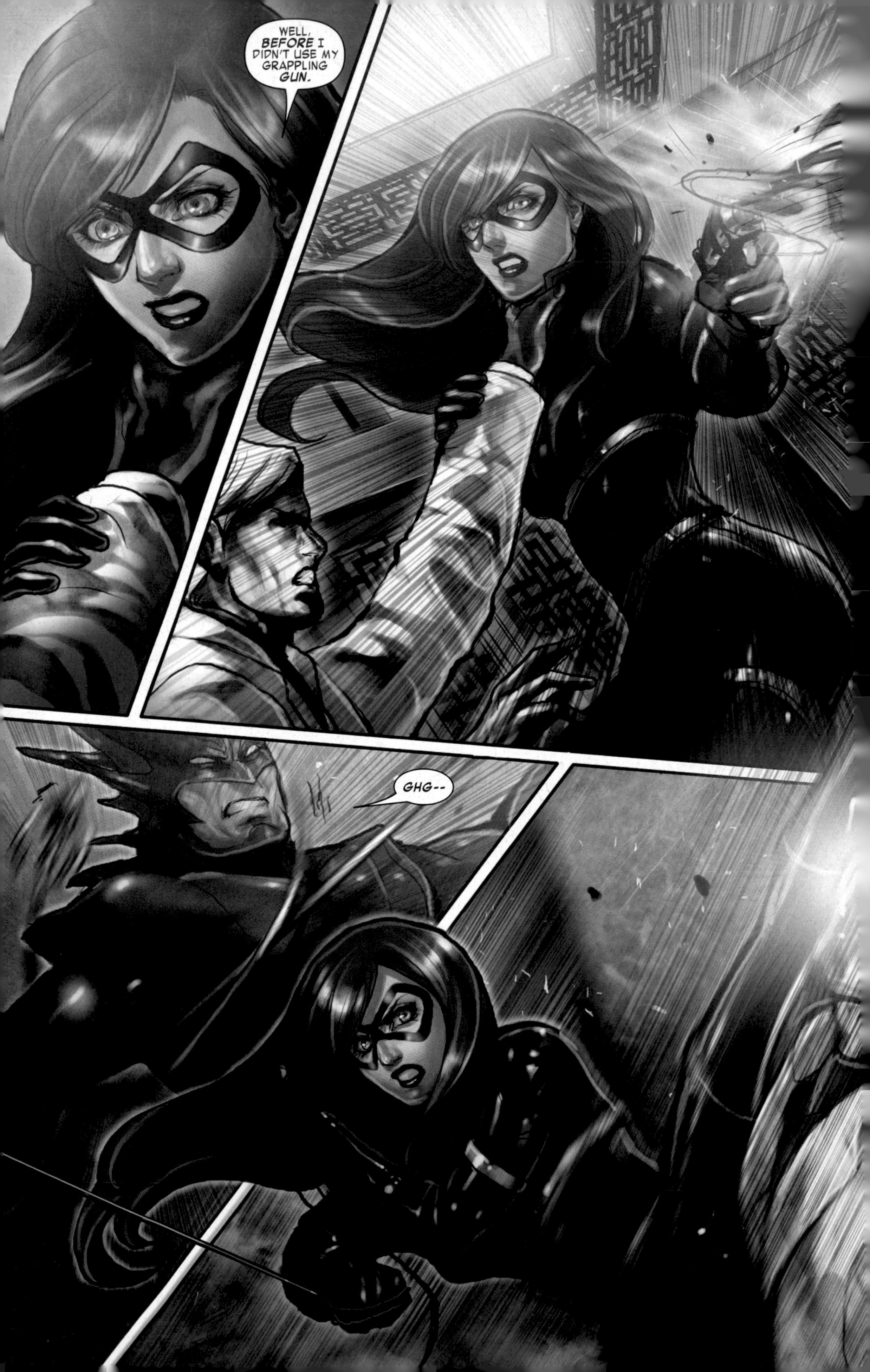
WELL, BEFORE I DIDN'T USE MY GRAPPLING GUN.
GHG--

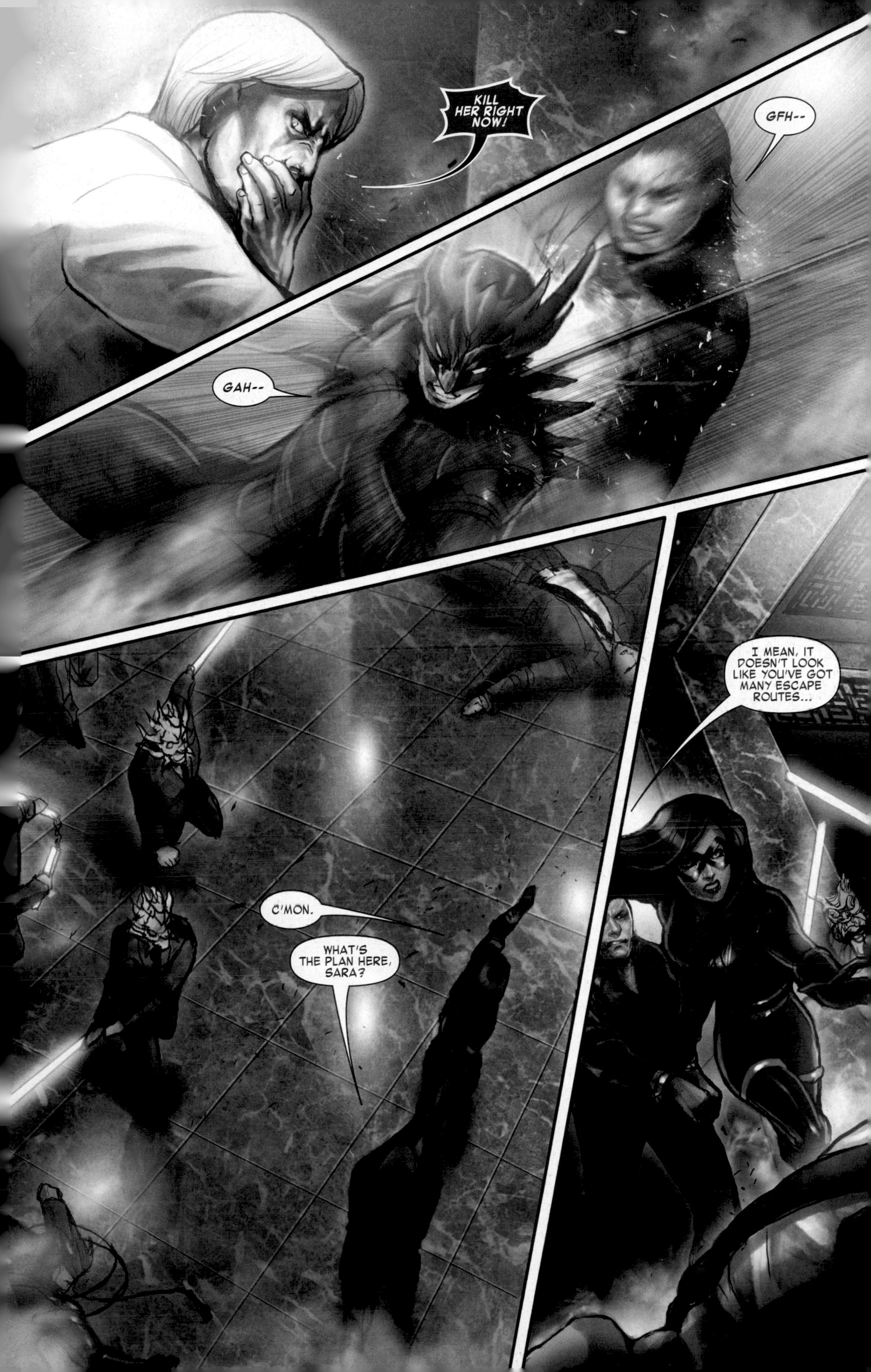
KILL HER RIGHT NOW!
GFH--
GAH--
I MEAN, IT DOESN'T LOOK LIKE YOU'VE GOT MANY ESCAPE ROUTES...
C'MON.
WHAT'S THE PLAN HERE, SARA?

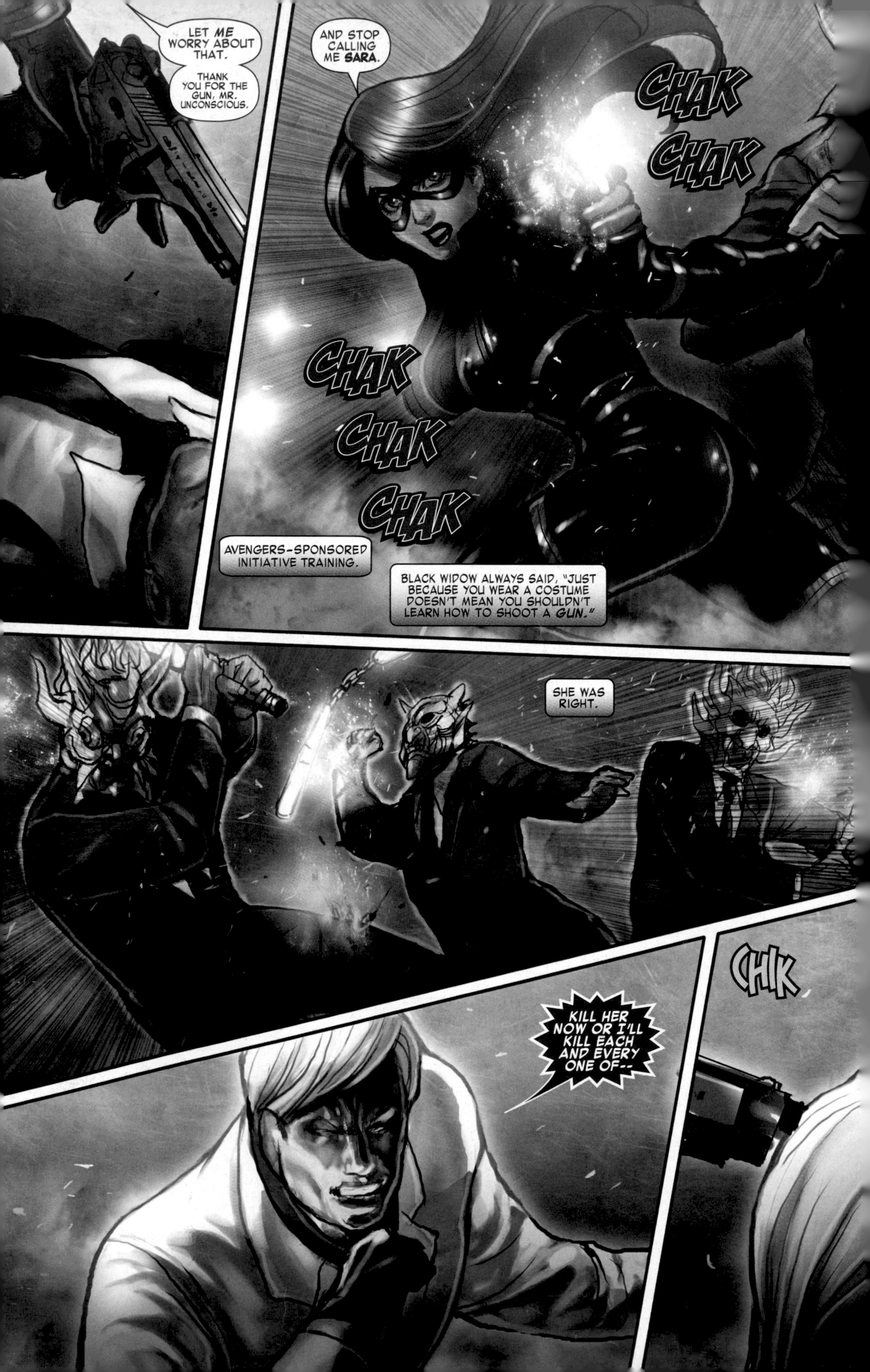
LET ME WORRY ABOUT THAT.
THANK YOU FOR THE GUN, MR. UNCONSCIOUS.
AND STOP CALLING ME SARA.
CHAK
CHAK
CHAK
CHAK
CHAK
AVENGERS-SPONSORED INITIATIVE TRAINING.
BLACK WIDOW ALWAYS SAID, "JUST BECAUSE YOU WEAR A COSTUME DOESN'T MEAN YOU SHOULDN'T LEARN HOW TO SHOOT A GUN."
SHE WAS RIGHT.
CHIK
KILL HER NOW OR I'LL KILL EACH AND EVERY ONE OF--

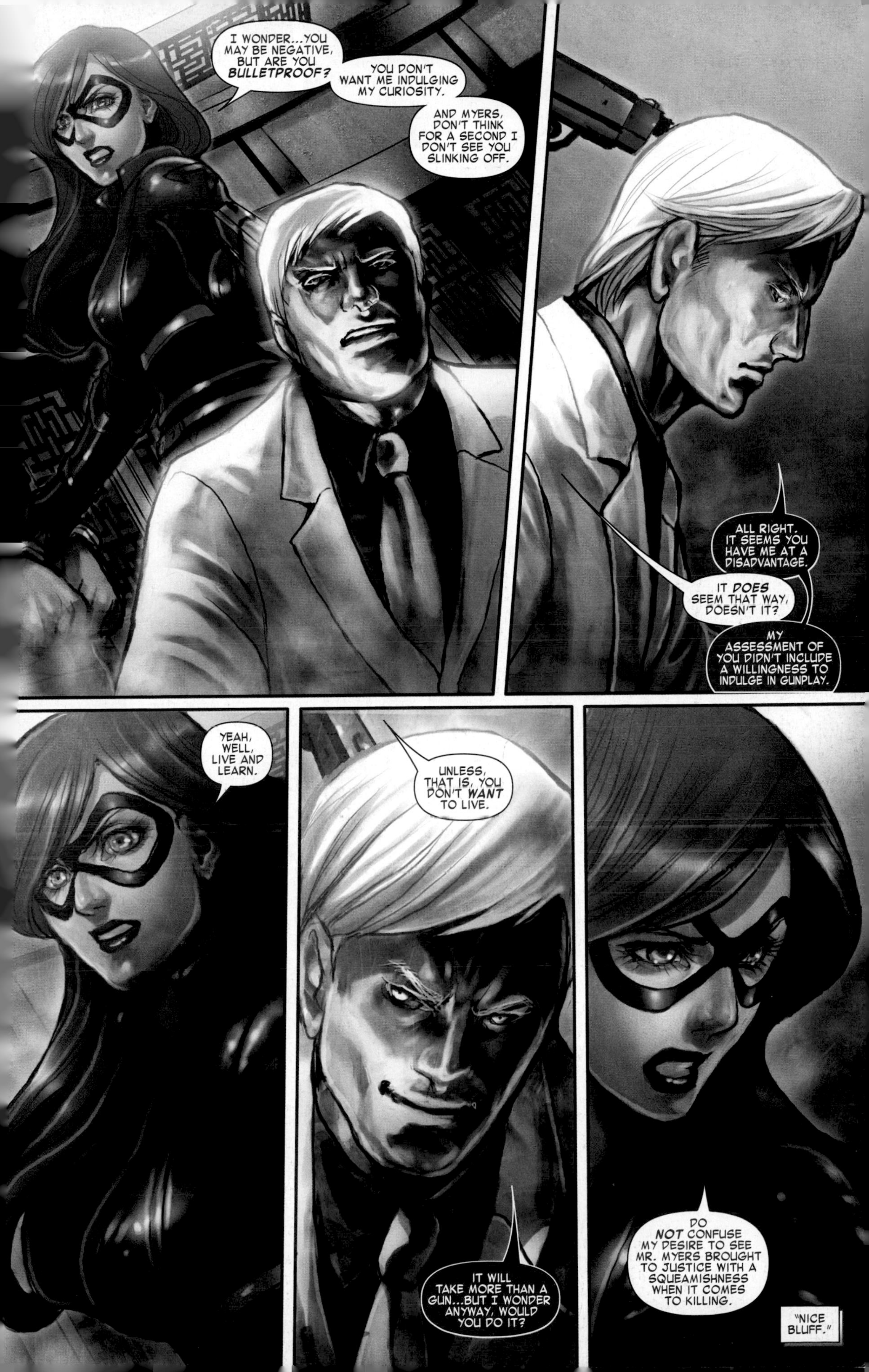
I WONDER...YOU MAY BE NEGATIVE, BUT ARE YOU BULLETPROOF?
YOU DON'T WANT ME INDULGING MY CURIOSITY.
AND MYERS, DON'T THINK FOR A SECOND I DON'T SEE YOU SLINKING OFF.
ALL RIGHT. IT SEEMS YOU HAVE ME AT A DISADVANTAGE.
IT DOES SEEM THAT WAY, DOESN'T IT?
MY ASSESSMENT OF YOU DIDN'T INCLUDE A WILLINGNESS TO INDULGE IN GUNPLAY.
YEAH, WELL, LIVE AND LEARN.
UNLESS, THAT IS, YOU DON'T WANT TO LIVE.
IT WILL TAKE MORE THAN A GUN...BUT I WONDER ANYWAY, WOULD YOU DO IT?
DO NOT CONFUSE MY DESIRE TO SEE MR. MYERS BROUGHT TO JUSTICE WITH A SQUEAMISHNESS WHEN IT COMES TO KILLING.
"NICE BLUFF."

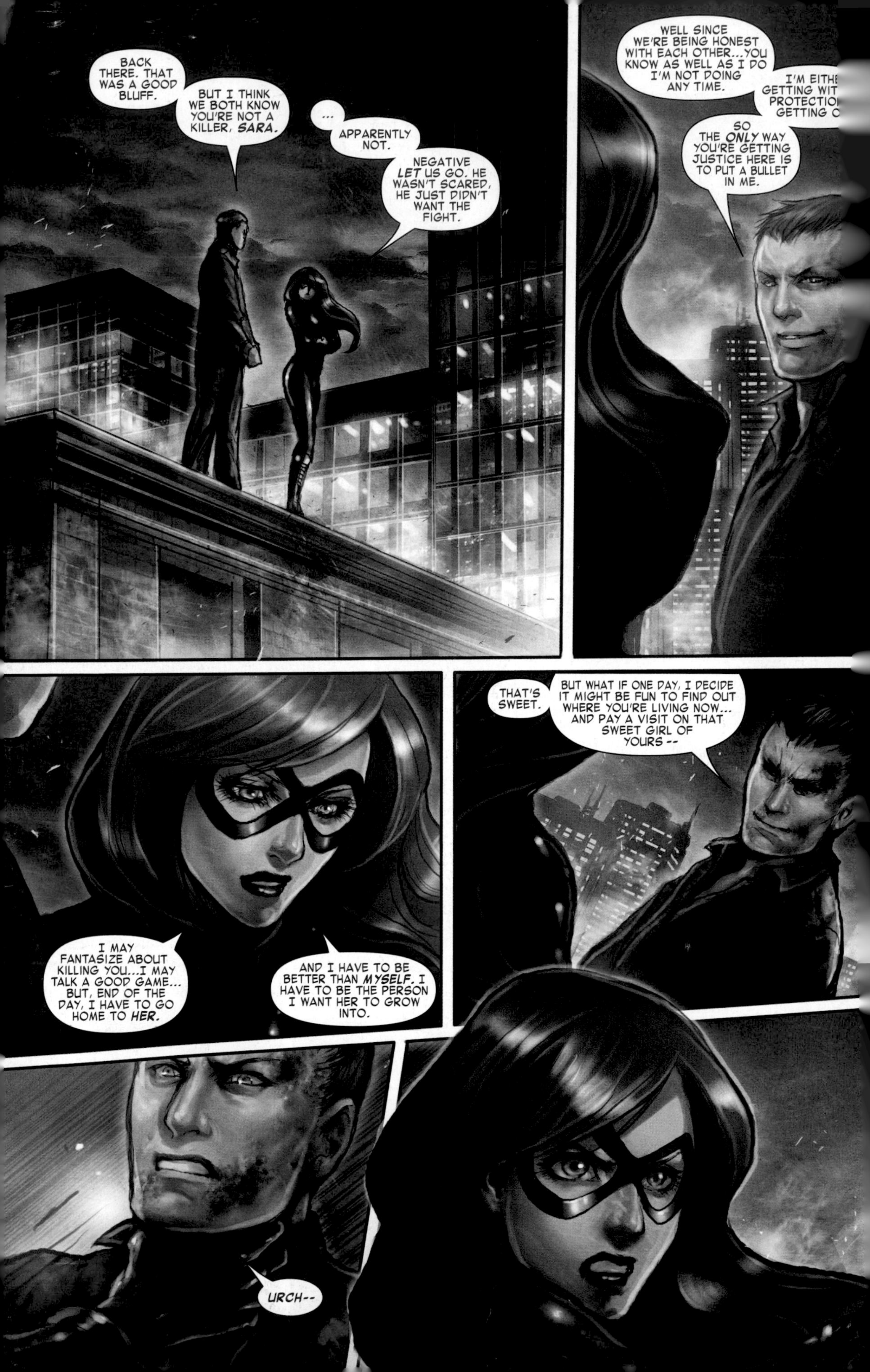
BACK THERE. THAT WAS A GOOD BLUFF.
BUT I THINK WE BOTH KNOW YOU'RE NOT A KILLER, SARA.
...
APPARENTLY NOT.
NEGATIVE LET US GO. HE WASN'T SCARED, HE JUST DIDN'T WANT THE FIGHT.
WELL SINCE WE'RE BEING HONEST WITH EACH OTHER...YOU KNOW AS WELL AS I DO I'M NOT DOING ANY TIME.
I'M EITHE GETTING WIT PROTECTIO GETTING O
SO THE ONLY WAY YOU'RE GETTING JUSTICE HERE IS TO PUT A BULLET IN ME.
THAT'S SWEET.
BUT WHAT IF ONE DAY, I DECIDE IT MIGHT BE FUN TO FIND OUT WHERE YOU'RE LIVING NOW... AND PAY A VISIT ON THAT SWEET GIRL OF YOURS --
I MAY FANTASIZE ABOUT KILLING YOU...I MAY TALK A GOOD GAME... BUT, END OF THE DAY, I HAVE TO GO HOME TO HER.
AND I HAVE TO BE BETTER THAN MYSELF. I HAVE TO BE THE PERSON I WANT HER TO GROW INTO.
URCH--

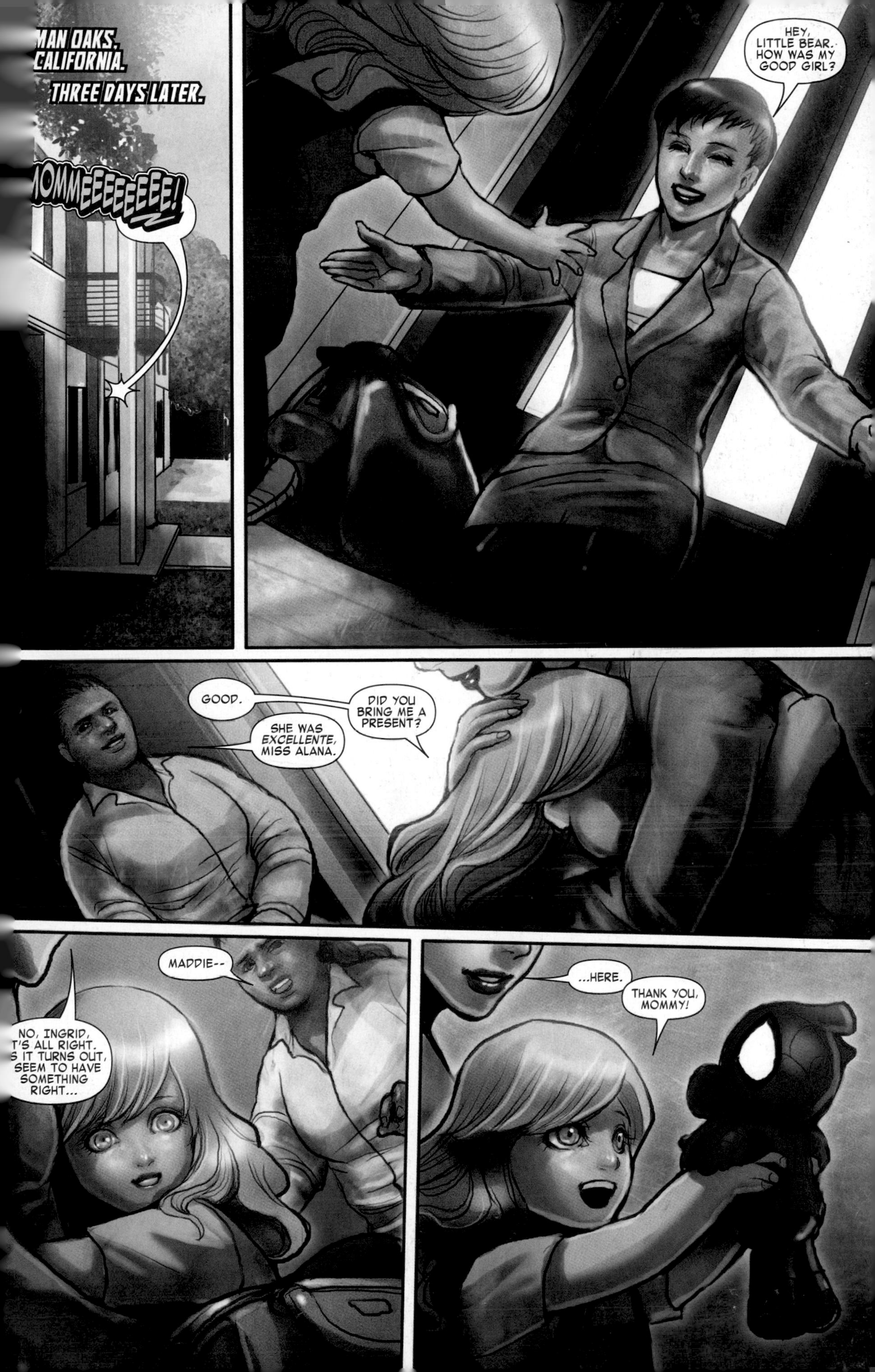

MAN OAKS, CALIFORNIA.
THREE DAYS LATER.
MOMMEEEEEEEE!
HEY, LITTLE BEAR. HOW WAS MY GOOD GIRL?
GOOD.
DID YOU BRING ME A PRESENT?
SHE WAS EXCELLENTE, MISS ALANA.
MADDIE--
NO, INGRID, IT'S ALL RIGHT. S IT TURNS OUT, SEEM TO HAVE SOMETHING RIGHT...
...HERE.
THANK YOU, MOMMY!

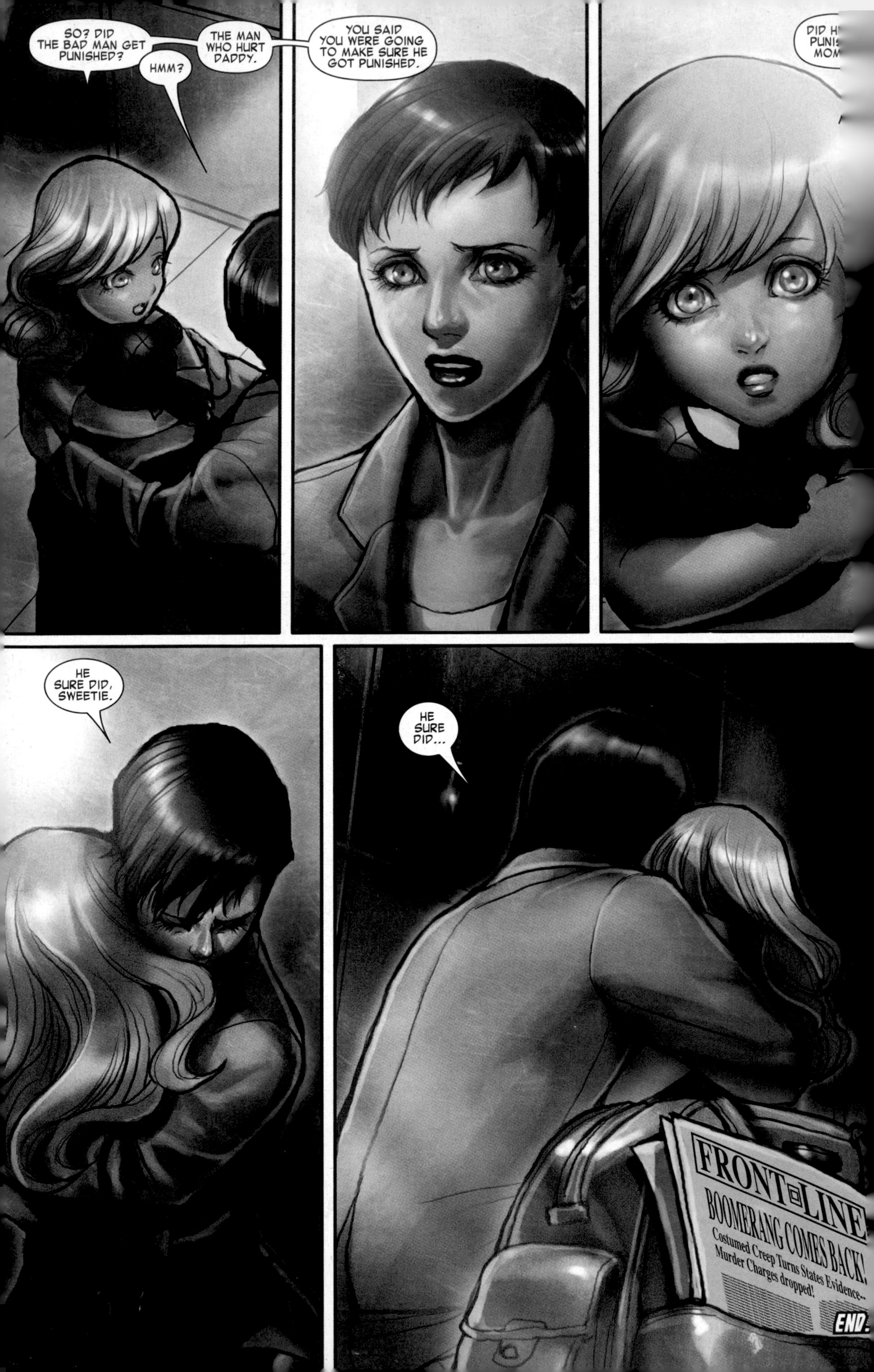

SO? DID THE BAD MAN GET PUNISHED?
HMM?
THE MAN WHO HURT DADDY.
YOU SAID YOU WERE GOING TO MAKE SURE HE GOT PUNISHED.
DID H
PUNIS
MOM
HE SURE DID, SWEETIE.
HE SURE DID...
FRONT LINE
BOOMERANG COMES BACK!
Costumed Creep Turns States Evidence--
Murder Charges dropped!
END.

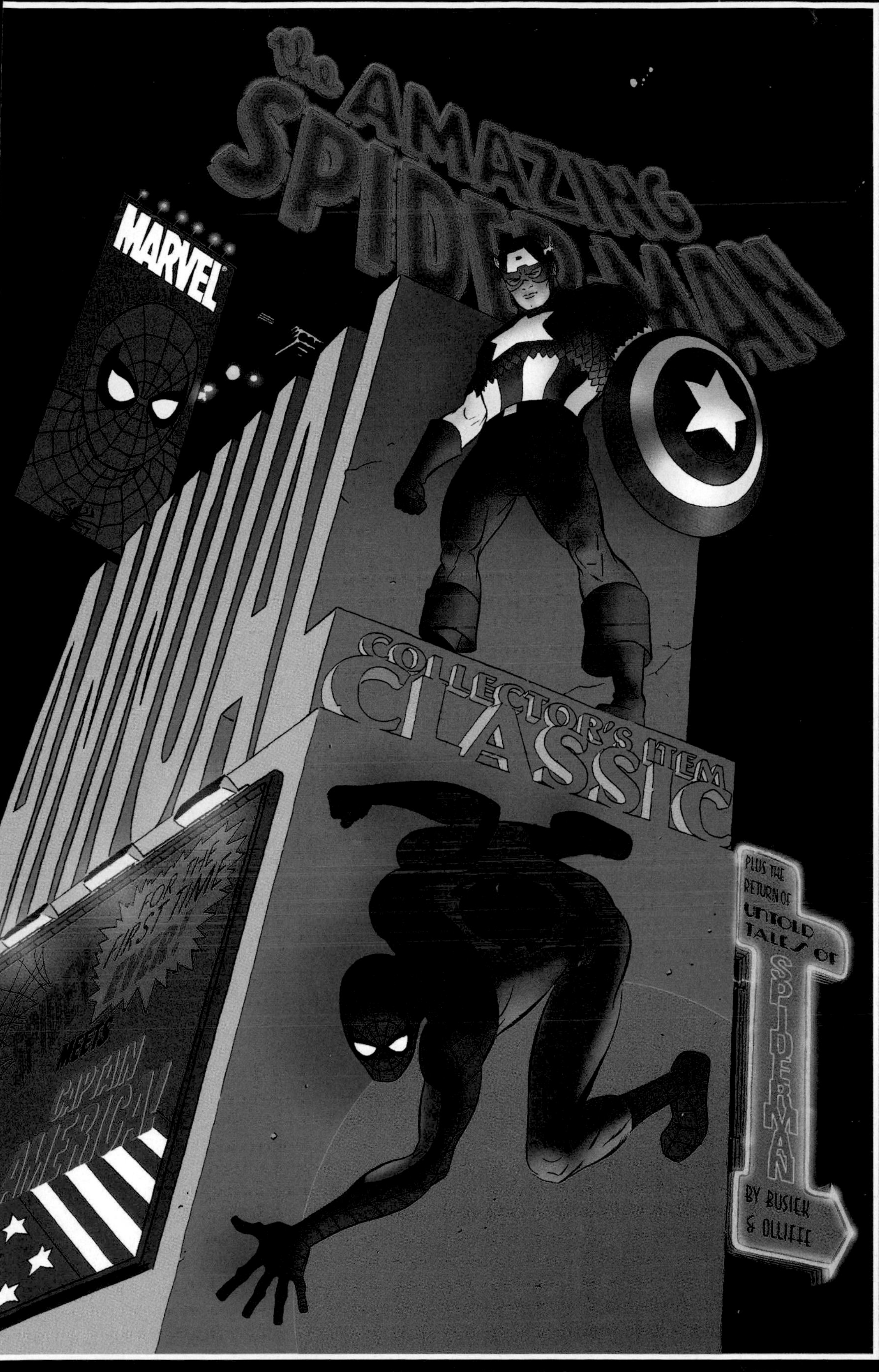
the AMAZING SPIDER-MAN
MARVEL
COLLECTOR'S ITEM CLASSIC
FOR THE FIRST TIME EVER!
MEETS
CAPTAIN AMERICA!
PLUS THE RETURN OF UNTOLD TALES OF SPIDER-MAN
BY BUSIEK & OLLIFFE

AMAZING SPIDER-MAN ANNUAL #37

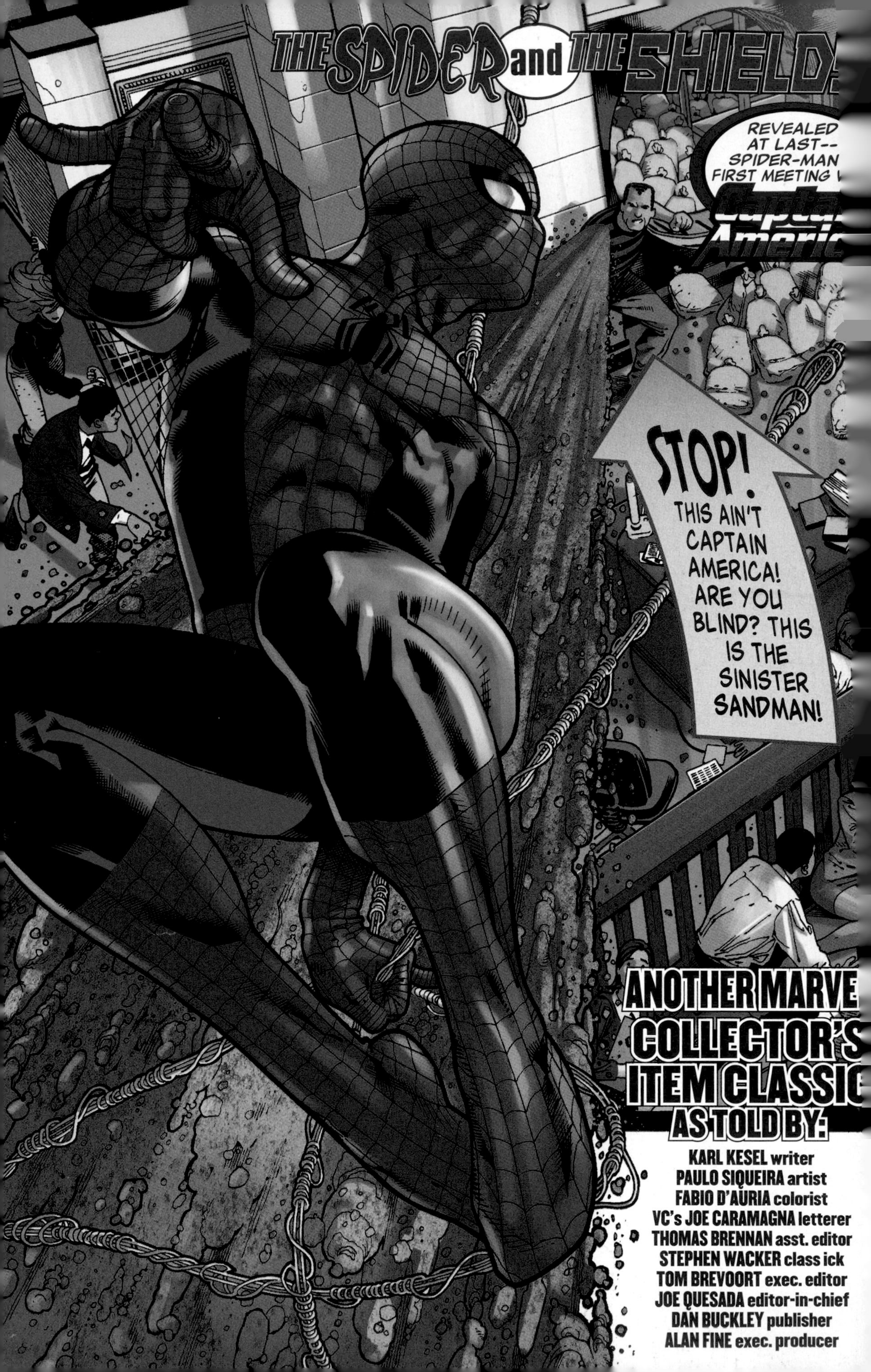

THE SPIDER and THE SHIELD
REVEALED AT LAST-- SPIDER-MAN FIRST MEETING
STOP! THIS AIN'T CAPTAIN AMERICA! ARE YOU BLIND? THIS IS THE SINISTER SANDMAN!
ANOTHER MARVE
COLLECTOR'S
ITEM CLASSIC
AS TOLD BY:
KARL KESEL writer
PAULO SIQUEIRA artist
FABIO D'AURIA colorist
VC's JOE CARAMAGNA letterer
THOMAS BRENNAN asst. editor
STEPHEN WACKER class ick
TOM BREVOORT exec. editor
JOE QUESADA editor-in-chief
DAN BUCKLEY publisher
ALAN FINE exec. producer

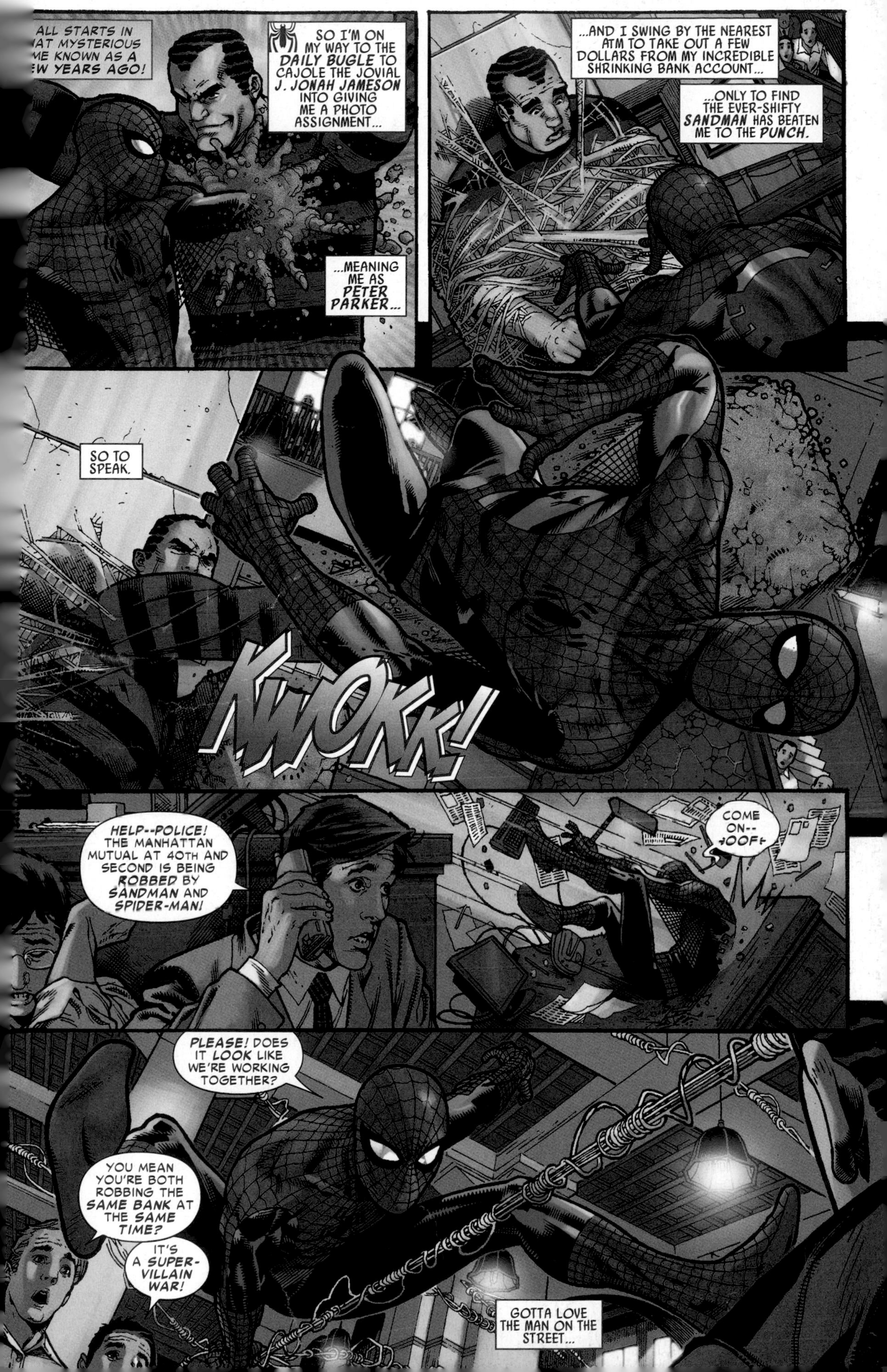
ALL STARTS IN
AT MYSTERIOUS
ME KNOWN AS A
EW YEARS AGO!
SO I'M ON MY WAY TO THE DAILY BUGLE TO CAJOLE THE JOVIAL J. JONAH JAMESON INTO GIVING ME A PHOTO ASSIGNMENT...
...MEANING ME AS PETER PARKER...
...AND I SWING BY THE NEAREST ATM TO TAKE OUT A FEW DOLLARS FROM MY INCREDIBLE SHRINKING BANK ACCOUNT...
...ONLY TO FIND THE EVER-SHIFTY SANDMAN HAS BEATEN ME TO THE PUNCH.
SO TO SPEAK.
KWOKK!
HELP--POLICE! THE MANHATTAN MUTUAL AT 40TH AND SECOND IS BEING ROBBED BY SANDMAN AND SPIDER-MAN!
COME ON-- OOF
PLEASE! DOES IT LOOK LIKE WE'RE WORKING TOGETHER?
YOU MEAN YOU'RE BOTH ROBBING THE SAME BANK AT THE SAME TIME?
IT'S A SUPER-VILLAIN WAR!
GOTTA LOVE THE MAN ON THE STREET...

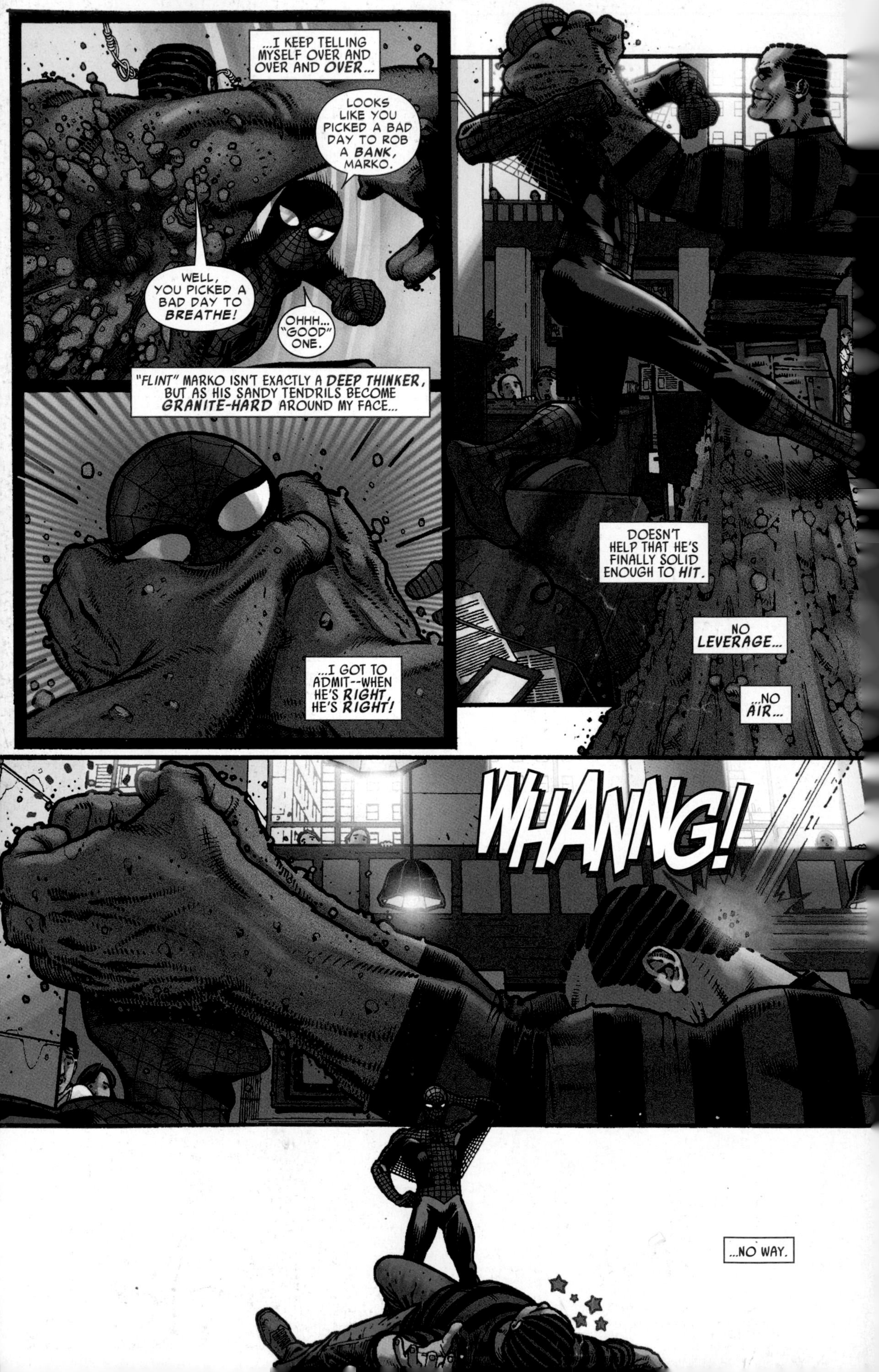

...I KEEP TELLING MYSELF OVER AND OVER AND OVER...
LOOKS LIKE YOU PICKED A BAD DAY TO ROB A BANK, MARKO.
WELL, YOU PICKED A BAD DAY TO BREATHE!
OHHH... "GOOD" ONE.
"FLINT" MARKO ISN'T EXACTLY A DEEP THINKER, BUT AS HIS SANDY TENDRILS BECOME GRANITE-HARD AROUND MY FACE...
...I GOT TO ADMIT--WHEN HE'S RIGHT, HE'S RIGHT!
DOESN'T HELP THAT HE'S FINALLY SOLID ENOUGH TO HIT.
NO LEVERAGE...
...NO AIR...
WHANNG!
...NO WAY.

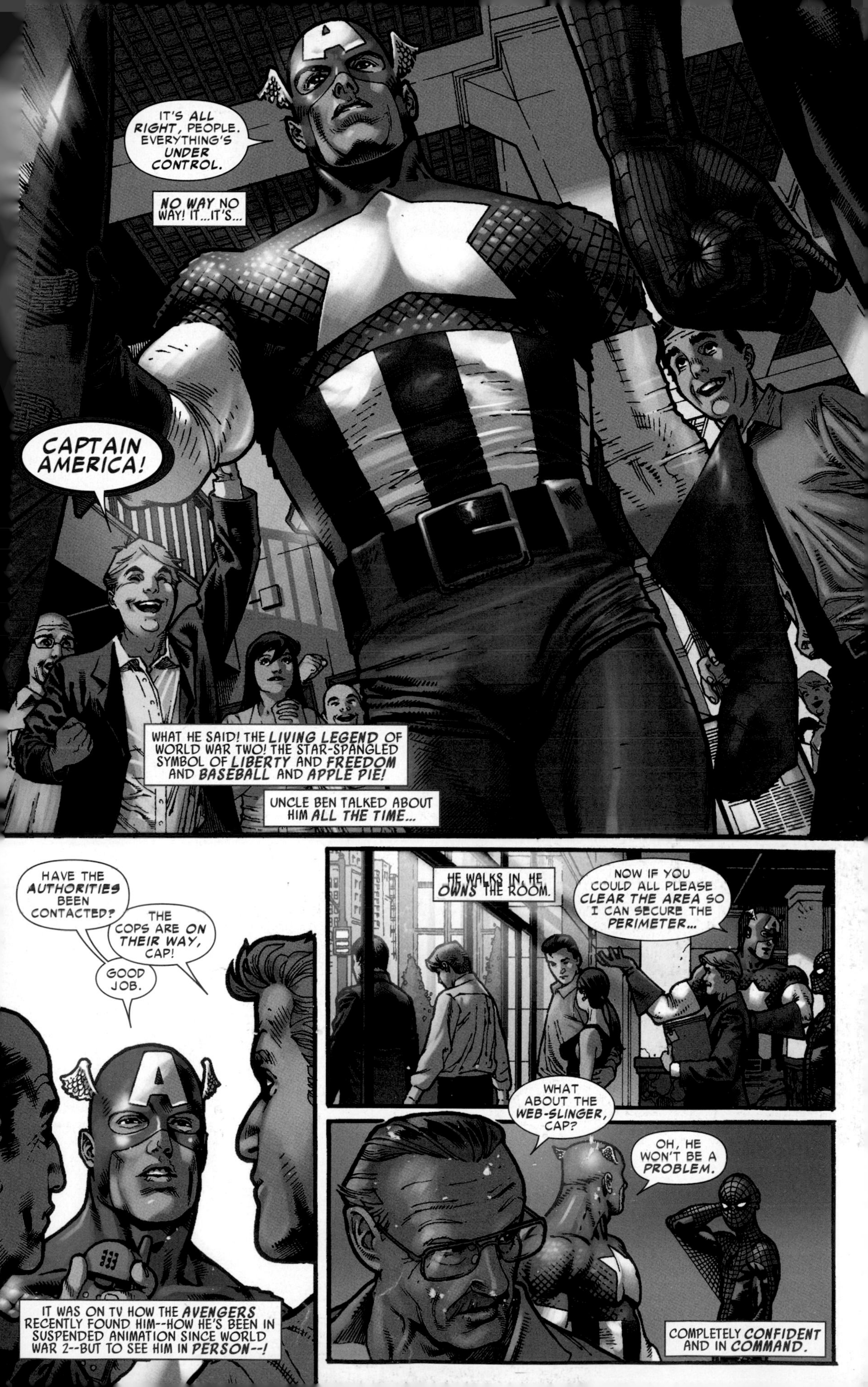

IT'S ALL RIGHT, PEOPLE. EVERYTHING'S UNDER CONTROL.
NO WAY NO WAY! IT...IT'S...
CAPTAIN AMERICA!
WHAT HE SAID! THE LIVING LEGEND OF WORLD WAR TWO! THE STAR-SPANGLED SYMBOL OF LIBERTY AND FREEDOM AND BASEBALL AND APPLE PIE!
UNCLE BEN TALKED ABOUT HIM ALL THE TIME...
HAVE THE AUTHORITIES BEEN CONTACTED?
THE COPS ARE ON THEIR WAY, CAP!
GOOD JOB.
IT WAS ON TV HOW THE AVENGERS RECENTLY FOUND HIM--HOW HE'S BEEN IN SUSPENDED ANIMATION SINCE WORLD WAR 2--BUT TO SEE HIM IN PERSON--!
HE WALKS IN, HE OWNS THE ROOM.
NOW IF YOU COULD ALL PLEASE CLEAR THE AREA SO I CAN SECURE THE PERIMETER...
WHAT ABOUT THE WEB-SLINGER, CAP?
OH, HE WON'T BE A PROBLEM.
COMPLETELY CONFIDENT AND IN COMMAND.

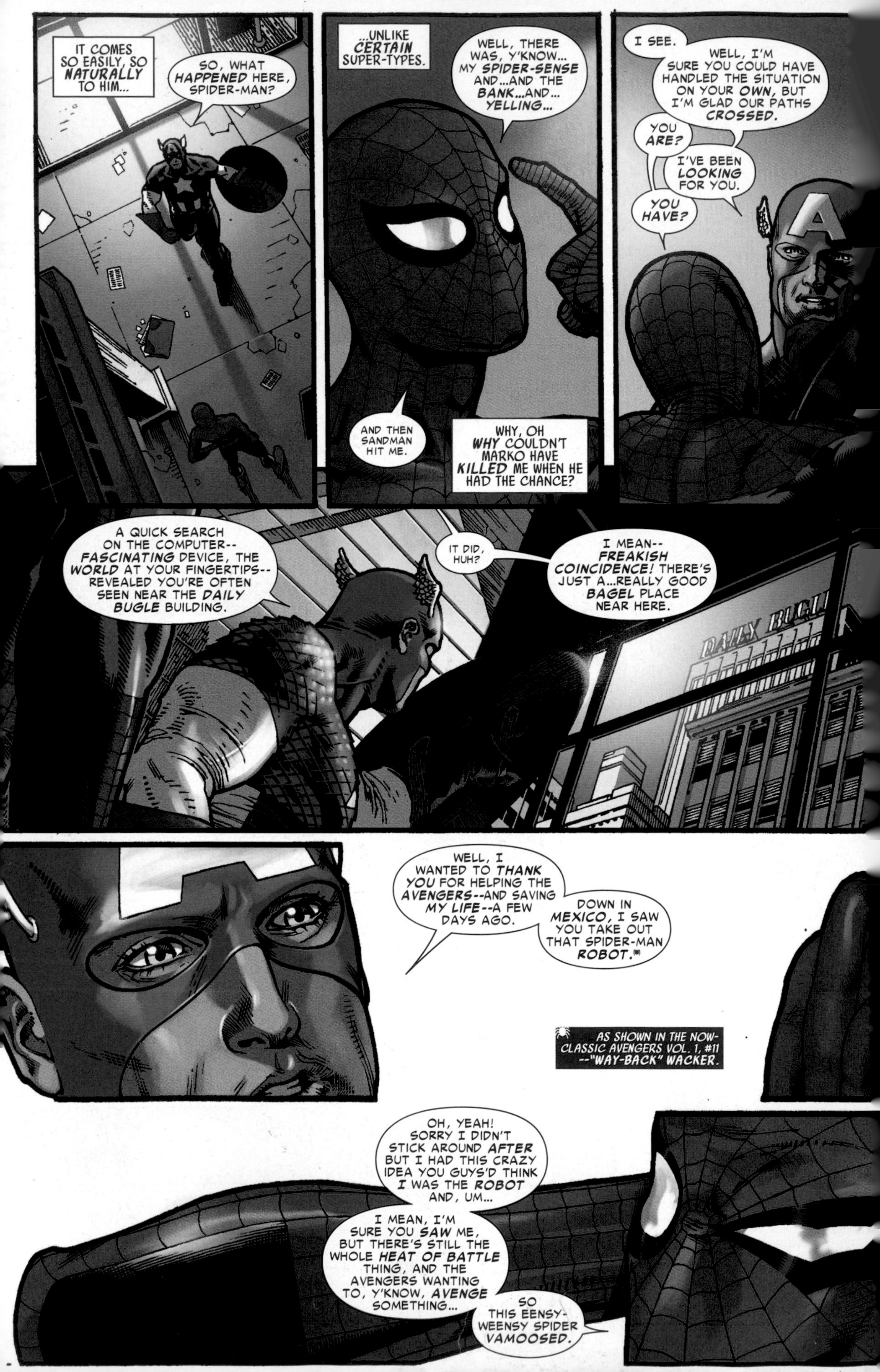
IT COMES SO EASILY, SO NATURALLY TO HIM...
SO, WHAT HAPPENED HERE, SPIDER-MAN?
...UNLIKE CERTAIN SUPER-TYPES.
WELL, THERE WAS, Y'KNOW... MY SPIDER-SENSE AND...AND THE BANK...AND... YELLING...
AND THEN SANDMAN HIT ME.
WHY, OH WHY COULDN'T MARKO HAVE KILLED ME WHEN HE HAD THE CHANCE?
I SEE.
WELL, I'M SURE YOU COULD HAVE HANDLED THE SITUATION ON YOUR OWN, BUT I'M GLAD OUR PATHS CROSSED.
YOU ARE?
I'VE BEEN LOOKING FOR YOU.
YOU HAVE?
A QUICK SEARCH ON THE COMPUTER-- FASCINATING DEVICE, THE WORLD AT YOUR FINGERTIPS-- REVEALED YOU'RE OFTEN SEEN NEAR THE DAILY BUGLE BUILDING.
IT DID, HUH?
I MEAN-- FREAKISH COINCIDENCE! THERE'S JUST A...REALLY GOOD BAGEL PLACE NEAR HERE.
WELL, I WANTED TO THANK YOU FOR HELPING THE AVENGERS--AND SAVING MY LIFE--A FEW DAYS AGO.
DOWN IN MEXICO, I SAW YOU TAKE OUT THAT SPIDER-MAN ROBOT.
AS SHOWN IN THE NOW-CLASSIC AVENGERS VOL. 1, #11 --"WAY-BACK" WACKER.
OH, YEAH! SORRY I DIDN'T STICK AROUND AFTER BUT I HAD THIS CRAZY IDEA YOU GUYS'D THINK I WAS THE ROBOT AND, UM...
I MEAN, I'M SURE YOU SAW ME, BUT THERE'S STILL THE WHOLE HEAT OF BATTLE THING, AND THE AVENGERS WANTING TO, Y'KNOW, AVENGE SOMETHING...
SO THIS EENSY-WEENSY SPIDER VAMOOSED.

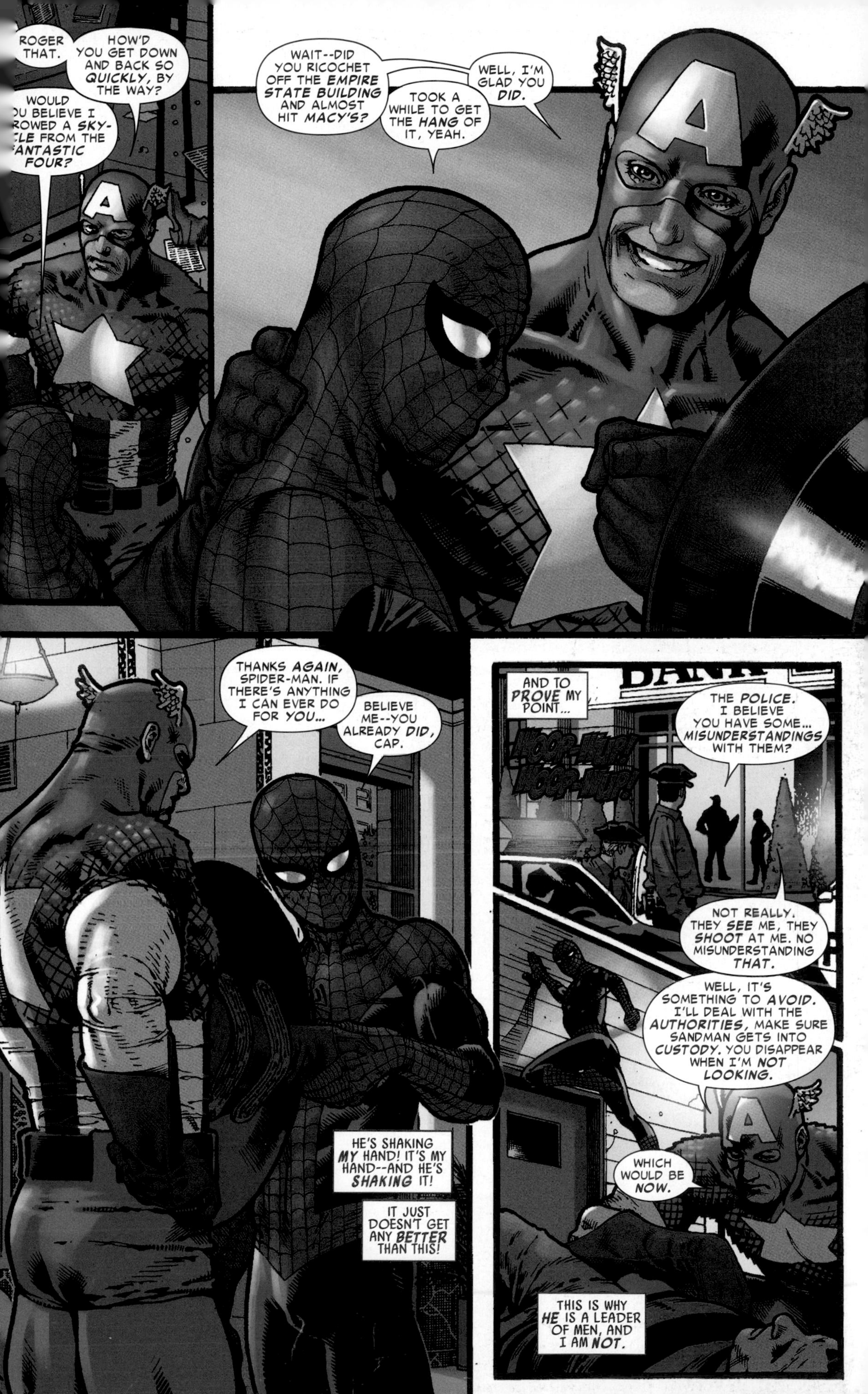
ROGER THAT.
HOW'D YOU GET DOWN AND BACK SO QUICKLY, BY THE WAY?
WOULD YOU BELIEVE I BORROWED A SKY-CYCLE FROM THE FANTASTIC FOUR?
WAIT--DID YOU RICOCHET OFF THE EMPIRE STATE BUILDING AND ALMOST HIT MACY'S?
TOOK A WHILE TO GET THE HANG OF IT, YEAH.
WELL, I'M GLAD YOU DID.
THANKS AGAIN, SPIDER-MAN. IF THERE'S ANYTHING I CAN EVER DO FOR YOU...
BELIEVE ME--YOU ALREADY DID, CAP.
HE'S SHAKING MY HAND! IT'S MY HAND--AND HE'S SHAKING IT!
IT JUST DOESN'T GET ANY BETTER THAN THIS!
AND TO PROVE MY POINT...
WHOOP-WHUP! WHOOP-WHUP!
THE POLICE. I BELIEVE YOU HAVE SOME... MISUNDERSTANDINGS WITH THEM?
NOT REALLY. THEY SEE ME, THEY SHOOT AT ME. NO MISUNDERSTANDING THAT.
WELL, IT'S SOMETHING TO AVOID. I'LL DEAL WITH THE AUTHORITIES, MAKE SURE SANDMAN GETS INTO CUSTODY. YOU DISAPPEAR WHEN I'M NOT LOOKING.
WHICH WOULD BE NOW.
THIS IS WHY HE IS A LEADER OF MEN, AND I AM NOT.

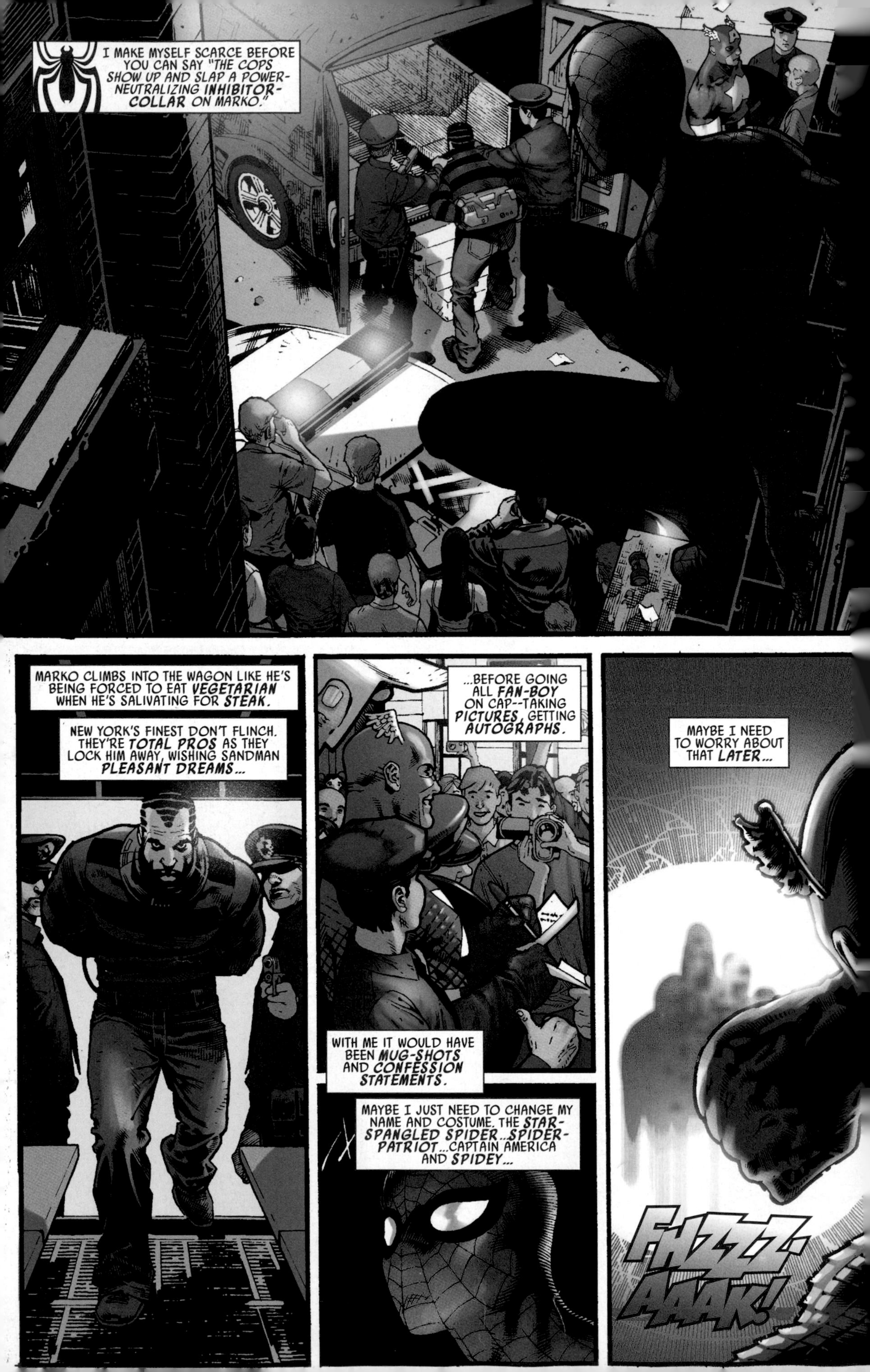
I MAKE MYSELF SCARCE BEFORE YOU CAN SAY "THE COPS SHOW UP AND SLAP A POWER-NEUTRALIZING INHIBITOR-COLLAR ON MARKO."
MARKO CLIMBS INTO THE WAGON LIKE HE'S BEING FORCED TO EAT VEGETARIAN WHEN HE'S SALIVATING FOR STEAK.
NEW YORK'S FINEST DON'T FLINCH. THEY'RE TOTAL PROS AS THEY LOCK HIM AWAY, WISHING SANDMAN PLEASANT DREAMS...
...BEFORE GOING ALL FAN-BOY ON CAP--TAKING PICTURES, GETTING AUTOGRAPHS.
WITH ME IT WOULD HAVE BEEN MUG-SHOTS AND CONFESSION STATEMENTS.
MAYBE I JUST NEED TO CHANGE MY NAME AND COSTUME. THE STAR-SPANGLED SPIDER...SPIDER-PATRIOT...CAPTAIN AMERICA AND SPIDEY...
MAYBE I NEED TO WORRY ABOUT THAT LATER...
FHZZZ-AAAK!

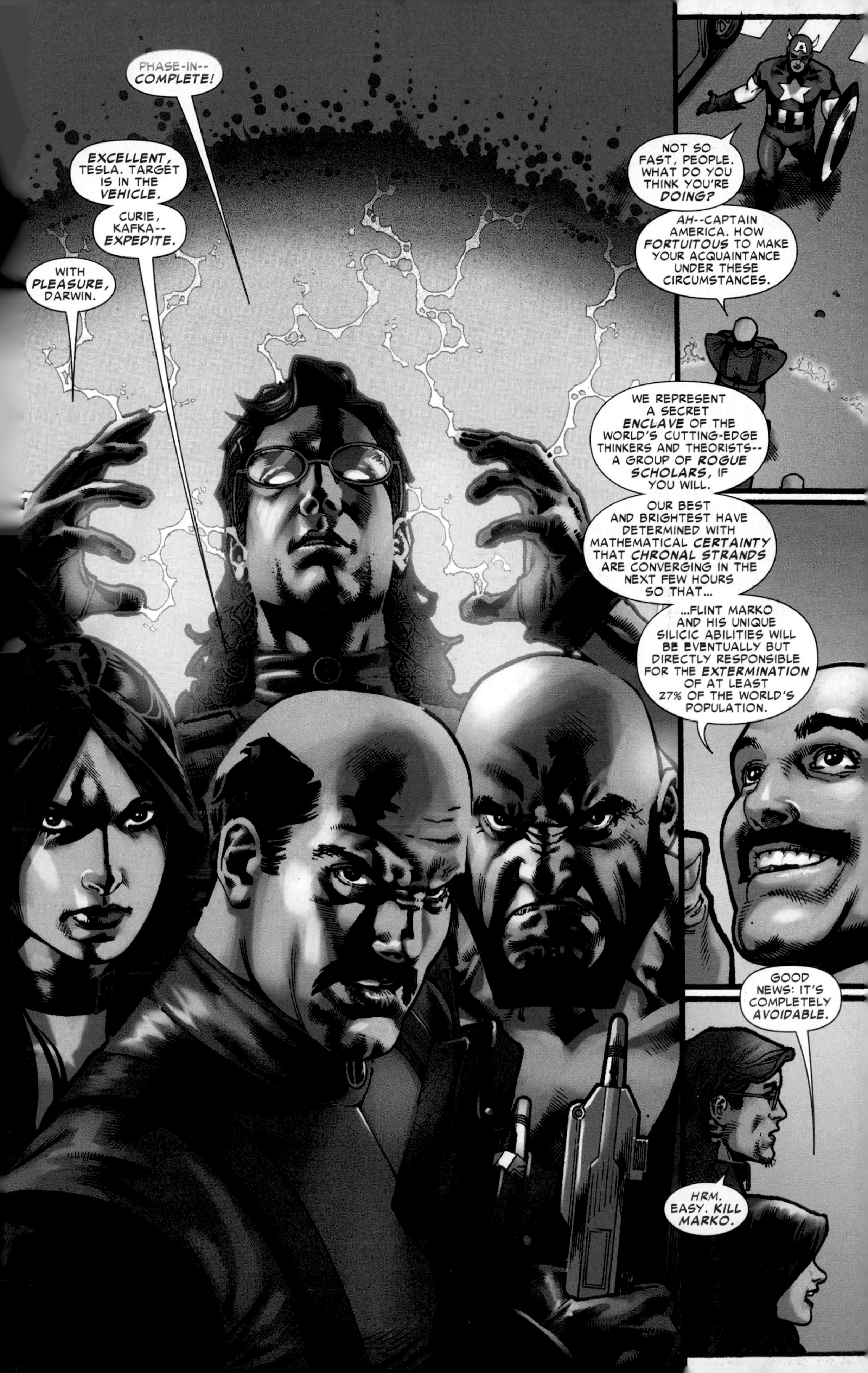

PHASE-IN--COMPLETE!
EXCELLENT, TESLA. TARGET IS IN THE VEHICLE.
CURIE, KAFKA--EXPEDITE.
WITH PLEASURE, DARWIN.
NOT SO FAST, PEOPLE. WHAT DO YOU THINK YOU'RE DOING?
AH--CAPTAIN AMERICA. HOW FORTUITOUS TO MAKE YOUR ACQUAINTANCE UNDER THESE CIRCUMSTANCES.
WE REPRESENT A SECRET ENCLAVE OF THE WORLD'S CUTTING-EDGE THINKERS AND THEORISTS--A GROUP OF ROGUE SCHOLARS, IF YOU WILL.
OUR BEST AND BRIGHTEST HAVE DETERMINED WITH MATHEMATICAL CERTAINTY THAT CHRONAL STRANDS ARE CONVERGING IN THE NEXT FEW HOURS SO THAT...
...FLINT MARKO AND HIS UNIQUE SILICIC ABILITIES WILL BE EVENTUALLY BUT DIRECTLY RESPONSIBLE FOR THE EXTERMINATION OF AT LEAST 27% OF THE WORLD'S POPULATION.
GOOD NEWS: IT'S COMPLETELY AVOIDABLE.
HRM. EASY. KILL MARKO.

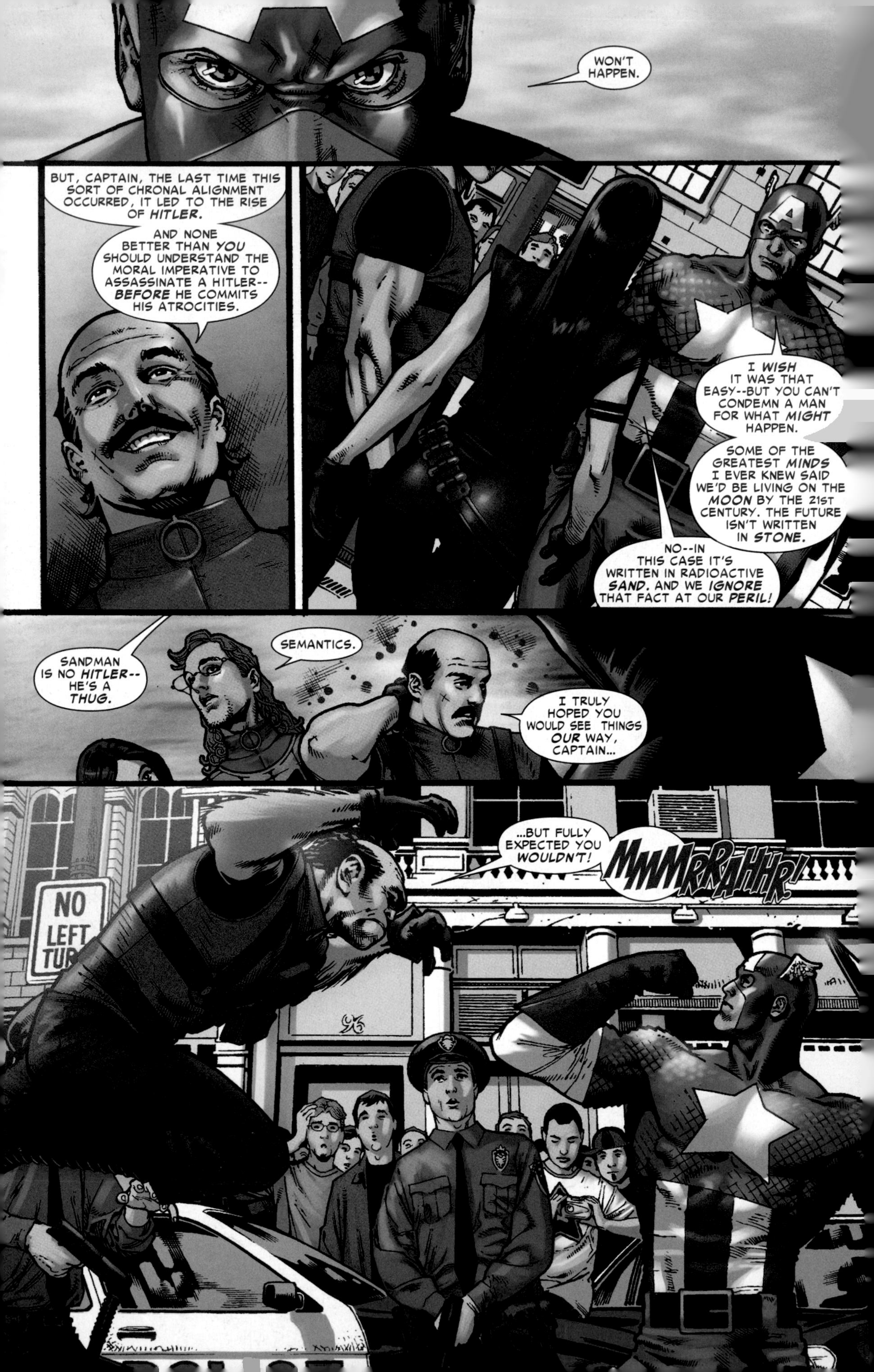
WON'T HAPPEN.
BUT, CAPTAIN, THE LAST TIME THIS SORT OF CHRONAL ALIGNMENT OCCURRED, IT LED TO THE RISE OF HITLER.
AND NONE BETTER THAN YOU SHOULD UNDERSTAND THE MORAL IMPERATIVE TO ASSASSINATE A HITLER-- BEFORE HE COMMITS HIS ATROCITIES.
I WISH IT WAS THAT EASY--BUT YOU CAN'T CONDEMN A MAN FOR WHAT MIGHT HAPPEN.
SOME OF THE GREATEST MINDS I EVER KNEW SAID WE'D BE LIVING ON THE MOON BY THE 21ST CENTURY. THE FUTURE ISN'T WRITTEN IN STONE.
NO--IN THIS CASE IT'S WRITTEN IN RADIOACTIVE SAND. AND WE IGNORE THAT FACT AT OUR PERIL!
SANDMAN IS NO HITLER-- HE'S A THUG.
SEMANTICS.
I TRULY HOPED YOU WOULD SEE THINGS OUR WAY, CAPTAIN...
...BUT FULLY EXPECTED YOU WOULDN'T!
MMMRRAHHR!
NO LEFT TUR

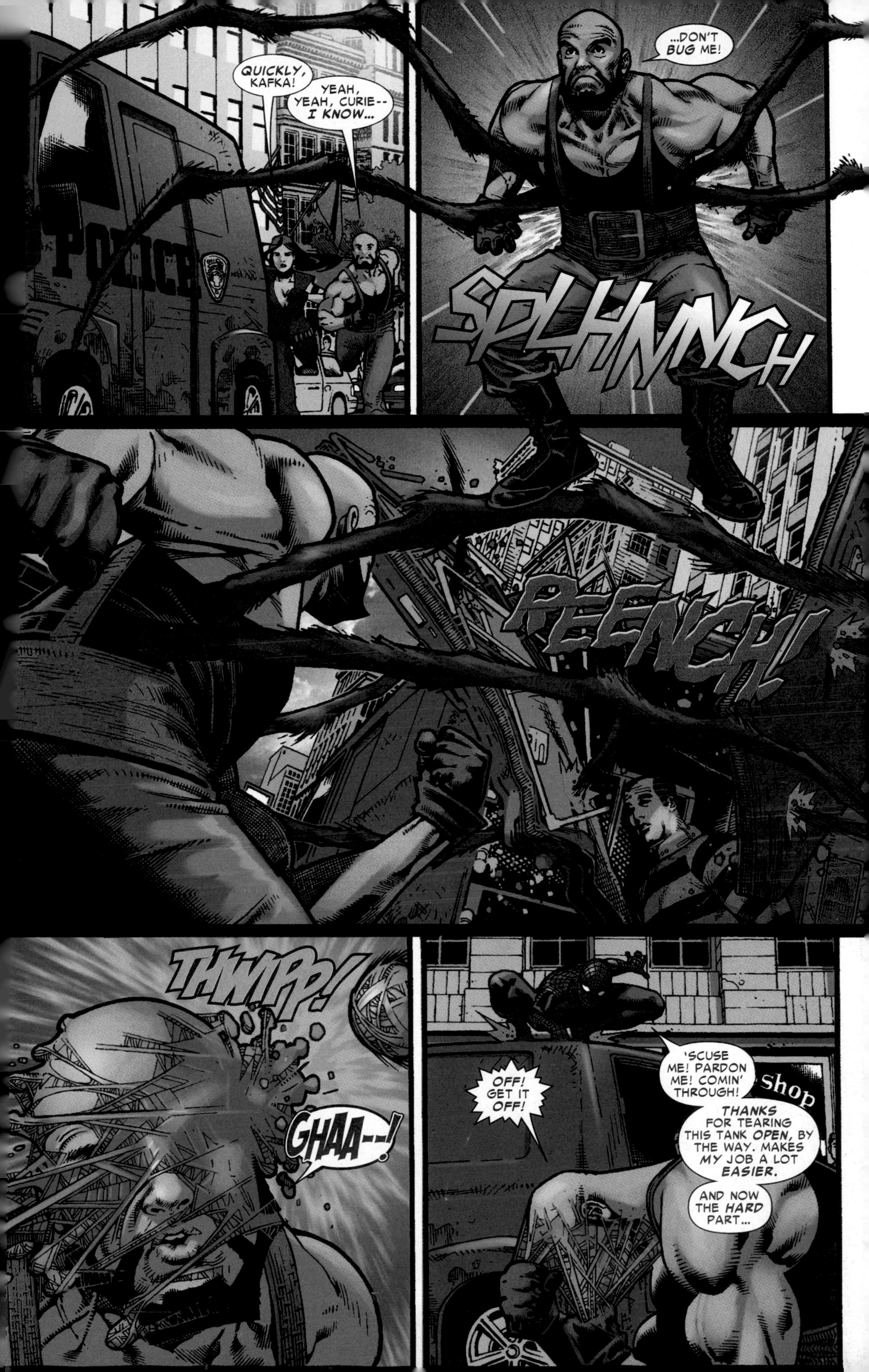
QUICKLY, KAFKA!
YEAH, YEAH, CURIE-- I KNOW...
POLICE
...DON'T BUG ME!
SPLHNNCH
RREENCH!
THWIPP!
GHAA--!
OFF! GET IT OFF!
'SCUSE ME! PARDON ME! COMIN' THROUGH!
THANKS FOR TEARING THIS TANK OPEN, BY THE WAY. MAKES MY JOB A LOT EASIER.
AND NOW THE HARD PART...
Shop

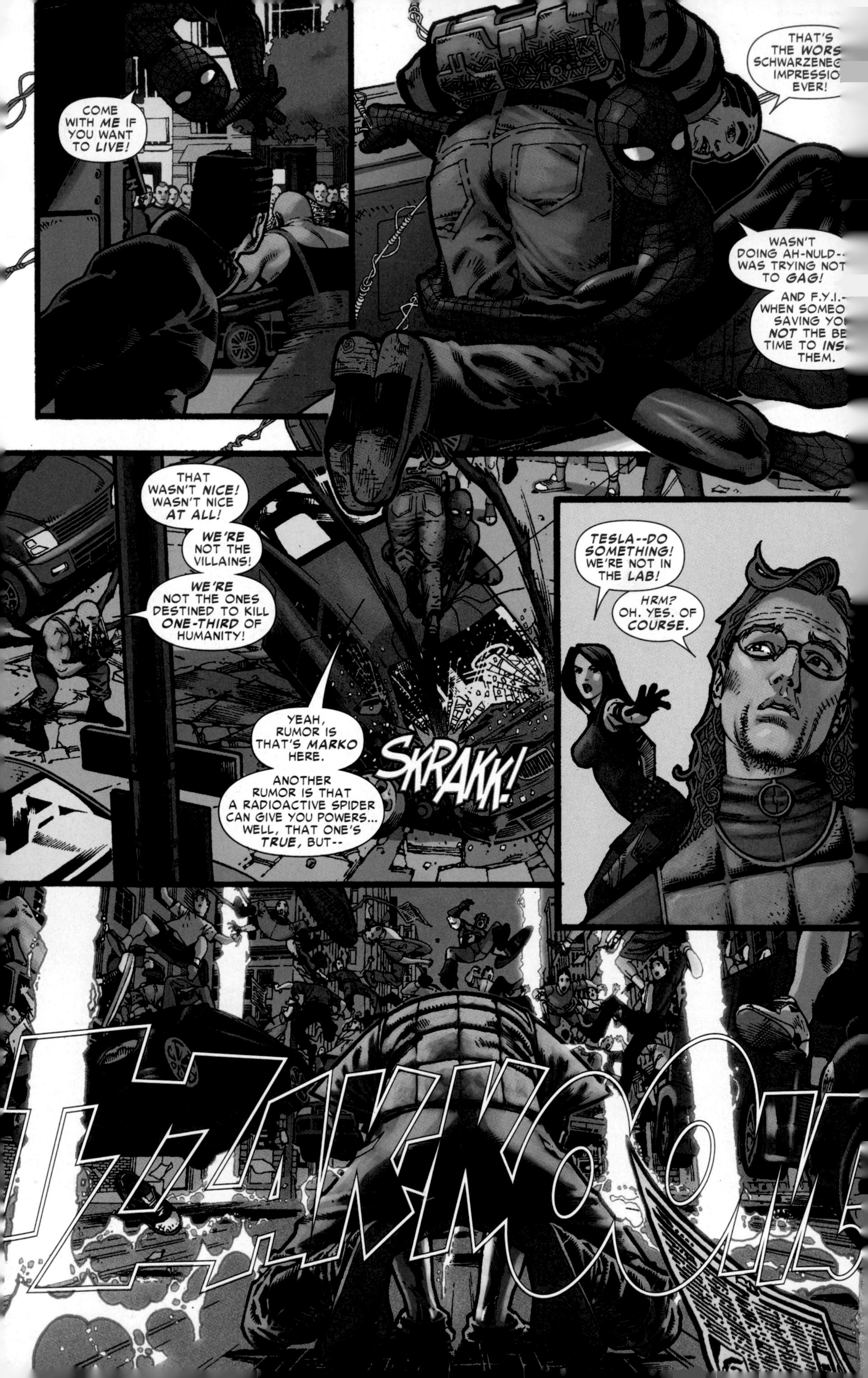

COME WITH ME IF YOU WANT TO LIVE!
THAT'S THE WORS SCHWARZENEG IMPRESSIO EVER!
WASN'T DOING AH-NULD-- WAS TRYING NOT TO GAG!
AND F.Y.I.- WHEN SOMEO SAVING YO NOT THE BE TIME TO INS THEM.
THAT WASN'T NICE! WASN'T NICE AT ALL!
WE'RE NOT THE VILLAINS!
WE'RE NOT THE ONES DESTINED TO KILL ONE-THIRD OF HUMANITY!
YEAH, RUMOR IS THAT'S MARKO HERE.
ANOTHER RUMOR IS THAT A RADIOACTIVE SPIDER CAN GIVE YOU POWERS... WELL, THAT ONE'S TRUE, BUT--
SKRAKK!
TESLA--DO SOMETHING! WE'RE NOT IN THE LAB!
HRM? OH. YES. OF COURSE.

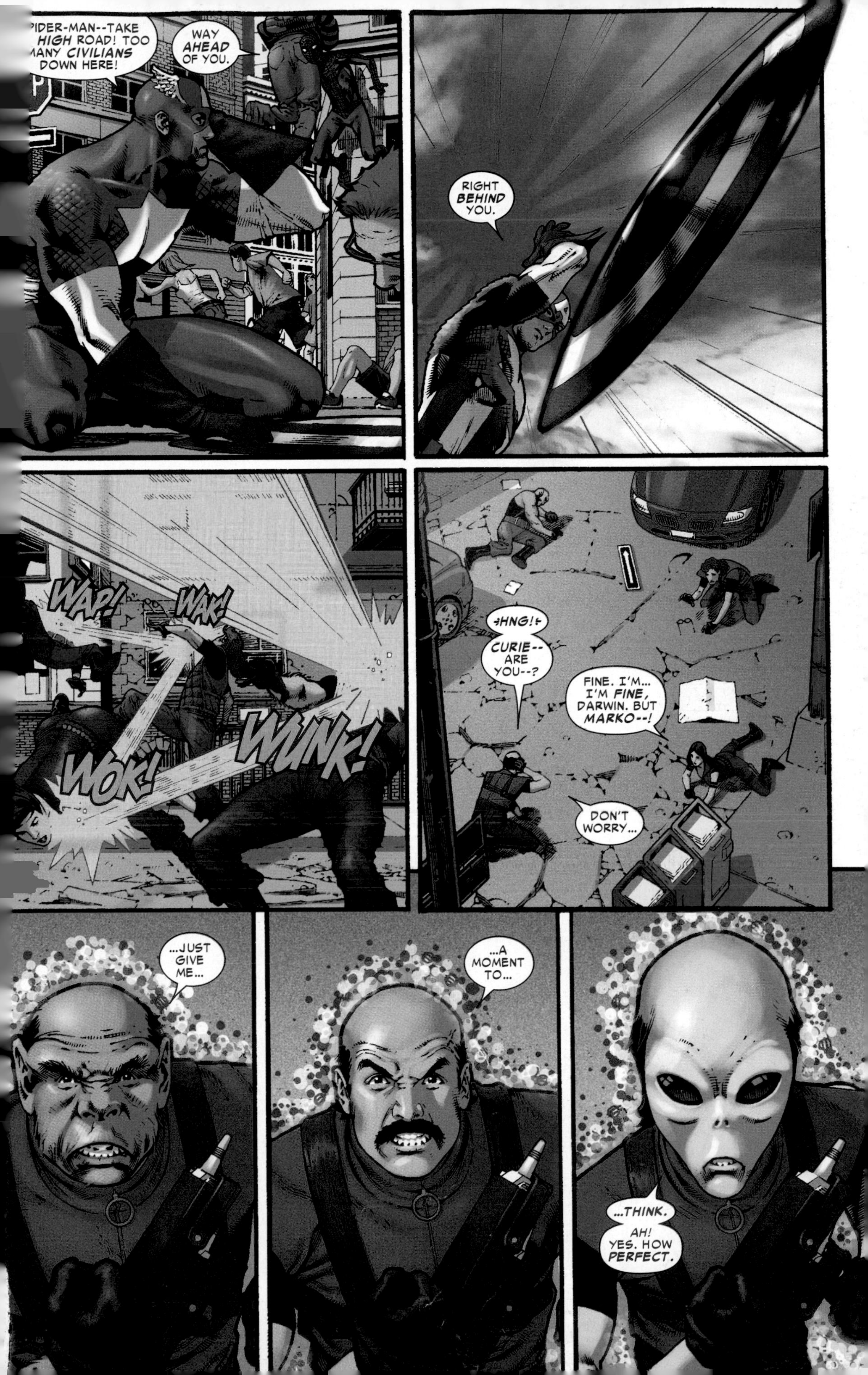

SPIDER-MAN--TAKE THE HIGH ROAD! TOO MANY CIVILIANS DOWN HERE!
WAY AHEAD OF YOU.
RIGHT BEHIND YOU.
WAP!
WAK!
WUNK!
WOK!
HNG!
CURIE--ARE YOU--?
FINE. I'M... I'M FINE, DARWIN. BUT MARKO--!
DON'T WORRY...
...JUST GIVE ME...
...A MOMENT TO...
...THINK.
AH! YES. HOW PERFECT.

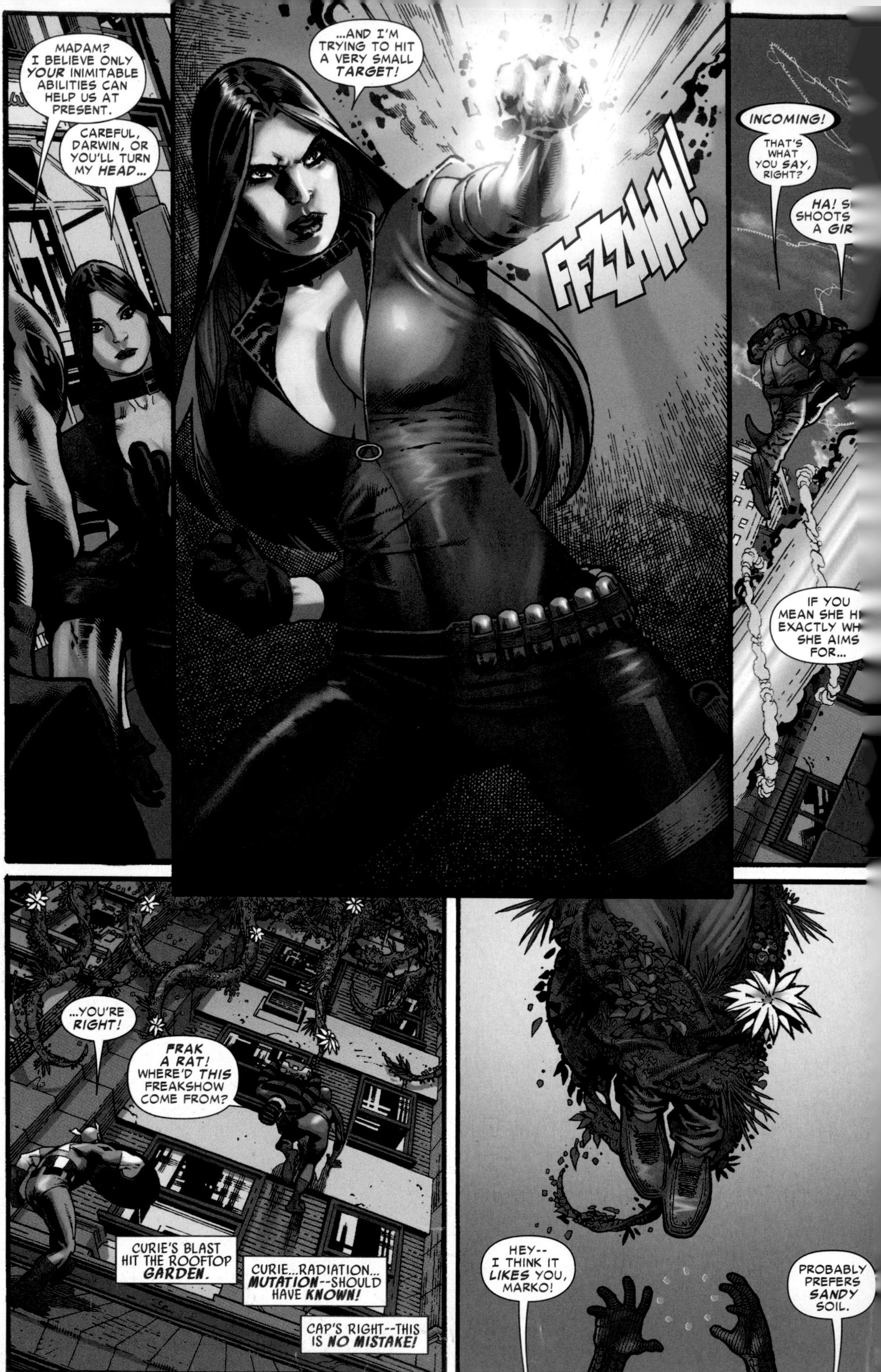
MADAM? I BELIEVE ONLY YOUR INIMITABLE ABILITIES CAN HELP US AT PRESENT.
CAREFUL, DARWIN, OR YOU'LL TURN MY HEAD...
...AND I'M TRYING TO HIT A VERY SMALL TARGET!
FFZZHHH!
INCOMING!
THAT'S WHAT YOU SAY, RIGHT?
HA! S SHOOTS A GIR
IF YOU MEAN SHE H EXACTLY WH SHE AIMS FOR...
...YOU'RE RIGHT!
FRAK A RAT! WHERE'D THIS FREAKSHOW COME FROM?
CURIE'S BLAST HIT THE ROOFTOP GARDEN.
CURIE...RADIATION... MUTATION--SHOULD HAVE KNOWN!
CAP'S RIGHT--THIS IS NO MISTAKE!
HEY-- I THINK IT LIKES YOU, MARKO!
PROBABLY PREFERS SANDY SOIL.

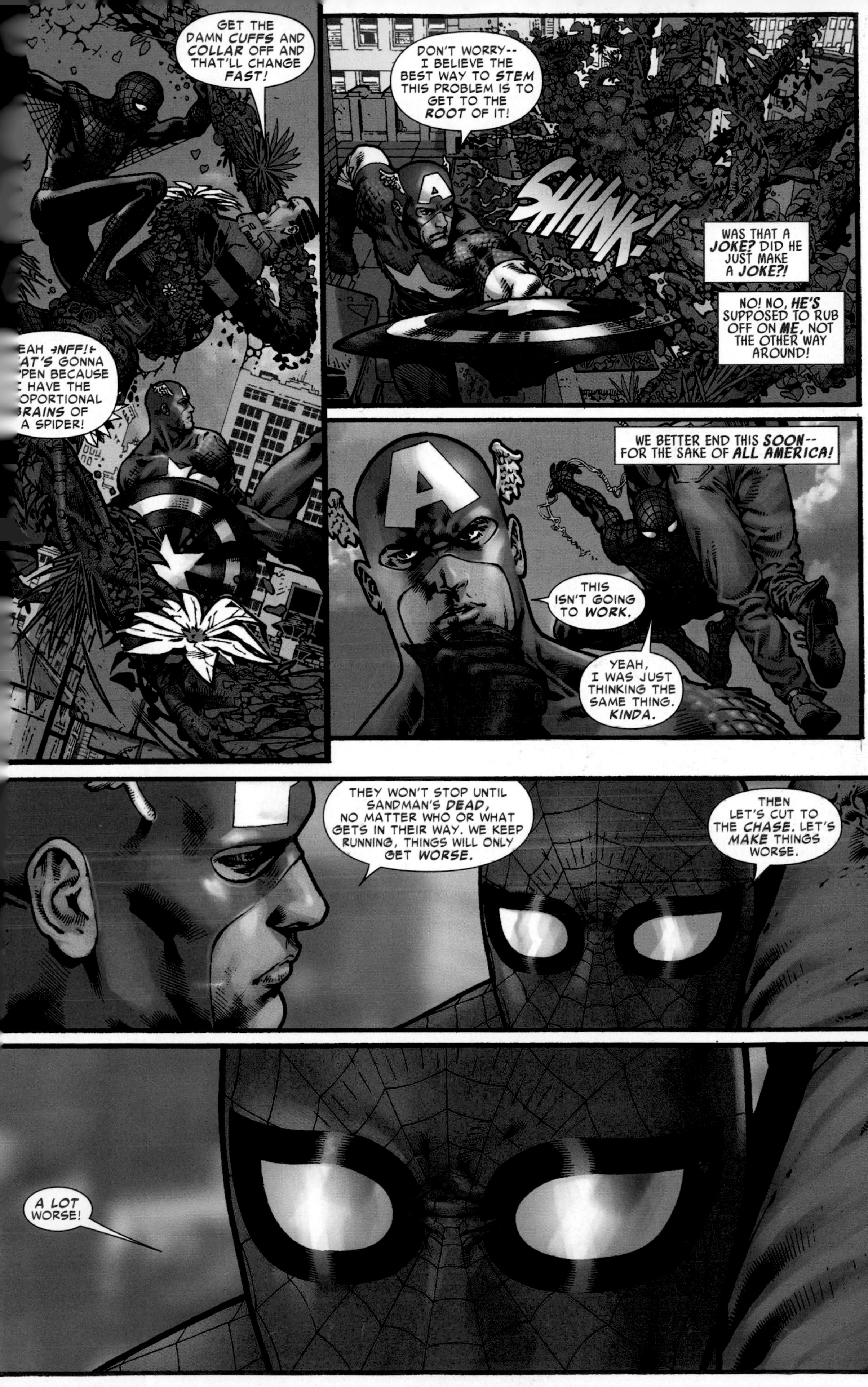
GET THE DAMN CUFFS AND COLLAR OFF AND THAT'LL CHANGE FAST!
EAH -NFF!- AT'S GONNA PEN BECAUSE HAVE THE OPORTIONAL BRAINS OF A SPIDER!
DON'T WORRY-- I BELIEVE THE BEST WAY TO STEM THIS PROBLEM IS TO GET TO THE ROOT OF IT!
SHHNK!
WAS THAT A JOKE? DID HE JUST MAKE A JOKE?!
NO! NO, HE'S SUPPOSED TO RUB OFF ON ME, NOT THE OTHER WAY AROUND!
WE BETTER END THIS SOON-- FOR THE SAKE OF ALL AMERICA!
THIS ISN'T GOING TO WORK.
YEAH, I WAS JUST THINKING THE SAME THING. KINDA.
THEY WON'T STOP UNTIL SANDMAN'S DEAD, NO MATTER WHO OR WHAT GETS IN THEIR WAY. WE KEEP RUNNING, THINGS WILL ONLY GET WORSE.
THEN LET'S CUT TO THE CHASE. LET'S MAKE THINGS WORSE.
A LOT WORSE!

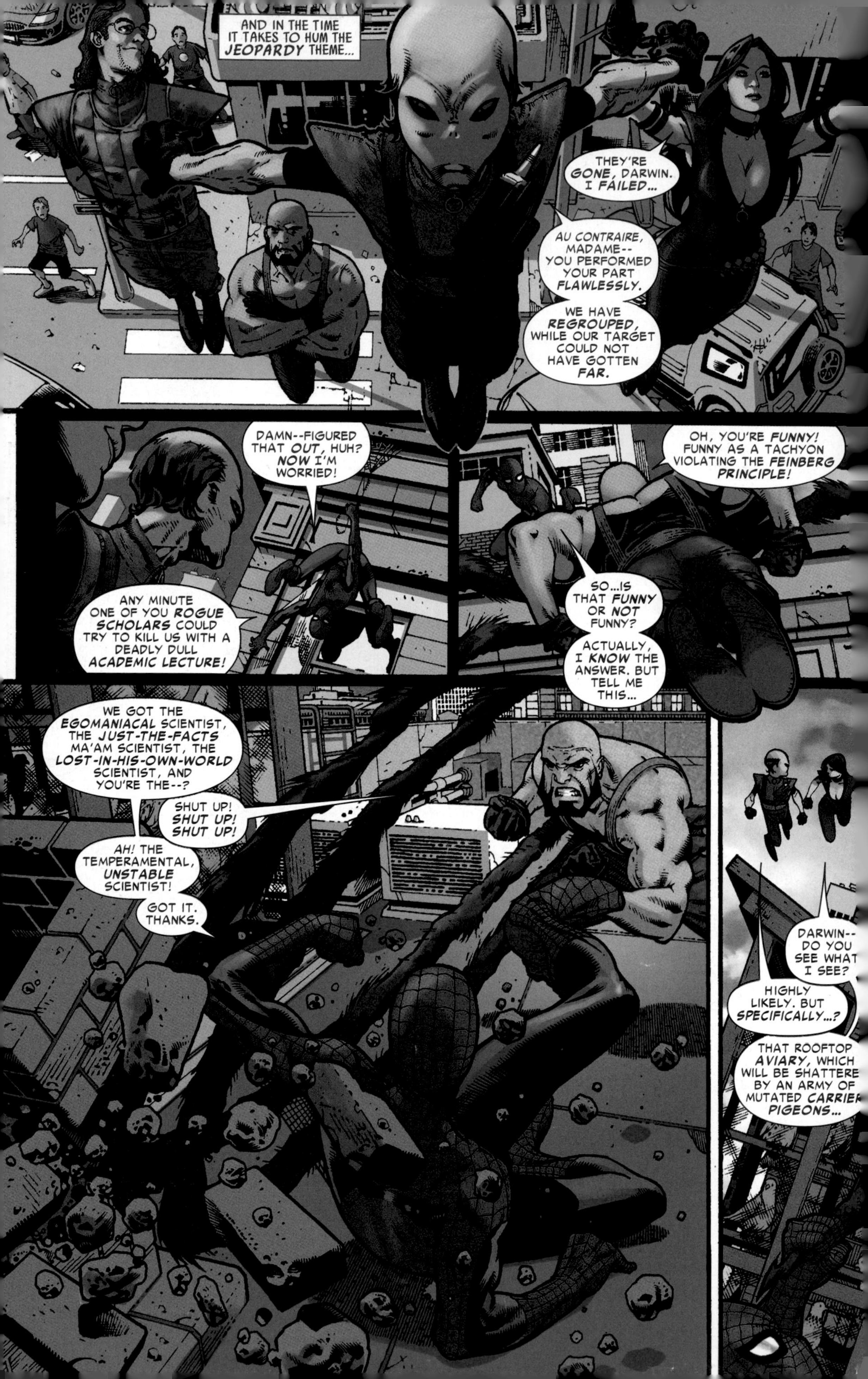
AND IN THE TIME IT TAKES TO HUM THE JEOPARDY THEME...
THEY'RE GONE, DARWIN. I FAILED...
AU CONTRAIRE, MADAME--YOU PERFORMED YOUR PART FLAWLESSLY.
WE HAVE REGROUPED, WHILE OUR TARGET COULD NOT HAVE GOTTEN FAR.
DAMN--FIGURED THAT OUT, HUH? NOW I'M WORRIED!
ANY MINUTE ONE OF YOU ROGUE SCHOLARS COULD TRY TO KILL US WITH A DEADLY DULL ACADEMIC LECTURE!
OH, YOU'RE FUNNY! FUNNY AS A TACHYON VIOLATING THE FEINBERG PRINCIPLE!
SO...IS THAT FUNNY OR NOT FUNNY?
ACTUALLY, I KNOW THE ANSWER. BUT TELL ME THIS...
WE GOT THE EGOMANIACAL SCIENTIST, THE JUST-THE-FACTS MA'AM SCIENTIST, THE LOST-IN-HIS-OWN-WORLD SCIENTIST, AND YOU'RE THE--?
SHUT UP! SHUT UP! SHUT UP!
AH! THE TEMPERAMENTAL, UNSTABLE SCIENTIST!
GOT IT. THANKS.
DARWIN--DO YOU SEE WHAT I SEE?
HIGHLY LIKELY. BUT SPECIFICALLY...?
THAT ROOFTOP AVIARY, WHICH WILL BE SHATTERE BY AN ARMY OF MUTATED CARRIEI PIGEONS...

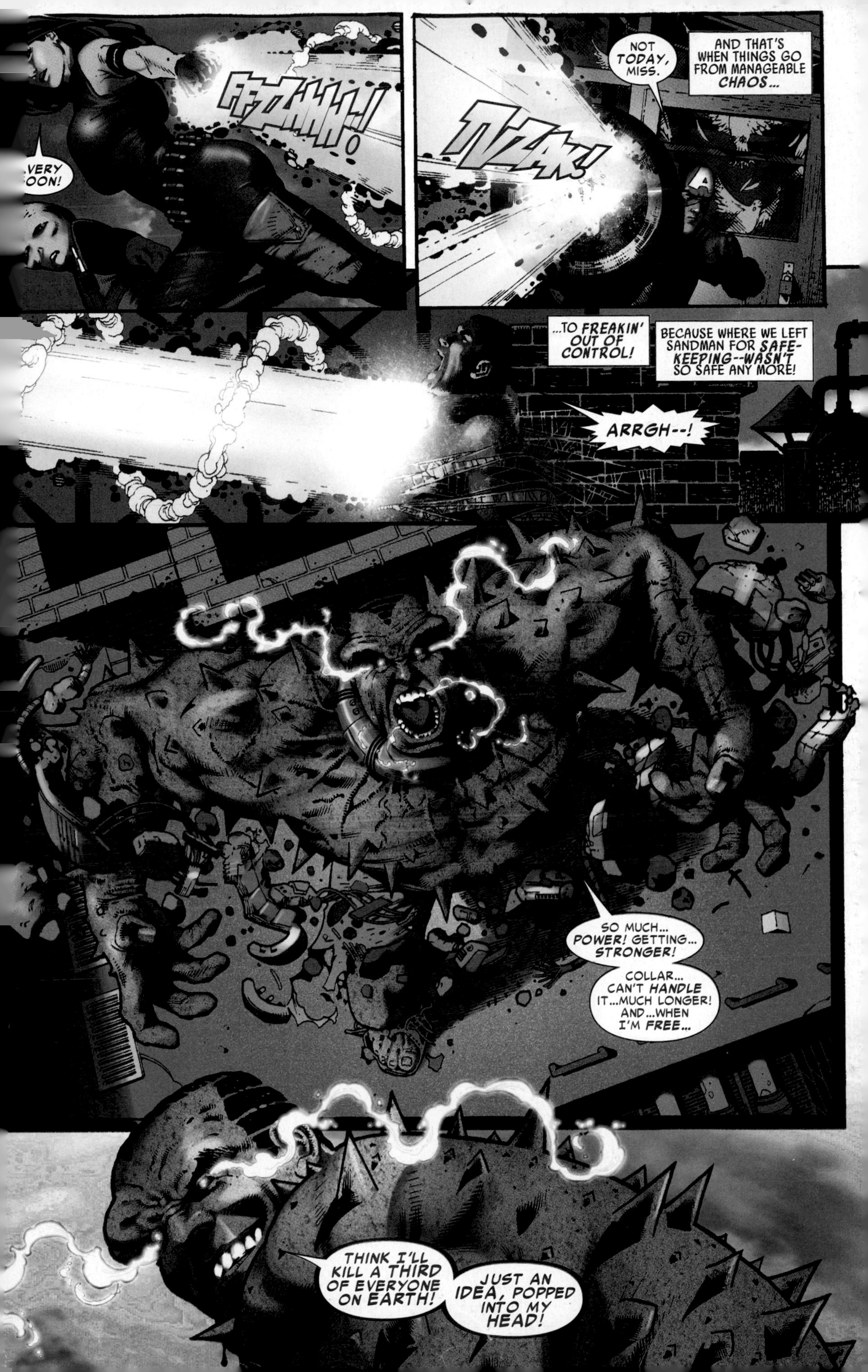
VERY
SOON!
FFZZAKK-!
NOT TODAY, MISS.
TVZAK!
AND THAT'S WHEN THINGS GO FROM MANAGEABLE CHAOS...
...TO FREAKIN' OUT OF CONTROL!
BECAUSE WHERE WE LEFT SANDMAN FOR SAFE-KEEPING--WASN'T SO SAFE ANY MORE!
ARRGH--!
SO MUCH... POWER! GETTING... STRONGER!
COLLAR... CAN'T HANDLE IT...MUCH LONGER! AND...WHEN I'M FREE...
THINK I'LL KILL A THIRD OF EVERYONE ON EARTH!
JUST AN IDEA, POPPED INTO MY HEAD!

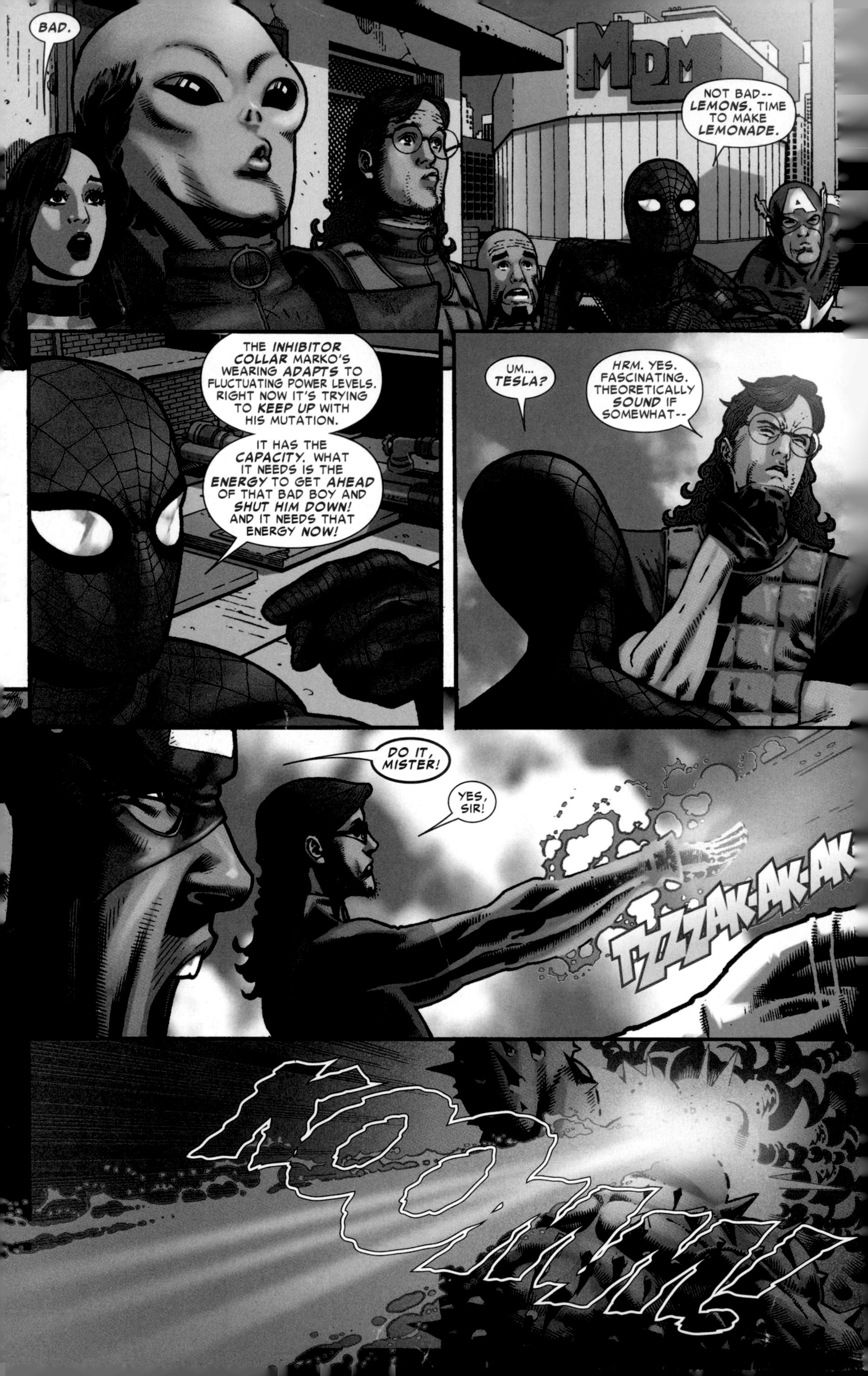
BAD.
NOT BAD-- LEMONS. TIME TO MAKE LEMONADE.
THE INHIBITOR COLLAR MARKO'S WEARING ADAPTS TO FLUCTUATING POWER LEVELS. RIGHT NOW IT'S TRYING TO KEEP UP WITH HIS MUTATION.
IT HAS THE CAPACITY. WHAT IT NEEDS IS THE ENERGY TO GET AHEAD OF THAT BAD BOY AND SHUT HIM DOWN! AND IT NEEDS THAT ENERGY NOW!
UM... TESLA?
HRM. YES. FASCINATING. THEORETICALLY SOUND IF SOMEWHAT--
DO IT, MISTER!
YES, SIR!
TZZZAK-AK-AK

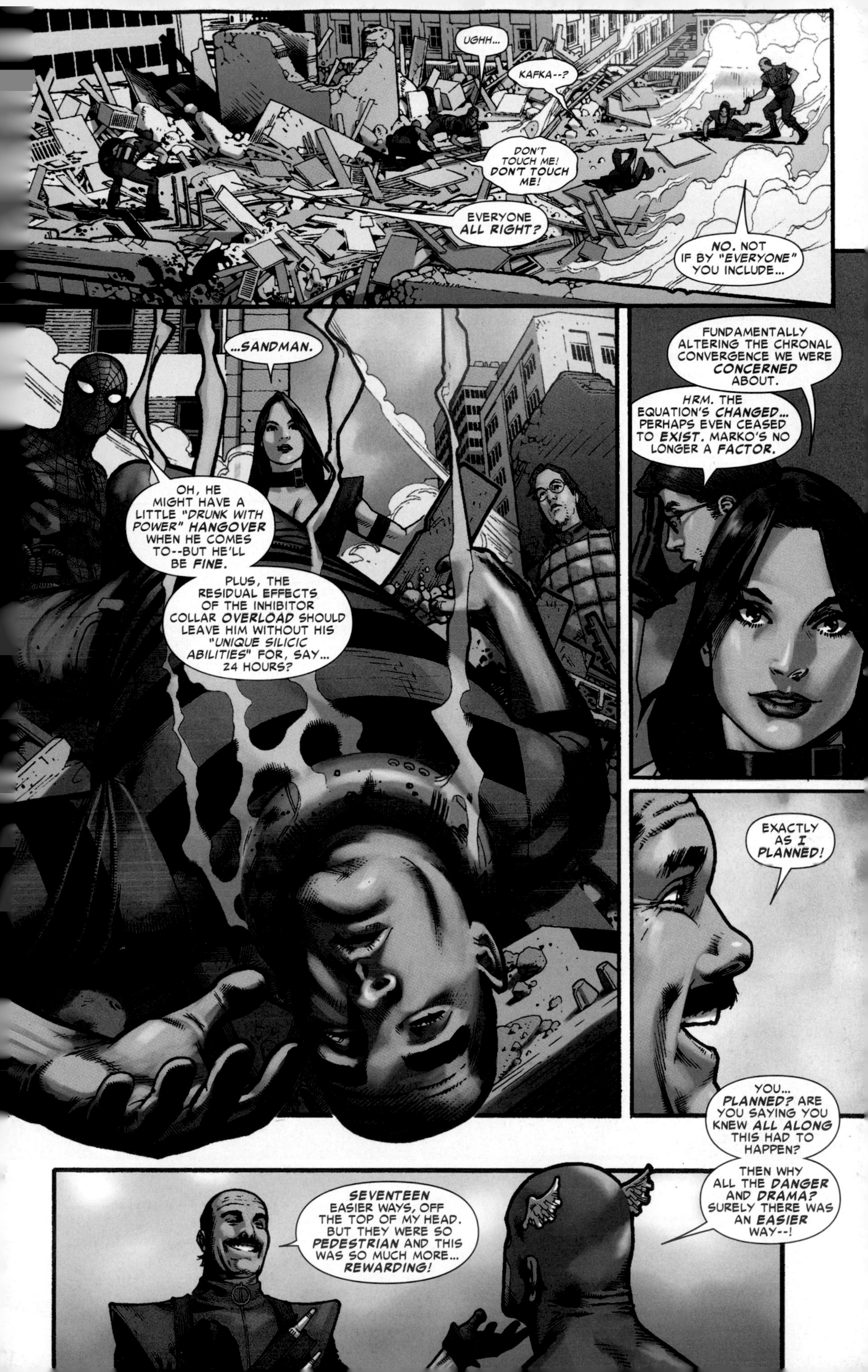
UGHH...
KAFKA--?
DON'T TOUCH ME! DON'T TOUCH ME!
EVERYONE ALL RIGHT?
NO. NOT IF BY "EVERYONE" YOU INCLUDE...
...SANDMAN.
OH, HE MIGHT HAVE A LITTLE "DRUNK WITH POWER" HANGOVER WHEN HE COMES TO--BUT HE'LL BE FINE.
PLUS, THE RESIDUAL EFFECTS OF THE INHIBITOR COLLAR OVERLOAD SHOULD LEAVE HIM WITHOUT HIS "UNIQUE SILICIC ABILITIES" FOR, SAY... 24 HOURS?
FUNDAMENTALLY ALTERING THE CHRONAL CONVERGENCE WE WERE CONCERNED ABOUT.
HRM. THE EQUATION'S CHANGED... PERHAPS EVEN CEASED TO EXIST. MARKO'S NO LONGER A FACTOR.
EXACTLY AS I PLANNED!
YOU... PLANNED? ARE YOU SAYING YOU KNEW ALL ALONG THIS HAD TO HAPPEN?
THEN WHY ALL THE DANGER AND DRAMA? SURELY THERE WAS AN EASIER WAY--!
SEVENTEEN EASIER WAYS, OFF THE TOP OF MY HEAD. BUT THEY WERE SO PEDESTRIAN AND THIS WAS SO MUCH MORE... REWARDING!

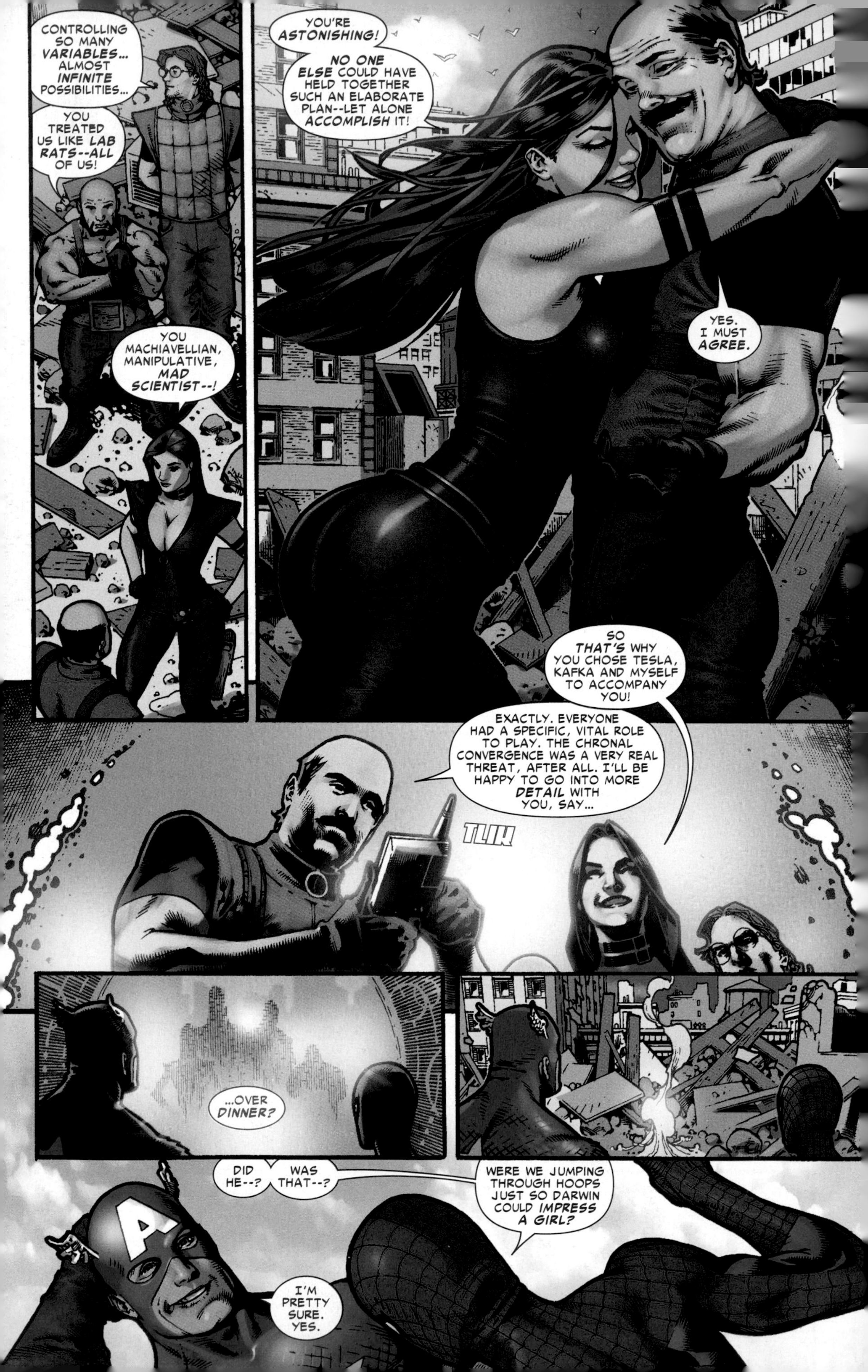

CONTROLLING SO MANY VARIABLES... ALMOST INFINITE POSSIBILITIES...
YOU TREATED US LIKE LAB RATS--ALL OF US!
YOU MACHIAVELLIAN, MANIPULATIVE, MAD SCIENTIST--!
YOU'RE ASTONISHING!
NO ONE ELSE COULD HAVE HELD TOGETHER SUCH AN ELABORATE PLAN--LET ALONE ACCOMPLISH IT!
YES. I MUST AGREE.
SO THAT'S WHY YOU CHOSE TESLA, KAFKA AND MYSELF TO ACCOMPANY YOU!
EXACTLY. EVERYONE HAD A SPECIFIC, VITAL ROLE TO PLAY. THE CHRONAL CONVERGENCE WAS A VERY REAL THREAT, AFTER ALL. I'LL BE HAPPY TO GO INTO MORE DETAIL WITH YOU, SAY...
TLIK
...OVER DINNER?
DID HE--?
WAS THAT--?
WERE WE JUMPING THROUGH HOOPS JUST SO DARWIN COULD IMPRESS A GIRL?
I'M PRETTY SURE. YES.

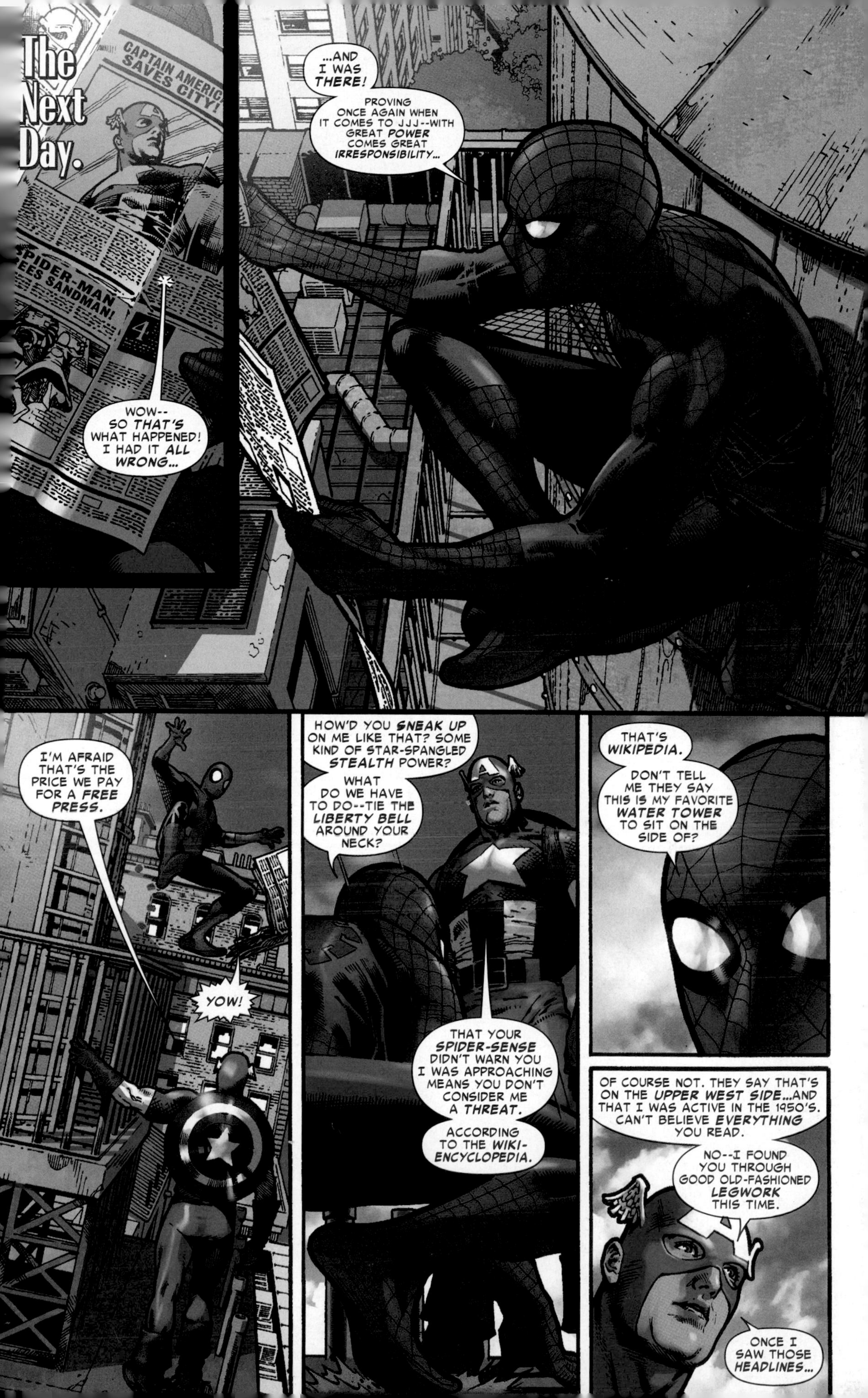
The Next Day.
CAPTAIN AMERICA SAVES CITY!
SPIDER-MAN FLEES SANDMAN!
WOW-- SO THAT'S WHAT HAPPENED! I HAD IT ALL WRONG...
...AND I WAS THERE!
PROVING ONCE AGAIN WHEN IT COMES TO JJJ--WITH GREAT POWER COMES GREAT IRRESPONSIBILITY...
I'M AFRAID THAT'S THE PRICE WE PAY FOR A FREE PRESS.
YOW!
HOW'D YOU SNEAK UP ON ME LIKE THAT? SOME KIND OF STAR-SPANGLED STEALTH POWER?
WHAT DO WE HAVE TO DO--TIE THE LIBERTY BELL AROUND YOUR NECK?
THAT YOUR SPIDER-SENSE DIDN'T WARN YOU I WAS APPROACHING MEANS YOU DON'T CONSIDER ME A THREAT.
ACCORDING TO THE WIKI-ENCYCLOPEDIA.
THAT'S WIKIPEDIA.
DON'T TELL ME THEY SAY THIS IS MY FAVORITE WATER TOWER TO SIT ON THE SIDE OF?
OF COURSE NOT. THEY SAY THAT'S ON THE UPPER WEST SIDE...AND THAT I WAS ACTIVE IN THE 1950'S. CAN'T BELIEVE EVERYTHING YOU READ.
NO--I FOUND YOU THROUGH GOOD OLD-FASHIONED LEGWORK THIS TIME.
ONCE I SAW THOSE HEADLINES...

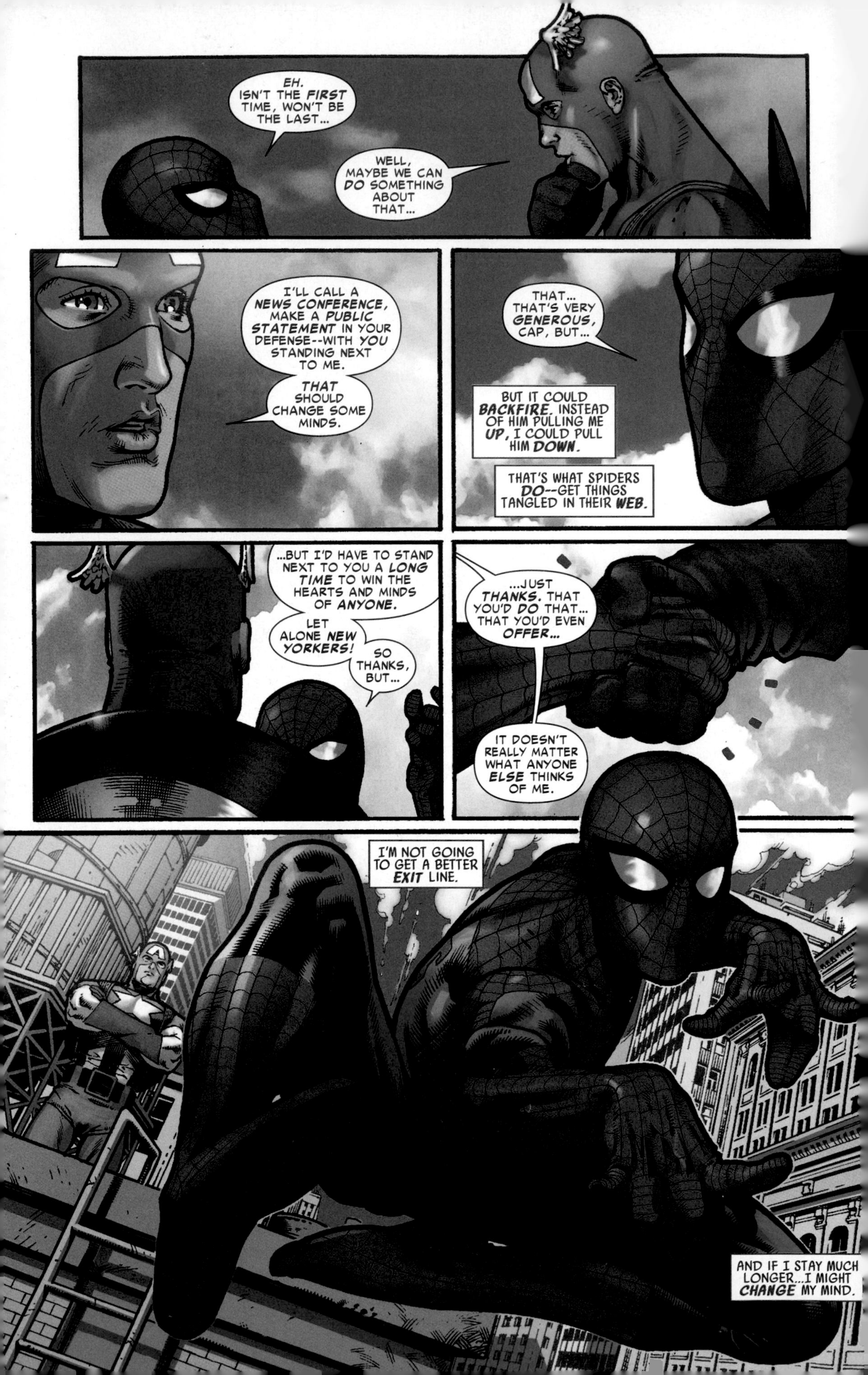

EH. ISN'T THE FIRST TIME, WON'T BE THE LAST...
WELL, MAYBE WE CAN DO SOMETHING ABOUT THAT...
I'LL CALL A NEWS CONFERENCE, MAKE A PUBLIC STATEMENT IN YOUR DEFENSE--WITH YOU STANDING NEXT TO ME.
THAT SHOULD CHANGE SOME MINDS.
THAT... THAT'S VERY GENEROUS, CAP, BUT...
BUT IT COULD BACKFIRE. INSTEAD OF HIM PULLING ME UP, I COULD PULL HIM DOWN.
THAT'S WHAT SPIDERS DO--GET THINGS TANGLED IN THEIR WEB.
...BUT I'D HAVE TO STAND NEXT TO YOU A LONG TIME TO WIN THE HEARTS AND MINDS OF ANYONE.
LET ALONE NEW YORKERS!
SO THANKS, BUT...
...JUST THANKS. THAT YOU'D DO THAT... THAT YOU'D EVEN OFFER...
IT DOESN'T REALLY MATTER WHAT ANYONE ELSE THINKS OF ME.
I'M NOT GOING TO GET A BETTER EXIT LINE.
AND IF I STAY MUCH LONGER...I MIGHT CHANGE MY MIND.

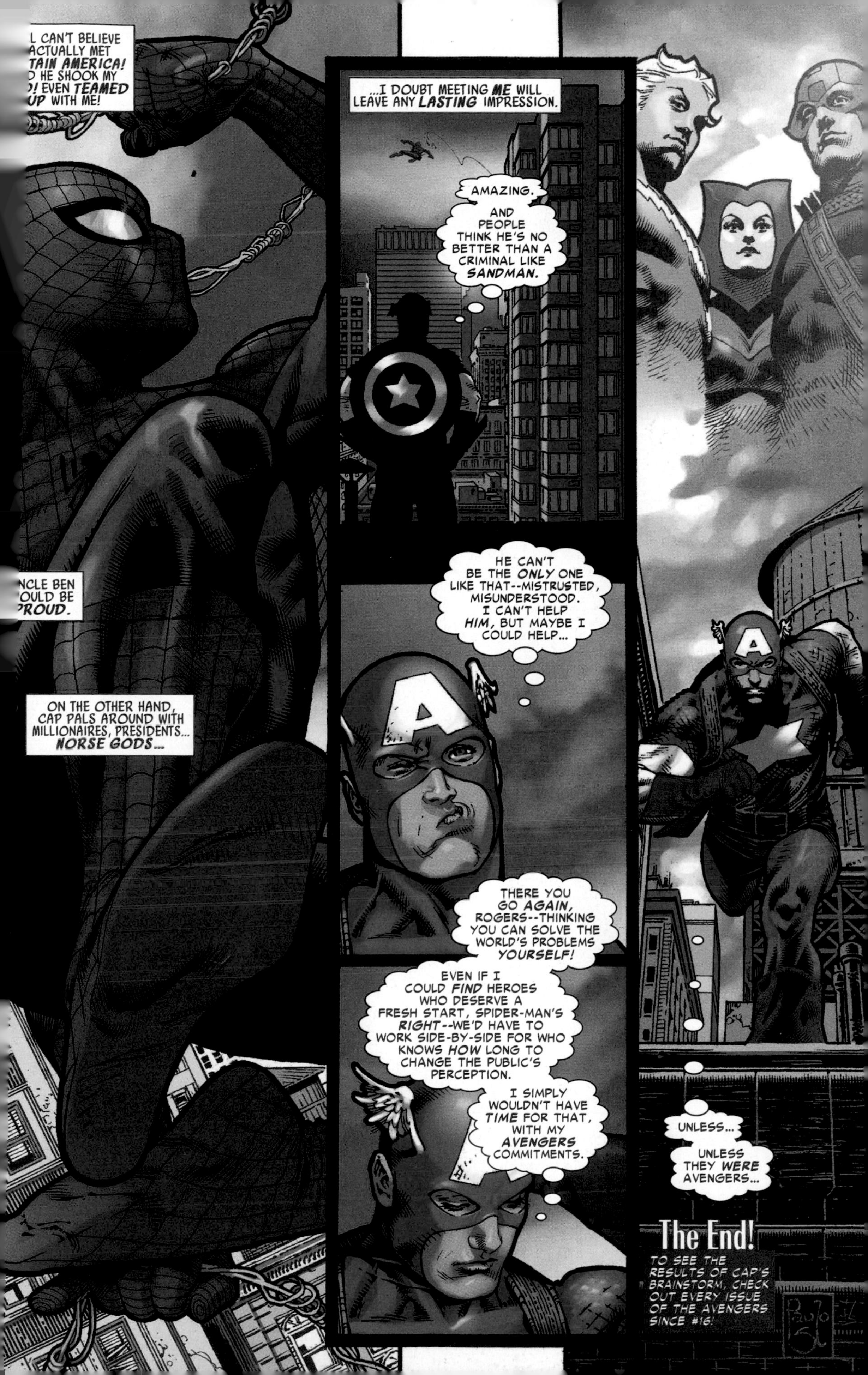
L CAN'T BELIEVE ACTUALLY MET TAIN AMERICA! D HE SHOOK MY ! EVEN TEAMED UP WITH ME!
...I DOUBT MEETING ME WILL LEAVE ANY LASTING IMPRESSION.
AMAZING.
AND PEOPLE THINK HE'S NO BETTER THAN A CRIMINAL LIKE SANDMAN.
NCLE BEN OULD BE PROUD.
HE CAN'T BE THE ONLY ONE LIKE THAT--MISTRUSTED, MISUNDERSTOOD. I CAN'T HELP HIM, BUT MAYBE I COULD HELP...
ON THE OTHER HAND, CAP PALS AROUND WITH MILLIONAIRES, PRESIDENTS... NORSE GODS...
THERE YOU GO AGAIN, ROGERS--THINKING YOU CAN SOLVE THE WORLD'S PROBLEMS YOURSELF!
EVEN IF I COULD FIND HEROES WHO DESERVE A FRESH START, SPIDER-MAN'S RIGHT--WE'D HAVE TO WORK SIDE-BY-SIDE FOR WHO KNOWS HOW LONG TO CHANGE THE PUBLIC'S PERCEPTION.
I SIMPLY WOULDN'T HAVE TIME FOR THAT, WITH MY AVENGERS COMMITMENTS.
UNLESS...
UNLESS THEY WERE AVENGERS...
The End!
TO SEE THE RESULTS OF CAP'S BRAINSTORM, CHECK OUT EVERY ISSUE OF THE AVENGERS SINCE #16!

DATELINE: 1995!

Toy Story topped the Box Office, Microsoft releases *Windows 95*, Assistant Editor Tom Brennan got his fi rejection from a girl, Senior Editor Stephen Wacker was born and Executive Editor Tom Brevoort, in his 8 year in comics, teamed Kurt Busiek and Patrick Olliffe on *Untold Tales of Spider-Man*!

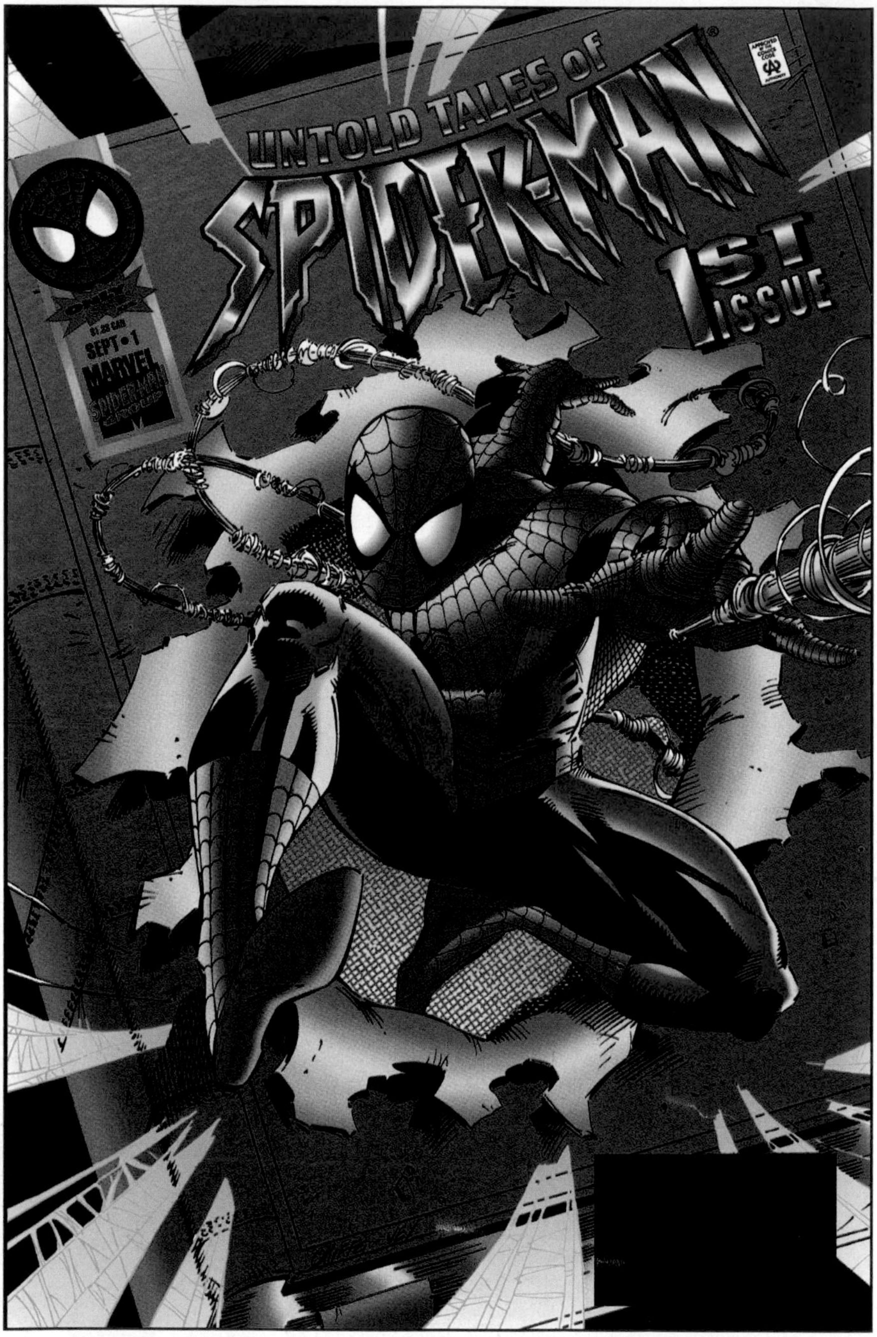
UNTOLD TALES OF
SPIDER-MAN
1ST ISSUE
SEPT • 1
MARVEL

Untold Tales was a unique book, telling stories of Peter Parker's early days in webs. But while most throw-back books either re-told original stories or gave a new spin on old content, *Untold Tales* gave you brand ne stories about the webbed wonder's first exploits.

Through 25 issues, Kurt and Pat (with a little help from Roger Stern, Tom DeFalco and Ron Frenz) brought some of the most fun Spider-Man comics of the decade. The Spidey Office is pleased to bring that team back together for one more *Untold Tale of Spider-Man*!

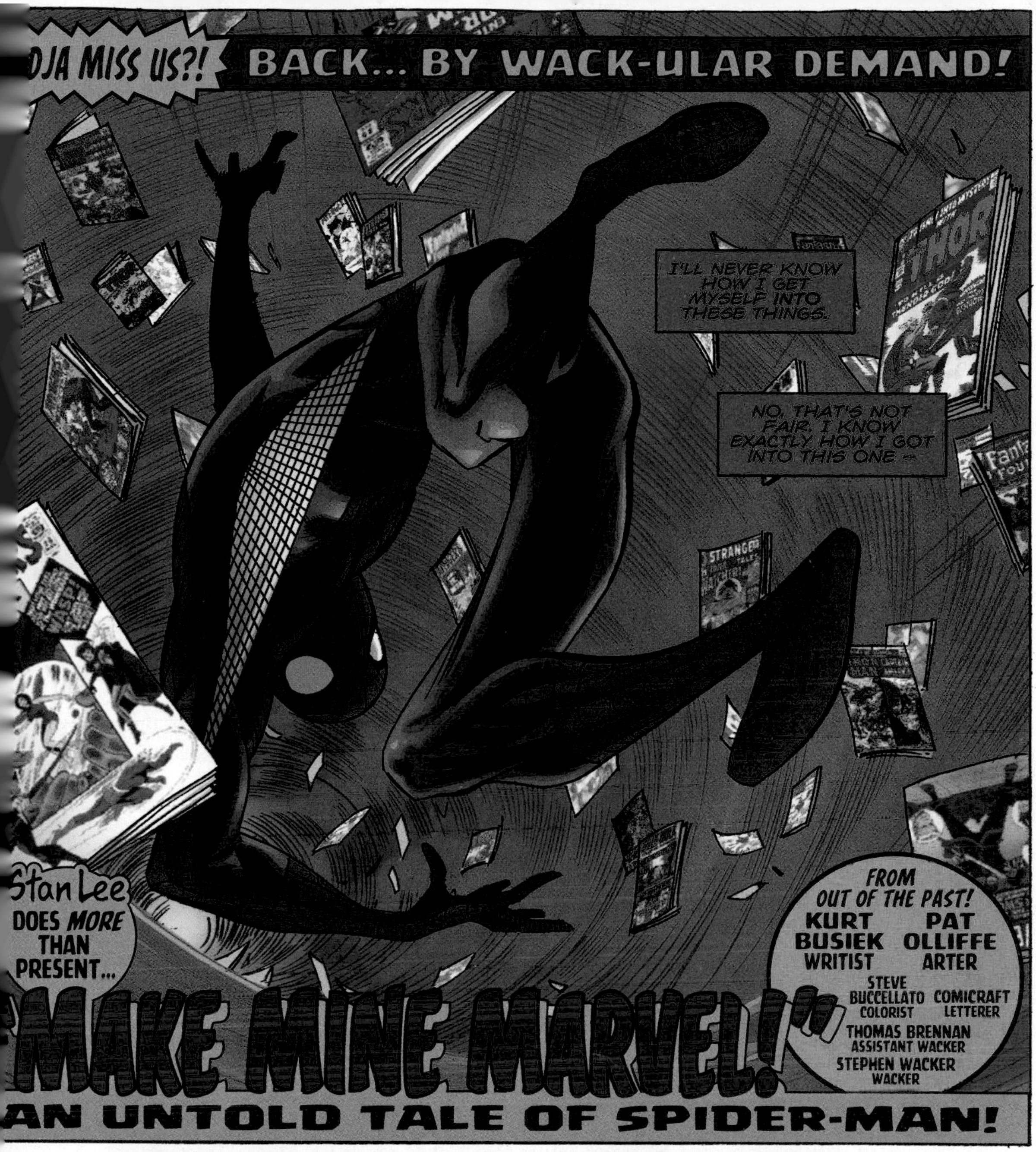
DJA MISS US?!
BACK... BY WACK-ULAR DEMAND!
I'LL NEVER KNOW HOW I GET MYSELF INTO THESE THINGS.
NO, THAT'S NOT FAIR. I KNOW EXACTLY HOW I GOT INTO THIS ONE --
THOR
STRANGE TALES
Stan Lee DOES MORE THAN PRESENT...
"MAKE MINE MARVEL!"
FROM OUT OF THE PAST!
KURT BUSIEK WRITIST
PAT OLLIFFE ARTER
STEVE BUCCELLATO COLORIST
COMICRAFT LETTERER
THOMAS BRENNAN ASSISTANT WACKER
STEPHEN WACKER WACKER
AN UNTOLD TALE OF SPIDER-MAN!

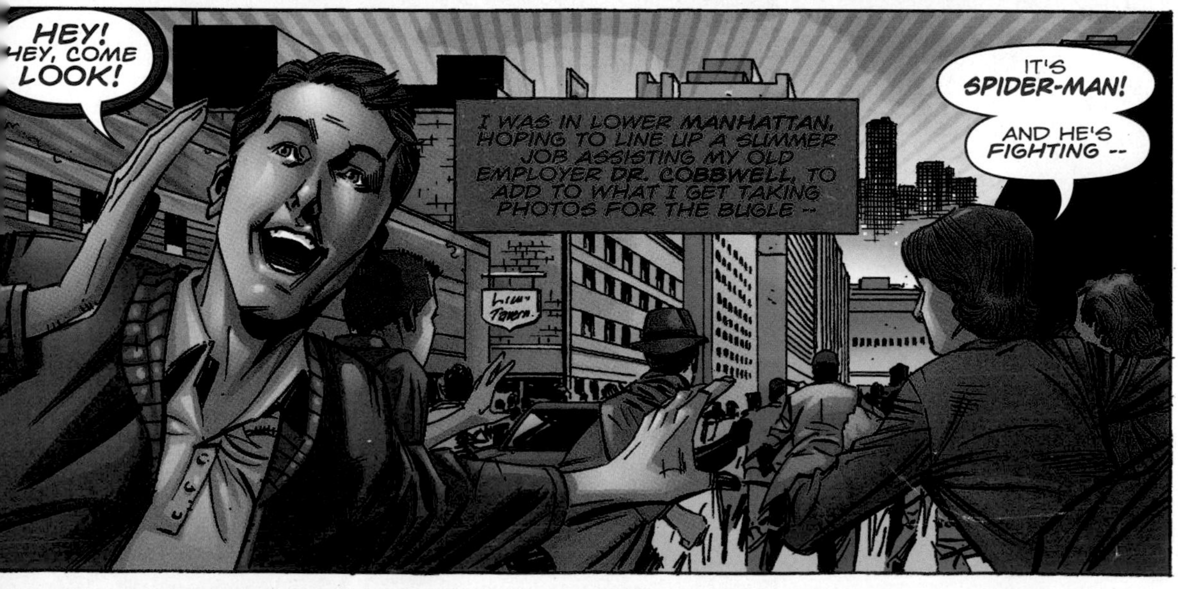
HEY! HEY, COME LOOK!
I WAS IN LOWER MANHATTAN, HOPING TO LINE UP A SUMMER JOB ASSISTING MY OLD EMPLOYER DR. COBBWELL, TO ADD TO WHAT I GET TAKING PHOTOS FOR THE BUGLE --
IT'S SPIDER-MAN!
AND HE'S FIGHTING --

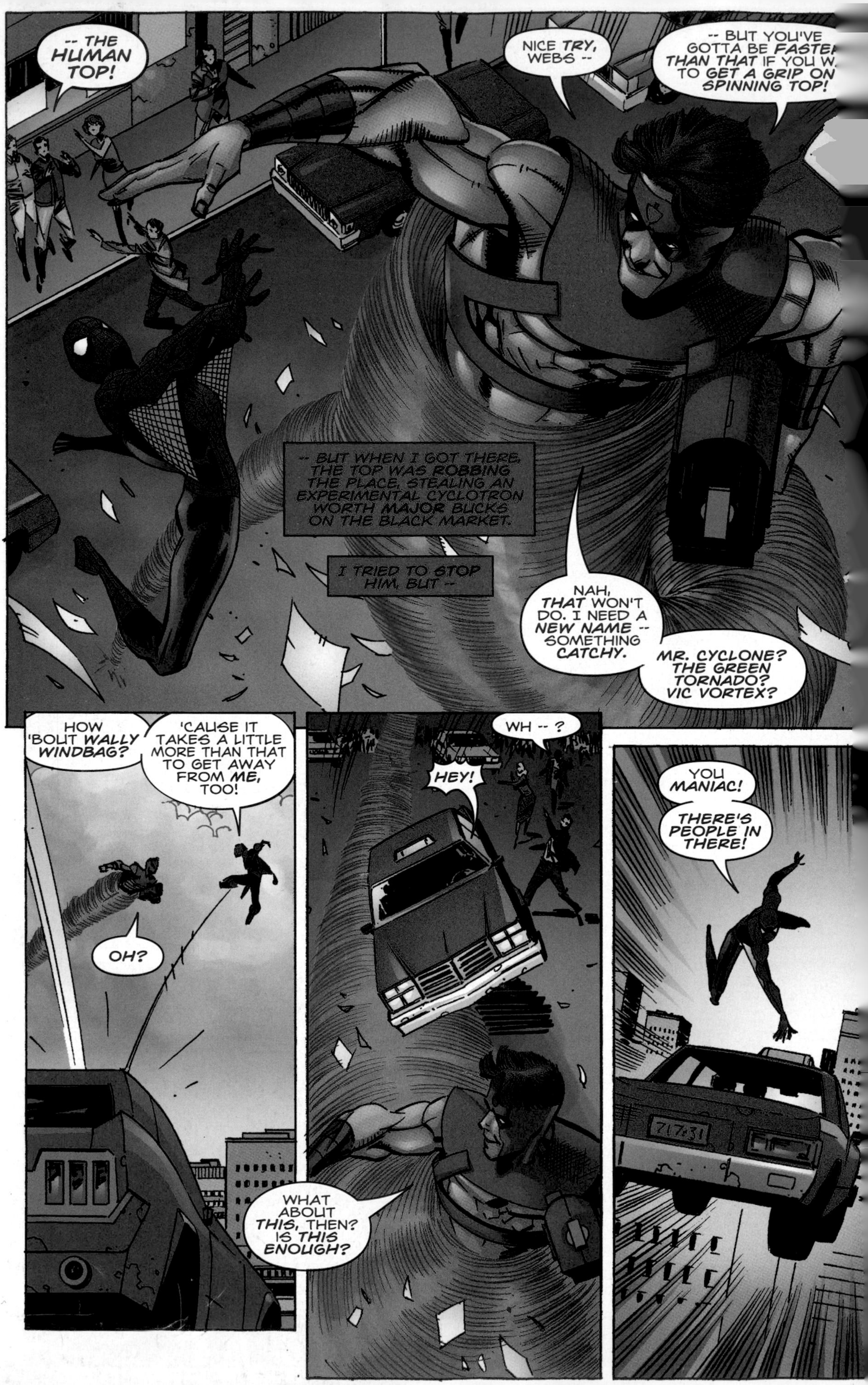
-- THE HUMAN TOP!
NICE TRY, WEBS --
-- BUT YOU'VE GOTTA BE FASTER THAN THAT IF YOU WANT TO GET A GRIP ON SPINNING TOP!
-- BUT WHEN I GOT THERE, THE TOP WAS ROBBING THE PLACE, STEALING AN EXPERIMENTAL CYCLOTRON WORTH MAJOR BUCKS ON THE BLACK MARKET.
I TRIED TO STOP HIM, BUT --
NAH, THAT WON'T DO. I NEED A NEW NAME -- SOMETHING CATCHY.
MR. CYCLONE? THE GREEN TORNADO? VIC VORTEX?
HOW 'BOUT WALLY WINDBAG?
'CAUSE IT TAKES A LITTLE MORE THAN THAT TO GET AWAY FROM ME, TOO!
OH?
WH -- ?
HEY!
WHAT ABOUT THIS, THEN? IS THIS ENOUGH?
YOU MANIAC!
THERE'S PEOPLE IN THERE!

THERE WASN'T ANY TIME TO THINK. I JUST STARTED THWIPPING OUT WEBS, AS FAST AS MY WEB-SHOOTERS COULD MANAGE, AND --

THWIP! WIP WIP WIPP

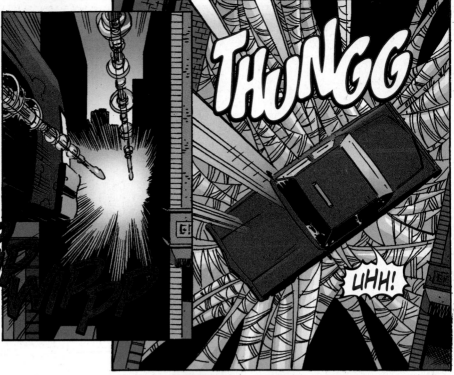

THUNGG

UHH!

HA! THERE'S YOUR PROBLEM *RIGHT THERE* -- YOU LET YOURSELF GET *DISTRACTED*, WHILE I TAKE CARE OF BUSINESS!

NOW BEFORE YOU CAN *REACH* ME, I'LL BE TOO FAR AWAY TO --

YEAH?

AND YOUR PROBLEM'S BEING *CALLOUS, MURDEROUS SCUM* -- AND A *KNOTHEAD* BESIDES!

FRANKLY...

...I LIKE MY PROBLEM BETTER!

HUH?

TO BE HONEST, THE SPEED HE WAS MOVING, IT WAS A LUCKY SHOT. BUT I GOT IT, AND --

THAT TEARS IT!

I WAS ONLY PLAYING WITH YOU BEFORE, SPIDER-MAN! BUT NOW YOU'VE EARNED THE WRATH OF -- OF --

MR. SPINNY GUY? DIZZY DAN? THE *ROTATOR?*

WH--?

I MEAN, YOU WANT TO STICK AROUND AND *TANGO,* THAT'S FINE --

-- MY WEBS'LL DISSOLVE IN AN *HOUR,* AND I'M *SURE* THERE WON'T BE ZILLIONS OF *COPS* AROUND BY THEN!

GNAH! YOU HA HEARD THE L OF ME, HER YOU'LL PA FOR THAT

SURE, SURE...

...JUST LET ME KNOW WHO TO MAKE THE *CHECK* OUT TO, NAMELESS!

I WISH I COULD HAVE GONE AFTER HIM, BUT I HAD TO CHECK ON THE MEN IN THE CAB. BESIDES, THAT WAS THE LAST OF MY WEBBING...!

YOU'RE *OKAY,* MAC. JUST A LITTLE SHOOK UP.

AB. AB DAB AB...

AND *YOU,* SIR?

ME? COULDN'T BE *BETTER,* SPIDEY.

I SHOULD DO THAT EVERY MORNING -- BETTER THAN THREE CUPS OF *COFFEE* AND A *FIRE ALARM* FOR GETTING THE BLOOD PUMPING, I'LL TELL YOU!

GLAD I WAS WEARING MY *SEAT BELT,* THOUGH.

YOU, AH, DON'T SEEM TOO *UPSET* AT BEING THROWN THROUGH THE AIR, MR....

CALL ME *STAN.*

AND IN *MY* LINE OF WORK -- AND CONSIDERING *WHO* I WAS COMING TO MEET -- I'VE GOT TO LEARN TO TAKE THINGS LIKE THAT IN *STRIDE.*

WHO YOU WERE COMING TO *MEET...?*

RIGHT *BEHIND* YOU, SON.

HUH?

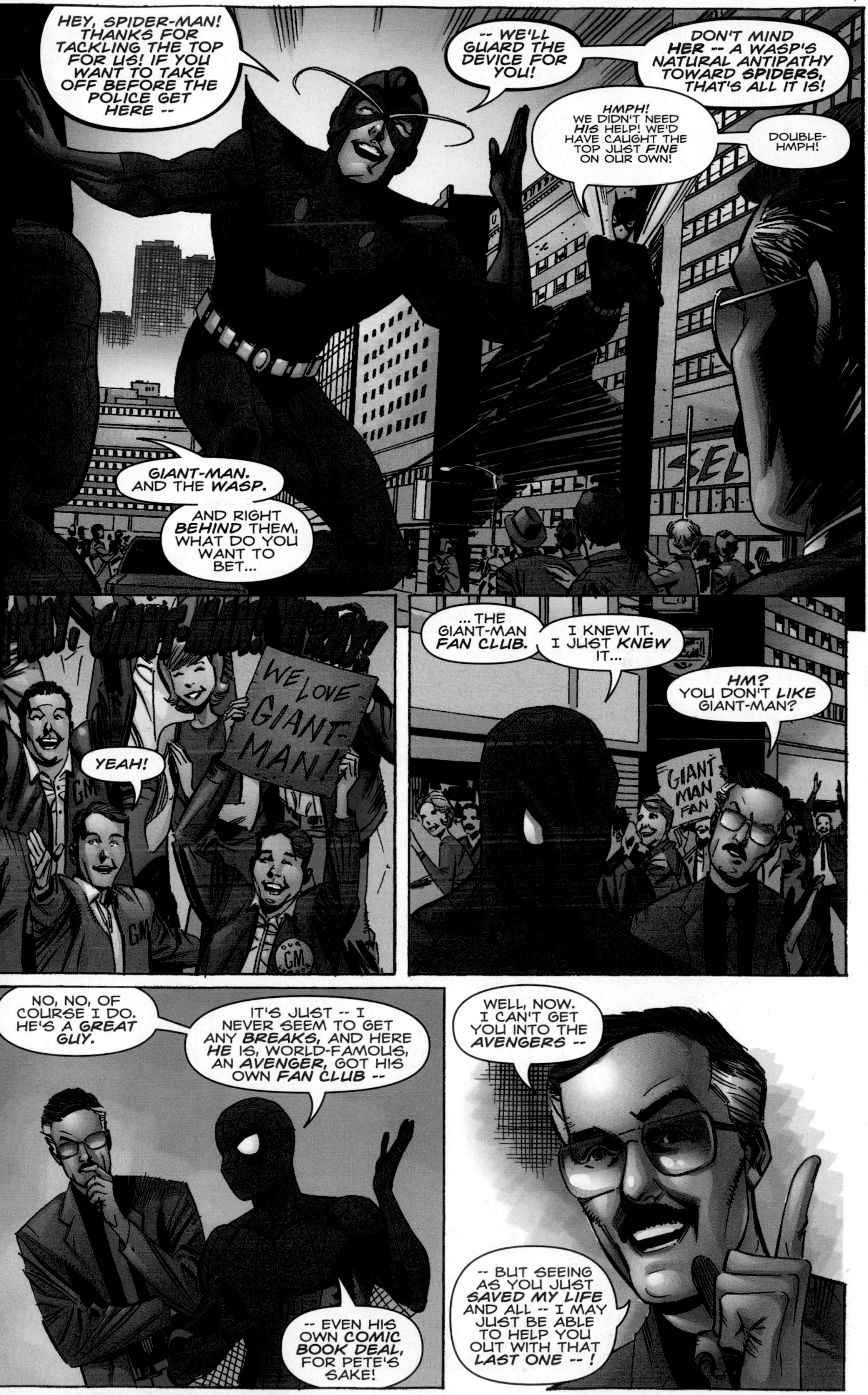
HEY, SPIDER-MAN! THANKS FOR TACKLING THE TOP FOR US! IF YOU WANT TO TAKE OFF BEFORE THE POLICE GET HERE --
-- WE'LL GUARD THE DEVICE FOR YOU!
DON'T MIND HER -- A WASP'S NATURAL ANTIPATHY TOWARD SPIDERS, THAT'S ALL IT IS!
HMPH! WE DIDN'T NEED HIS HELP! WE'D HAVE CAUGHT THE TOP JUST FINE ON OUR OWN!
DOUBLE-HMPH!
GIANT-MAN. AND THE WASP.
AND RIGHT BEHIND THEM, WHAT DO YOU WANT TO BET...
WE LOVE GIANT-MAN!
YEAH!
... THE GIANT-MAN FAN CLUB.
I KNEW IT. I JUST KNEW IT...
HM? YOU DON'T LIKE GIANT-MAN?
GIANT MAN FAN
NO, NO, OF COURSE I DO. HE'S A GREAT GUY.
IT'S JUST -- I NEVER SEEM TO GET ANY BREAKS, AND HERE HE IS, WORLD-FAMOUS, AN AVENGER, GOT HIS OWN FAN CLUB --
-- EVEN HIS OWN COMIC BOOK DEAL, FOR PETE'S SAKE!
WELL, NOW. I CAN'T GET YOU INTO THE AVENGERS --
-- BUT SEEING AS YOU JUST SAVED MY LIFE AND ALL -- I MAY JUST BE ABLE TO HELP YOU OUT WITH THAT LAST ONE -- !

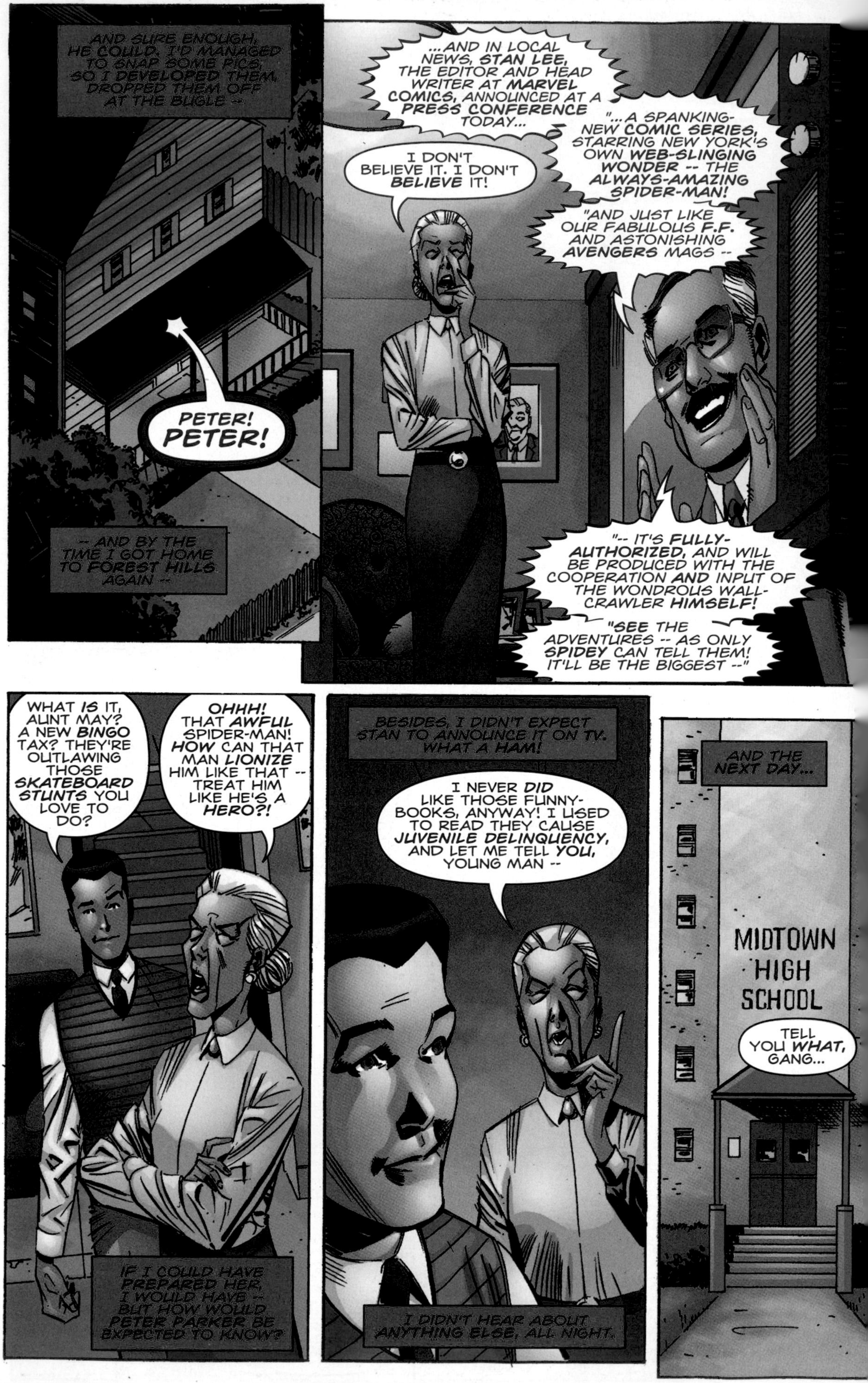
AND SURE ENOUGH, HE COULD. I'D MANAGED TO SNAP SOME PICS, SO I DEVELOPED THEM, DROPPED THEM OFF AT THE BUGLE --
-- AND BY THE TIME I GOT HOME TO FOREST HILLS AGAIN --
PETER! PETER!
...AND IN LOCAL NEWS, STAN LEE, THE EDITOR AND HEAD WRITER AT MARVEL COMICS, ANNOUNCED AT A PRESS CONFERENCE TODAY...
"...A SPANKING-NEW COMIC SERIES, STARRING NEW YORK'S OWN WEB-SLINGING WONDER -- THE ALWAYS-AMAZING SPIDER-MAN!
"AND JUST LIKE OUR FABULOUS F.F. AND ASTONISHING AVENGERS MAGS --
I DON'T BELIEVE IT. I DON'T BELIEVE IT!
"-- IT'S FULLY-AUTHORIZED, AND WILL BE PRODUCED WITH THE COOPERATION AND INPUT OF THE WONDROUS WALL-CRAWLER HIMSELF!
"SEE THE ADVENTURES -- AS ONLY SPIDEY CAN TELL THEM! IT'LL BE THE BIGGEST --"
WHAT IS IT, AUNT MAY? A NEW BINGO TAX? THEY'RE OUTLAWING THOSE SKATEBOARD STUNTS YOU LOVE TO DO?
OHHH! THAT AWFUL SPIDER-MAN! HOW CAN THAT MAN LIONIZE HIM LIKE THAT -- TREAT HIM LIKE HE'S A HERO?!
IF I COULD HAVE PREPARED HER, I WOULD HAVE -- BUT HOW WOULD PETER PARKER BE EXPECTED TO KNOW?
BESIDES, I DIDN'T EXPECT STAN TO ANNOUNCE IT ON TV. WHAT A HAM!
I NEVER DID LIKE THOSE FUNNY-BOOKS, ANYWAY! I USED TO READ THEY CAUSE JUVENILE DELINQUENCY, AND LET ME TELL YOU, YOUNG MAN --
I DIDN'T HEAR ABOUT ANYTHING ELSE, ALL NIGHT.
AND THE NEXT DAY...
MIDTOWN HIGH SCHOOL
TELL YOU WHAT, GANG...

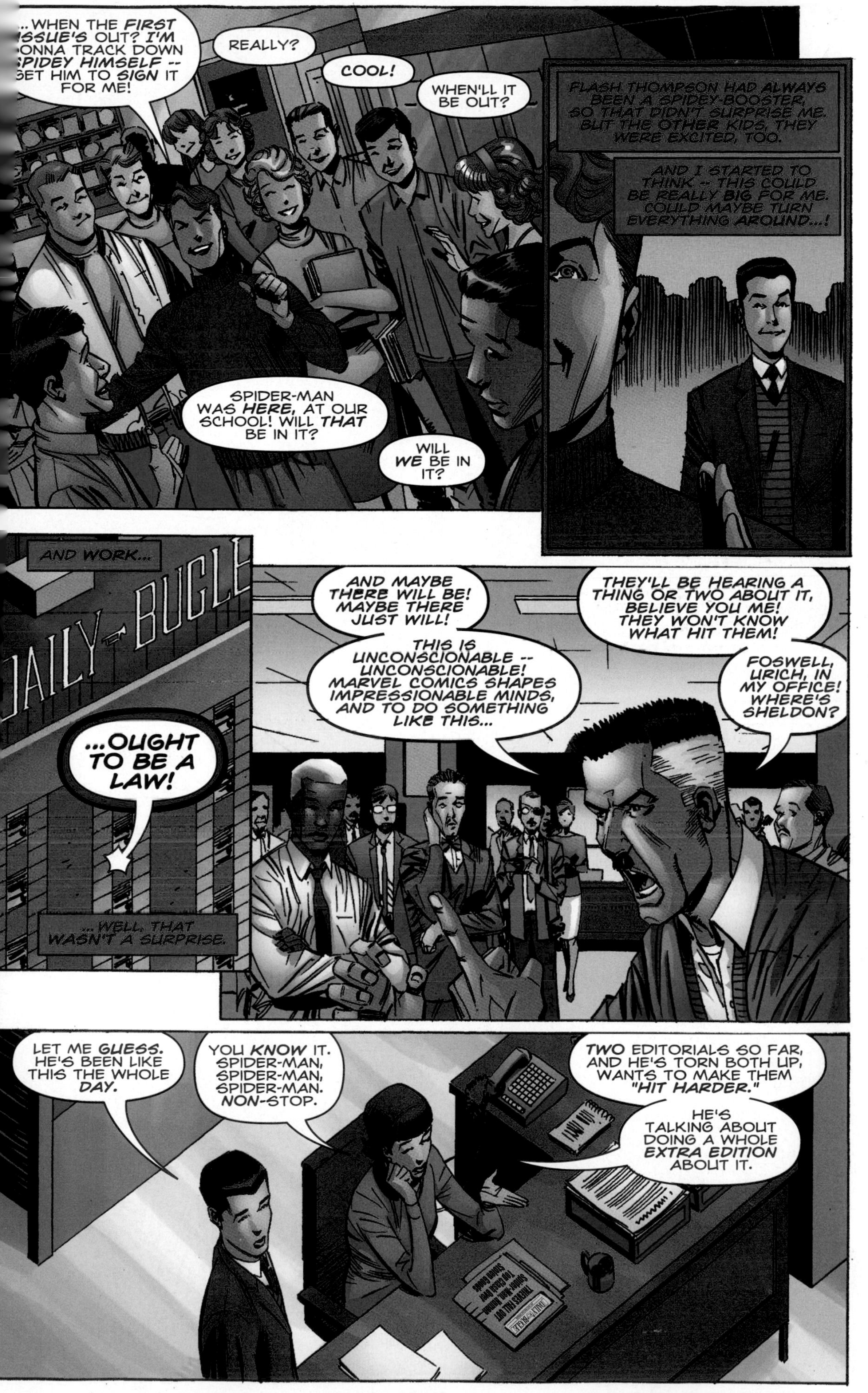
...WHEN THE FIRST ISSUE'S OUT? I'M GONNA TRACK DOWN SPIDEY HIMSELF -- GET HIM TO SIGN IT FOR ME!
REALLY?
COOL!
WHEN'LL IT BE OUT?
SPIDER-MAN WAS HERE, AT OUR SCHOOL! WILL THAT BE IN IT?
WILL WE BE IN IT?
FLASH THOMPSON HAD ALWAYS BEEN A SPIDEY-BOOSTER, SO THAT DIDN'T SURPRISE ME. BUT THE OTHER KIDS, THEY WERE EXCITED, TOO.
AND I STARTED TO THINK -- THIS COULD BE REALLY BIG FOR ME. COULD MAYBE TURN EVERYTHING AROUND...!
AND WORK...
DAILY BUGLE
...OUGHT TO BE A LAW!
...WELL, THAT WASN'T A SURPRISE.
AND MAYBE THERE WILL BE! MAYBE THERE JUST WILL!
THIS IS UNCONSCIONABLE -- UNCONSCIONABLE! MARVEL COMICS SHAPES IMPRESSIONABLE MINDS, AND TO DO SOMETHING LIKE THIS...
THEY'LL BE HEARING A THING OR TWO ABOUT IT, BELIEVE YOU ME! THEY WON'T KNOW WHAT HIT THEM!
FOSWELL, URICH, IN MY OFFICE! WHERE'S SHELDON?
LET ME GUESS. HE'S BEEN LIKE THIS THE WHOLE DAY.
YOU KNOW IT. SPIDER-MAN, SPIDER-MAN, SPIDER-MAN. NON-STOP.
TWO EDITORIALS SO FAR, AND HE'S TORN BOTH UP, WANTS TO MAKE THEM "HIT HARDER."
HE'S TALKING ABOUT DOING A WHOLE EXTRA EDITION ABOUT IT.

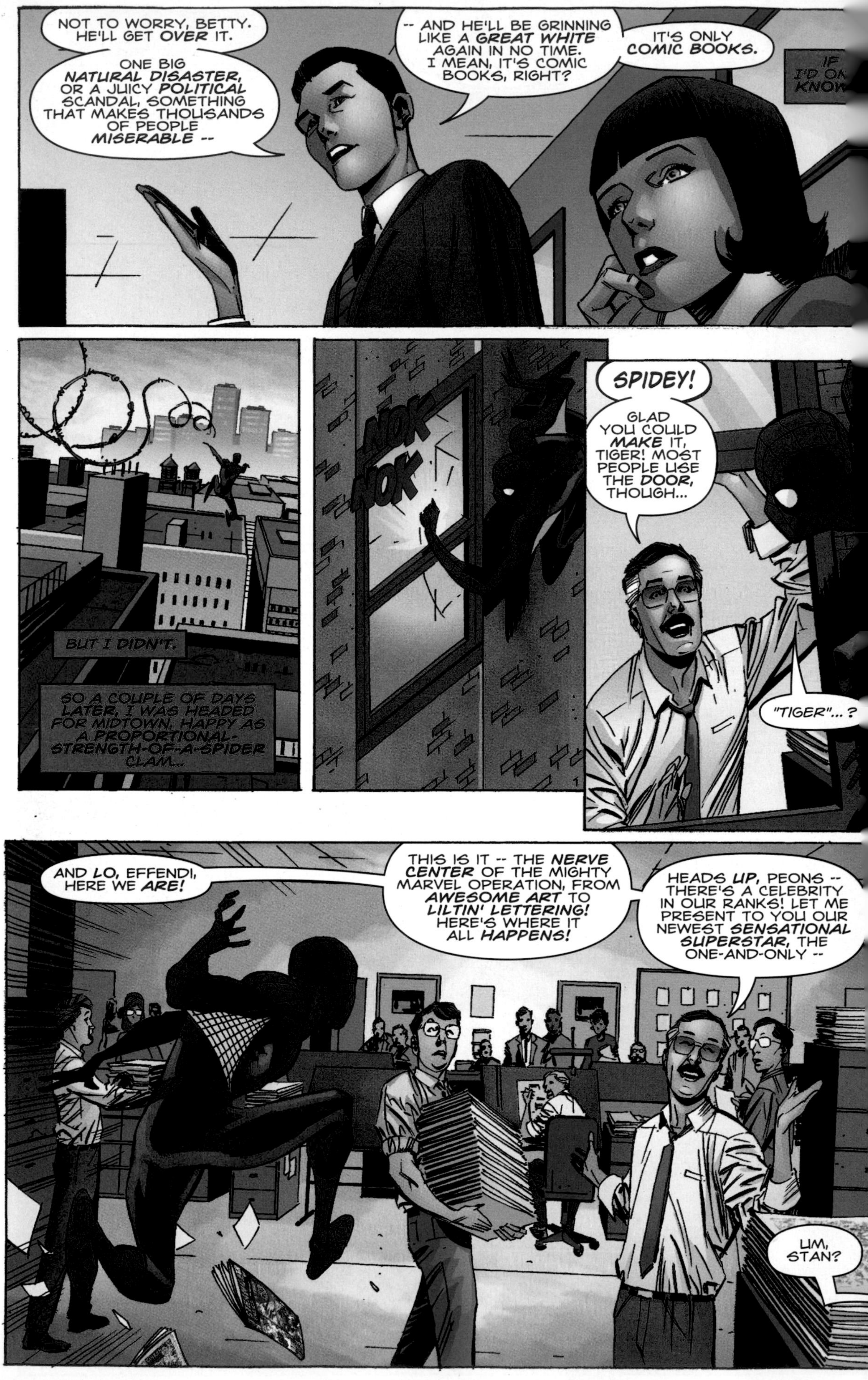
NOT TO WORRY, BETTY. HE'LL GET OVER IT.
ONE BIG NATURAL DISASTER, OR A JUICY POLITICAL SCANDAL, SOMETHING THAT MAKES THOUSANDS OF PEOPLE MISERABLE --
-- AND HE'LL BE GRINNING LIKE A GREAT WHITE AGAIN IN NO TIME. I MEAN, IT'S COMIC BOOKS, RIGHT?
IT'S ONLY COMIC BOOKS.
IF
BUT I DIDN'T.
SO A COUPLE OF DAYS LATER, I WAS HEADED FOR MIDTOWN, HAPPY AS A PROPORTIONAL-STRENGTH-OF-A-SPIDER CLAM...
NOK NOK
SPIDEY!
GLAD YOU COULD MAKE IT, TIGER! MOST PEOPLE USE THE DOOR, THOUGH...
"TIGER"...?
AND LO, EFFENDI, HERE WE ARE!
THIS IS IT -- THE NERVE CENTER OF THE MIGHTY MARVEL OPERATION, FROM AWESOME ART TO LILTIN' LETTERING! HERE'S WHERE IT ALL HAPPENS!
HEADS UP, PEONS -- THERE'S A CELEBRITY IN OUR RANKS! LET ME PRESENT TO YOU OUR NEWEST SENSATIONAL SUPERSTAR, THE ONE-AND-ONLY --
UM, STAN?

I THINK YOU SHOULD *SEE* THIS...

UH. THANKS, FLO.

DAILY BUGLE
NEW YORK'S FINEST DAILY NEWSPAPER

CORRUPTION OF THE INNOCENT

What Are Comic Books Teaching Your Children?

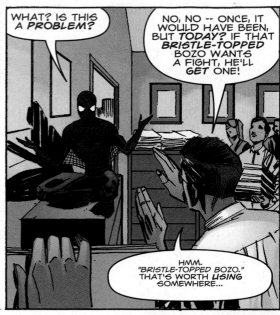

WHAT? IS THIS A *PROBLEM?*

NO, NO -- ONCE, IT WOULD HAVE BEEN, BUT *TODAY?* IF THAT *BRISTLE-TOPPED* BOZO WANTS A FIGHT, HE'LL *GET* ONE!

HMM. "BRISTLE-TOPPED BOZO." THAT'S WORTH *USING* SOMEWHERE...

ON'T *WORRY* ABOUT IT. JST STEP INTO MY -- OH, YOU'RE ALREADY IN.

HAVE A *CHAIR,* IF YOU LIKE.

I'M FINE *HERE.* HOW DO WE START?

JUST A FEW *QUESTIONS.*

SHOOT.

OKAY, FIRST OFF, I GOTTA GET TO *KNOW* YOU. JUST WHO *ARE* YOU, UNDER THAT MASK?

WHAT?! I *CAN'T TELL YOU THAT!*

IF YOU KNEW MY REAL NAME, IT'D --

EASY, *EASY!* WE'D NEVER *PUBLISH* YOUR SECRET IDENTITY. UT, THEN -- WHAT SORT OF THING DO YOU *DO* WHEN YOU'RE NOT WEB-SLINGING?

SCIENTIST? ATHLETE? *GOVERNMENT AGENT?*

UM.

CAN I... *PASS* ON THAT FOR NOW?

SURE. AN *EASIER* ONE, THEN.

THOSE WEB-SHOOTERS. ARE THEY *PART* OF YOU? ARE THEY *GADGETS?* HOW DO THEY WORK?

UM...

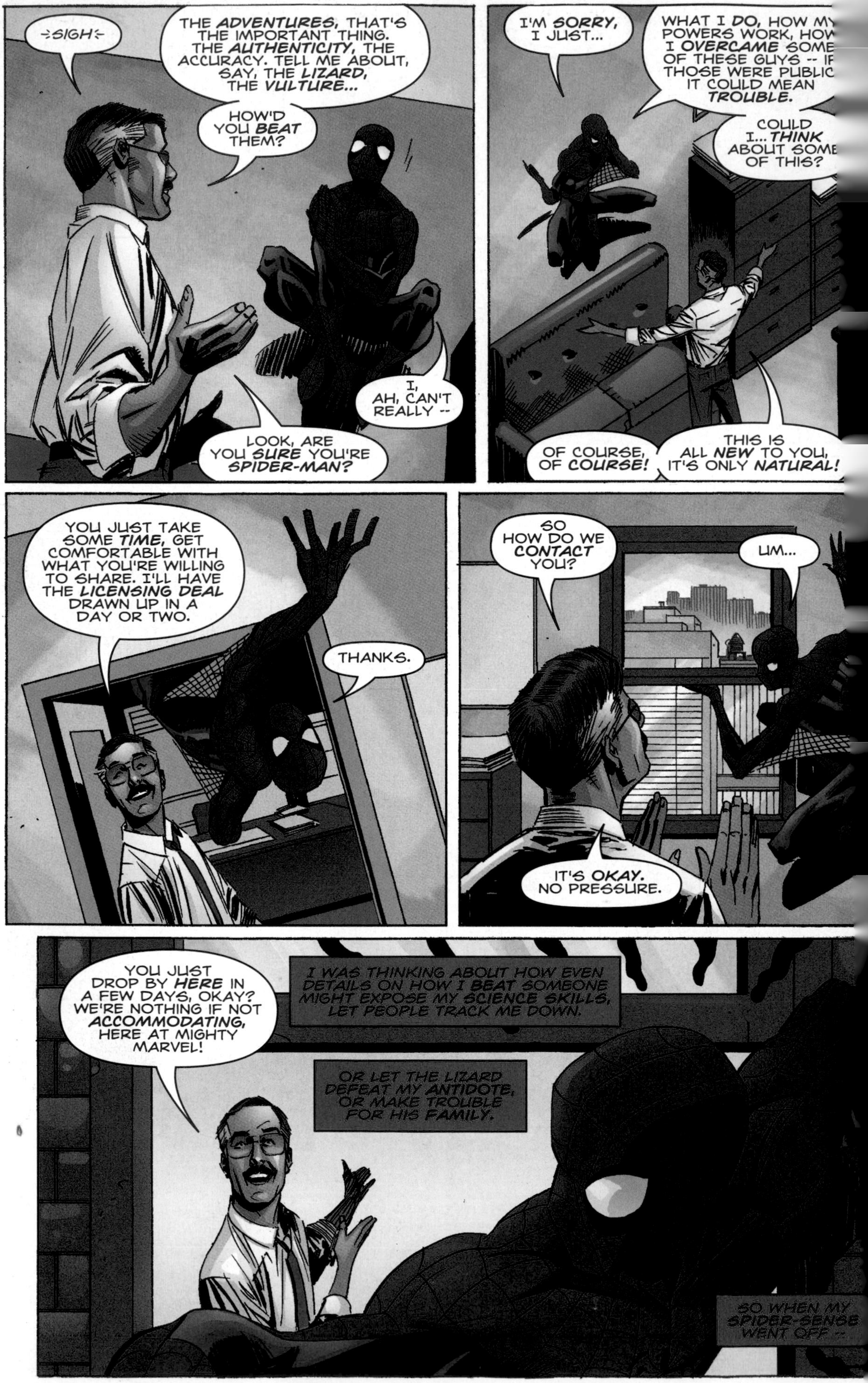

-SIGH-
THE ADVENTURES, THAT'S THE IMPORTANT THING. THE AUTHENTICITY, THE ACCURACY. TELL ME ABOUT, SAY, THE LIZARD, THE VULTURE...
HOW'D YOU BEAT THEM?
I, AH, CAN'T REALLY --
LOOK, ARE YOU SURE YOU'RE SPIDER-MAN?
I'M SORRY, I JUST...
WHAT I DO, HOW MY POWERS WORK, HOW I OVERCAME SOME OF THESE GUYS -- IF THOSE WERE PUBLIC IT COULD MEAN TROUBLE.
COULD I...THINK ABOUT SOME OF THIS?
OF COURSE, OF COURSE!
THIS IS ALL NEW TO YOU, IT'S ONLY NATURAL!
YOU JUST TAKE SOME TIME, GET COMFORTABLE WITH WHAT YOU'RE WILLING TO SHARE. I'LL HAVE THE LICENSING DEAL DRAWN UP IN A DAY OR TWO.
THANKS.
SO HOW DO WE CONTACT YOU?
UM...
IT'S OKAY. NO PRESSURE.
YOU JUST DROP BY HERE IN A FEW DAYS, OKAY? WE'RE NOTHING IF NOT ACCOMMODATING, HERE AT MIGHTY MARVEL!
I WAS THINKING ABOUT HOW EVEN DETAILS ON HOW I BEAT SOMEONE MIGHT EXPOSE MY SCIENCE SKILLS, LET PEOPLE TRACK ME DOWN.
OR LET THE LIZARD DEFEAT MY ANTIDOTE, OR MAKE TROUBLE FOR HIS FAMILY.
SO WHEN MY SPIDER-SENSE WENT OFF --

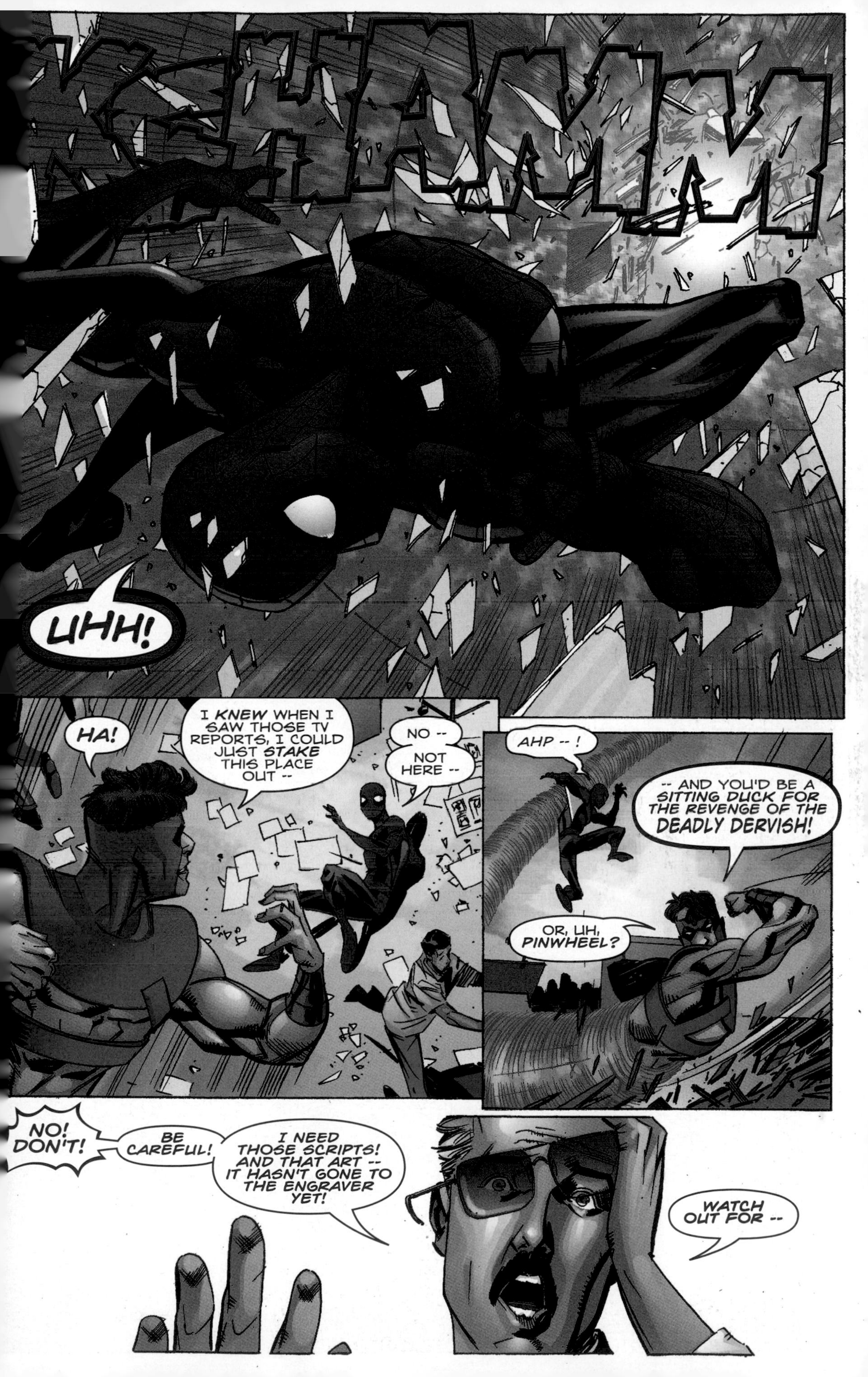
KRAKOOM
UHH!
HA!
I KNEW WHEN I SAW THOSE TV REPORTS, I COULD JUST STAKE THIS PLACE OUT --
NO -- NOT HERE --
AHP -- !
-- AND YOU'D BE A SITTING DUCK FOR THE REVENGE OF THE DEADLY DERVISH!
OR, UH, PINWHEEL?
NO! DON'T!
BE CAREFUL!
I NEED THOSE SCRIPTS! AND THAT ART -- IT HASN'T GONE TO THE ENGRAVER YET!
WATCH OUT FOR --

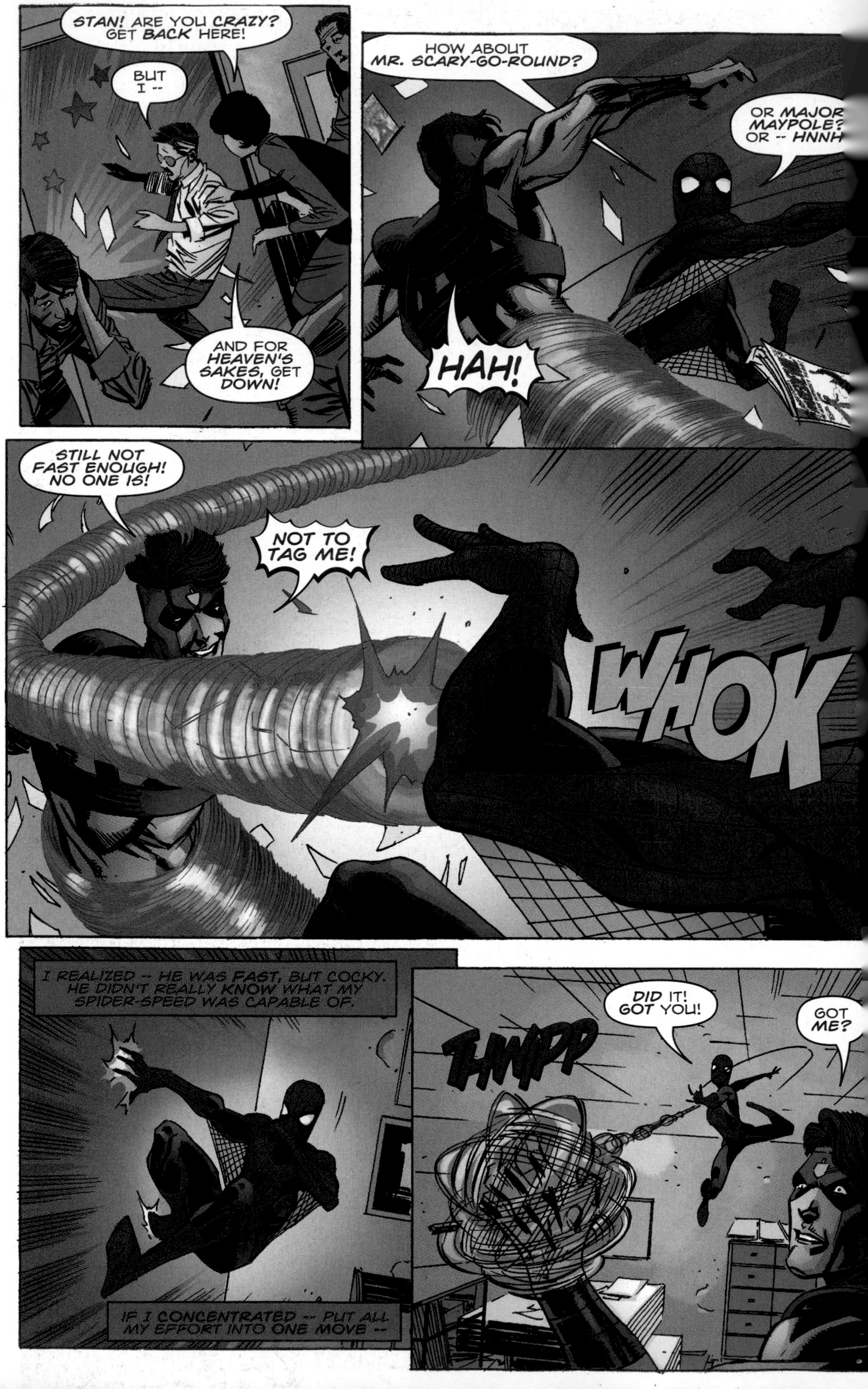
STAN! ARE YOU CRAZY? GET BACK HERE!
BUT I --
AND FOR HEAVEN'S SAKES, GET DOWN!
HOW ABOUT MR. SCARY-GO-ROUND?
OR MAJOR MAYPOLE? OR -- HNNH
HAH!
STILL NOT FAST ENOUGH! NO ONE IS!
NOT TO TAG ME!
WHOK
I REALIZED -- HE WAS FAST, BUT COCKY. HE DIDN'T REALLY KNOW WHAT MY SPIDER-SPEED WAS CAPABLE OF.
IF I CONCENTRATED -- PUT ALL MY EFFORT INTO ONE MOVE --
THWPP
DID IT! GOT YOU!
GOT ME?

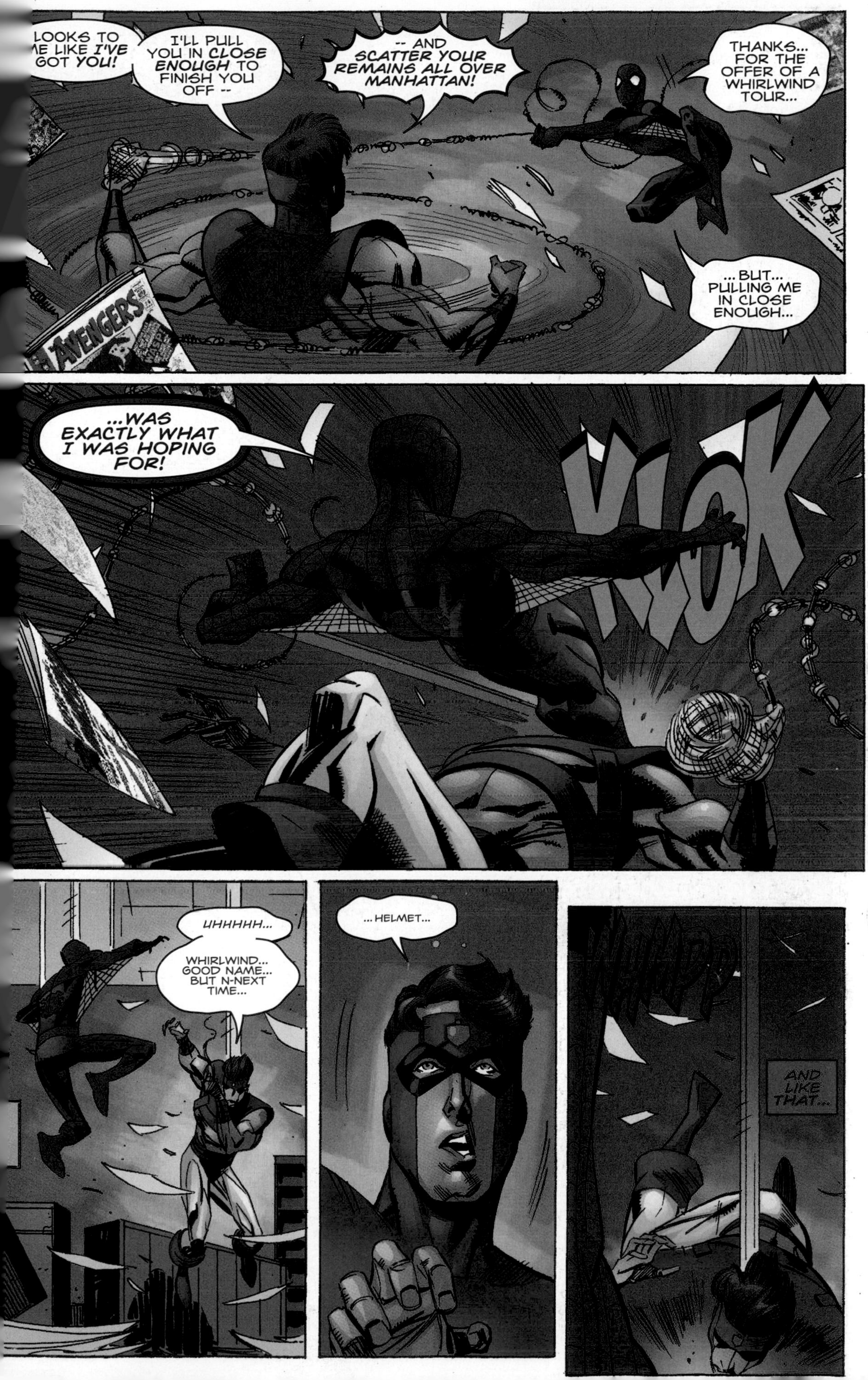
LOOKS TO ME LIKE I'VE GOT YOU!
I'LL PULL YOU IN CLOSE ENOUGH TO FINISH YOU OFF --
-- AND SCATTER YOUR REMAINS ALL OVER MANHATTAN!
THANKS... FOR THE OFFER OF A WHIRLWIND TOUR...
... BUT... PULLING ME IN CLOSE ENOUGH...
AVENGERS
...WAS EXACTLY WHAT I WAS HOPING FOR!
UHHHHH...
WHIRLWIND... GOOD NAME... BUT N-NEXT TIME...
... HELMET...
AND LIKE THAT...

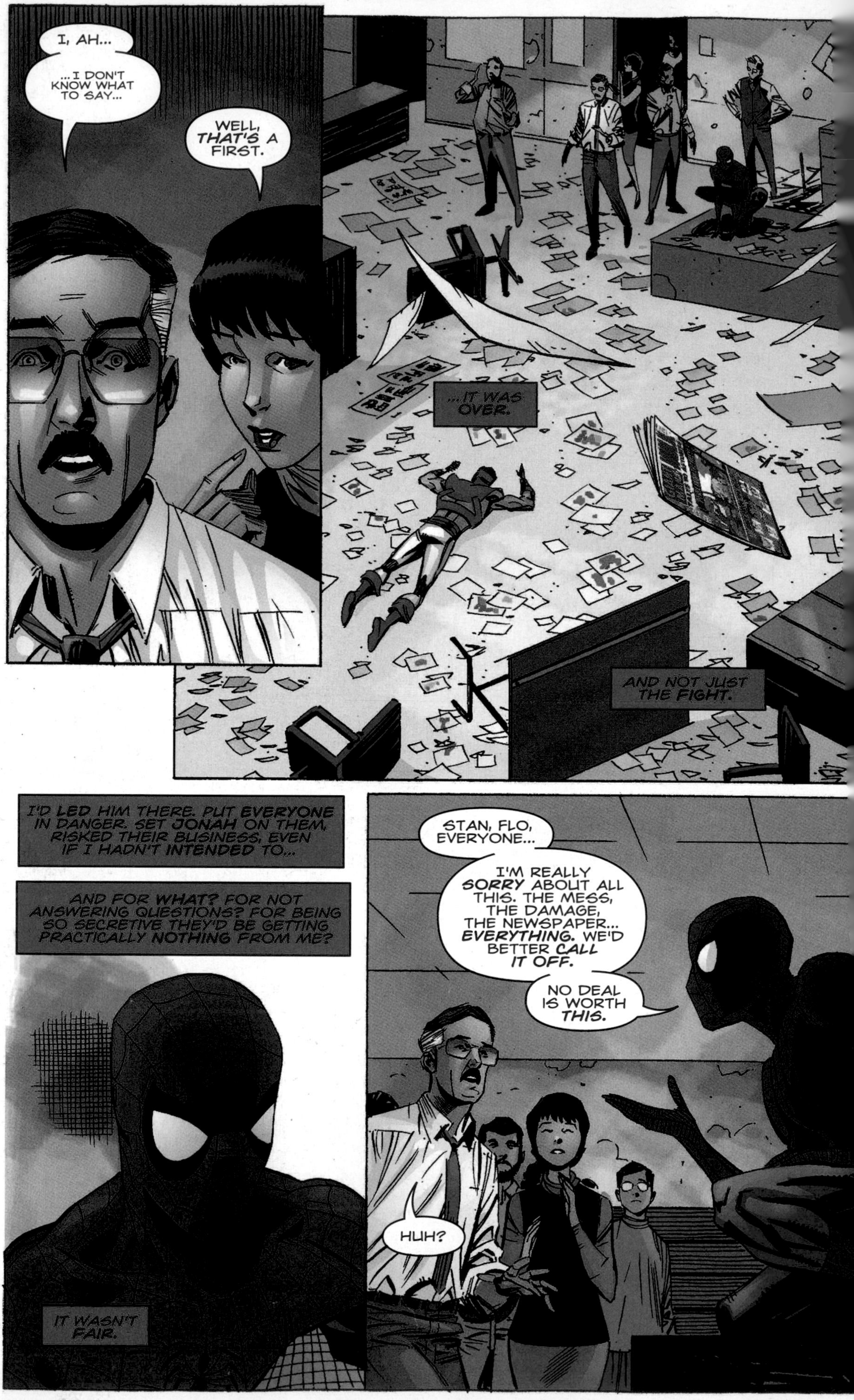

I, AH...
...I DON'T KNOW WHAT TO SAY...
WELL, THAT'S A FIRST.
...IT WAS OVER.
AND NOT JUST THE FIGHT.
I'D LED HIM THERE. PUT EVERYONE IN DANGER. SET JONAH ON THEM, RISKED THEIR BUSINESS, EVEN IF I HADN'T INTENDED TO...
AND FOR WHAT? FOR NOT ANSWERING QUESTIONS? FOR BEING SO SECRETIVE THEY'D BE GETTING PRACTICALLY NOTHING FROM ME?
IT WASN'T FAIR.
STAN, FLO, EVERYONE...
I'M REALLY SORRY ABOUT ALL THIS. THE MESS, THE DAMAGE, THE NEWSPAPER... EVERYTHING. WE'D BETTER CALL IT OFF.
NO DEAL IS WORTH THIS.
HUH?

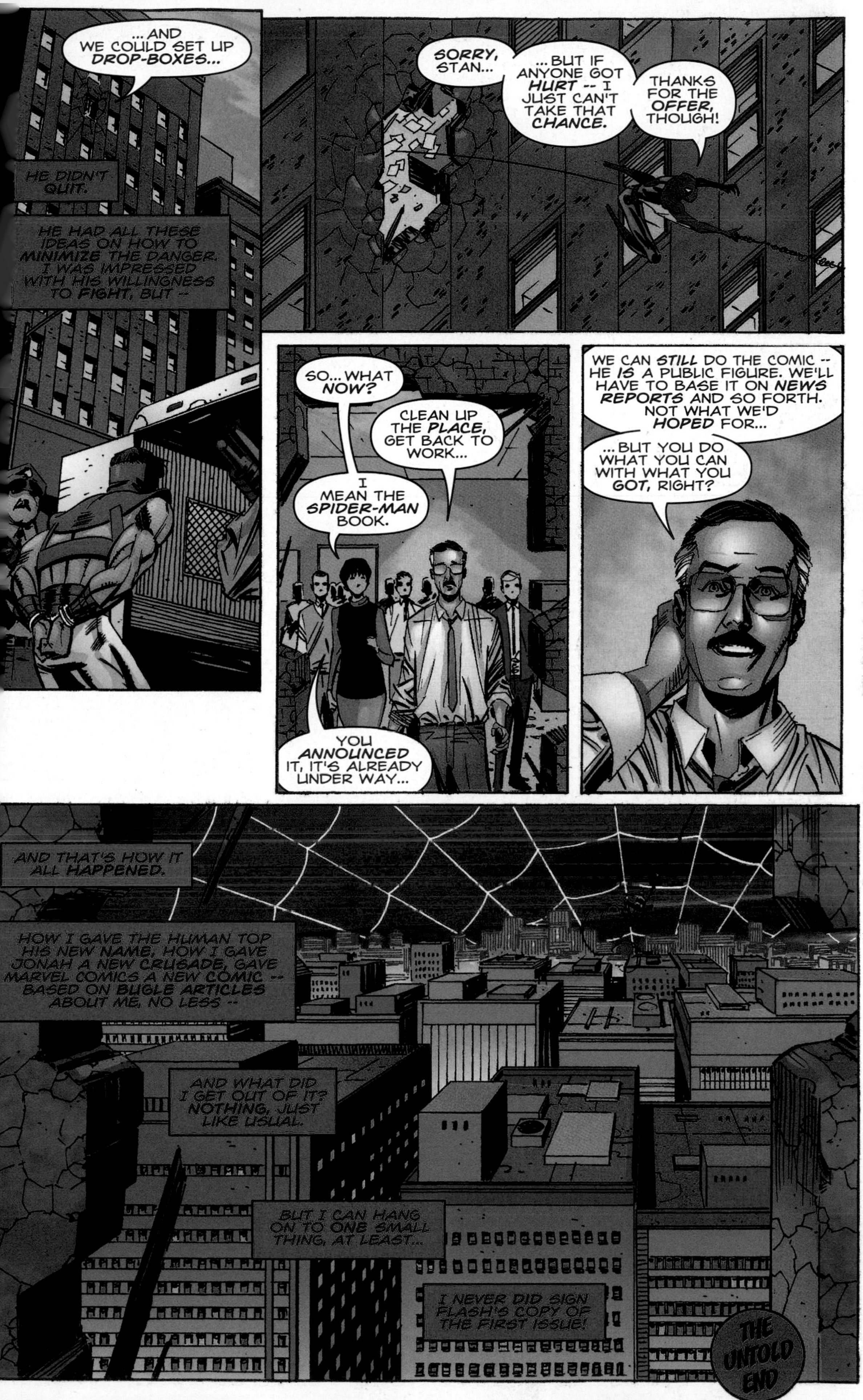
...AND WE COULD SET UP DROP-BOXES...
HE DIDN'T QUIT.
HE HAD ALL THESE IDEAS ON HOW TO MINIMIZE THE DANGER. I WAS IMPRESSED WITH HIS WILLINGNESS TO FIGHT, BUT --
SORRY, STAN...
...BUT IF ANYONE GOT HURT -- I JUST CAN'T TAKE THAT CHANCE.
THANKS FOR THE OFFER, THOUGH!
SO...WHAT NOW?
CLEAN UP THE PLACE, GET BACK TO WORK...
I MEAN THE SPIDER-MAN BOOK.
YOU ANNOUNCED IT, IT'S ALREADY UNDER WAY...
WE CAN STILL DO THE COMIC -- HE IS A PUBLIC FIGURE. WE'LL HAVE TO BASE IT ON NEWS REPORTS AND SO FORTH. NOT WHAT WE'D HOPED FOR...
...BUT YOU DO WHAT YOU CAN WITH WHAT YOU GOT, RIGHT?
AND THAT'S HOW IT ALL HAPPENED.
HOW I GAVE THE HUMAN TOP HIS NEW NAME, HOW I GAVE JONAH A NEW CRUSADE, GAVE MARVEL COMICS A NEW COMIC -- BASED ON BUGLE ARTICLES ABOUT ME, NO LESS --
AND WHAT DID I GET OUT OF IT? NOTHING, JUST LIKE USUAL.
BUT I CAN HANG ON TO ONE SMALL THING, AT LEAST...
I NEVER DID SIGN FLASH'S COPY OF THE FIRST ISSUE!
THE UNTOLD END

GOT A SHORT ATTENTION SPAN?

A BRAND NEW 12-CHAPTER SERIES WITH ONLY *TWO* PAGES A MONTH, BUT FILLED WITH ALL THE FUN AND EXCITEMENT YOU'D EXPECT IN *TWO-AND-A-HALF* PAGES A MONTH! AS USUAL, MARVEL BREAKS THE MOLD!

THEIR NICKNAMES ARE "BRAIN" AND "BULL." IF YOU CAN'T TELL WHY, YOU SHOULDN'T BE READING COMICS!

HEY, BRAIN, WHY CAN'T WE LEAVE THIS DUMP?

I AIN'T *MUGGED* NO ONE ALL WEEK!

HOW DID A GENIUS LIKE ME TEAM UP WITH SUCH AN *IGNORAMUS?*

HEY, THAT AIN'T NICE! I DON' MAKE FUN'A *YOUR* RELIGION.

HOW ABOUT I READ A *COMIC BOOK?*

NO! I NEED THEM FOR MY *INVENTION!*

YOU'RE SO CLUMSY YOU MIGHT *RIP* ONE!

THEY GOT TOO MANY *BIG* WORDS ANYWAY.

THERE! MY INVENTION IS *FINISHED!*

WHAT'JA INVENT, BRAIN?

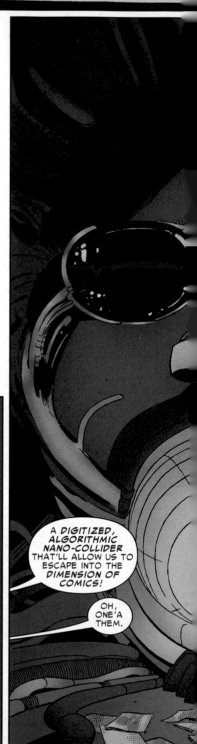

A DIGITIZED, ALGORITHMIC NANO-COLLIDER THAT'LL ALLOW US TO ESCAPE INTO THE *DIMENSION OF COMICS!*

OH, ONE'A THEM.

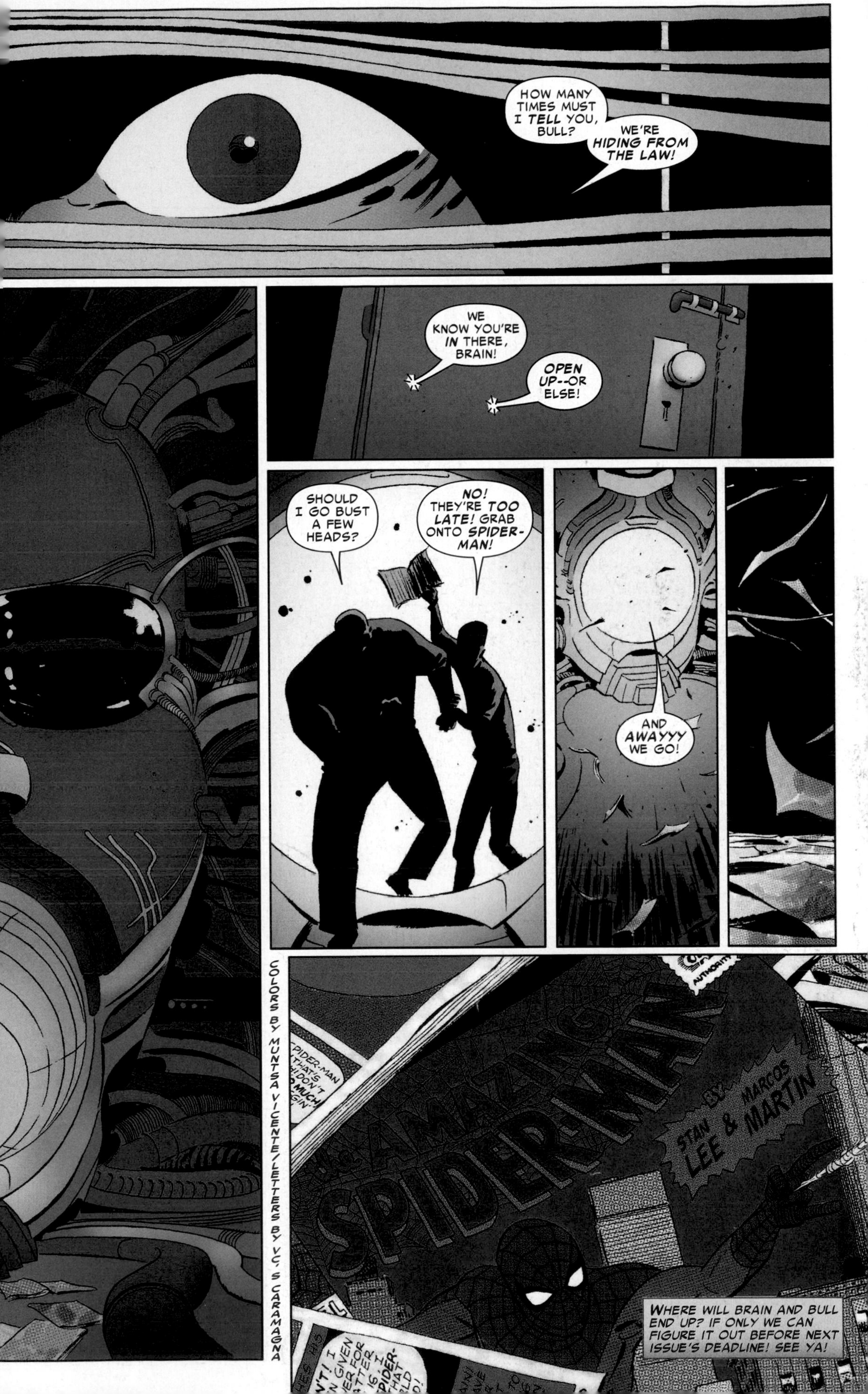
HOW MANY TIMES MUST I TELL YOU, BULL?
WE'RE HIDING FROM THE LAW!
WE KNOW YOU'RE IN THERE, BRAIN!
OPEN UP--OR ELSE!
SHOULD I GO BUST A FEW HEADS?
NO! THEY'RE TOO LATE! GRAB ONTO SPIDER-MAN!
AND AWAYYY WE GO!
COLORS BY MUNTSA VICENTE/LETTERS BY VC'S CARAMAGNA
SPIDER-MAN
STAN LEE & MARCOS MARTIN
WHERE WILL BRAIN AND BULL END UP? IF ONLY WE CAN FIGURE IT OUT BEFORE NEXT ISSUE'S DEADLINE! SEE YA!

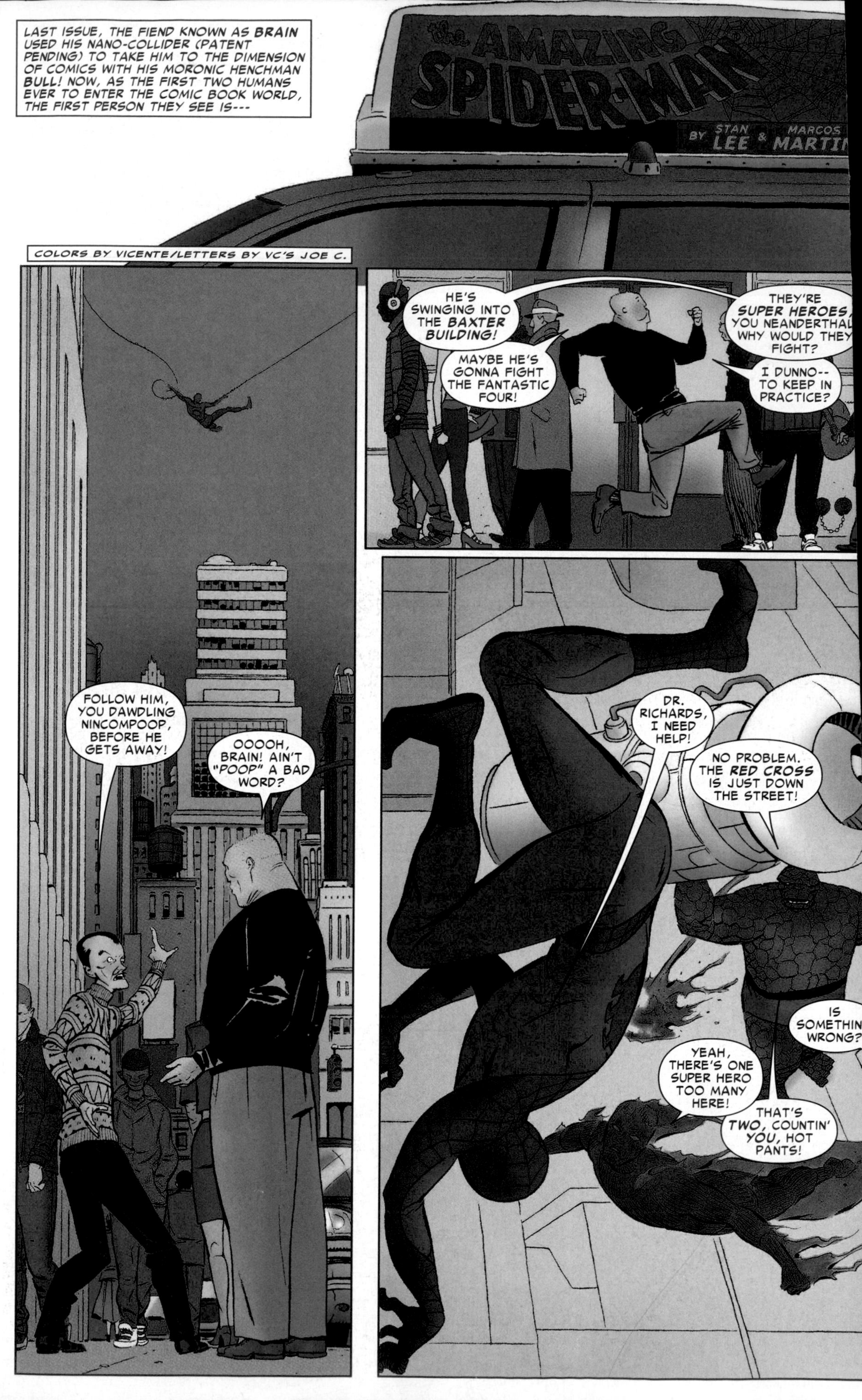
LAST ISSUE, THE FIEND KNOWN AS BRAIN USED HIS NANO-COLLIDER (PATENT PENDING) TO TAKE HIM TO THE DIMENSION OF COMICS WITH HIS MORONIC HENCHMAN BULL! NOW, AS THE FIRST TWO HUMANS EVER TO ENTER THE COMIC BOOK WORLD, THE FIRST PERSON THEY SEE IS---
THE AMAZING SPIDER-MAN
BY STAN LEE & MARCOS MARTIN
COLORS BY VICENTE/LETTERS BY VC'S JOE C.
FOLLOW HIM, YOU DAWDLING NINCOMPOOP, BEFORE HE GETS AWAY!
OOOOH, BRAIN! AIN'T "POOP" A BAD WORD?
HE'S SWINGING INTO THE BAXTER BUILDING!
MAYBE HE'S GONNA FIGHT THE FANTASTIC FOUR!
THEY'RE SUPER HEROES, YOU NEANDERTHAL! WHY WOULD THEY FIGHT?
I DUNNO-- TO KEEP IN PRACTICE?
DR. RICHARDS, I NEED HELP!
NO PROBLEM. THE RED CROSS IS JUST DOWN THE STREET!
IS SOMETHING WRONG?
YEAH, THERE'S ONE SUPER HERO TOO MANY HERE!
THAT'S TWO, COUNTIN' YOU, HOT PANTS!

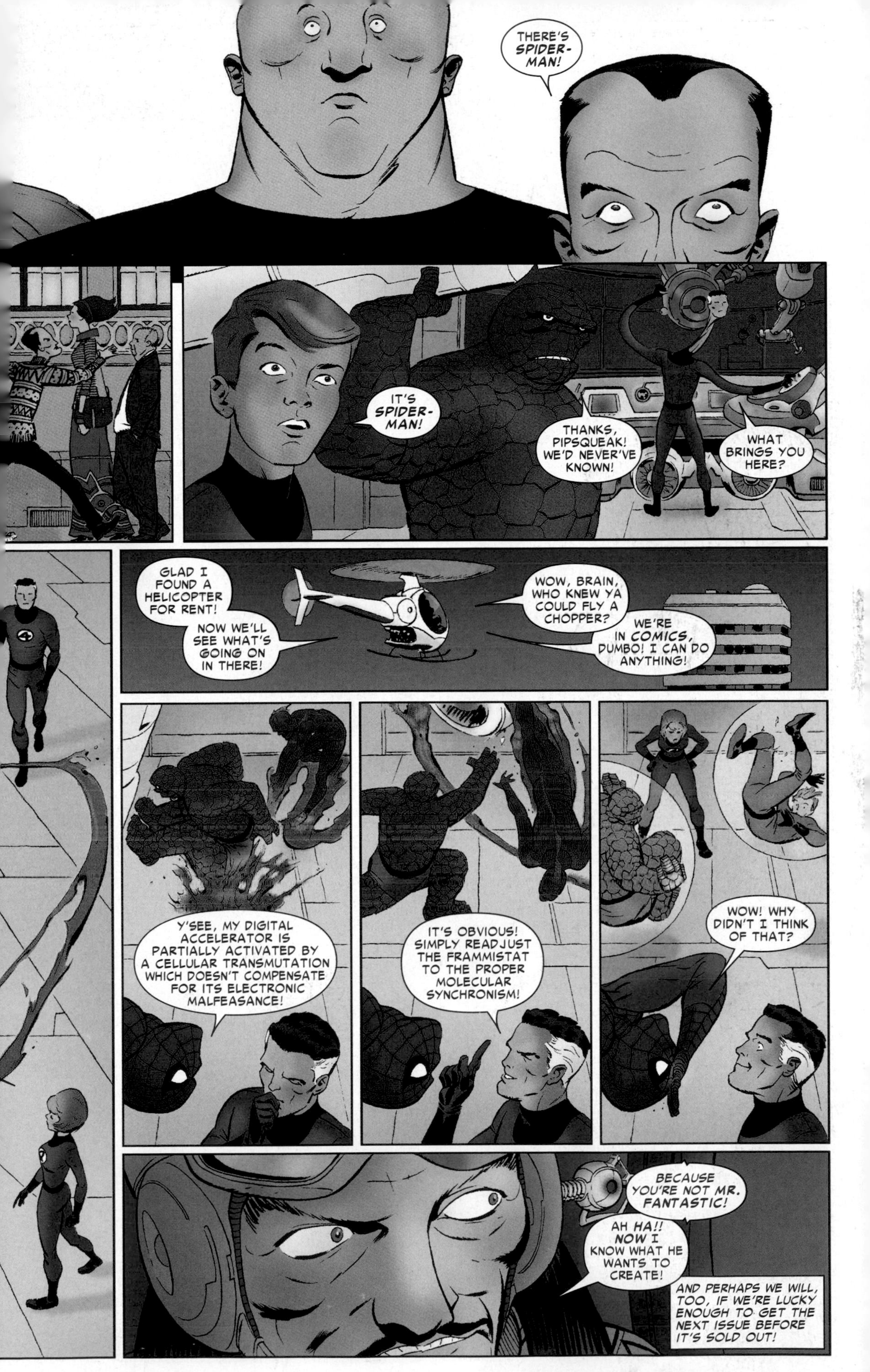
THERE'S SPIDER-MAN!
IT'S SPIDER-MAN!
THANKS, PIPSQUEAK! WE'D NEVER'VE KNOWN!
WHAT BRINGS YOU HERE?
GLAD I FOUND A HELICOPTER FOR RENT!
NOW WE'LL SEE WHAT'S GOING ON IN THERE!
WOW, BRAIN, WHO KNEW YA COULD FLY A CHOPPER?
WE'RE IN COMICS, DUMBO! I CAN DO ANYTHING!
Y'SEE, MY DIGITAL ACCELERATOR IS PARTIALLY ACTIVATED BY A CELLULAR TRANSMUTATION WHICH DOESN'T COMPENSATE FOR ITS ELECTRONIC MALFEASANCE!
IT'S OBVIOUS! SIMPLY READJUST THE FRAMMISTAT TO THE PROPER MOLECULAR SYNCHRONISM!
WOW! WHY DIDN'T I THINK OF THAT?
BECAUSE YOU'RE NOT MR. FANTASTIC!
AH HA!! NOW I KNOW WHAT HE WANTS TO CREATE!
AND PERHAPS WE WILL, TOO, IF WE'RE LUCKY ENOUGH TO GET THE NEXT ISSUE BEFORE IT'S SOLD OUT!

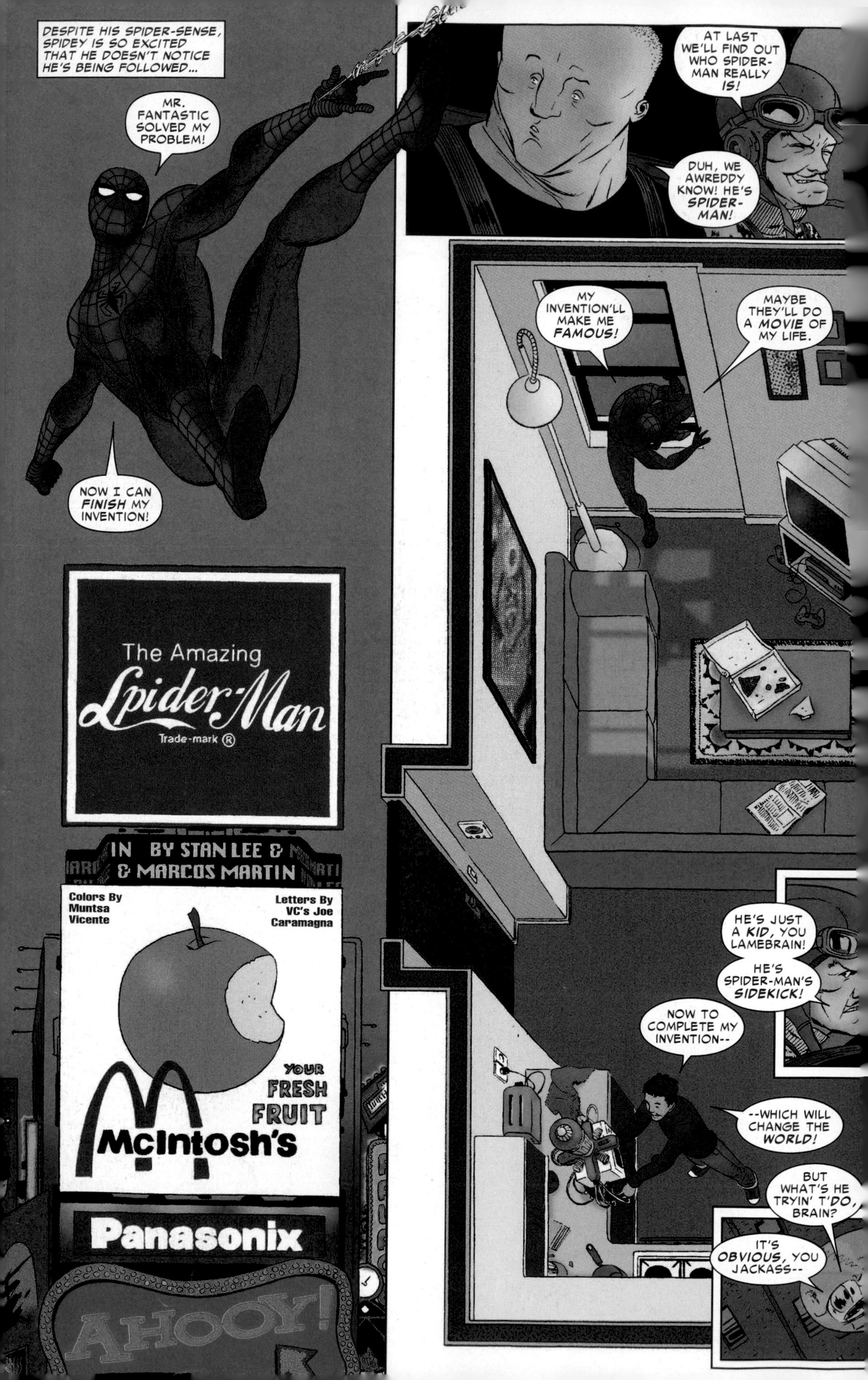

DESPITE HIS SPIDER-SENSE, SPIDEY IS SO EXCITED THAT HE DOESN'T NOTICE HE'S BEING FOLLOWED...
MR. FANTASTIC SOLVED MY PROBLEM!
NOW I CAN FINISH MY INVENTION!
AT LAST WE'LL FIND OUT WHO SPIDER-MAN REALLY IS!
DUH, WE AWREDDY KNOW! HE'S SPIDER-MAN!
MY INVENTION'LL MAKE ME FAMOUS!
MAYBE THEY'LL DO A MOVIE OF MY LIFE.
The Amazing
Spider-Man
Trade-mark ®
IN BY STAN LEE &
& MARCOS MARTIN
Colors By Muntsa Vicente
Letters By VC's Joe Caramagna
YOUR FRESH FRUIT
McIntosh's
Panasonix
AHOOY!
HE'S JUST A KID, YOU LAMEBRAIN!
HE'S SPIDER-MAN'S SIDEKICK!
NOW TO COMPLETE MY INVENTION--
--WHICH WILL CHANGE THE WORLD!
BUT WHAT'S HE TRYIN' T'DO, BRAIN?
IT'S OBVIOUS, YOU JACKASS--

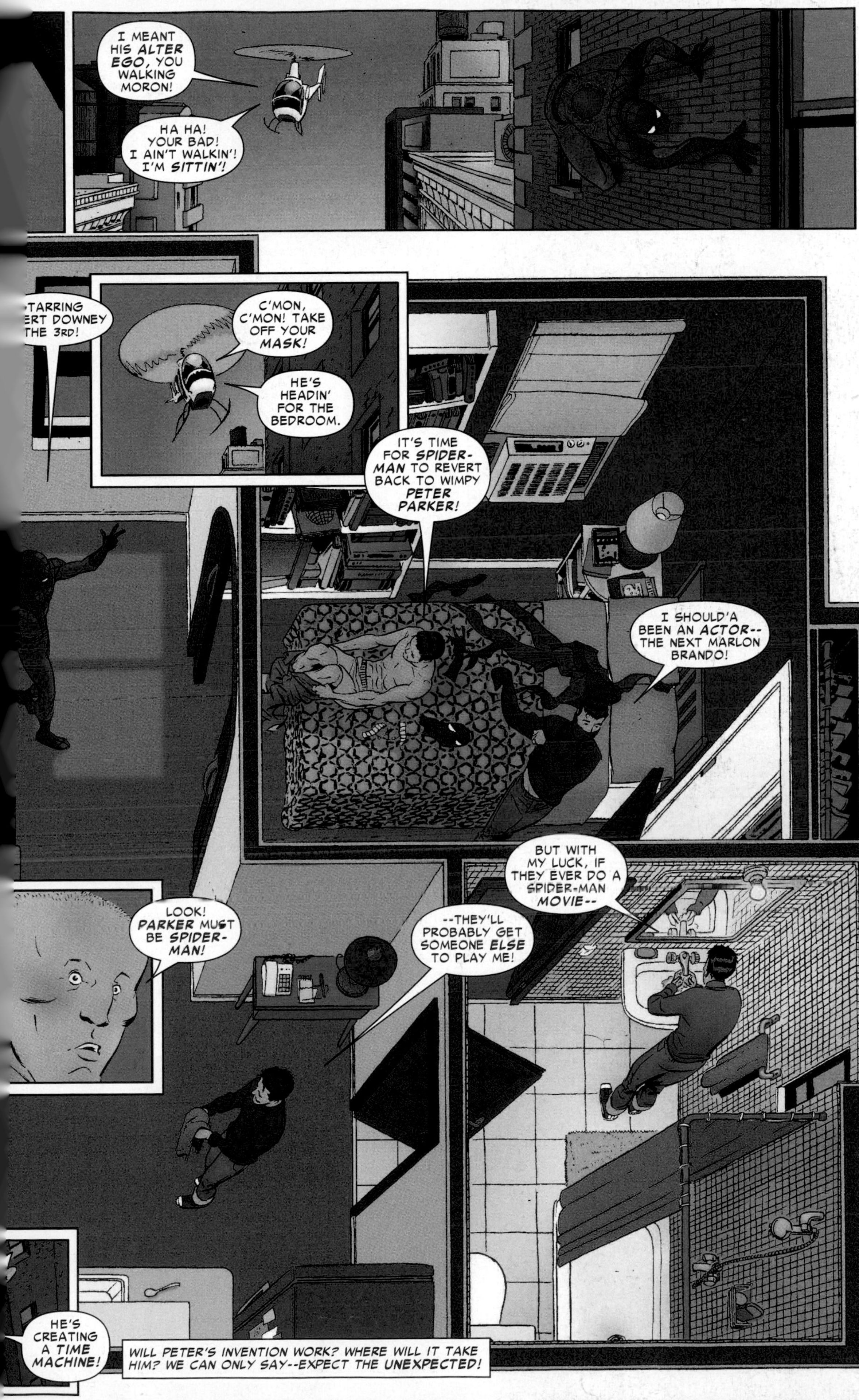
I MEANT HIS ALTER EGO, YOU WALKING MORON!
HA HA! YOUR BAD! I AIN'T WALKIN'! I'M SITTIN'!
STARRING ERT DOWNEY THE 3RD!
C'MON, C'MON! TAKE OFF YOUR MASK!
HE'S HEADIN' FOR THE BEDROOM.
IT'S TIME FOR SPIDER-MAN TO REVERT BACK TO WIMPY PETER PARKER!
I SHOULD'A BEEN AN ACTOR-- THE NEXT MARLON BRANDO!
BUT WITH MY LUCK, IF THEY EVER DO A SPIDER-MAN MOVIE--
--THEY'LL PROBABLY GET SOMEONE ELSE TO PLAY ME!
LOOK! PARKER MUST BE SPIDER-MAN!
HE'S CREATING A TIME MACHINE!
WILL PETER'S INVENTION WORK? WHERE WILL IT TAKE HIM? WE CAN ONLY SAY--EXPECT THE UNEXPECTED!

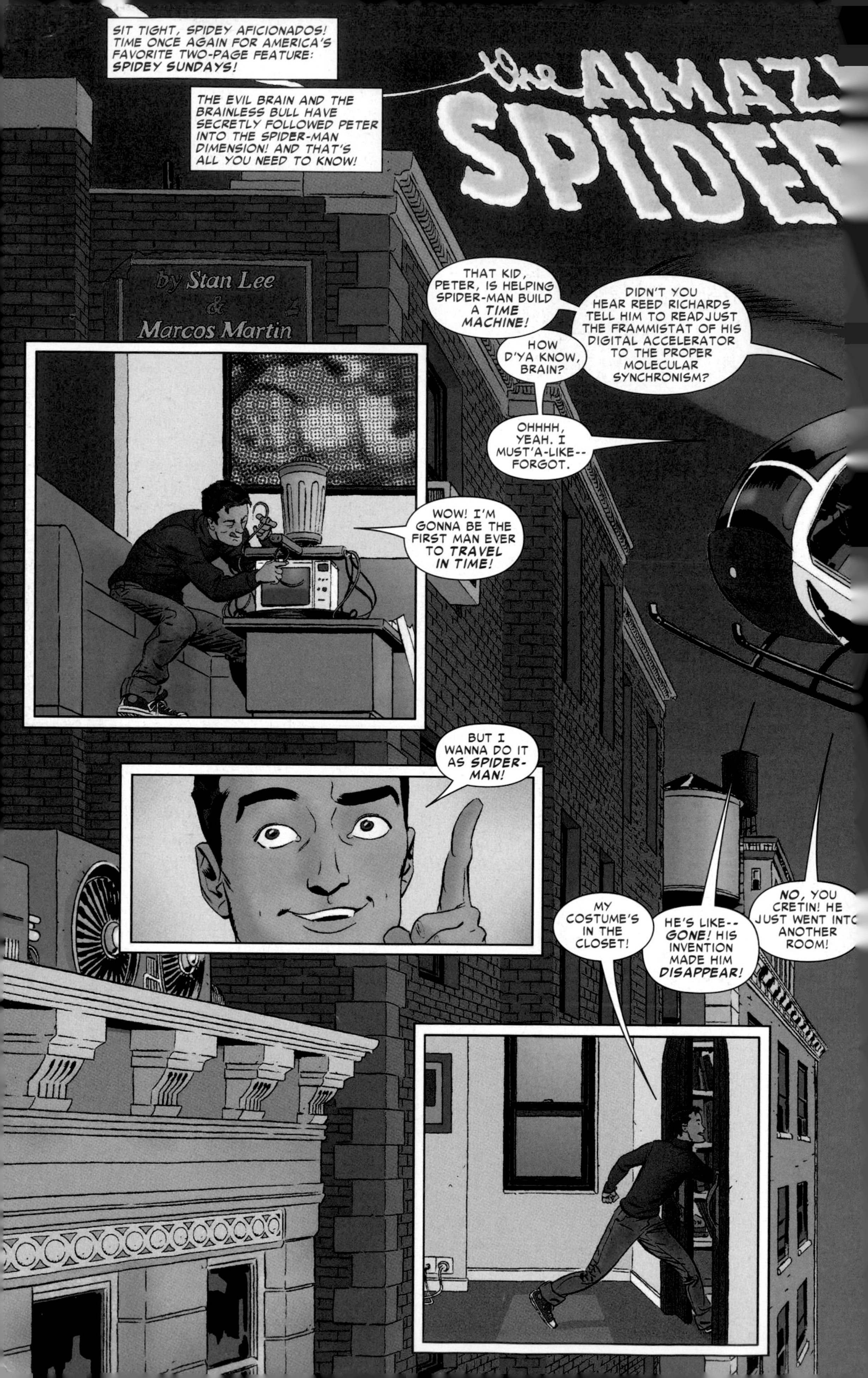
SIT TIGHT, SPIDEY AFICIONADOS! TIME ONCE AGAIN FOR AMERICA'S FAVORITE TWO-PAGE FEATURE: SPIDEY SUNDAYS!
THE EVIL BRAIN AND THE BRAINLESS BULL HAVE SECRETLY FOLLOWED PETER INTO THE SPIDER-MAN DIMENSION! AND THAT'S ALL YOU NEED TO KNOW!
The AMAZ SPIDE
by Stan Lee & Marcos Martin
THAT KID, PETER, IS HELPING SPIDER-MAN BUILD A TIME MACHINE!
HOW D'YA KNOW, BRAIN?
DIDN'T YOU HEAR REED RICHARDS TELL HIM TO READJUST THE FRAMMISTAT OF HIS DIGITAL ACCELERATOR TO THE PROPER MOLECULAR SYNCHRONISM?
OHHHH, YEAH. I MUST'A-LIKE--FORGOT.
WOW! I'M GONNA BE THE FIRST MAN EVER TO TRAVEL IN TIME!
BUT I WANNA DO IT AS SPIDER-MAN!
MY COSTUME'S IN THE CLOSET!
HE'S LIKE--GONE! HIS INVENTION MADE HIM DISAPPEAR!
NO, YOU CRETIN! HE JUST WENT INTO ANOTHER ROOM!

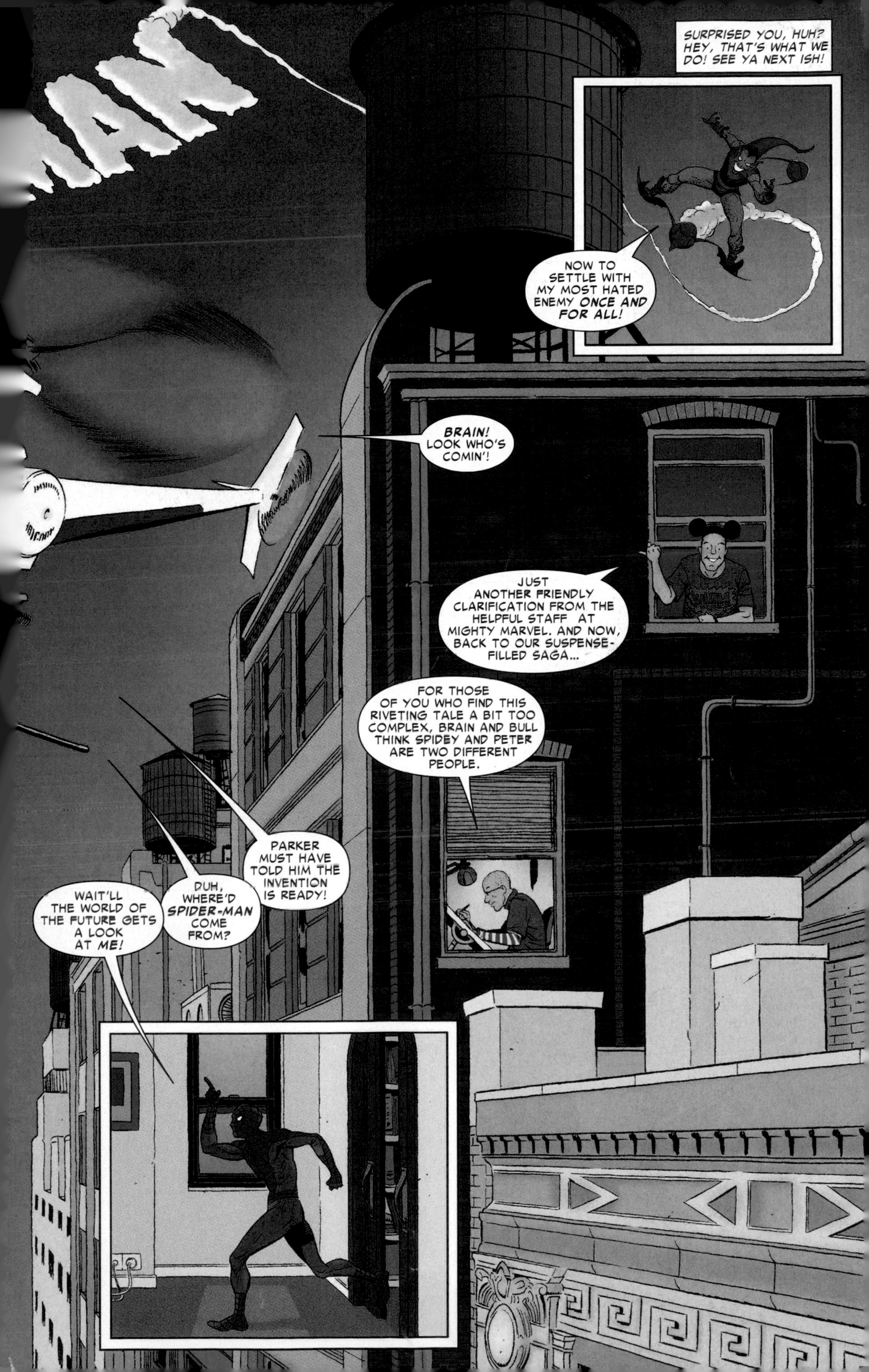

MAN
SURPRISED YOU, HUH? HEY, THAT'S WHAT WE DO! SEE YA NEXT ISH!
NOW TO SETTLE WITH MY MOST HATED ENEMY ONCE AND FOR ALL!
BRAIN! LOOK WHO'S COMIN'!
JUST ANOTHER FRIENDLY CLARIFICATION FROM THE HELPFUL STAFF AT MIGHTY MARVEL. AND NOW, BACK TO OUR SUSPENSE-FILLED SAGA...
FOR THOSE OF YOU WHO FIND THIS RIVETING TALE A BIT TOO COMPLEX, BRAIN AND BULL THINK SPIDEY AND PETER ARE TWO DIFFERENT PEOPLE.
PARKER MUST HAVE TOLD HIM THE INVENTION IS READY!
DUH, WHERE'D SPIDER-MAN COME FROM?
WAIT'LL THE WORLD OF THE FUTURE GETS A LOOK AT ME!

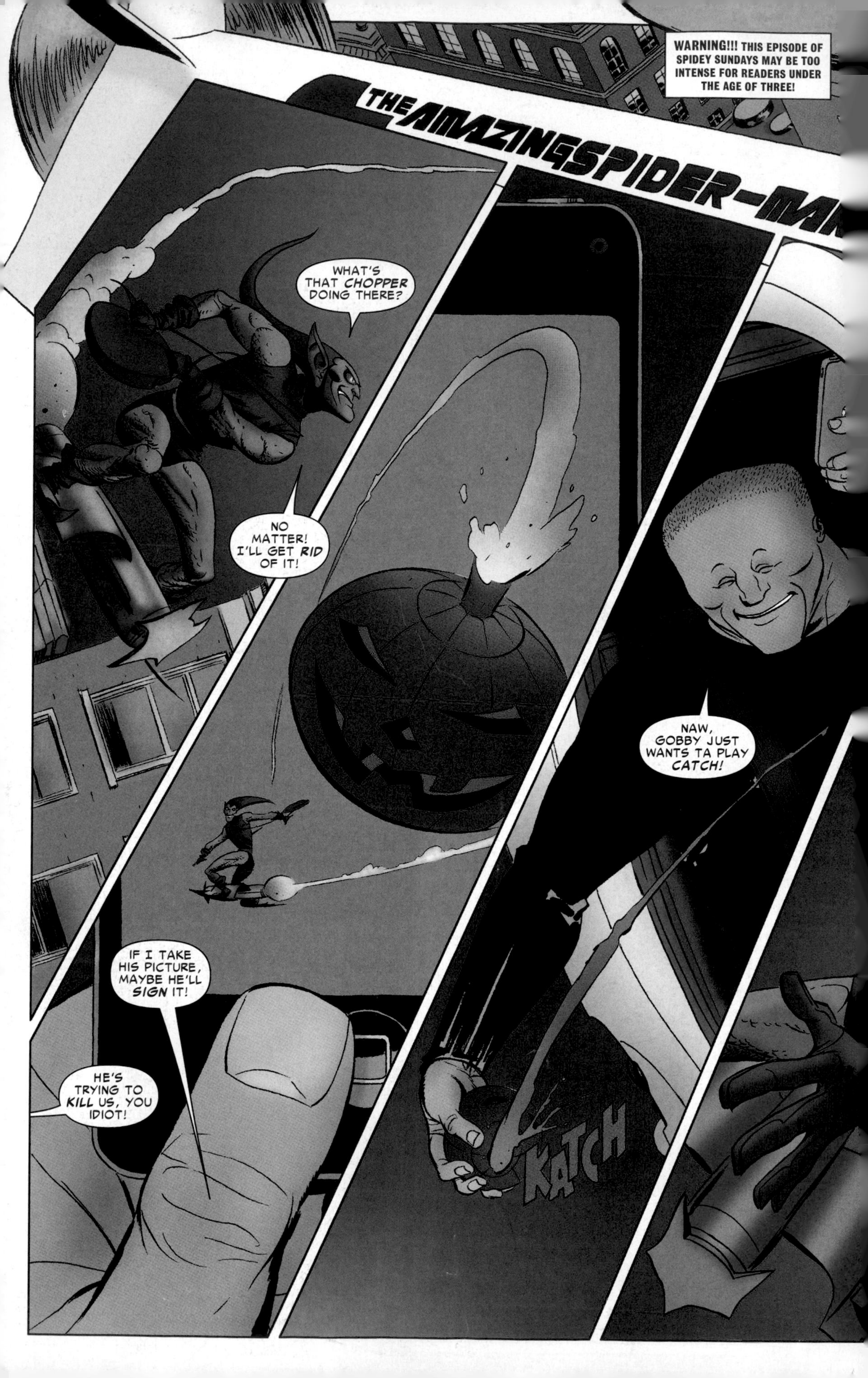
WARNING!!! THIS EPISODE OF SPIDEY SUNDAYS MAY BE TOO INTENSE FOR READERS UNDER THE AGE OF THREE!
THE AMAZING SPIDER-MAN
WHAT'S THAT CHOPPER DOING THERE?
NO MATTER! I'LL GET RID OF IT!
IF I TAKE HIS PICTURE, MAYBE HE'LL SIGN IT!
HE'S TRYING TO KILL US, YOU IDIOT!
NAW, GOBBY JUST WANTS TA PLAY CATCH!
KATCH

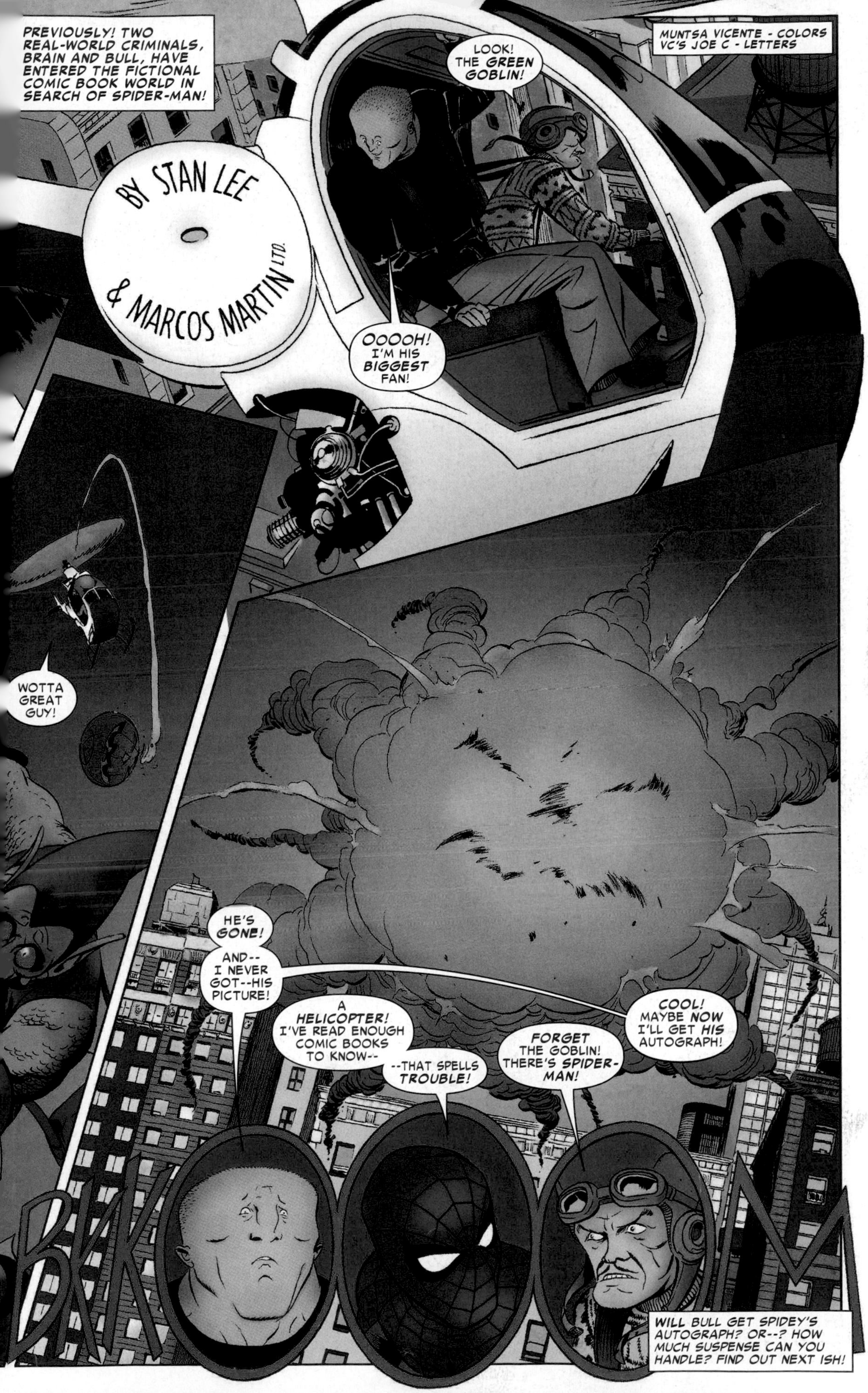

PREVIOUSLY! TWO REAL-WORLD CRIMINALS, BRAIN AND BULL, HAVE ENTERED THE FICTIONAL COMIC BOOK WORLD IN SEARCH OF SPIDER-MAN!
MUNTSA VICENTE - COLORS
VC'S JOE C - LETTERS
LOOK! THE GREEN GOBLIN!
BY STAN LEE & MARCOS MARTIN LTD.
OOOOH! I'M HIS BIGGEST FAN!
WOTTA GREAT GUY!
HE'S GONE!
AND-- I NEVER GOT--HIS PICTURE!
A HELICOPTER! I'VE READ ENOUGH COMIC BOOKS TO KNOW--
--THAT SPELLS TROUBLE!
FORGET THE GOBLIN! THERE'S SPIDER-MAN!
COOL! MAYBE NOW I'LL GET HIS AUTOGRAPH!
BKKOOOM
WILL BULL GET SPIDEY'S AUTOGRAPH? OR--? HOW MUCH SUSPENSE CAN YOU HANDLE? FIND OUT NEXT ISH!

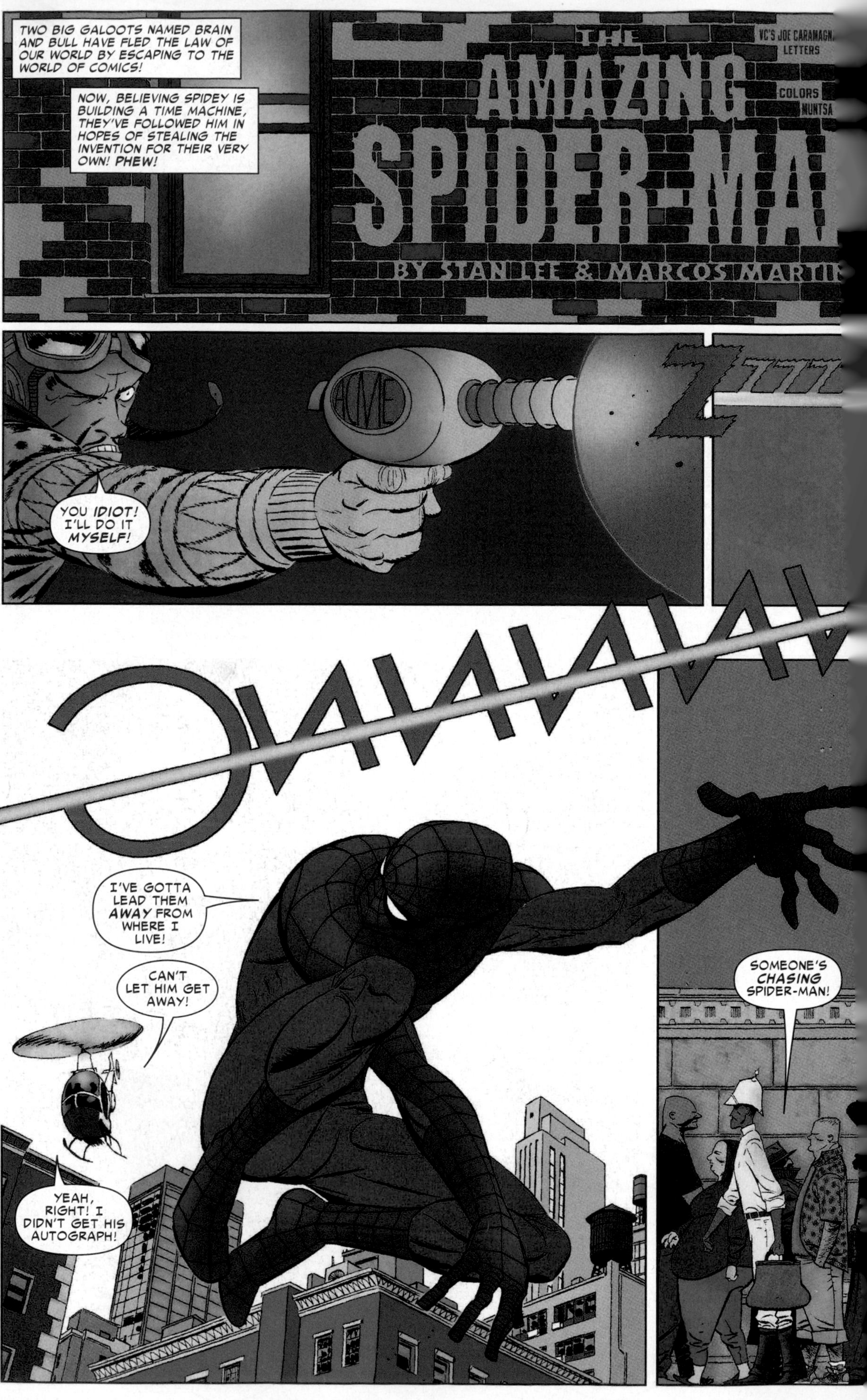
TWO BIG GALOOTS NAMED BRAIN AND BULL HAVE FLED THE LAW OF OUR WORLD BY ESCAPING TO THE WORLD OF COMICS!
NOW, BELIEVING SPIDEY IS BUILDING A TIME MACHINE, THEY'VE FOLLOWED HIM IN HOPES OF STEALING THE INVENTION FOR THEIR VERY OWN! PHEW!
THE AMAZING SPIDER-MA
BY STAN LEE & MARCOS MARTI
VC'S JOE CARAMAGN
LETTERS
COLORS
MUNTSA
ACME
YOU IDIOT! I'LL DO IT MYSELF!
I'VE GOTTA LEAD THEM AWAY FROM WHERE I LIVE!
CAN'T LET HIM GET AWAY!
YEAH, RIGHT! I DIDN'T GET HIS AUTOGRAPH!
SOMEONE'S CHASING SPIDER-MAN!

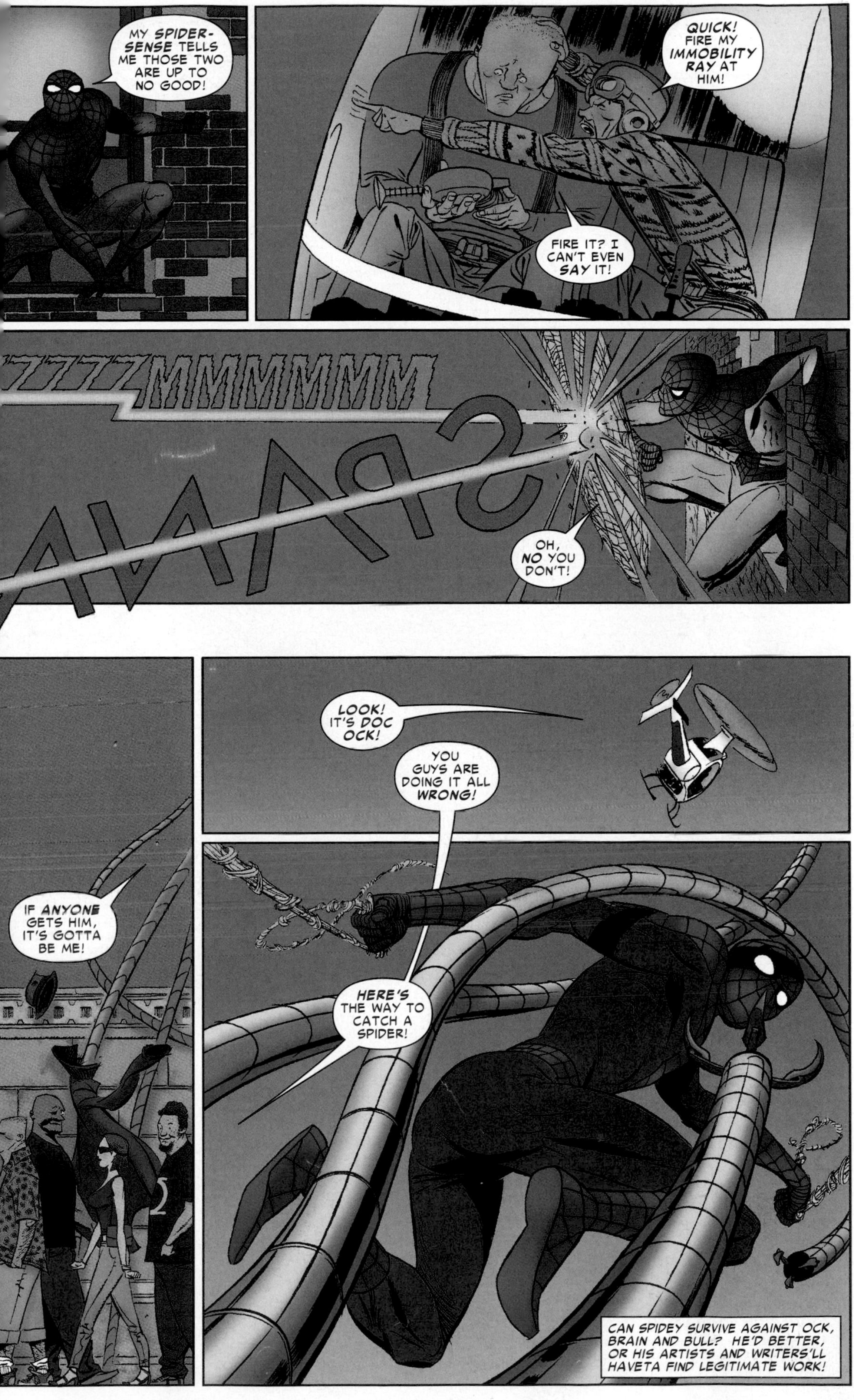
MY SPIDER-SENSE TELLS ME THOSE TWO ARE UP TO NO GOOD!
QUICK! FIRE MY IMMOBILITY RAY AT HIM!
FIRE IT? I CAN'T EVEN SAY IT!
OH, NO YOU DON'T!
IF ANYONE GETS HIM, IT'S GOTTA BE ME!
LOOK! IT'S DOC OCK!
YOU GUYS ARE DOING IT ALL WRONG!
HERE'S THE WAY TO CATCH A SPIDER!
CAN SPIDEY SURVIVE AGAINST OCK, BRAIN AND BULL? HE'D BETTER, OR HIS ARTISTS AND WRITERS'LL HAVETA FIND LEGITIMATE WORK!

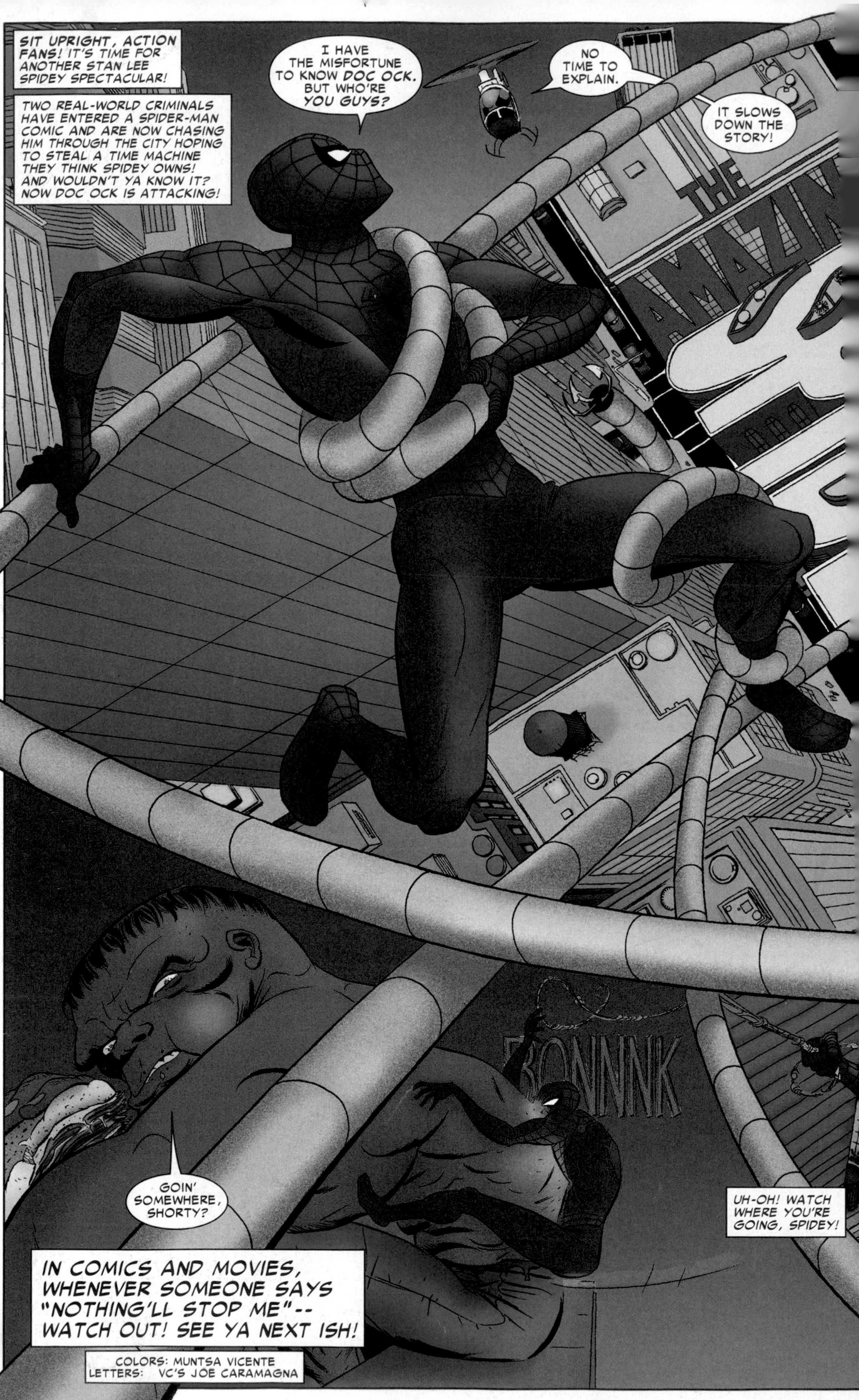
SIT UPRIGHT, ACTION FANS! IT'S TIME FOR ANOTHER STAN LEE SPIDEY SPECTACULAR!
TWO REAL-WORLD CRIMINALS HAVE ENTERED A SPIDER-MAN COMIC AND ARE NOW CHASING HIM THROUGH THE CITY HOPING TO STEAL A TIME MACHINE THEY THINK SPIDEY OWNS! AND WOULDN'T YA KNOW IT? NOW DOC OCK IS ATTACKING!
I HAVE THE MISFORTUNE TO KNOW DOC OCK. BUT WHO'RE YOU GUYS?
NO TIME TO EXPLAIN.
IT SLOWS DOWN THE STORY!
BONNNK
GOIN' SOMEWHERE, SHORTY?
UH-OH! WATCH WHERE YOU'RE GOING, SPIDEY!
IN COMICS AND MOVIES, WHENEVER SOMEONE SAYS "NOTHING'LL STOP ME"-- WATCH OUT! SEE YA NEXT ISH!
COLORS: MUNTSA VICENTE
LETTERS: VC'S JOE CARAMAGNA

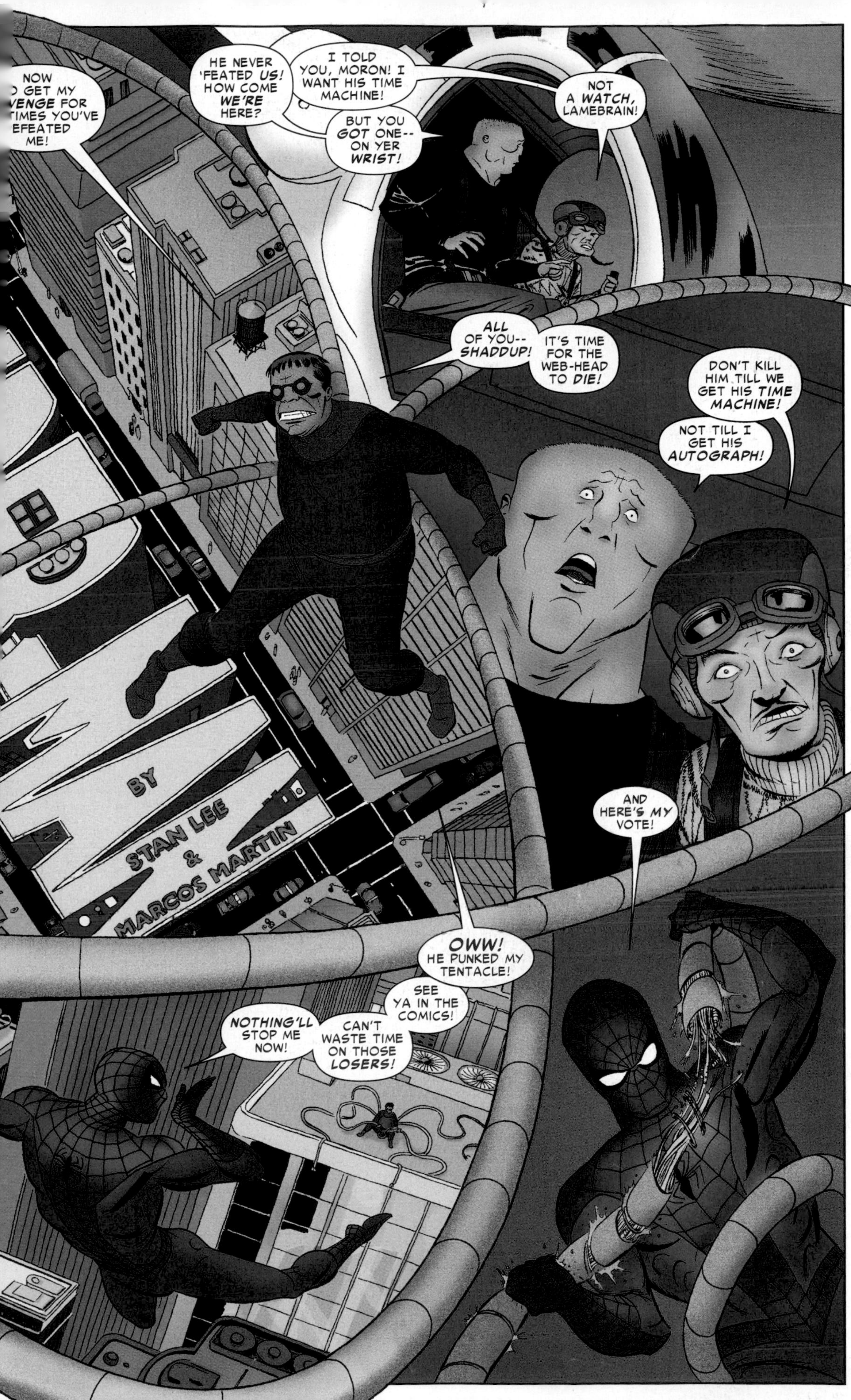
NOW
D GET MY
VENGE FOR
TIMES YOU'VE
EFEATED
ME!
HE NEVER 'FEATED *US!* HOW COME *WE'RE* HERE?
I TOLD YOU, MORON! I WANT HIS TIME MACHINE!
BUT YOU *GOT* ONE-- ON YER *WRIST!*
NOT A *WATCH,* LAMEBRAIN!
ALL OF YOU-- *SHADDUP!*
IT'S TIME FOR THE WEB-HEAD TO *DIE!*
DON'T KILL HIM TILL WE GET HIS *TIME MACHINE!*
NOT TILL I GET HIS *AUTOGRAPH!*
BY
STAN LEE
&
MARCOS MARTIN
AND HERE'S *MY* VOTE!
OWW! HE PUNKED MY TENTACLE!
SEE YA IN THE COMICS!
CAN'T WASTE TIME ON THOSE *LOSERS!*
NOTHING'LL STOP ME NOW!

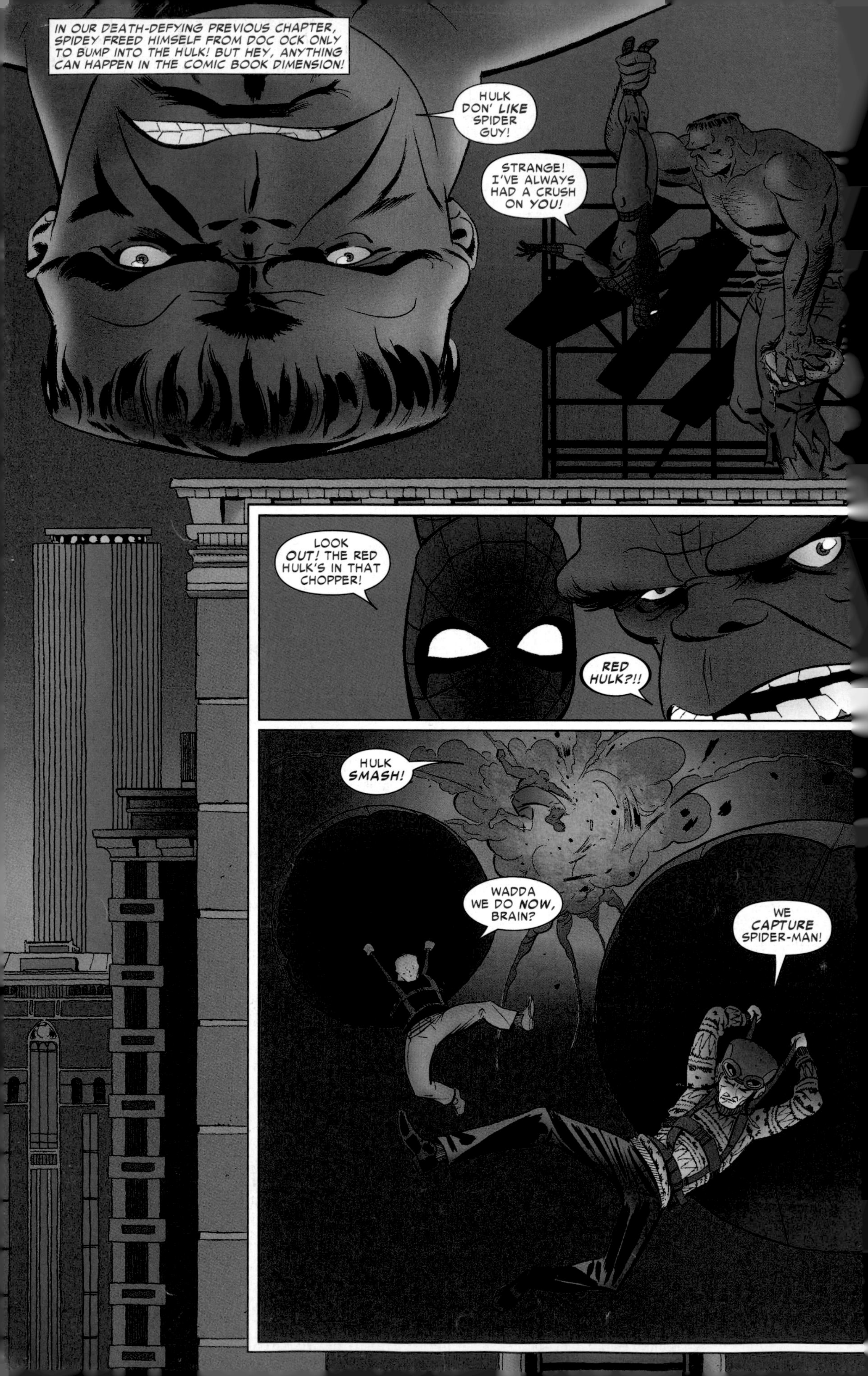
IN OUR DEATH-DEFYING PREVIOUS CHAPTER, SPIDEY FREED HIMSELF FROM DOC OCK ONLY TO BUMP INTO THE HULK! BUT HEY, ANYTHING CAN HAPPEN IN THE COMIC BOOK DIMENSION!
HULK DON' LIKE SPIDER GUY!
STRANGE! I'VE ALWAYS HAD A CRUSH ON YOU!
LOOK OUT! THE RED HULK'S IN THAT CHOPPER!
RED HULK?!!
HULK SMASH!
WADDA WE DO NOW, BRAIN?
WE CAPTURE SPIDER-MAN!

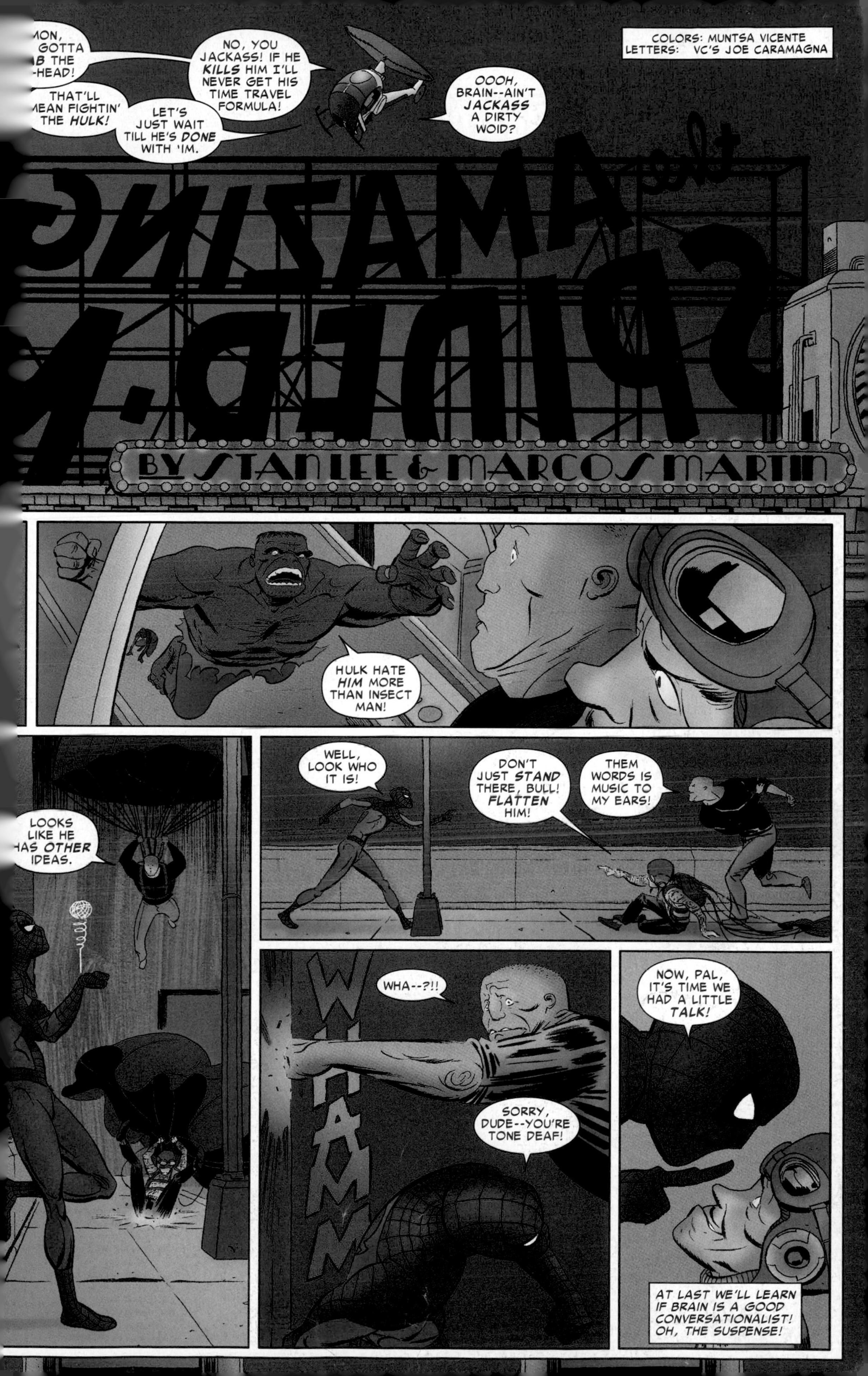
COLORS: MUNTSA VICENTE
LETTERS: VC'S JOE CARAMAGNA
MON, GOTTA B THE -HEAD!
THAT'LL MEAN FIGHTIN' THE HULK!
NO, YOU JACKASS! IF HE KILLS HIM I'LL NEVER GET HIS TIME TRAVEL FORMULA!
LET'S JUST WAIT TILL HE'S DONE WITH 'IM.
OOOH, BRAIN--AIN'T JACKASS A DIRTY WOID?
BY STAN LEE & MARCOS MARTIN
HULK HATE HIM MORE THAN INSECT MAN!
LOOKS LIKE HE HAS OTHER IDEAS.
WELL, LOOK WHO IT IS!
DON'T JUST STAND THERE, BULL! FLATTEN HIM!
THEM WORDS IS MUSIC TO MY EARS!
WHAMM
WHA--?!!
SORRY, DUDE--YOU'RE TONE DEAF!
NOW, PAL, IT'S TIME WE HAD A LITTLE TALK!
AT LAST WE'LL LEARN IF BRAIN IS A GOOD CONVERSATIONALIST! OH, THE SUSPENSE!

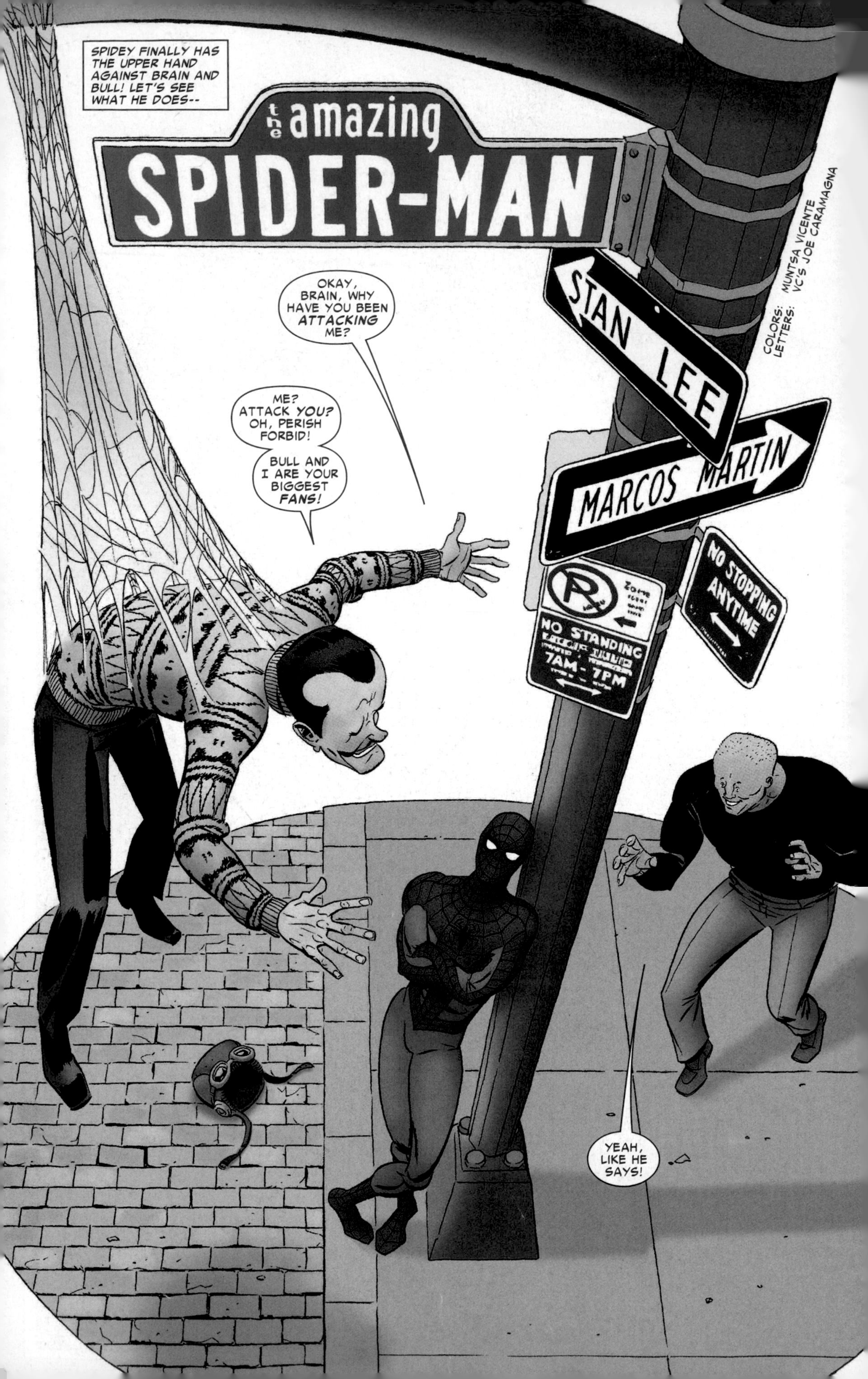
SPIDEY FINALLY HAS THE UPPER HAND AGAINST BRAIN AND BULL! LET'S SEE WHAT HE DOES--
the amazing SPIDER-MAN
STAN LEE
MARCOS MARTIN
COLORS: MUNTSA VICENTE
LETTERS: VC'S JOE CARAMAGNA
OKAY, BRAIN, WHY HAVE YOU BEEN ATTACKING ME?
ME? ATTACK YOU? OH, PERISH FORBID!
BULL AND I ARE YOUR BIGGEST FANS!
NO STOPPING ANYTIME
NO STANDING
7AM - 7PM
YEAH, LIKE HE SAYS!

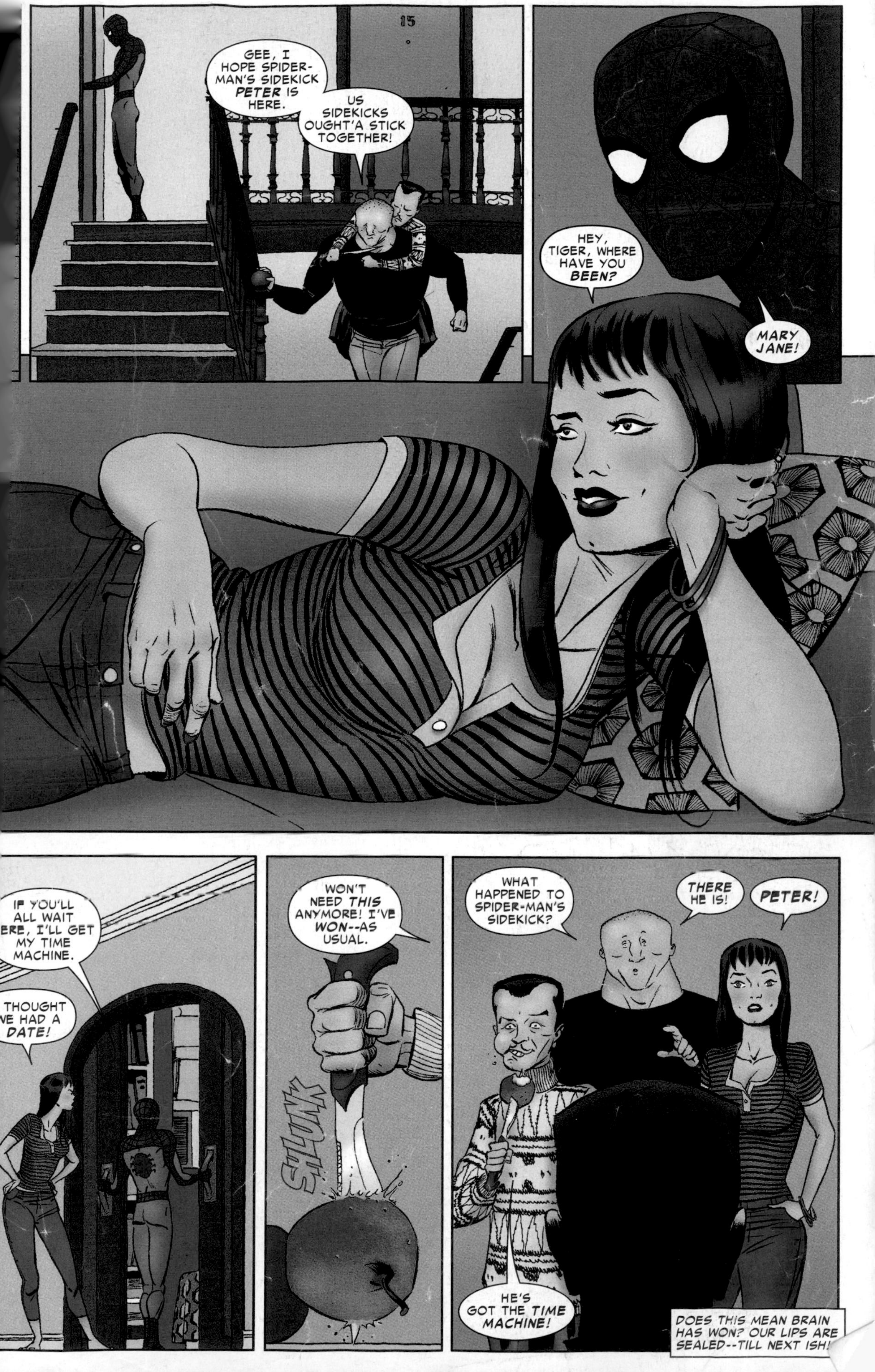
15
GEE, I HOPE SPIDER-MAN'S SIDEKICK PETER IS HERE.
US SIDEKICKS OUGHT'A STICK TOGETHER!
HEY, TIGER, WHERE HAVE YOU BEEN?
MARY JANE!
IF YOU'LL ALL WAIT ERE, I'LL GET MY TIME MACHINE.
THOUGHT WE HAD A DATE!
WON'T NEED THIS ANYMORE! I'VE WON--AS USUAL.
SHUNK
WHAT HAPPENED TO SPIDER-MAN'S SIDEKICK?
THERE HE IS!
PETER!
HE'S GOT THE TIME MACHINE!
DOES THIS MEAN BRAIN HAS WON? OUR LIPS ARE SEALED--TILL NEXT ISH!

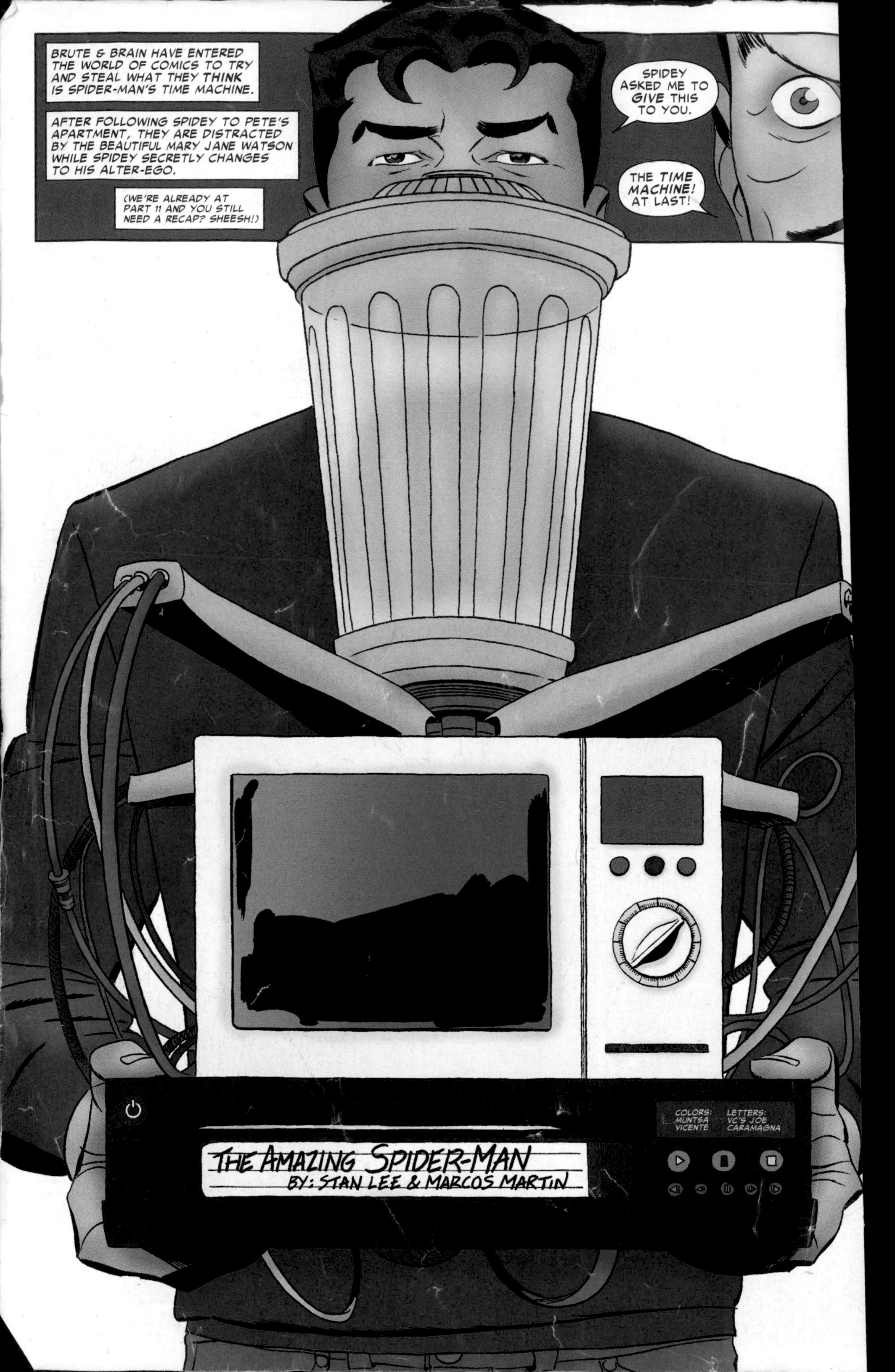
BRUTE & BRAIN HAVE ENTERED THE WORLD OF COMICS TO TRY AND STEAL WHAT THEY THINK IS SPIDER-MAN'S TIME MACHINE.
AFTER FOLLOWING SPIDEY TO PETE'S APARTMENT, THEY ARE DISTRACTED BY THE BEAUTIFUL MARY JANE WATSON WHILE SPIDEY SECRETLY CHANGES TO HIS ALTER-EGO.
(WE'RE ALREADY AT PART 11 AND YOU STILL NEED A RECAP? SHEESH!)
SPIDEY ASKED ME TO GIVE THIS TO YOU.
THE TIME MACHINE! AT LAST!
COLORS: MUNTSA VICENTE
LETTERS: VC'S JOE CARAMAGNA
THE AMAZING SPIDER-MAN
BY: STAN LEE & MARCOS MARTIN

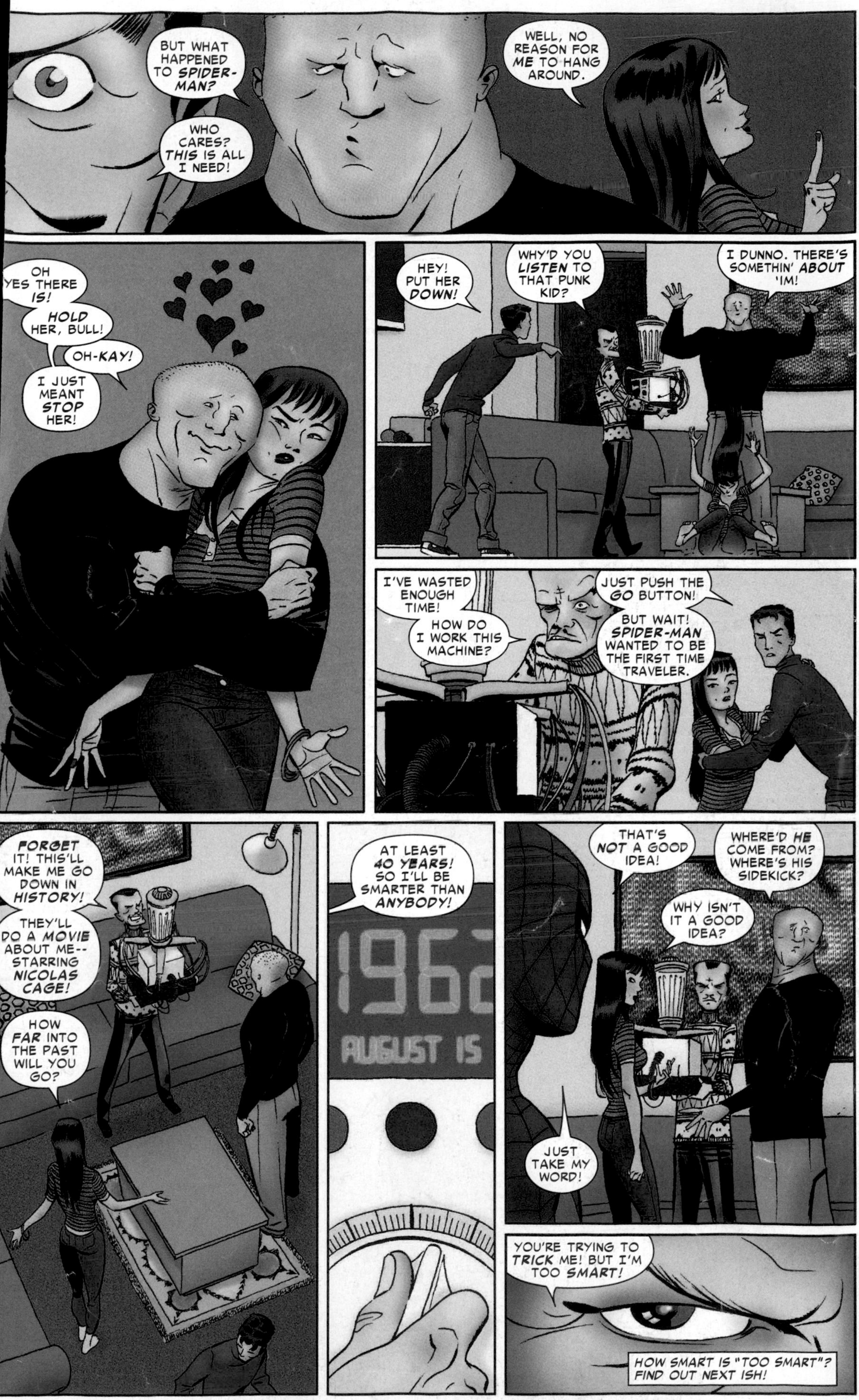
BUT WHAT HAPPENED TO SPIDER-MAN?
WHO CARES? THIS IS ALL I NEED!
WELL, NO REASON FOR ME TO HANG AROUND.
OH YES THERE IS! HOLD HER, BULL!
OH-KAY!
I JUST MEANT STOP HER!
HEY! PUT HER DOWN!
WHY'D YOU LISTEN TO THAT PUNK KID?
I DUNNO. THERE'S SOMETHIN' ABOUT 'IM!
I'VE WASTED ENOUGH TIME!
HOW DO I WORK THIS MACHINE?
JUST PUSH THE GO BUTTON!
BUT WAIT! SPIDER-MAN WANTED TO BE THE FIRST TIME TRAVELER.
FORGET IT! THIS'LL MAKE ME GO DOWN IN HISTORY!
THEY'LL DO A MOVIE ABOUT ME-- STARRING NICOLAS CAGE!
HOW FAR INTO THE PAST WILL YOU GO?
AT LEAST 40 YEARS! SO I'LL BE SMARTER THAN ANYBODY!
1962
AUGUST 15
THAT'S NOT A GOOD IDEA!
WHERE'D HE COME FROM? WHERE'S HIS SIDEKICK?
WHY ISN'T IT A GOOD IDEA?
JUST TAKE MY WORD!
YOU'RE TRYING TO TRICK ME! BUT I'M TOO SMART!
HOW SMART IS "TOO SMART"? FIND OUT NEXT ISH!

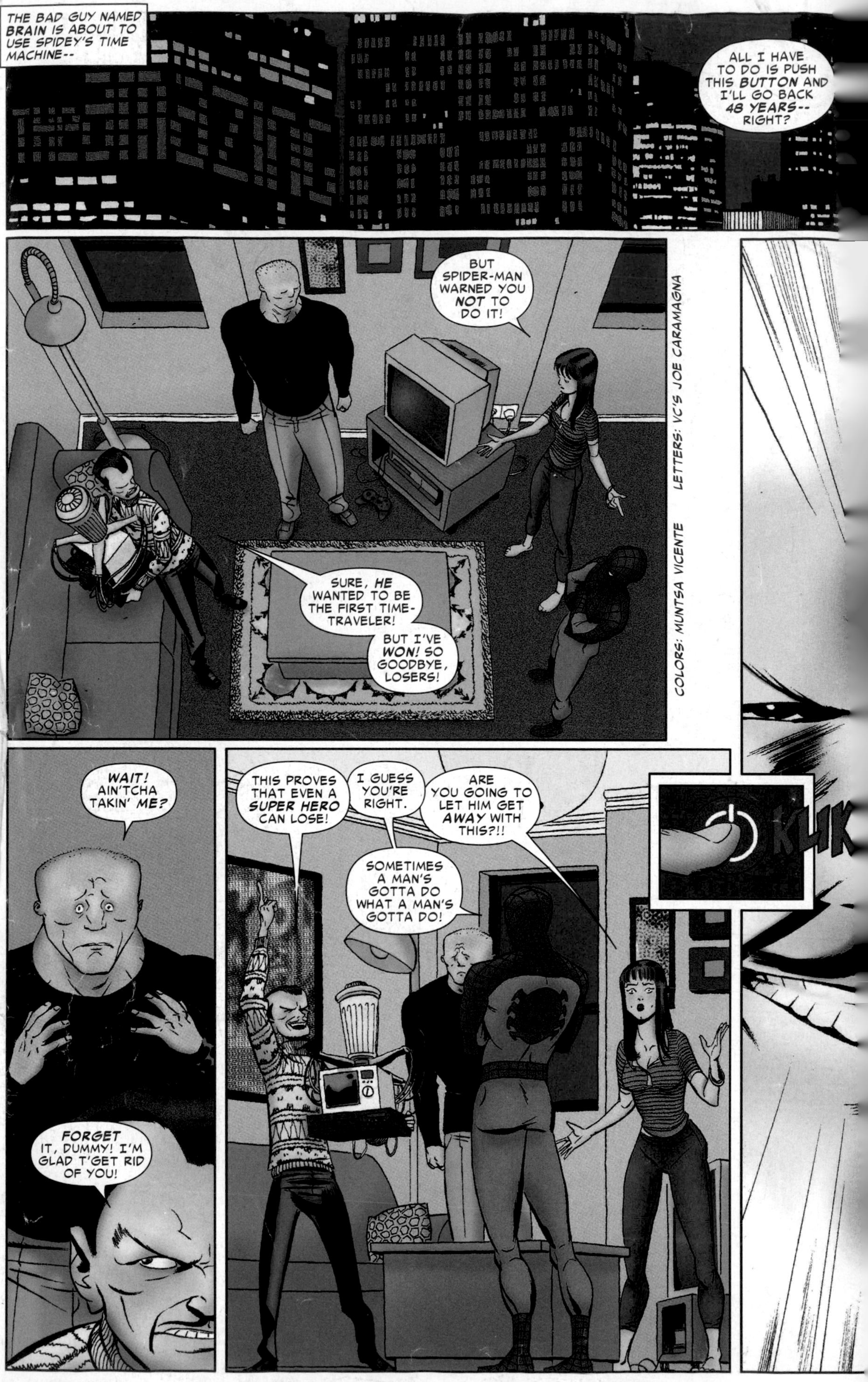
THE BAD GUY NAMED BRAIN IS ABOUT TO USE SPIDEY'S TIME MACHINE--
ALL I HAVE TO DO IS PUSH THIS BUTTON AND I'LL GO BACK 48 YEARS-- RIGHT?
BUT SPIDER-MAN WARNED YOU NOT TO DO IT!
SURE, HE WANTED TO BE THE FIRST TIME-TRAVELER!
BUT I'VE WON! SO GOODBYE, LOSERS!
COLORS: MUNTSA VICENTE LETTERS: VC'S JOE CARAMAGNA
WAIT! AIN'TCHA TAKIN' ME?
FORGET IT, DUMMY! I'M GLAD T'GET RID OF YOU!
THIS PROVES THAT EVEN A SUPER HERO CAN LOSE!
I GUESS YOU'RE RIGHT.
SOMETIMES A MAN'S GOTTA DO WHAT A MAN'S GOTTA DO!
ARE YOU GOING TO LET HIM GET AWAY WITH THIS?!!

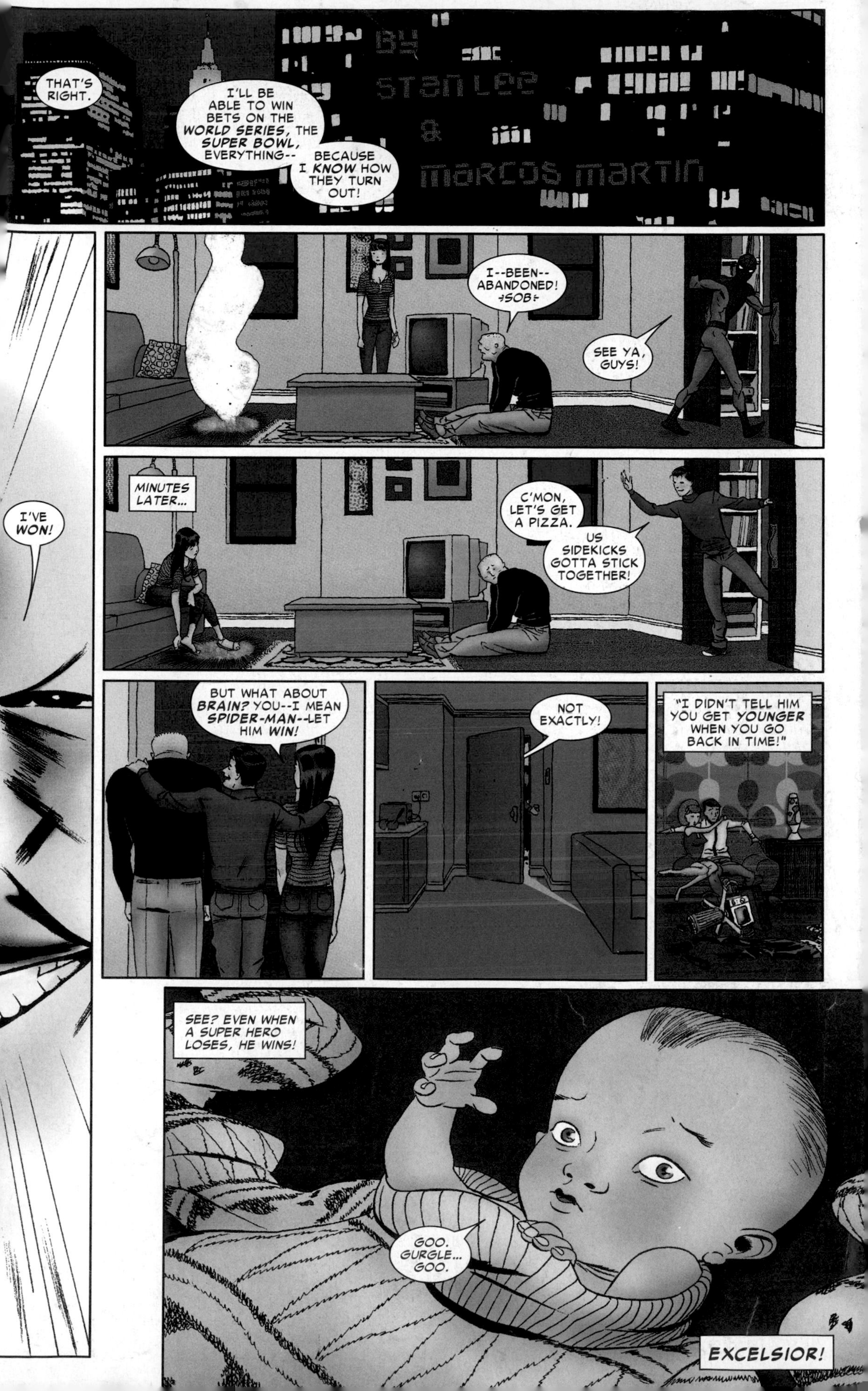

THAT'S RIGHT.
I'LL BE ABLE TO WIN BETS ON THE WORLD SERIES, THE SUPER BOWL, EVERYTHING--
BECAUSE I KNOW HOW THEY TURN OUT!
BY STAN LEE & MARCOS MARTIN
I'VE WON!
I--BEEN--ABANDONED! SOB
SEE YA, GUYS!
MINUTES LATER...
C'MON, LET'S GET A PIZZA.
US SIDEKICKS GOTTA STICK TOGETHER!
BUT WHAT ABOUT BRAIN? YOU--I MEAN SPIDER-MAN--LET HIM WIN!
NOT EXACTLY!
"I DIDN'T TELL HIM YOU GET YOUNGER WHEN YOU GO BACK IN TIME!"
SEE? EVEN WHEN A SUPER HERO LOSES, HE WINS!
GOO. GURGLE... GOO.
EXCELSIOR!

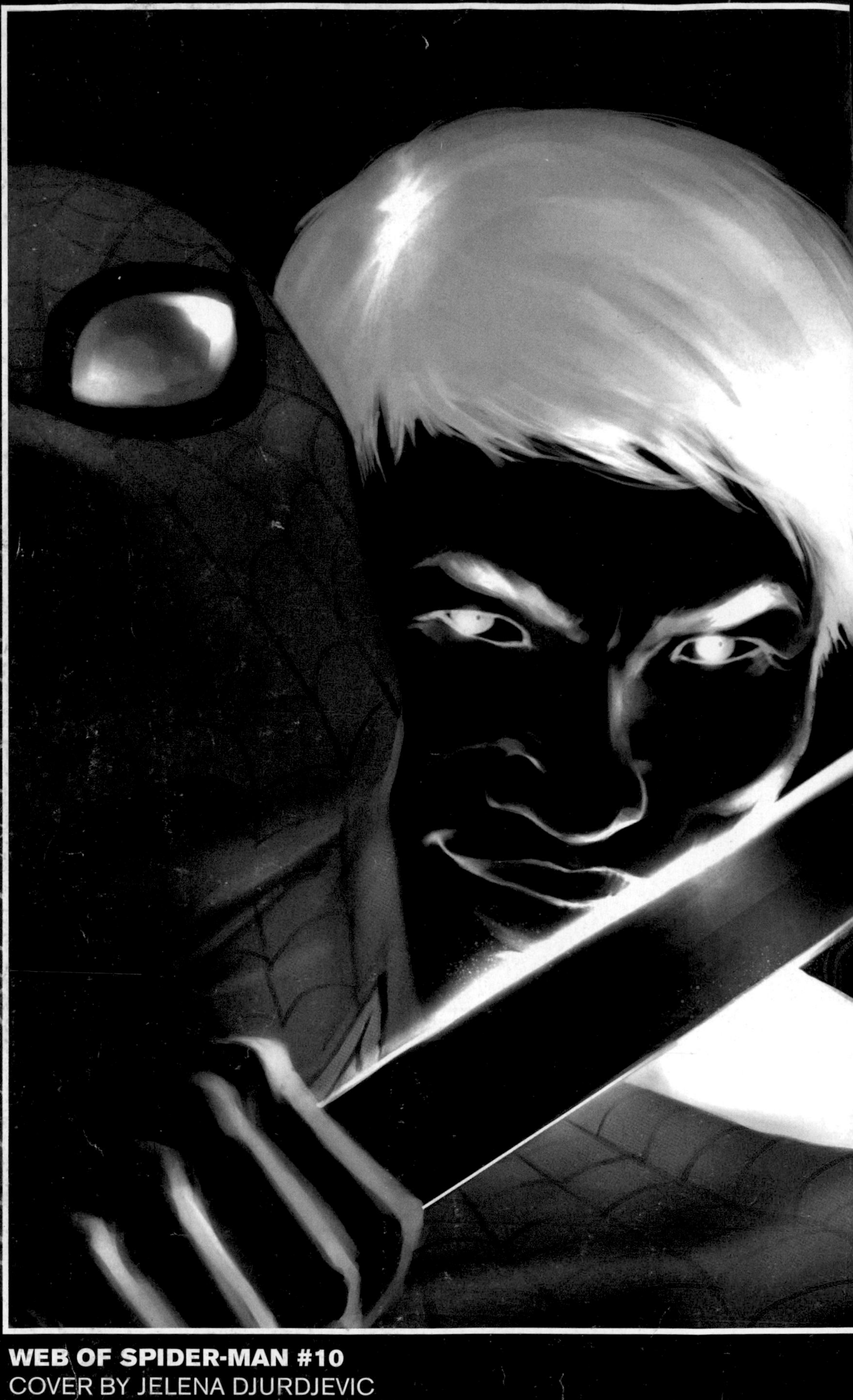

WEB OF SPIDER-MAN #10
COVER BY JELENA DJURDJEVIC